# Scott Foresman - Addison Wesley
# MATH

## AUTHORS

**Randall I. Charles**

**Dinah Chancellor   Lalie Harcourt   Debbie Moore   Jane F. Schielack**
**John Van de Walle   Ricki Wortzman**

Linda Bailey • Carne S. Barnett • Diane J. Briars • Dwight A. Cooley • Warren D. Crown
Martin L. Johnson • Steven J. Leinwand • Pearl Ling • Shauna Lund
Freddie Lee Renfro • Mary Thompson

Scott Foresman
Addison Wesley

Editorial Offices: Menlo Park, California • Glenview, Illinois
Sales Offices: Reading, Massachusetts • Atlanta, Georgia • Glenview, Illinois
Carrollton, Texas • Menlo Park, California

http://www.sf.aw.com

**Cover artist:** Robert Silvers was taking photographs and playing with computers by the time he was ten. Eventually he melded his interests in computer programming and photography to produce a program that divides images into a grid and matches them with images from a database. The results are mosaics such as the one on this cover.

2001 Impression
Copyright © 1999 Addison Wesley Longman, Inc.

Printed in the United States of America

ISBN 0-201-36379-8

17 18 19 20 21 22 -V064- 12 11 10 09 08 07

# CHAPTER 1

# Numbers and Graphing
## Theme: All About Us   1

**CHAPTER 2**

# Addition and Subtraction: Patterns and Concepts
## Theme: The Big Picnic   37

### Connections
Math in Your World,
Math and Reading,
Math at Home

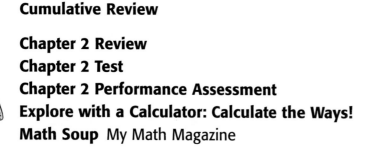

**0  1  2  3  4  5  6  7  8  9  10  11  12**

CHAPTER 3

# Addition and Subtraction Facts and Strategies
### Theme: Fun and Games   79

**Problem Solving**
Make a List, Critical Thinking,
Visual Thinking,
Patterns

**Connections**
Math at Home,
Journal, Algebra Readiness

**Problem Solving**
Group Decision Making,
Visual Thinking

**Connections**
Mental Math,
Tell a Math Story,
Write About It,
Reading for Math, Journal,
Algebra Readiness

**Connections**
Math in Your World,
Math and Social Studies,
Math at Home

**CHAPTER 4**

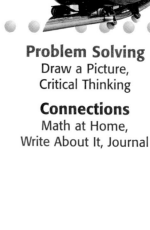

# Using Addition and Subtraction
### Theme: Fun at the Fair 117

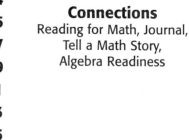

**Problem Solving**
Draw a Picture,
Critical Thinking

**Connections**
Math at Home,
Write About It, Journal

**Problem Solving**
Multiple-Step Problems,
Patterns

**Connections**
Reading for Math, Journal,
Tell a Math Story,
Algebra Readiness

**Connections**
Math in Your World,
Math and Social Studies,
Math at Home

© Scott Foresman Addison Wesley

# Place Value and Patterns to 100
## Theme: Colorful Collections    155

 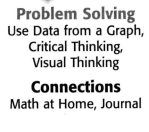

**Connections**
Math in Your World,
Math and Social Studies,
Math at Home

# Money
## Theme: What's for Sale? 197

# CHAPTER 7

## Time
### Theme: All Around Town  231

**CHAPTER**

**8**

# Two-Digit Addition
## Theme: What a Ride!   267

# CHAPTER 9

## Two-Digit Subtraction
### Theme: Creatures and Critters  311

**Problem Solving**
Choose a Computation
Method, Patterns, Estimation,
Critical Thinking,
Visual Thinking

**Connections**
Math at Home, Journal,
Algebra Readiness

**Problem Solving**
Too Much Information,
Visual Thinking,
Critical Thinking

**Connections**
Reading for Math, Journal

**Connections**
Math in Your World,
Math and Health,
Math at Home

# CHAPTER 10

## Numbers to 1,000
### Theme: Crafty Numbers  355

**Problem Solving**
Group Decision Making,
Visual Thinking, Patterns,
Critical Thinking, Estimation

**Connections**
Math at Home, Journal,
Write About It,
Algebra Readiness

**Problem Solving**
Use Data from a Picture,
Patterns, Critical Thinking

**Connections**
Write About It,
Reading for Math, Journal,
Algebra Readiness

**Connections**
Math in Your World,
Math and Art,
Math at Home

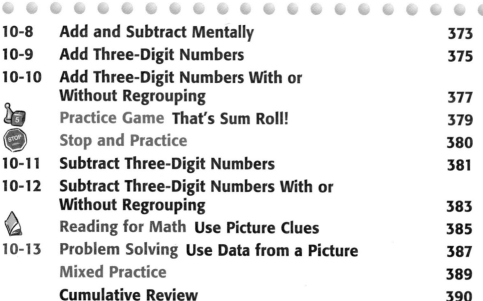

**CHAPTER**

**11**

# Measurement
### Theme: Sizing Up Your World   399

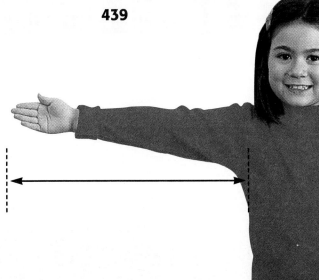

**CHAPTER**

**12**

# Geometry and Fractions
## Theme: Food Festival   443

**Connections**
Math in Your World,
Math and Art,
Math at Home

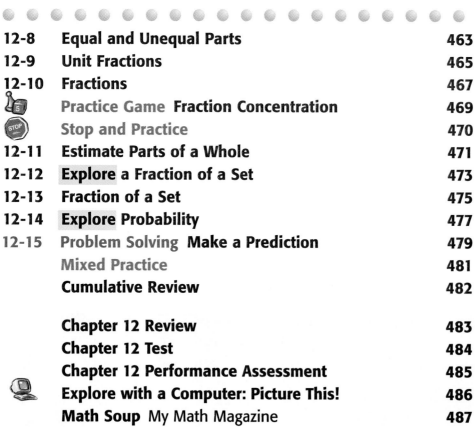

## CHAPTER 13

# Multiplication and Division Concepts
### Theme: Summer Fun 491

**Problem Solving**
Choose a Strategy,
Visual Thinking, Patterns,
Estimation

**Connections**
Math at Home, Journal,
Algebra Readiness

**Problem Solving**
Choose an Operation

**Connections**
Reading for Math, Journal,
Tell a Math Story

**Connections**
Math in Your World,
Math and Physical
Education,
Math at Home

MATHmatazz
Tree House

Welcome

# Numbers and Graphing

**All About Us**

Where would you put your picture?

Ron Matthews

Yasuko Masami

Nituna Totno

Rebecca Nuñez

Mark Robbins

Julia Ponti

Miguel Flores

Karen Kaspar

Anne Martin

Daniel Wozniak

Araba Stevenson

Colin Thomas

| Art | Sports | Reading | Music |

**Notes for Home:** Your child described what is in the pictures and what the graph shows.
*Home Activity:* Ask your child to tell you how many children picked reading as their favorite activity. (2)

# Math at Home

Dear Family,
Our class is starting Chapter 1. We will be learning about numbers, patterns, and graphing. We will count objects, compare numbers, and make different types of graphs. Together, we can do these activities.

## Counting Quickly

Gather 20 items, such as pennies or buttons. Have your child count to find out how many. Ask your child if he or she can think of a faster way to count the items; for example, counting by 2s.

## In the News

Show your child graphs in a newspaper or magazine. Point out the titles of the graphs. Talk about the numbers used in the graphs.

## Community Connection

Help your child count items outside of the home, such as the number of grocery items purchased or the number of buildings passed on the way to school. When counting large quantities, count by 2s, 5s, or 10s.

**Visit our Web site. www.parent.mathsurf.com**

Name _____

**Explore** ● ● ● ● ● ● ● ● ● ● ● ● ● ● ● ● ● ● ● ● ● ● ● ● ● ● ● ● ●

How many girls and boys are in your class?

Use ⬤ ⬭ to show how many.

**1** How many girls are in your class? _____

**2** How many boys are in your class? _____

**3** Which group has more? _____

**4** Which group has fewer? _____

**Share** ● ● ● ● ● ● ● ● ● ● ● ● ● ● ● ● ● ● ● ● ● ● ● ● ● ● ● ● ●

How did you decide which group has more?

**Notes for Home:** Your child counted the number of boys and girls in his or her class.
*Home Activity:* Set up two groups of objects, such as spoons and forks. Ask your child to find the number of objects in each group. Ask which group has more.

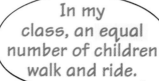

In my class, more children walk to school. Fewer children ride.

In my class, an equal number of children walk and ride.

How many children in your class walk to school?
How many ride?

Use   to show how many.

**5** How many children walk to school? _____

**6** How many children ride to school? _____

**7** Which group has more? _____

**8** Which group has fewer? _____

**Journal**

**9** Tell how you know if two groups are equal.

**Notes for Home:** Your child practiced counting and comparing numbers using <u>more</u>, <u>fewer</u>, and <u>equal</u>. *Home Activity:* Ask your child <u>more</u>, <u>fewer</u> and <u>equal</u> questions using sets of objects such as beans and buttons.

Name _____

# More or Fewer

Which name has more letters? Which name has fewer letters?

How many letters?

First Name | M | a | r | k | | | | | | |    4

Last Name | R | o | b | b | i | n | s | | | |    7

Circle the name that has more letters.    **Mark**    **Robbins**

Count how many more. __3__ more letters

Circle the name that has fewer letters.    **Mark**    **Robbins**

Count how many fewer. __3__ fewer letters

How many letters?

**1**  Write the letters in your name.

First Name | | | | | | | | | | | |    ____

Last Name | | | | | | | | | | | |    ____

**2**  Which name has fewer letters? _____

**3**  Count how many fewer. _____ fewer letters

**Talk About It**  Compare the number of letters in **Sue** and **Jim**.

**Notes for Home:** Your child used <u>more</u> and <u>fewer</u> to compare sets. *Home Activity:* Ask your child to write the first names of family members. Use the words <u>more</u> and <u>fewer</u> to ask questions about the number of letters in the names.

**PRACTICE**

**4** How many letters are in each name? Put the names in order from the fewest to the most number of letters.

How many letters?

S u                                                                    2

_____

_____

_____

_____

_____

## Problem Solving

Solve.

**5** Keesha has 3 sports cards. Ana has 5 sports cards. How many fewer cards does Keesha have than Ana?

_____ fewer cards

**6** Brad has 7 books. Su has 4 books. How many more books does Brad have than Su?

_____ more books

**Notes for Home:** Your child practiced comparing sets. *Home Activity:* Ask your child to use <u>most</u> and <u>fewest</u> to compare three different sets of objects.

Name _____

**Learn** • • • • • • • • • • • • • • • • • • • • • • • • • • • • •

How many eyes?

Count by 2s. Write the numbers.

2    4    6    8    10    12    ___    ___    ___

___    ___    ___    ___    ___    ___    ___ eyes

**Check** • • • • • • • • • • • • • • • • • • • • • • • • • • • • •

❶ How many fingers?

Count by 5s. Write the numbers.

5    10    ___    ___    ___ fingers

❷ How many toes?

Count by 10s. Write the numbers.

10    20    ___    ___    ___ toes

**Talk About It** Count the toes by 5s.

Do you get a different answer? Why or why not?

**Notes for Home:** Your child counted by 2s, 5s, and 10s. *Home Activity:* Ask your child to count by 2s to find the total number of objects in a group, such as the number of eggs in a carton.

**3** How many shoes?
Count by 2s. Write the numbers.

2   4   _____   _____   _____   _____

_____   _____   _____   _____   _____   _____ shoes

**4** How many dots are on the dominoes?
Count by 10s. Write the numbers.

   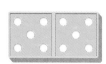 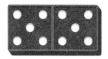

10   _____   _____   _____   _____ dots

Count by 2s, 5s, or 10s.
Write the numbers.

**5** 5, 10, 15, _____, _____

**6** 10, 20, _____, _____, _____

**7** 4, 6, _____, _____, _____

**8** 30, 35, _____, _____, _____

## Problem Solving Estimation

How many ears are there in your class?
Estimate the number of ears.
Then count the ears. Count by 2s.

**9** Estimate: _____ ears

**10** Count: _____ ears

 **Notes for Home:** Your child counted by 2s, 5s, and 10s. *Home Activity:* Ask your child to count 30 items, such as beans or buttons, by 2s, then 5s, then 10s.

**For additional practice, see Skills Practice Bank, page 527, Set 1.**

Name _____

## Charts

Columns go up and down.

Rows go across.

Read the chart.

1. How many rows are there? _____

2. How many columns are there? _____

3. Find the orange row.
   What is in the second column? _____

4. Finish the first 3 columns.

5. Create your own column.

   What will you draw? _____

**Talk About It** How could you tell someone
where the orange heart is?

**Notes for Home:** Your child looked at the rows and columns in a chart. *Home Activity:* Ask your child
to tell you how a row is different from a column.

| 1 | 2 | 3 | 4 | 5 | 6 | 7 | 8 | 9 | 10 |
|---|---|---|---|---|---|---|---|---|---|
| 11 | 12 | 13 | 14 | 15 | 16 | 17 | 18 | 19 | 20 |
| 21 | 22 | 23 | 24 | 25 | 26 | 27 | 28 | 29 | 30 |
| 31 | 32 | 33 | 34 | 35 | 36 | 37 | 38 | 39 | 40 |
| 41 | 42 | 43 | 44 | 45 | 46 | 47 | 48 | 49 | 50 |

Read the chart.

**6** What number is in the first column and in the first row?

**7** What number is in the third column and in the third row?

_____

_____

Use one color.

**8** Color the box in the first column and first row.

**9** Color the box in the second column and second row.

**10** Color the box in the third column and third row.

**11** What pattern do you see? Finish coloring the pattern.

## Critical Thinking

**12** The boxes you have shaded make a diagonal.
Use a different color to shade another diagonal on your chart.
Describe the pattern in your diagonal.

**Notes for Home:** Your child made diagonal patterns on a number chart. *Home Activity:* Ask your child to show and describe some other diagonal patterns on the chart.

Name _____

## Problem Solving: Look for a Pattern

**Learn** • • • • • • • • • • • • •

**PROBLEM SOLVING GUIDE**
Understand • Plan • Solve • Look Back

What pattern do you see?

| 1 | 2 | 3 | 4 | 5 | 6 | 7 | 8 | 9 | 10 |
|---|---|---|---|---|---|---|---|---|---|
| 11 | 12 | 13 | 14 | 15 | 16 | 17 | 18 | 19 | 20 |
| 21 | 22 | 23 | 24 | 25 | 26 | 27 | 28 | 29 | 30 |
| 31 | 32 | 33 | 34 | 35 | 36 | 37 | 38 | 39 | 40 |
| 41 | 42 | 43 | 44 | 45 | 46 | 47 | 48 | 49 | 50 |

What number comes next in the pattern? __21__
Continue the pattern. Color the numbers.

**Check** • • • • • • • • • • • • • • • • • • • • • • • • •

1. Continue the pattern. Color the numbers.

| 1 | 2 | 3 | 4 | 5 | 6 | 7 | 8 | 9 | 10 |
|---|---|---|---|---|---|---|---|---|---|
| 11 | 12 | 13 | 14 | 15 | 16 | 17 | 18 | 19 | 20 |
| 21 | 22 | 23 | 24 | 25 | 26 | 27 | 28 | 29 | 30 |
| 31 | 32 | 33 | 34 | 35 | 36 | 37 | 38 | 39 | 40 |
| 41 | 42 | 43 | 44 | 45 | 46 | 47 | 48 | 49 | 50 |

**Talk About It** What pattern do you see in each chart?

**Notes for Home:** Your child found and continued patterns in which he or she counted by 3s and 5s.
*Home Activity:* Ask your child to find his or her birthday on a calendar, and tell the row and column the date is in.

**PROBLEM SOLVING**

Continue the patterns. Color the numbers.

**2**

| 1 | 2 | 3 | 4 | 5 | 6 | 7 | 8 | 9 | 10 |
|---|---|---|---|---|---|---|---|---|----|
| 11 | 12 | 13 | 14 | 15 | 16 | 17 | 18 | 19 | 20 |
| 21 | 22 | 23 | 24 | 25 | 26 | 27 | 28 | 29 | 30 |
| 31 | 32 | 33 | 34 | 35 | 36 | 37 | 38 | 39 | 40 |
| 41 | 42 | 43 | 44 | 45 | 46 | 47 | 48 | 49 | 50 |

**3**

| 1 | 2 | 3 | 4 | 5 | 6 | 7 | 8 | 9 | 10 |
|---|---|---|---|---|---|---|---|---|----|
| 11 | 12 | 13 | 14 | 15 | 16 | 17 | 18 | 19 | 20 |
| 21 | 22 | 23 | 24 | 25 | 26 | 27 | 28 | 29 | 30 |
| 31 | 32 | 33 | 34 | 35 | 36 | 37 | 38 | 39 | 40 |
| 41 | 42 | 43 | 44 | 45 | 46 | 47 | 48 | 49 | 50 |

## Visual Thinking

**4** Make your own pattern. Color to show how it begins.
Ask a friend to finish it.

| 1 | 2 | 3 | 4 | 5 | 6 | 7 | 8 | 9 | 10 |
|---|---|---|---|---|---|---|---|---|----|
| 11 | 12 | 13 | 14 | 15 | 16 | 17 | 18 | 19 | 20 |
| 21 | 22 | 23 | 24 | 25 | 26 | 27 | 28 | 29 | 30 |

**Notes for Home:** Your child continued number patterns. *Home Activity:* Ask your child to describe the pattern in each chart on this page. (Exercise 2: counting by 2s, Exercise 3: counting by 4s)

**For additional practice, see Skills Practice Bank, page 527, Set 2.**

# Mixed Practice
## Lessons 1–4

## Concepts and Skills

① Circle the color that has more cubes.   **red**   **blue**

② Circle the color that has fewer cubes.   **red**   **blue**

Use the chart to answer the questions.

③ Are there more girls or boys?

_____

④ How many more?  _____ more

Count by 2s or 5s. Write the numbers.

⑤ 2, 4, 6, 8, ____, ____, ____, ____, ____

⑥ 10, 15, 20, ____, ____, ____, ____, ____

## Problem Solving

⑦ Continue the pattern. Color the numbers.

| 1 | 2 | 3 | 4 | 5 | 6 | 7 | 8 | 9 | 10 |
|---|---|---|---|---|---|---|---|---|----|
| 11 | 12 | 13 | 14 | 15 | 16 | 17 | 18 | 19 | 20 |
| 21 | 22 | 23 | 24 | 25 | 26 | 27 | 28 | 29 | 30 |

## Journal

⑧ Draw a picture of 2 groups. Circle the group that has more.

**Notes for Home:** Your child practiced comparing numbers and completing counting patterns.
*Home Activity:* Ask your child to count by 2s, then 5s, then 10s.

MIXED PRACTICE

Name _____

# Cumulative Review
## Chapter 1

## Concepts and Skills

Count how many. Write the numbers.

**1**

_____

**2**

_____

**3** Which group has more, the books or the drums?

_____

**4** How many more?

_____ more

**5** Which name has more letters?

_____

| M | a | r | i | a | n | | |
|---|---|---|---|---|---|---|---|
| D | a | n | | | | | |

**6** How many more? _____ more

## Test Prep

Fill in the ○ for the correct answer.

**7** What number comes next?

26, 27, 28, 29, _____

| 30 | 32 | 35 | 210 |
|----|----|----|-----|
| ○  | ○  | ○  | ○   |

**8** What number comes next?

41, 42, 43, 44, _____

| 40 | 50 | 45 | 5 |
|----|----|----|---|
| ○  | ○  | ○  | ○ |

**Notes for Home:** Your child reviewed number groups to 9, comparing numbers, and counting patterns.
*Home Activity:* Ask your child to say the next five numbers in Exercise 7. (31, 32, 33, 34, 35)

**Learn**  • • • • • • • • • • • • • • • • • • • • • • • • • • • • •

*Graphs can help to compare groups.*

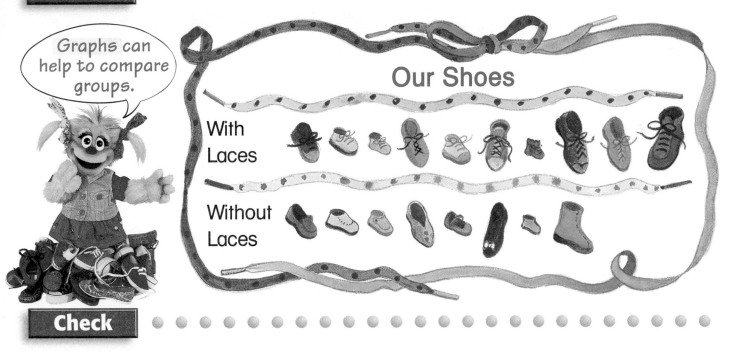

**Our Shoes**

With Laces

Without Laces

**Check**  • • • • • • • • • • • • • • • • • • • • • • • • • • • • •

Use the graph to answer the questions.

1. How many children wear shoes with laces? ___10___

2. How many children wear shoes without laces? _____

3. Do more children wear shoes with laces or without laces? _____

4. How many more? _____ more

Use the graph to answer the questions.

5. Do more children write with their right or left hand?

   _____

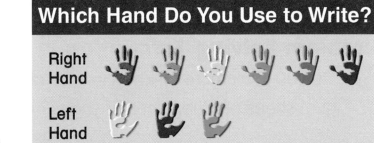

**Which Hand Do You Use to Write?**

Right Hand

Left Hand

6. How many more? _____ more

**Talk About It** How can the graphs help you compare?

**Notes for Home:** Your child read graphs and answered questions about them. *Home Activity:* Ask your child to explain the graph at the top of the page.

Use the graphs to answer the questions.

**7** How many children drink juice?

_____

**8** How many more children drink milk than juice?

_____ more

## What Do You Drink at Lunch?

| Juice | |
| --- | --- |
| Milk | |

**9** Which foods do an equal number of children like best? Circle the foods.

**10** Which food was picked the least number of times?

_____

**11** 🙂 **Write your own** question about one of the graphs.

## What Is Your Favorite Lunch?

Taco      Pizza      Sandwich

## Problem Solving Estimation

**12** Do you think more children in your class are wearing gym shoes or other kinds of shoes? Circle your estimate.

**gym shoes      other shoes**

You can make a graph to check your estimate.

**Notes for Home:** Your child answered questions about graphs. *Home Activity:* Ask your child to make a graph using common objects, such as forks and spoons.

Name _____

**Learn** • • • • • • • • • • • • • • • • • • • • • • • • • • • • •

Each 🛉 means I child.

How many children like winter best? ___3___

Which season is the favorite of most children? ___Summer___

**Check** • • • • • • • • • • • • • • • • • • • • • • • • • • • • •

1   Which season does your class like best? Make a guess. _____
    Make a pictograph to find out. Complete the graph below.

Each 🛉 means I child.

2   Do more children in your class like spring or summer best? _____

3   Which season do children in your class like best? _____

**Talk About It** Why do you think this graph is called a pictograph?

**Notes for Home:** Your child made a pictograph. *Home Activity:* Ask your child to explain the graph that he or she made.

**Practice**

Use the graph. Give each answer.

**4** How many children like soccer best?

_____

**5** Which sport is the favorite of most children?

_____

Each 👤 means 1 child.

## Mixed Practice

Count to find each answer.

**6** How many children like apples best?

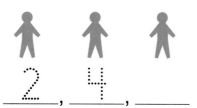

2, 4, ____

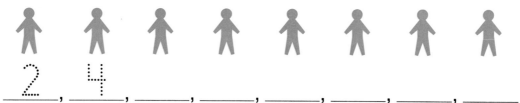

Each 👤 means 2 children.

**7** How many children like oranges best?

2, 4, ____, ____, ____, ____, ____, ____

## Mental Math

**8** How many more children picked basketball than soccer in the graph above?

_____ more

 **Notes for Home:** Your child answered questions about pictographs. *Home Activity:* Ask your child to think of a question that compares two items in one of the graphs. [Sample: How many more children like bananas than apples? (6)]

18  eighteen

# Experiment and Tally

**Learn** • • • • • • • • • • • • • • • • • • • • • • • • • • • • •

Charles tossed a counter 10 times.
Hideo showed his results with tally marks.

It was red
4 times.

It was yellow
6 times.

**Check** • • • • • • • • • • • • • • • • • • • • • • • • • • • • •

**1** Toss a counter 25 times. Use a tally to mark **red** or **yellow**.

Remember,
I means 1.
HHt means 5.

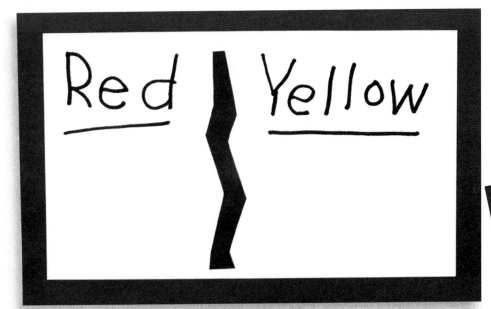

**2** Circle the color that has more.    **red    yellow**

**3** How many more red or yellow did you toss? _____ more

**Talk About It** Tally marks can show groups of 5.

How else can you show groups of 5?

**Notes for Home:** Your child tossed a counter and used tallies to show the results.
*Home Activity:* Choose a number between 10 and 25. Ask your child to show it using tallies.

Here are some other tallies.

Count how many red, how many yellow, and how many in all.

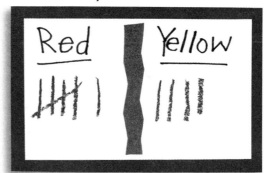

④ How many red? __3__

⑤ How many yellow? _____

⑥ How many in all? _____

⑦ How many red? _____

⑧ How many yellow? _____

⑨ How many in all? _____

Show the tallies for each chart.

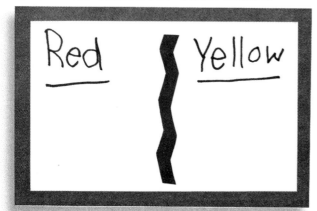

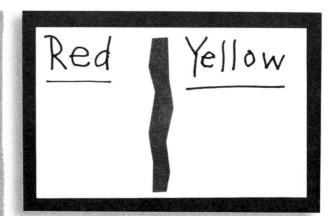

⑩ Show 8 red.

⑪ Show 12 yellow.

⑫ How many in all? _____

⑬ Show 15 red.

⑭ Show 15 yellow.

⑮ How many in all? _____

## Problem Solving Critical Thinking

⑯ If you toss a counter 10 times, could it land on red 10 times? Why or why not?

**Notes for Home:** Your child read tally charts. *Home Activity:* Ask your child to tell you which chart shows the most red tosses and which shows the fewest red tosses.

Name _____

**Learn**

Number of Letters in Our Names

*I colored two boxes for 7 on the bar graph.*

Number of Letters In Our Names

| 1 | 2 | 3 | 4 | 5 |
|---|---|---|---|---|
| I | II | IIII | ΗΗΗ | ΗΗΗ I |
| 6 | 7 | 8 | 9 | 10 |
| IIII | II | III | I | I |

*I counted two tally marks for the names with 7 letters.*

**Check**

1   How many children have 5 letters in their names? __6__

2   How many spaces would you color above 8 on the graph? _____

3   How many letters does the greatest number of names have? _____

**Talk About It** Which numbers on the graph will have 1 space colored?

**Notes for Home:** Your child analyzed data using a tally chart and a bar graph. *Home Activity:* Ask your child how many names on the graph have 3 letters. (1)

**PRACTICE**

**4** How many letters are there in the first names in your class?
Make tally marks.

### Number of Letters in Our Names

| 1 | 2 | 3 | 4 | 5 | 6 |
|---|---|---|---|---|---|
|   |   |   |   |   |   |

| 7 | 8 | 9 | 10 | 11 | 12 |
|---|---|---|----|----|----|
|   |   |   |    |    |    |

**5** Make a bar graph. Color one space for each tally mark.

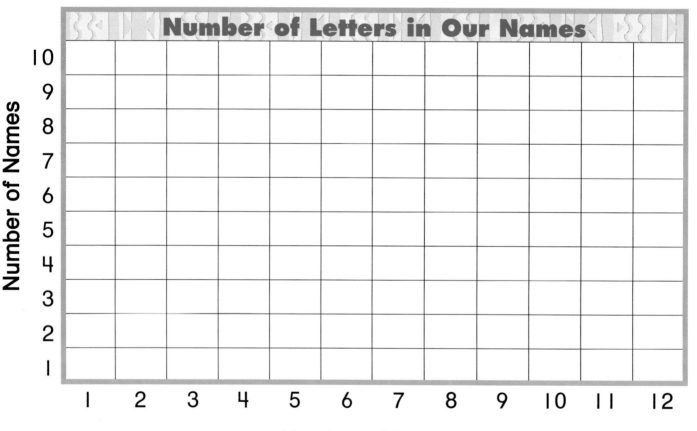

### Number of Letters in Our Names

Number of Names

Number of Letters

## Problem Solving Critical Thinking

**6** In another class, 5 children have 4 letters in their names.
Explain how you would show this on a bar graph.

**Notes for Home:** Your child has gathered and shown data using tally marks and a bar graph.
*Home Activity:* Ask your child to add the first names of people in his or her family to the graph.

**For additional practice, see Skills Practice Bank, page 527, Set 3.**

Name _____

# Race to the Top

**Players** 2

## What You Need

1 number cube
6 crayons in different colors

## How to Play

1. Toss the number cube.

2. Color a square on the graph to show the number you rolled.

3. Use a different color crayon for each number.

4. Roll until one number is colored to the top.
   That number wins.

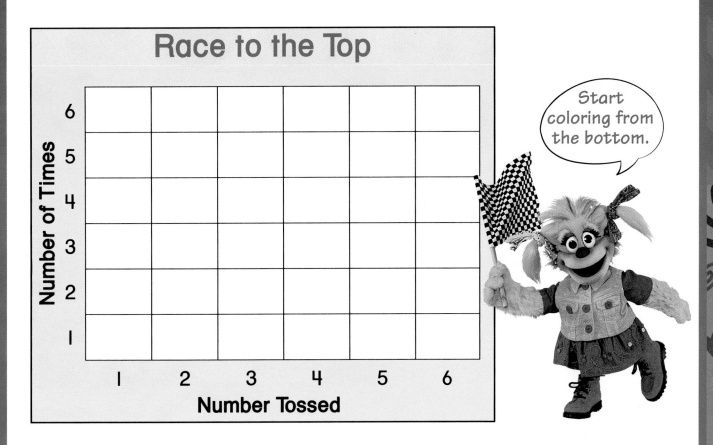

Race to the Top

Number of Times

6
5
4
3
2
1

1  2  3  4  5  6
**Number Tossed**

Start coloring from the bottom.

**Notes For Home:** Your child played a game to practice graphing.
*Home Activity:* Ask your child to tell which number was rolled the least number of times.

Name _____

Compare the numbers in each group.

**1** Are there more scissors or brushes?

_____

**2** Count how many more.

_____ more

Count by 5s or 10s. Write the numbers.

**3** 5, 10, 15, _____, _____, _____, _____, _____, _____, _____

**4** 10, 20, 30, _____, _____, _____, _____, _____, _____

**5** Use the tally marks. Make a bar graph.

| Which Cereal is Your Favorite? | | | |
|---|---|---|---|
| Fruit Crunch | Cornies | Raisin-O's | Loops |
| ||| | |||| | ////// | ///// / |

Which Cereal is Your Favorite?

| 6 | | | | |
| 5 | | | | |
| 4 | | | | |
| 3 | | | | |
| 2 | | | | |
| 1 | | | | |
| | Fruit Crunch | Cornies | Raisin-O's | Loops |

**6** How many children picked Loops?

_____

**7** Which cereal was picked the least?

_____

**Notes for Home:** Your child practiced comparing groups, counting, and making bar graphs.
*Home Activity:* Ask your child which cereal was chosen 4 times. (Cornies)

Name _____

**Learn** ● ● ● ● ● ● ● ● ● ● ● ● ●

**PROBLEM SOLVING GUIDE**
Understand • Plan • Solve • Look Back

These children showed their
data using a diagram.

### Do you like skating, biking, or both?

Derek

Juanita

Jessie

Zubin

Kwame

Isabel

Lizzie

Trevor

Hank

Aimee

Luisa

Jevon

↑ Likes skating    ↑ Likes both    ↑ Likes biking

**Check** ● ● ● ● ● ● ● ● ● ● ● ● ● ● ● ● ● ● ● ● ● ● ● ● ● ● ● ●

PROBLEM SOLVING

**1** How many children like both skating and biking? _3_

**2** How many children like skating? _____

**3** How many children like skating but not biking? _____

**4** How many children like biking? _____

**5** How many children like biking but not skating? _____

**Talk About It** Do more children like skating or biking?
Tell how you know.

**Notes for Home:** Your child studied how to organize data using a diagram. *Home Activity:* Ask your
child to use the diagram to tell you what Jessie, Luisa, and Lizzie like to do. (Jessie likes skating, but not
biking; Luisa likes biking, but not skating; Lizzie likes both.)

⑥ Show data for 7 classmates using a diagram.

## Do you like skating, biking, or both?

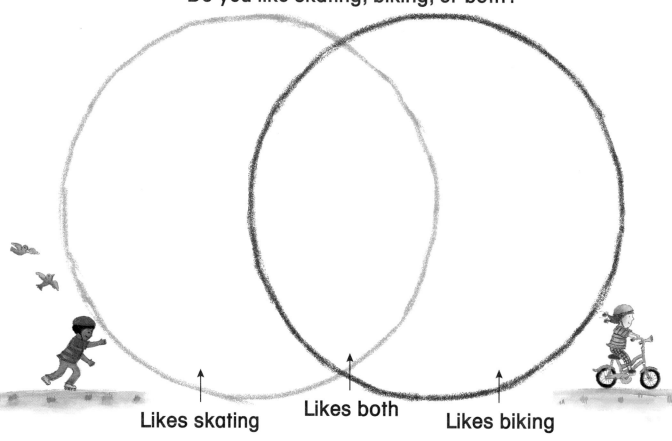

Likes skating          Likes both          Likes biking

Use your diagram to answer the questions.

⑦ How many children like both skating and biking? _____

⑧ How many children like skating?

_____

⑨ How many children like skating but not biking?

_____

⑩ How many children like biking?

_____

⑪ How many children like biking but not skating?

_____

## Tell a Math Story

⑫ Draw your own diagram. Ask a friend to tell a story about your diagram.

**PROBLEM SOLVING**

Name _____

# Mixed Practice
## Lessons 5–9

## Concepts and Skills

Use the graph to answer the questions.

**1** How many children liked purple best? _____

**2** Did more children like green or blue? _____

| Favorite Color | |
|---|---|
| Purple | ♀ ♀ ♀ ♀ ♀ ♀ ♀ |
| Green | ♀ ♀ ♀ |
| Red | ♀ ♀ ♀ ♀ |
| Blue | ♀ ♀ ♀ ♀ ♀ |

Each ♀ means I child.

Use the graph to answer the questions.

**3** Which pet was picked most often? _____

**4** Which pet was picked the least number of times? _____

| Favorite Pet | 1 | 2 | 3 | 4 | 5 | 6 | 7 | 8 | 9 |
|---|---|---|---|---|---|---|---|---|---|
| Dog | | | | | | | | | |
| Cat | | | | | | | | | |
| Fish | | | | | | | | | |
| Bird | | | | | | | | | |

**5** How many children liked cats best? _____

## Problem Solving

Look at the diagram.
Answer the questions.

**6** How many children like softball but not soccer? _____

**7** How many children like both soccer and softball? _____

Do you like soccer, softball, or both?

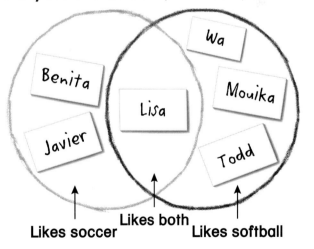

Likes soccer    Likes both    Likes softball

## Journal

**8** Write a question about the diagram.
Ask a friend to answer your question.

**Notes for Home:** Your child practiced using graphs and diagrams to compare information.
*Home Activity:* Ask your child to add his or her vote to the graph about a favorite color.

MIXED PRACTICE

Name _____

# Cumulative Review
## Chapter 1

## Concepts and Skills

Circle the number
that is greater.

Circle the number
that is less.

**1**   4    8    **2**   16   11      **3**   15   12   **4**   7    9

## Problem Solving

Solve.

**5**   There are 6 drums.
There are 4 flutes.
Which group has more?

_____

**6**   There are 5 guitars.
There are 8 violins.
Which group has fewer?

_____

---

### Test Prep

Fill in the ○ for the correct answer.

**7**   Count by 5s.
Mark the number
that comes next.

5, 10, 15, 20, _____

| 21 | 22 | 25 | 30 |
|----|----|----|----|
| ○  | ○  | ○  | ○  |

**8**   Count by 10s.
Mark the number
that comes next.

10, 20, 30, 40, _____

○ 41
○ 42
○ 45
○ 50

 **Notes for Home:** Your child reviewed comparing numbers and skip counting.
*Home Activity:* Ask your child to find two groups of objects at home that are equal in number.

CUMULATIVE REVIEW

# Chapter 1 Review

## Vocabulary

**1** Which group has more counters?

red    yellow

**2** Count how many more. _____ more

---

**3** How many votes?
Count the tally marks.

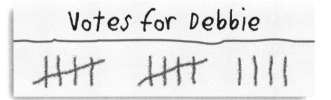

_____ votes

---

## Concepts and Skills

Count by 2s or 5s. Write the numbers.

**4** 2, 4, 6, _____, _____, _____, _____, _____, _____, _____

**5** 5, 10, 15, _____, _____, _____, _____, _____, _____, _____

---

## Problem Solving

Use the graph.
Answer the questions.

**6** How many kickball games were played?

_____

**7** Which game was played the most?

_____

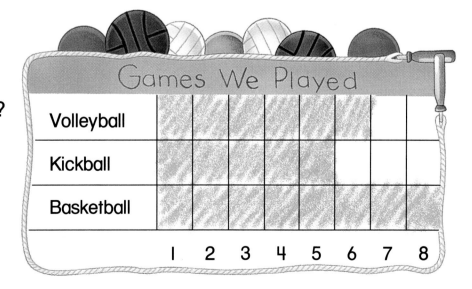

**Notes for Home:** Your child reviewed the vocabulary, skills, concepts, and problem solving taught in Chapter 1. *Home Activity:* Ask your child to use tally marks to count the number of windows in your home.

Name _____

# Chapter 1 Test

Use the graph. Answer the questions.

**1** Do more children get to school by bus or bike?

_____

**2** How many more?

_____ more

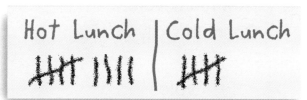

| How We Get to School | |
|---|---|
| Bus | 🧍🧍🧍🧍🧍🧍 |
| Bike | 🧍🧍🧍 |
| Walk | 🧍🧍🧍🧍 |

Each 🧍 means 1 child.

---

**3** How many children picked hot lunch? Count the tally marks.

_____ children

| Hot Lunch | Cold Lunch |
|---|---|
| 卌 \|\|\|\| | 卌 |

---

Count by 10s. Write the numbers.

**4** 10, 20, _____, _____, _____

---

Use the graph. Answer the question.

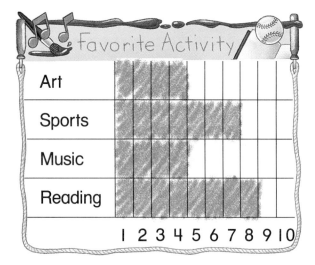

Favorite Activity

| | 1 2 3 4 5 6 7 8 9 10 |
|---|---|
| Art | |
| Sports | |
| Music | |
| Reading | |

**5** Which activity do most of these children like best?

_____

Use the diagram. Answer the question.

Do you like milk, juice, or both?

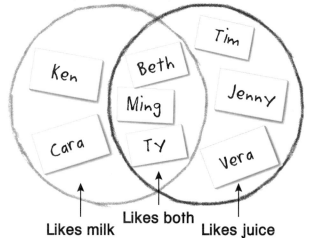

Ken  Beth  Tim
Ming  Jenny
Cara  TY  Vera

↑ Likes milk   ↑ Likes both   ↑ Likes juice

**6** How many of these children like only juice?

_____

**Notes for Home:** Your child was tested on Chapter 1 concepts, skills, and problem solving. *Home Activity:* Ask your child to look at the diagram in Exercise 6 and name the children who like only milk. (Ken, Cara)

Name _____

# Performance Assessment
## Chapter 1

Put I red, I blue,
I yellow, and I green
cube in a bag.

Pick a cube from the bag.
What color is it?

Color a box in
the graph to show
the cube you picked.

Put the cube back each time.
Do this until one color has
been picked 5 times.

**1** How many times was
red picked?

_____ times

**2** How many times was
green picked?

_____ times

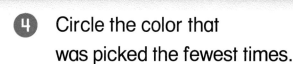

What color did you pick?

Number of Times

5
4
3
2
I

Color Picked

**3** Circle the color
that was picked the most.

**4** Circle the color that
was picked the fewest times.

## Problem Solving Critical Thinking

**5** How else could you show which cubes you picked?

Notes for Home: Your child did an activity that assessed Chapter 1 skills, concepts, and problem
solving. *Home Activity:* Ask your child to use the words <u>more</u> and <u>fewer</u> to tell about his or her graph.

Name _____

## Use the World Wide Web

### Computer Skills You Will Need

You can use the Internet to get different kinds of information.

**1** Go to: **www.mathsurf.com/2** . **Click** on Chapter 1.

This activity can tell you about favorite things of second graders.

**2** **Click** [Forward →] and [← Backward] to get from screen to screen.

**3** What did you learn from this activity?

_____

Use the information you found on the Internet.
Write 2 questions that you could ask about favorite topics.

**4** _____

_____

**5** _____

_____

**6** Exchange your questions with a friend.
Answer each other's questions.

**Tech Talk** How is clicking  and  like turning a page in a book? How is it different?

💻💻 **Visit our Web site.** www.parent.mathsurf.com

## Math at Home

# Mystery Jar

To win many contests, you must guess the number of things in a jar. Have your own contest at home. Make your own Mystery Jar.

**1** Fill a container with marbles. Do not count them.

**2** Have people guess how many. Write the numbers.

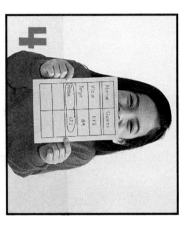

**3** Count the marbles. Try counting by 2s, 5s, or 10s.

**4** The nearest guess wins.

**Fold down**

Scott Foresman · Addison Wesley    My Math Magazine    No. 1

**MathSurf**

Jumping Gym Shoes

**How Many Bananas Are Needed?**

| | |
|---|---|
| Biking | 🍌 🍌 🍌 |
| Swimming | 🍌 🍌 |
| Reading | 🍌 |
| Running | 🍌 🍌 🍌 🍌 |

Each 🍌 means 1 banana

# Show Your Shoes

A diagram can show all the places children wear gym shoes. Use the diagram to answer these questions.

1 How many children wear gym shoes at school, at home, and for outdoor activities?

_____

2 How many children do not wear gym shoes at school?

_____

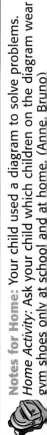

Notes for Home: Your child used a diagram to solve problems. Home Activity: Ask your child which children on the diagram wear gym shoes only at school and at home. (Anne Bruno)

2

# Banana Power

Bananas help to give you energy. The graph shows how many bananas you need to do different activities for an hour. Use the graph to solve the problems.

1 How many bananas do you need to swim for 1 hour?

_____ bananas

2 How many more bananas do you need to run for 1 hour than to swim?

_____ more bananas

3 Make up your own question. Give it to a friend to answer.

Notes for Home: Your child used a graph to solve problems. *Home Activity:* Ask your child which activity requires more energy from food, swimming or biking. (swimming)

## Where Do You Wear Gym Shoes?

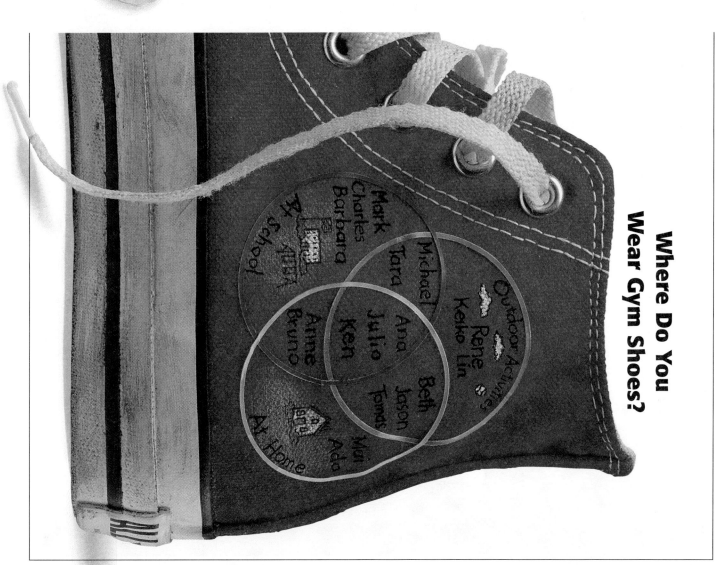

© Scott Foresman Addison Wesley

## Math Fun

# Far Out Friends

Imagine if you had a friend from Mars!
What would he or she be like? Use this chart
to compare yourself to your imaginary friend
from Mars.

Use this space to
draw a picture of
your friend.

· My Friend From Mars ·

Use this space
to draw a picture
of yourself.

Me.

| | You | Friend From Mars | Who Has More? | How Many More? |
|---|---|---|---|---|
| Eyes | 2 | 5 | Friend | 3 |
| Fingers | | | | |
| Arms | | | | |
| Noses | | | | |
| Legs | | | | |

Your friend from Mars has 7 friends, each
with 5 eyes. How many eyes would the
7 friends have in all? Count by 5s.

**Notes for Home:** Your child completed a chart and used that chart to
draw pictures. *Home Activity:* Ask your child how many arms 5 friends
from Mars would have.

Dear Family,
Our class is starting Chapter 2. We will learn about patterns, adding, and subtracting. We will tell math stories about numbers to 12. We can do these activities together at home.

### Give and Take

Ask your child to make up addition and subtraction stories using items in your home. For example: I have 8 books on the table. I take 2 off. I have 6 left.

### The Name Game

Find 8 common objects, such as spoons. Ask your child to find different ways to put the objects into two groups (for example, 2 and 6, 3 and 5). Repeat the activity with 9 objects.

### Community Connection

While you are waiting in line at a store, ask your child to count how many adults and how many children are in the line. Then add to find the total. What is another way to group the people in line?

 **Visit our Web site. www.parent.mathsurf.com**

Name _____

# Explore Addition Stories

Use 🥚🥚 to show two groups of ants.

Tell addition stories about a picnic.

Show your story.

Tell your story.

**Notes for Home:** Your child used counters to tell addition stories about a picnic.
*Home Activity:* Ask your child to tell you an addition story using small objects.

**EXPLORE**

5  .

4 more  .

5 and 4 is 9.

Solve each problem. You can use  .

**1** 3  on a plate.

4 more  are added.

How many  in all?

___3___ and ___4___ is ___7___ .

**2** 6  on Mia's plate.

4  on Kayla's plate.

How many  in all?

_____ and _____ is _____ .

**3** 7  .

Lee brings 2 more  .

How many  in all?

_____ and _____ is _____ .

**4** 3  .

Bob brings 1 more  .

How many  in all?

_____ and _____ is _____ .

**Talk About It** Tell a number story about the picture.

 **Notes for Home:** Your child solved addition problems. *Home Activity:* Ask your child to tell you an addition story about 2 ants and 4 ants.

EXPLORE

Name _____

## Join Groups to Add

**Learn** • • • • • • • • • • • • • • • • • • • • • •

3  on a leaf.

6  come.

How many
in all?

When you add, the answer is called the sum.

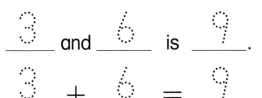

$\underline{3}$ and $\underline{6}$ is $\underline{9}$.

$\underline{3} + \underline{6} = \underline{9}$

**Check** • • • • • • • • • • • • • • • • • • • • •

Use  ⬤ ⬤ and ▭ to add.
Write the number sentence.

**1** 3  .

2 more  join them.

How many  in all?

$\underline{3}$ and $\underline{2}$ is $\underline{5}$.

$\underline{3} + \underline{2} = \underline{5}$

**2** 5  are eating.

5 more  come.

How many  in all?

_____ and _____ is _____.

_____ + _____ = _____

**3** 4  are on a leaf.

1 more  joins them.

How many  in all?

_____ and _____ is _____.

_____ + _____ = _____

**Talk About It** What is the greatest sum
in the problems above?

**Notes for Home:** Your child used counters to show math stories and wrote number sentences.
*Home Activity:* Ask your child to use objects, such as buttons, to show you how to solve Exercise 3.

**Chapter 2 Lesson 2**

forty-one **41**

You can use  and a .
Write the number sentence. Solve.

**4** 4  are near the food.

5 more  come.

How many  are there now?

$\underline{4} + \underline{5} = \underline{9}$

**5** 1  is on a flower.

2  fly to the flower.

How many  in all?

____ + ____ = ____

**6** 7  are playing.

2  come to play.

How many  in all?

____ + ____ = ____

**7** 6  are swimming.

6 more  come to swim.

How many  are swimming?

____ + ____ = ____

**8** Dave ate 4 .

Sal ate 2 .

How many  did they
eat in all?

____ + ____ = ____

**9** Dan has 3 .

He finds 8 more .

How many  does he
have now?

____ + ____ = ____

## Problem Solving Critical Thinking

Solve. You can use .

**10** There are 10  in all.

How many  are in the basket?

_____

 **Notes for Home:** Your child wrote number sentences for addition stories. *Home Activity:* Ask your child to tell you how he or she solved Exercise 8. (Sample answer: I put down 4 counters. Then I put down 2 more. 4 + 2 = 6)

# Count On and Add Zero

**Learn** ● ● ● ● ● ● ● ● ● ● ● ● ● ● ● ● ● ● ● ● ● ● ● ●

There are 7 forks.
Tia adds 2 more.
How many forks
are there now?

*Start at 0. Go to 7. Then count on 2 more: 7, ...8, 9.*

0  1  2  3  4  5  6  7  8  9  10  11  12

$$7 + 2 = \underline{9}$$

**Check** ● ● ● ● ● ● ● ● ● ● ● ● ● ● ● ● ● ● ● ● ● ● ● ●

0  1  2  3  4  5  6  7  8  9  10  11  12

Use the number line. Write the sum.

**1** $6 + 2 = \underline{8}$      $9 + 1 = \underline{\phantom{0}}$      $6 + 0 = \underline{\phantom{0}}$

**2** $8 + 2 = \underline{\phantom{0}}$      $8 + 3 = \underline{\phantom{0}}$      $7 + 2 = \underline{\phantom{0}}$

**3** $5 + 3 = \underline{\phantom{0}}$      $9 + 0 = \underline{\phantom{0}}$      $5 + 1 = \underline{\phantom{0}}$

**4**

| 4 | 9 | 8 | 7 | 9 | 8 | 6 |
|---|---|---|---|---|---|---|
| +2 | +3 | +0 | +3 | +2 | +1 | +3 |
| 6 | | | | | | |

**Talk About It** How can a number line help you add?

**Notes for Home:** Your child added 0, 1, 2, or 3 to numbers. *Home Activity:* Have your child use a small object, such as a penny, to find 8 + 2 on the number line.

<-----•---•---•---•---•---•---•---•---•---•---•---•---•----->
0   1   2   3   4   5   6   7   8   9   10   11   12

You can use the number line. Write the sum.

**5**  $8 + 3 = \underline{11}$        $6 + 2 = \underline{\phantom{00}}$

**6**  $9 + 2 = \underline{\phantom{00}}$        $7 + 3 = \underline{\phantom{00}}$

**7**  $9 + 3 = \underline{\phantom{00}}$        $6 + 0 = \underline{\phantom{00}}$

**8**  $8 + 1 = \underline{\phantom{00}}$        $4 + 3 = \underline{\phantom{00}}$

**9**  $7 + 2 = \underline{\phantom{00}}$        $5 + 3 = \underline{\phantom{00}}$

Add.

**10**
$$\begin{array}{r} 5 \\ +2 \\ \hline 7 \end{array} \quad \begin{array}{r} 7 \\ +1 \\ \hline \end{array} \quad \begin{array}{r} 6 \\ +3 \\ \hline \end{array} \quad \begin{array}{r} 4 \\ +3 \\ \hline \end{array} \quad \begin{array}{r} 5 \\ +1 \\ \hline \end{array} \quad \begin{array}{r} 3 \\ +0 \\ \hline \end{array} \quad \begin{array}{r} 11 \\ +0 \\ \hline \end{array}$$

**11**
$$\begin{array}{r} 5 \\ +0 \\ \hline \end{array} \quad \begin{array}{r} 10 \\ +2 \\ \hline \end{array} \quad \begin{array}{r} 6 \\ +1 \\ \hline \end{array} \quad \begin{array}{r} 10 \\ +0 \\ \hline \end{array} \quad \begin{array}{r} 4 \\ +2 \\ \hline \end{array} \quad \begin{array}{r} 9 \\ +1 \\ \hline \end{array} \quad \begin{array}{r} 11 \\ +1 \\ \hline \end{array}$$

**12**
$$\begin{array}{r} 8 \\ +2 \\ \hline \end{array} \quad \begin{array}{r} 9 \\ +0 \\ \hline \end{array} \quad \begin{array}{r} 7 \\ +2 \\ \hline \end{array} \quad \begin{array}{r} 4 \\ +0 \\ \hline \end{array} \quad \begin{array}{r} 10 \\ +1 \\ \hline \end{array} \quad \begin{array}{r} 6 \\ +2 \\ \hline \end{array} \quad \begin{array}{r} 9 \\ +2 \\ \hline \end{array}$$

## Problem Solving Critical Thinking

**13**  What do you notice about adding zero to a number?

**Notes for Home:** Your child practiced adding 0, 1, 2, or 3 to numbers. *Home Activity:* Have your child use the number line to show how to find the answers for two of the exercises on this page.

**For additional practice, see Skills Practice Bank, page 528, Set 1.**

# Turnaround Facts

**Learn** • • • • • • • • • • • • • • • • • • • • • • • • • • • • • • •

6 + 4 = 10
and
4 + 6 = 10
are called
turnaround facts.
Can you tell why?

**Check** • • • • • • • • • • • • • • • • • • • • • • • • • • • • • • •

Use  to make each train. Color.

**1**

3 + 4 = 7

4 + 3 = 7

**2**

2 + 7 = 9

7 + 2 = 9

**3**

8 + 3 = 11

3 + 8 = 11

**4**

6 + 2 = 8

2 + 6 = 8

**Talk About It** How are these alike? How are they different?

5 + 6 = 11
6 + 5 = 11

**Notes for Home:** Your child used turnaround facts, such as 6 + 2 and 2 + 6, to find sums.
*Home Activity:* Ask your child to write two addition sentences using the numbers 5, 6, and 11.
(5 + 6 = 11; 6 + 5 = 11)

Write the number sentence for each train.

**5**

$$4 + 7 = 11$$

$$7 + 4 = 11$$

**6**

_____

_____

**7**

_____

_____

**8**

_____

_____

Write the turnaround fact for each number sentence.

**9** $7 + 3 = 10$

_____

**10** $5 + 4 = 9$

_____

## Problem Solving

Write the number sentence. Solve.

**11** 8 children are playing baseball. 4 more children join them. How many children are playing in all?

____ + ____ = ____ children

**12** 4 children are eating lunch. 8 more children come to eat. Now how many children are eating lunch?

____ + ____ = ____ children

**Notes for Home:** Your child used turnaround facts to find sums to 12. *Home Activity:* Ask your child to tell you a pair of turnaround facts with the sum of 10. (Sample answer: 4 + 6 and 6 + 4)

# Ways to Make Numbers

**Learn** • • • • • • • • • • • • • • • • • • • • • • • • • •

You can show 5 in many ways.

| ⊞ 5 ◑ ·five | Ways to Make 5 | ··· ▭ 5 ▪ ◑ ≡ |
|---|---|---|
| [cubes] | $0 + 5 = 5$ | [child] |
| [cubes] | $1 + 4 = 5$ | [child] |
| [cubes] | $2 + 3 = 5$ | [child] |
| [cubes] | $3 + 2 = 5$ | [child] |
| [cubes] | $4 + 1 = 5$ | [child] |
| [cubes] | $5 + 0 = 5$ | [child] |

**Check** • • • • • • • • • • • • • • • • • • • • • • • • • •

Use 🟦🟦 . Show different ways to make 6.

Write the number sentences.

1

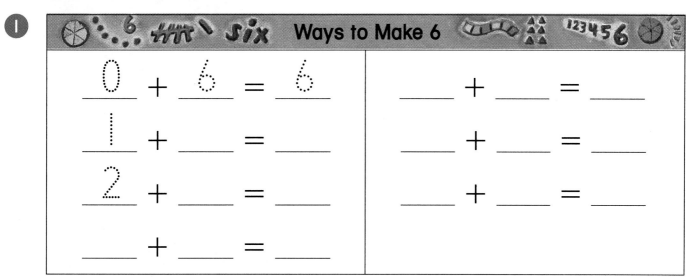

| ◑ ·6 ⊞ six | Ways to Make 6 | ▭ ▲ 123456 ◑ |
|---|---|---|

$$0 + 6 = 6 \qquad \_\_\_ + \_\_\_ = \_\_\_$$

$$1 + \_\_\_ = \_\_\_ \qquad \_\_\_ + \_\_\_ = \_\_\_$$

$$2 + \_\_\_ = \_\_\_ \qquad \_\_\_ + \_\_\_ = \_\_\_$$

$$\_\_\_ + \_\_\_ = \_\_\_$$

**Talk About It** What patterns do you see?

**Notes for Home:** Your child found all the pairs of numbers that add to make 6. *Home Activity:* Ask your child to tell you one way to make 6. (Sample answer: 2 + 4 = 6)

Use  . Show different ways to make 7.
Write the number sentences.

**2**

| | Ways to Make 7 | |
|---|---|---|

7 = 0 + 7      ___ = ___ + ___

___ = ___ + ___      ___ = ___ + ___

___ = ___ + ___      ___ = ___ + ___

___ = ___ + ___      ___ = ___ + ___

## Problem Solving Patterns

**3** How many ways are there to make 5? _____

**4** How many ways are there to make 6? _____

**5** How many ways are there to make 7? _____

**6** How many ways do you think there

are to make 8? _____

**7** How many ways do you think there

are to make 9? _____

**8** Why do you think so?

_____

_____

 **Notes for Home:** Your child found all the pairs of numbers that add to make 7. *Home Activity:* Ask your child what patterns he or she can find in the Ways to Make 7 chart. (Sample answer: The last number in each number sentence decreases by one.)

Name _____

# Spin to Win

Make your spinner like this!

## What You Need

paper clip ⬭

pencil ✏

## How to Play

① Play with a friend. Use your spinner.

② Spin 2 times for each turn. Use the numbers to make a number sentence.

③ Keep playing until you have 5 different number sentences.

④ Circle your greatest sum. The player with the greatest sum wins.

Player 1

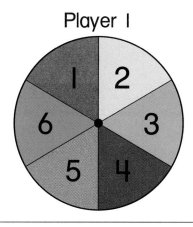

Player 2

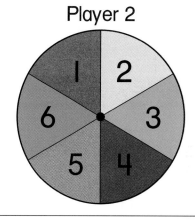

| Name _____ | Name _____ |
|---|---|
| 1. ____ + ____ = ____ | 1. ____ + ____ = ____ |
| 2. ____ + ____ = ____ | 2. ____ + ____ = ____ |
| 3. ____ + ____ = ____ | 3. ____ + ____ = ____ |
| 4. ____ + ____ = ____ | 4. ____ + ____ = ____ |
| 5. ____ + ____ = ____ | 5. ____ + ____ = ____ |

**Notes for Home:** Your child played a game to practice adding numbers with sums to 12.
*Home Activity:* Use the spinners to play the game with your child.

forty-nine **49**

Name _____

Choose 4 colors.
Color each crayon
a different color.

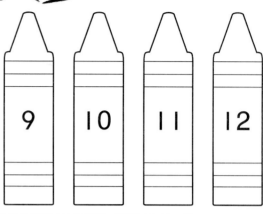

| 9 | 10 | 11 | 12 |

Use ⬤ ⬤ to find the sums.
Color the boxes to match the crayons.

**PRACTICE**

| | | | |
|---|---|---|---|
| **1** | 6 + 5 = 11 | 2 + 7 = ___ | 4 + 7 = ___ |
| **2** | 6 + 6 = ___ | 7 + 3 = ___ | 8 + 4 = ___ |
| **3** | 3 + 8 = ___ | 5 + 4 = ___ | 9 + 2 = ___ |
| **4** | 0 + 12 = ___ | 9 + 1 = ___ | 11 + 1 = ___ |
| **5** | 7 + 4 = ___ | 9 + 0 = ___ | 1 + 10 = ___ |
| **6** | 3 + 9 = ___ | 0 + 10 = ___ | 7 + 5 = ___ |
| **7** | 0 + 11 = ___ | 8 + 1 = ___ | 8 + 3 = ___ |
| **8** | 4 + 8 = ___ | 5 + 5 = ___ | 9 + 3 = ___ |

**Talk About It** Tell about the color patterns that you see.

**Notes for Home:** Your child practiced addition facts. *Home Activity:* Ask your child to say a number sentence with a sum of 8. (Sample answer: 5 + 3 = 8)

# Problem Solving: Write a Number Sentence

**Learn** ● ● ● ● ● ● ● ● ● ● ● ● ● ●

**PROBLEM SOLVING GUIDE**

Understand ● Plan ● Solve ● Look Back

Write a number sentence. Solve.

5 children are eating lunch.
2 children join them.
How many children are eating
lunch now?

$5 + 2 = 7$ children

**Check** ● ● ● ● ● ● ● ● ● ● ● ● ● ● ● ● ● ● ● ● ● ● ●

Write a number sentence. Solve. You can use 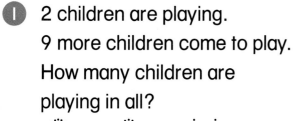.

**1** 2 children are playing.
9 more children come to play.
How many children are
playing in all?

$2 + 9 = 11$ children

**2** 6 children are riding bicycles.
4 children join them.
How many children are riding
bicycles now?

_____ children

**3** Luis found 8 🪵.

Ming found 4 🪵.

How many 🪵 did they
find in all?

_____

**4** 6 🪁 were stuck in the tree.

6 more 🪁 got stuck.

Then how many 🪁 were
stuck?

_____

**Talk About It** What other number sentence
could you use to solve the problem about bicycles?

**Notes for Home:** Your child wrote number sentences to solve story problems. *Home Activity:* Ask your
child to make up a story problem and tell a number sentence that can be used to solve it.

**Practice** ● ● ● ● ● ● ● ● ● ● ● ● ● ● ● ● ● ● ● ● ● ● ●

**Write your own.** Complete each sentence.

Write a number sentence. You can use  .

**5** _____ 🦆 are swimming.

_____ more 🦆 join them.

How many 🦆 are swimming now?

_____

**6** _____ 🐕 are playing.

_____ more 🐕 join them.

How many 🐕 are playing in all?

_____

**7** There are _____ 🐦 in a tree.

_____ more 🐦 fly to the tree.

How many 🐦 are in the tree now?

_____

**8** Pedro saw _____ 🦋 in a bush

and _____ 🦋 near the pond.

How many 🦋 did he see in all?

_____

## Tell a Math Story

**9** Use the picture. Tell an addition story to a friend. Ask your friend to solve it by writing a number sentence.

_____ + _____ = _____

**PROBLEM SOLVING**

Name _____

# Mixed Practice
## Lessons 1–6

## Concepts and Skills

Add. You can use 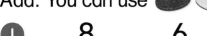 .

**1**
| 8 | 6 | 12 | 4 | 9 | 7 | 10 |
|---|---|----|---|---|---|----|
| + 3 | + 4 | + 0 | + 2 | + 3 | + 2 | + 1 |

These pictures show turnaround facts.
Write the number sentence for each picture.

**2**

_____

_____

**3**

_____

_____

## Problem Solving

Write a number sentence. Solve. You can use  .

**4** Tara saw 5 children at the swings.
She saw 4 children at the pond.
How many children did she
see in all?

____ + ____ = ____ children

**5** 2 children were playing tag.
5 more children came to play.
How many children played tag
in all?

____ + ____ = ____ children

## Journal

**6** How can you use turnaround facts to help you find sums?

**Notes for Home:** Your child practiced addition and problem-solving skills. *Home Activity:* Ask your child how the number sentences in Exercise 2 are alike and how they are different. (Sample answer: They both have the same sum; the numbers are in a different order.)

Name _____

# Cumulative Review
### Chapters 1–2

## Concepts and Skills

Count by ones. Write the numbers.

**1** 23, 24, 25, ____, ____, ____, ____, ____, ____, ____

Count back by ones. Write the numbers.

**2** 17, 16, 15, ____, ____, ____, ____, ____, ____, ____

## Problem Solving

**3** Use the tally marks to make a bar graph.

### Votes for Favorite Picnic Foods

|  |  |
|---|---|
| (chicken leg) II | (hamburger) ЖЖ II |
| (sandwich) ЖЖ | (hot dog) IIII |

**Favorite Picnic Foods**

| 8 |  |  |  |  |
|---|---|---|---|---|
| 7 |  |  |  |  |
| 6 |  |  |  |  |
| 5 |  |  |  |  |
| 4 |  |  |  |  |
| 3 |  |  |  |  |
| 2 |  |  |  |  |
| 1 |  |  |  |  |
|  | (chicken) | (hamburger) | (sandwich) | (hot dog) |

**4** How many people chose ? ____ people

**5** Which food was chosen the most? Circle the picture.

---

**Test Prep**

Fill in the ○ for the correct answer.

Find the missing number in the pattern.

**6** 3, 6, 9, ____, 15, 18, 21, 24

○ 10
○ 11
○ 12
○ 13

**Notes for Home:** Your child reviewed counting, using tally marks and graphs, and finding number patterns. *Home Activity:* Ask your child to tell which food was chosen more in Exercise 3, hamburger or hot dog. (hamburger)

## Separate Groups to Subtract

**Learn**

When you subtract, the answer is called the difference.

10  are in the tree.

3  leave.

How many  are still in the tree?

10 − 3 = 7

**Check**

Use  to subtract.
Write the number sentence.

**1** 9  are on a stick.

5  fly away.

How many  are there now?

9 − 5 = 4

**2** 8  are swimming.

2  swim away.

How many  are still there?

____ − ____ = ____

**3** 11  are in the bush.

2  fly away.

How many  are still in the bush?

____ − ____ = ____

**4** 12  are in the grass.

4  hop away.

How many  are still in the grass?

____ − ____ = ____

**Talk About It** Which problem above has the greatest difference?

 **Notes for Home:** Your child used counters and wrote number sentences to subtract.
*Home Activity:* Ask your child to use objects, such as pennies, to show 9 − 3 = 6.

Use  to subtract.
Write the number sentence.

**5** 7  are playing.

2  run away.

How many  are left?

7 – 2 = 5

**6** 10  are in a bowl.

Stan eats 5  .

How many  are left?

____ – ____ = ____

**7** 9  are in the grass.

6  run away.

How many  are left?

____ – ____ = ____

**8** 11  are on the plate.

Jo takes 4  away.

How many  are left?

____ – ____ = ____

## Problem Solving Visual Thinking

Draw a picture to solve.
Write the number sentence.

**9** First there were 8  .

Later, 3  were left on the tree.

How many  flew away?

____ – ____ = ____

 **Notes for Home:** Your child used counters to subtract and then wrote number sentences.
*Home Activity:* Ask your child to use small objects to act out a subtraction story.

# Count Back and Subtract Zero

**Learn** ● ● ● ● ● ● ● ● ● ● ● ● ● ● ● ● ● ● ● ● ● ● ● ● ● ●

There are 11 pretzel rods.

Sam takes 2 rods.

How many rods are still on the blanket?

On the number line I go to 11. Then I count back two: 11, ...10, 9.

◄——┼——┼——┼——┼——┼——┼——┼——┼——┼——┼——┼——┼——┼——►
0   1   2   3   4   5   6   7   8   9   10  11  12

There are 9 rods on the blanket.    $11 - 2 = 9$

**Check** ● ● ● ● ● ● ● ● ● ● ● ● ● ● ● ● ● ● ● ● ● ● ● ● ● ●

◄——┼——┼——┼——┼——┼——┼——┼——┼——┼——┼——┼——┼——┼——►
0   1   2   3   4   5   6   7   8   9   10  11  12

Use the number line. Write the difference

**1**
$$\begin{array}{cccccccc} 10 & 8 & 11 & 12 & 5 & 7 & 8 \\ -2 & -1 & -0 & -1 & -0 & -2 & -2 \\ \hline 8 \end{array}$$

**2**
$$\begin{array}{cccccccc} 9 & 4 & 12 & 8 & 6 & 3 & 7 \\ -2 & -0 & -2 & -0 & -1 & -0 & -1 \\ \hline \end{array}$$

**Talk About It** How can the number line help you subtract?

**Notes for Home:** Your child subtracted 0, 1, and 2 from numbers to 12. *Home Activity:* Have your child show you $10 - 2 = 8$ using the number line.

```
◄──┼───┼───┼───┼───┼───┼───┼───┼───┼───┼───┼───┼───┼──►
   0   1   2   3   4   5   6   7   8   9  10  11  12
```

You can use the number line. Write the difference.

③
| 9 | 11 | 7 | 6 | 10 | 9 | 5 |
|---|----|---|---|----|---|---|
| − 2 | − 1 | − 0 | − 2 | − 0 | − 0 | − 1 |
| 7 | | | | | | |

④
| 7 | 10 | 4 | 8 | 6 | 12 | 11 |
|---|----|---|---|---|----|----|
| − 2 | − 1 | − 2 | − 2 | − 0 | − 0 | − 2 |

⑤
| 5 | 10 | 5 | 9 | 11 | 7 | 6 |
|---|----|---|---|----|---|---|
| − 2 | − 2 | − 0 | − 1 | − 0 | − 1 | − 1 |

**Mixed Practice** Add or subtract.

⑥
| 7 | 1 | 11 | 3 | 8 | 3 | 8 |
|---|---|----|---|---|---|---|
| + 0 | + 9 | + 1 | − 1 | + 2 | − 2 | − 0 |
| 7 | | | | | | |

⑦
| 3 | 7 | 12 | 3 | 4 | 8 | 9 |
|---|---|----|---|---|---|---|
| + 5 | + 2 | − 2 | + 8 | − 0 | − 1 | + 3 |

## Problem Solving Critical Thinking

⑧ What do you notice about subtracting zero from a number?

**Notes for Home:** Your child practiced adding and subtracting. *Home Activity:* Ask your child to show 6 + 2 = 8 and 5 − 2 = 3 using the number line.

**For additional practice, see Skills Practice Bank, page 528, Set 2.**

Name _____

**Explore** • • • • • • • • • • • • • • • • • • • • • • • • • • • • • • •

Use ⬤ to show apples.

Use ⬤ to show bananas.

Tell a story about which group has more.

Use a different number of ⬤ and ⬤ to show food.

Tell new stories about which group has more.

Draw one of your stories.

**Share** • • • • • • • • • • • • • • • • • • • • • • • • • • • • • • •

Tell one of your stories.

**Notes for Home:** Your child told stories about comparing two groups using this picture.
*Home Activity:* Have your child tell you one of his or her stories.

I have 4 blue cups.
I have 3 red cups.

You have 1 more blue cup.

EXPLORE

Use ⬤ ⬭ to solve.

**1** There are 8 🔪 on the table.

There are 7 🍴 on the table.

How many more 🔪 are there?

_____ more

**2** There are 6 🥤 .

There are 4 🥤(straw) .

How many more 🥤 are there?

_____ more

**3** There are 10 🍽️ .

There are 5 🧻 .

How many more 🍽️ are there?

_____ more

**4** There are 9 🥣 .

There are 6 🥄 .

How many more 🥣 are there?

_____ more

## Problem Solving  Visual Thinking

**5** How many more 🥤 than 🍴 ?

_____ more

**6** How many more 🍴 than 🍽️ ?

_____ more

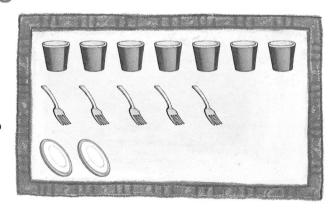

**Notes for Home:** Your child used counters to compare groups. *Home Activity:* Ask your child to take some spoons and some forks and compare how many are in the two groups.

Name _____

**Learn** • • • • • • • • • • • • • • • • • • • • • • • • • • • • •

How many more  than  ?

*I can see there are 4 more yellow.*

**4 more**

*I can subtract to find out.*

**7 − 3 = 4**

**Check** • • • • • • • • • • • • • • • • • • • • • • • • • • • • •

Write the number sentence. Solve.

You can use  .

**1** How many more  than  ?

9 − 8 = 1 more

____ − ____ = ____ more

**2** How many more  than  ?

____ − ____ = ____ more

**3** How many more  than  ?

____ − ____ = ____ more

**4** How many more  than  ?

____ − ____ = ____ more

**Talk About It** Can you solve these problems without writing a number sentence? Explain.

 **Notes for Home:** Your child used subtraction to compare groups. *Home Activity:* Ask your child to make a group of 9 objects and a group of 5 objects. Have your child write a number sentence to find which group has more. (9 − 5 = 4; 4 more)

Write the number sentence. Solve.

You can use .

**5** Jan found 10 .

Don found 3 .

How many more  did Jan find?

10 − 3 = 7 ____ more

**6** John had 11 .

Ben had 5 .

How many more  did John have than Ben?

____ − ____ = ____ more

**7** Al saw 12 .

Maria saw 7 .

How many more  did Al see than Maria?

____ − ____ = ____ more

**8** Jane saw 8 .

Pat saw 6 .

How many more  did Jane see?

____ − ____ = ____ more

## Problem Solving Visual Thinking

**9** Draw less than 10  on the .

How many more  than ?
Write a number sentence.

____ − ____ = ____ more

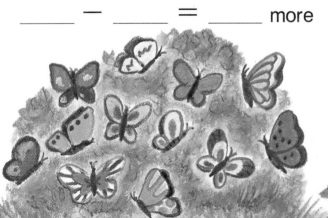
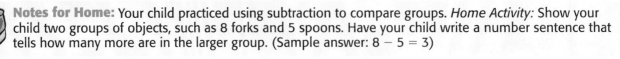

 **Notes for Home:** Your child practiced using subtraction to compare groups. *Home Activity:* Show your child two groups of objects, such as 8 forks and 5 spoons. Have your child write a number sentence that tells how many more are in the larger group. (Sample answer: 8 − 5 = 3)

Name _____

# Relate Addition and Subtraction

**Learn** ● ● ● ● ● ● ● ● ● ● ● ● ● ● ● ● ● ● ● ● ● ● ●

You have 7  . You get 4 more.

How many  in all?

$$\underline{7} + \underline{4} = \underline{11}$$

You have 11  . You give 4  away.

How many  do you have now?

$$\underline{11} - \underline{4} = \underline{7}$$

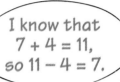

I know that
7 + 4 = 11,
so 11 − 4 = 7.

**Check** ● ● ● ● ● ● ● ● ● ● ● ● ● ● ● ● ● ● ● ● ● ●

Add or subtract.
Write the number sentence. Solve.

**1** Sam had 5  .

Carol came with 6 more.

How many  in all?

___ + ___ = ___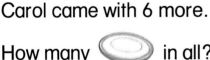

**2** Sam and Carol had 11  .

Carol took away 6  .

How many  did
Sam have left?

___ − ___ = ___

**Talk About It** How can you use addition
to help you solve 9 − 3?

 **Notes for Home:** Your child used related addition and subtraction facts to solve problems.
*Home Activity:* Use items, such as beans, to act out Exercises 1 and 2 with your child.

Add or subtract.

Write the number sentence. Solve.

**PRACTICE**

**3** 4  were on the table.

Lee came with 6 more.

How many  were there in all?

$\underline{4} + \underline{6} = \underline{10}$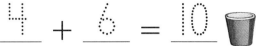

**4** 10  were on the table.

Lee took 6 .

How many  were left?

____ − ____ = ____

**5** Ken found 3 .

Eva found 9 .

How many  did they find in all?

____ + ____ = ____

**6** There were 12 .

Eva took 9 away.

How many  were left?

____ − ____ = ____

**7** Manny found 2 .

Lisa found 9 .

How many  did they find in all?

____ + ____ = ____

**8** There were 11 .

Lisa took 9 away.

How many  were left?

____ − ____ = ____

## Tell a Math Story

Look at the picture. Tell stories to match the number sentences.

**9** $2 + 5 = 7$

**10** $7 - 5 = 2$

**Notes for Home:** Your child solved word problems. *Home Activity:* Ask your child to say a related subtraction sentence for $2 + 7 = 9$. ($9 - 7 = 2$ or $9 - 2 = 7$)

Name ______________________

Reading for Math

# Compare and Contrast

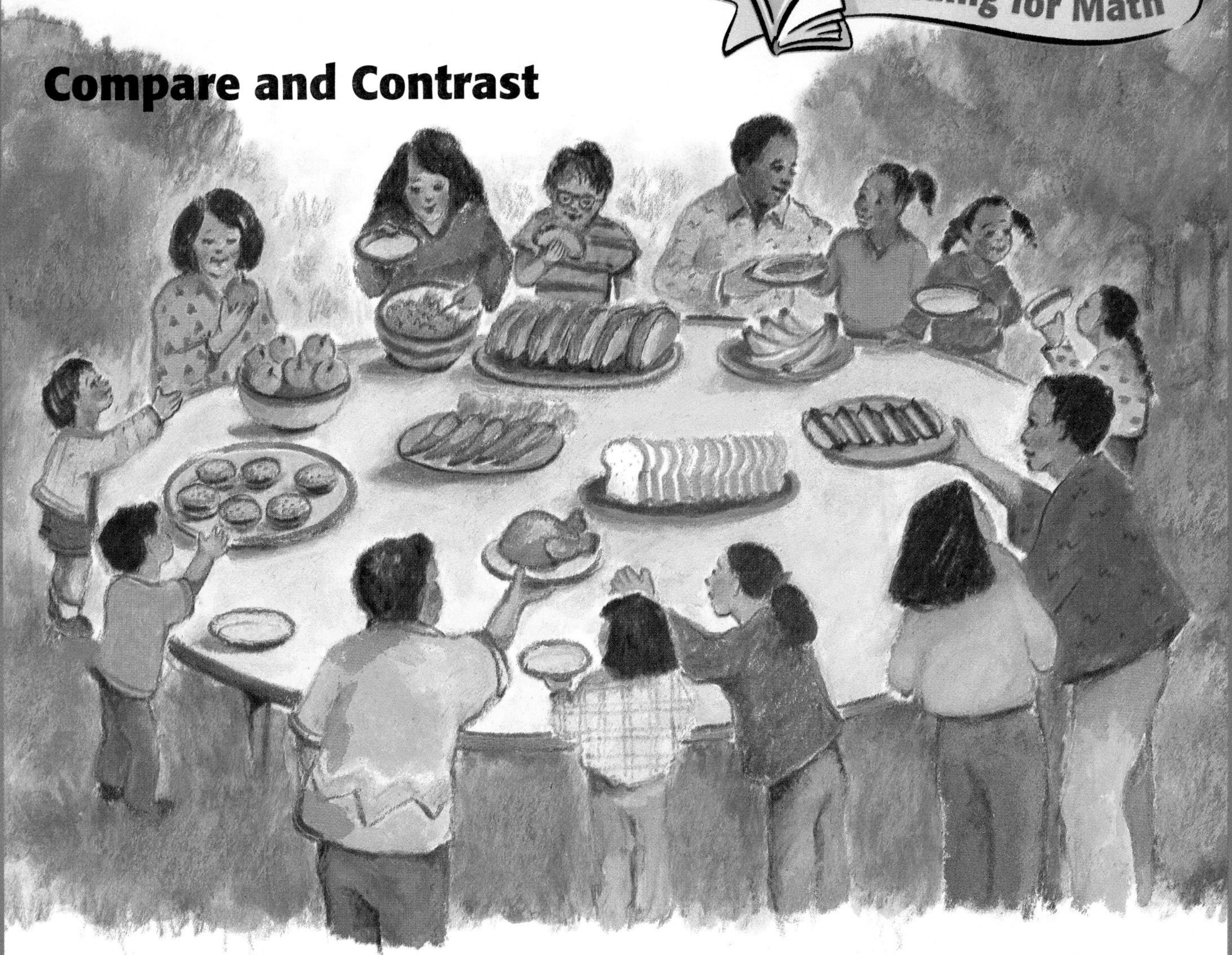

Use the picture.

Tell addition stories.

Tell subtraction stories.

1. How are addition and subtraction stories alike?

______________________

______________________

2. How are addition and subtraction stories different?

______________________

______________________

**Notes for Home:** Your child compared addition and subtraction stories. *Home Activity:* Show your child some items, such as pens and pencils. Ask your child to make up an addition story and a subtraction story using the items.

Use the picture. Tell an addition story.

**3**   How do you know it is an addition story?

_____

_____

Tell a subtraction story.

**4**   How do you know it is a subtraction story?

_____

_____

**Talk About It**  Tell an addition story and a subtraction story about the same group of people in the picture.

**Notes for Home:** Your child talked about the differences between addition and subtraction. *Home Activity:* Ask your child to draw a simple picture and tell addition and subtraction stories about it.

# Problem Solving: Choose an Operation

**Learn** • • • • • • • • • • • • • • • •

Two groups are joined together. Add.

Part of the group is taken away. Subtract.

5 children are flying kites.
3 more children join them.
How many children are flying kites in all?

$5 + 3 = 8$ _____ children

8 children are flying kites.
3 children go home.
How many children are left?

$8 - 3 = 5$ _____ children

**Check** • • • • • • • • • • • • • • • • • • • • • • • • • • • •

Circle **add** or **subtract**. Write the number sentence.
Solve. You can use ⬤ ⬤ .

1  10  are in the grass.

2  hop away.

How many  are still in the grass?

**add**   (**subtract**)

$10 - 2 = 8$
_____

2  There were 6  .

3 more  came.

How many  were there in all?

**add**     **subtract**

_____

**Talk About It** How did you decide whether
to add or subtract in the problem about bees?

**Notes for Home:** Your child chose addition or subtraction to solve problems. *Home Activity:* Ask your child to tell a math story that would be solved by adding.

Circle **add** or **subtract**.
Write the number sentence.
Solve. You can use  .

**3** 12 children were playing softball.
3 children went home.
How many children were left?

add ⟨ **subtract** ⟩

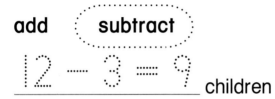 children

**4** Nora saw 2 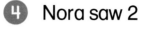 .

Lucy saw 8 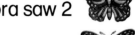 .

How many  did they
see in all?

add      subtract

_____

**5** Pam ate 7  .

Her sister ate 5 .

How many did they
eat all together?

add      subtract

_____

**6** 8 children played on the swings.
8 children got off.
How many children were left?

add      subtract

_____ children

## Write About It

**7** Make up your own story.
Have a friend write a number sentence to solve it.

 **Notes for Home:** Your child practiced choosing addition or subtraction to solve problems.
*Home Activity:* Ask your child to make up a problem that could be solved by subtracting.

     **For additional practice, see Skills Practice Bank, page 528, Set 3.**

Name _____

# Mixed Practice
**Lessons 7–12**

## Concepts and Skills

Subtract. You can use .

**❶**

| 5 | 9 | 4 | 2 | 12 | 5 | 11 |
|---|---|---|---|----|---|----|
| − 1 | − 3 | − 4 | − 1 | − 3 | − 3 | − 0 |

## Problem Solving

Subtract. Write the number sentence.

You can use .

**❷** Carl found 10 .

4 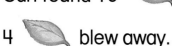 blew away.

How many  were left?

____ − ____ = ____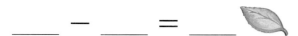

**❸** 8  are in the grass.

4  run away.

How many  are left?

____ − ____ = ____

Circle **add** or **subtract**. Write a number sentence.

Solve. You can use .

**❹** 8 children are riding bicycles.
4 children join them.
How many children are riding now?

**add**     **subtract**

_____ children

**❺** 7 children are on the swings.
2 children get off.
How many children are left?

**add**     **subtract**

_____ children

## Journal

**❻** Write your own word problem using the numbers
3, 5, and 8. Would you add or subtract to solve it?
Write the number sentence.

 **Notes for Home:** Your child practiced subtraction and problem-solving skills. *Home Activity:* Ask your child to use objects, such as buttons or beans and tell a math story that could be solved by adding.

MIXED PRACTICE

Name _____

# Cumulative Review
### Chapters 1–2

## Concepts and Skills

Write the number sentence. Solve.

**1** 9  are on the rock.

4  jump off.

How many  are still on the rock?

___ − ___ = ___

**2** 2  are on the table.

8  are in the basket.

How many  are there in all?

___ + ___ = ___

Count by ones. Write the numbers.

**3** 47, 48, 49, ____, ____, ____, ____, ____, ____

Count back by ones. Write the numbers.

**4** 24, 23, 22, ____, ____, ____, ____, ____, ____

## Test Prep

Fill in the ○ for the correct answer.

**5** Which train and number sentence show the turnaround fact for the train and number sentence below?

2 + 9 = 11

○  7 + 4 = 11

○  8 + 3 = 11

○  9 + 2 = 11

 **Notes for Home:** Your child reviewed addition and subtraction skills. *Home Activity:* Ask your child to tell what the next three numbers would be in Exercise 4. (Answer: 15, 14, 13)

**70** seventy

# Chapter 2 Review

## Vocabulary

**1** Find the sum.  $7 + 5 =$ _____

**2** Find the difference.  $10 - 4 =$ _____

**3** Write the turnaround fact.

$3 + 5 = 8$ _____

## Concepts and Skills

Write the number sentence. Solve.

**4** 4 children are playing catch.
5 more children join them.
How many children are
playing now?

_____ $+$ _____ $=$ _____ children

**5** Ben found 10 .

Ann found 2 .

How many more  did
Ben find than Ann?

_____ $-$ _____ $=$ _____ more

## Problem Solving

Write the number sentence. Solve.

**6** 12 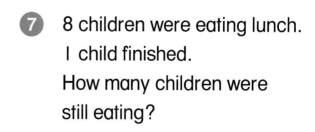 are on the table.

Sandy takes 5  away.

How many  are there now?

_____

**7** 8 children were eating lunch.
1 child finished.
How many children were
still eating?

_____ children

 **Notes for Home:** Your child reviewed Chapter 2 vocabulary, concepts, skills, and problem solving.
*Home Activity:* Ask your child to tell how he or she solved Exercise 5.

CHAPTER REVIEW

Name _____

# Chapter 2 Test

Write the turnaround fact. Solve.

**①** $5 + 3 = 8$

_____

**②** $9 + 1 = 10$

_____

Circle **add** or **subtract**.
Write a number sentence. Solve.

**③** Beth found 11  .

Eric found 3  .

How many more  did
Beth find than Eric?

**add**          **subtract**

_____ more

Add or subtract.

**④**

|  7  |  9  | 12  |  5  |  4  | 10  |  8  |
|-----|-----|-----|-----|-----|-----|-----|
| + 3 | − 0 | − 3 | + 1 | + 0 | − 2 | − 1 |

Show two ways to make 8.

**⑤** ___ + ___ = ___          **⑥** ___ + ___ = ___

Write the number sentence. Solve.

**⑦** There were 5 children on
the swings. 4 more children
got on. How many children
were there in all?

_____ children

**⑧** There were 9 children on
the swings. 4 children got off.
How many children were left?

_____ children

 **Notes for Home:** Your child was tested on Chapter 2 concepts, skills, and problem solving.
*Home Activity:* Ask your child how he or she decided what number sentence to write for Exercise 8.

Name _____

# Performance Assessment

## Chapter 2

Write a story problem.

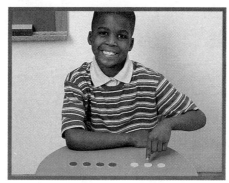

Use counters to show the problem.

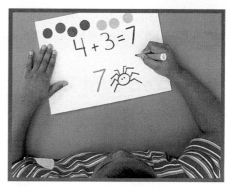

Draw your counters. Write the number sentence. Solve.

1. Write a story problem that uses addition.

_____

_____

_____

4. Write a story problem that uses subtraction.

_____

_____

_____

2. Draw your counters.

5. Draw your counters.

3. Write the number sentence. Solve.

____ + ____ = ____

6. Write the number sentence. Solve.

____ − ____ = ____

## Critical Thinking

7. Tell another story problem using one of your number sentences.

**Notes for Home:** Your child did an activity that tested Chapter 2 skills, concepts, and problem solving. *Home Activity:* Ask your child to make up a story problem and write a number sentence to solve it.

Name _____

## Calculate the Ways!

**Keys You Will Use** [ON/C] [+] [=]

Use your 🖩 to show one way to make 10.

Press [ON/C] [2] [+] [2] [+] [1] [+] [5] [=] [10.]

Use your 🖩 to find more ways to make 10.

Write the number sentences.

*What number do I need to write here?*

1  [3] + [4] + [1] + [ ] = [10.]

2  [ ] + [ ] + [ ] + [ ] = [10.]

3  [ ] + [ ] + [ ] = [10.]

4  [ ] + [ ] + [ ] + [ ] = [10.]

Use your 🖩 to find ways to make 12.

Write the number sentences.

5  [ ] + [ ] + [ ] + [ ] = [12.]

6  [ ] + [ ] + [ ] + [ ] = [12.]

7  [ ] + [ ] + [ ] + [ ] = [12.]

**Tech Talk** How did you find the last number in each number sentence?

💻 **Visit our Web site. www.parent.mathsurf.com**

# NumberShuffle

**Players** 2

## What You Need
12 cards numbered 1-12

## How to Play
1 Put the cards facedown. Spread them apart.

2 Turn over 3 cards. Try to make an addition or subtraction sentence using the numbers.

3 If you cannot make an addition or subtraction sentence, put the cards back. If you can make an addition or subtraction sentence, keep the cards and take another turn.

4 The player with the most cards wins!

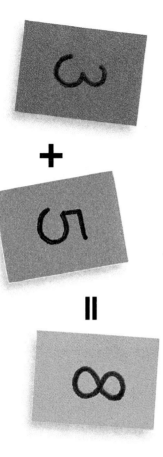

$$3 + 5 = 8$$

**Fold down**

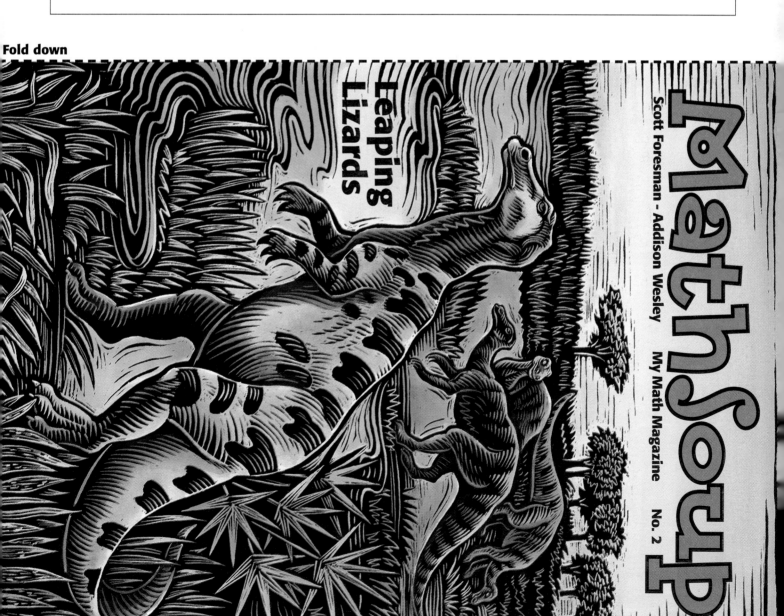

Leaping Lizards

Scott Foresman - Addison Wesley   My Math Magazine   No. 2

MathSoup

You can write numbers greater than 9 in Braille. To write 10, the dot patterns for 1 and 0 are shown next to each other.

| 10 |
| :-: |
| 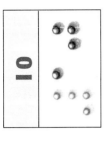 |

Write the numbers for these Braille dot patterns.

1

2

_____

Write the dot patterns below these numbers.

3    37

4    48

_____

5    Pick your own number and write the dot pattern for it.

---

## Math in Your World

# Lizzie's Lizard

Imagine having a dinosaur named after you! That happened to nine-year-old Lizzie Williams. How did it happen? While hiking with her family in Alaska, Lizzie found some strange-looking rocks. The rocks turned out to be Hadrosaur fossils. A scientist named the fossil bones "Lizzie."

Look at these dinosaur bones.

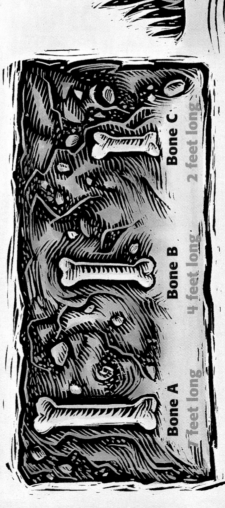

**Bone A**  7 feet long    **Bone B**  4 feet long    **Bone C**  2 feet long

1  How much longer is Bone A than Bone B? ____ feet

2  If Bones B and C were placed end to end, how long would they be? ____ feet

**Notes for Home:** Your child solved problems about dinosaur bones. *Home Activity:* Ask your child to make up a story problem about the dinosaur bones. Then ask him or her to solve the problem.

# Read It with Feeling

Braille is a written language for the blind. Patterns of raised dots stand for letters and numbers. People read the dots by touching them. This dot pattern means that a number comes next:

The dots below stand for numbers.

| 0 | 1 | 2 | 3 | 4 |
|---|---|---|---|---|

| 5 | 6 | 7 | 8 | 9 |
|---|---|---|---|---|

What has a long neck, three wheels, and weighs more than a ton?

Answer: A dinosaur riding a tricycle.

# Join the Team

This is a picture of the Troopers soccer team.
Use the names and numbers in the picture to
answer the riddles.

## Who Am I?

I am standing. When you subtract my
shirt number from 11, the difference is 6.
My name is _____.

## Who Are We?

We are both sitting. The sum of our shirt
numbers is 17. Our names are
_____ and _____.

Make up your own riddles using the picture.
Ask a friend to solve them.

 **Notes for Home:** Your child used logical reasoning, addition, and
subtraction to solve problems. *Home Activity:* Ask your child to tell you
how he or she solved one of the riddles.

# Addition and Subtraction Facts and Strategies

Fun and Games

Dear
I am having a great time.
I learned to play 3 new
games from different
countries. I flew kites and
saw beautiful gardens.
Miss you,
Sandra

I got some postcards in the mail. Let's tell some math stories.

**Notes for Home:** Your child told addition and subtraction stories about groups in the picture. *Home Activity:* Ask your child to tell you an addition story and a subtraction story about the children playing games.

Dear Family,
Our class is starting Chapter 3. We will add numbers with sums (totals) to 18. We will also subtract from numbers up to 18. Here are some activities we can do together.

### Flash Card Fun
Make flash cards for addition and subtraction facts. Ask your child to match the addition fact with a related subtraction fact, such as $7 + 8 = 15$ and $15 - 8 = 7$.

### Finding Facts
Help your child practice facts. Find two groups of objects, each with 1–9 items. Add to find how many there are in all.

$$\begin{array}{r} 7 \\ +\ 8 \\ \hline 15 \end{array} \qquad \begin{array}{r} 15 \\ -\ 8 \\ \hline 7 \end{array}$$

### Community Connection

Take your child to the park. Look for situations that show addition and subtraction. For example: 6 children are playing on the slide. 4 children are swinging. How many children are playing in all?

Visit our Web site. www.parent.mathsurf.com

Name _____

**Explore** ● ● ● ● ● ● ● ● ● ● ● ● ● ● ● ● ● ● ● ● ● ● ● ● ● ●

You will need: 18  .

Take some cubes.
Write how many in all.

Make a train.

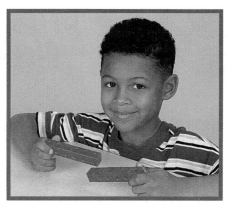

Try to break the train
into 2 equal groups.

| How many  in all? | Can you break the train into 2 equal groups? | How many  in each of the 2 groups? |
|---|---|---|
| **1** _____ | yes          no | _____ and _____ |
| **2** _____ | yes          no | _____ and _____ |
| **3** _____ | yes          no | _____ and _____ |
| **4** _____ | yes          no | _____ and _____ |

**Share** ● ● ● ● ● ● ● ● ● ● ● ● ● ● ● ● ● ● ● ● ● ● ● ● ● ●

How can you build a train that will break into two equal groups?

**Notes for Home:** Your child explored doubles facts (such as 6 + 6 = 12) with Snap Cubes.
*Home Activity:* Ask your child if a train of 8 cubes can be broken into two equal groups.
(Yes; 2 groups of 4 cubes each)

$$7 + 7 = 14$$

$$7 + 7 \qquad 8 + 8 \qquad 9 + 9$$

Add. Write the sums. You can use 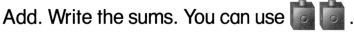.

**5**  $7 + 7 = \underline{14}$    $8 + 8 = \underline{\phantom{00}}$    $9 + 9 = \underline{\phantom{00}}$

**6**  $1 + 1 = \underline{\phantom{00}}$    $2 + 2 = \underline{\phantom{00}}$    $3 + 3 = \underline{\phantom{00}}$

**7**  $4 + 4 = \underline{\phantom{00}}$    $5 + 5 = \underline{\phantom{00}}$    $6 + 6 = \underline{\phantom{00}}$

**8**
$$\begin{array}{ccccccc} 3 & 4 & 5 & 6 & 7 & 8 & 9 \\ +3 & +4 & +5 & +6 & +7 & +8 & +9 \\ \hline \end{array}$$

**Talk About It**  Look at the last row of facts. What pattern do you see in the sums?

**Notes for Home:** Your child found the sums for doubles facts such as 6 + 6 = 12.
*Home Activity:* Ask your child if 8 + 7 = 15 is a doubles fact and to explain how he or she knows.
(Sample Answer: No, because 8 and 7 are two different numbers.)

## Use Doubles Plus One

**Learn**

6 + 7 is 1 more than 6 + 6.
6 + 7 is a double plus one.

| Double | Double Plus One | Turnaround Fact |
|---|---|---|

6 + 6 = _12_          6 + _7_ = _13_          7 + _6_ = _13_

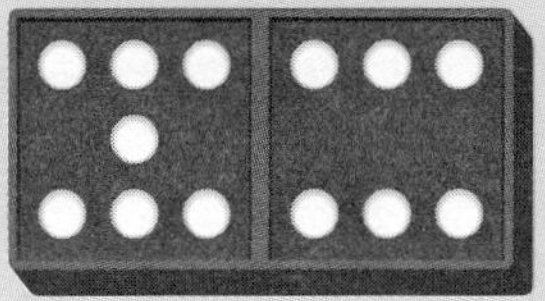

**Check**

Complete the number sentences.

**1**

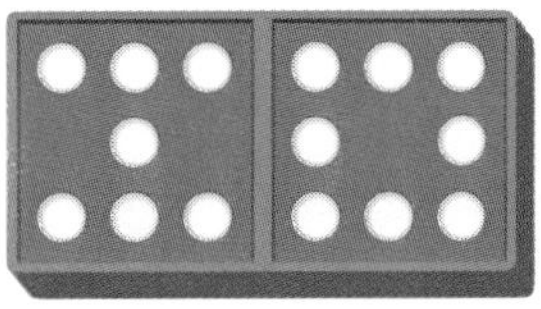

7 + 7 = _14_     7 + _8_ = _15_     8 + _7_ = _15_

**2**
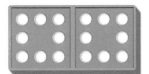

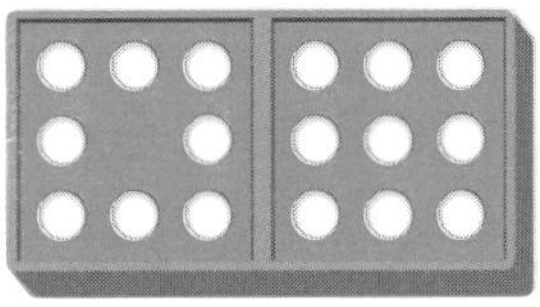

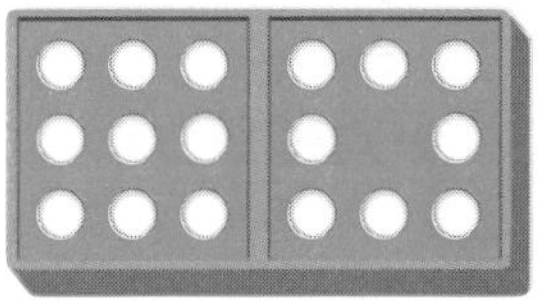

8 + 8 = ___     8 + ___ = ___     9 + ___ = ___

**3**

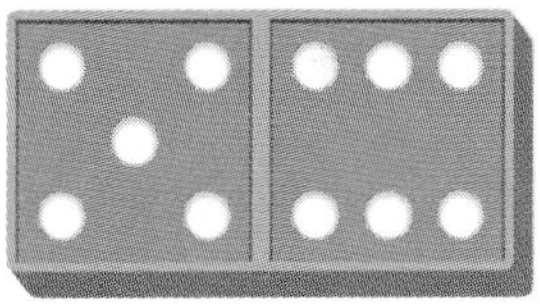

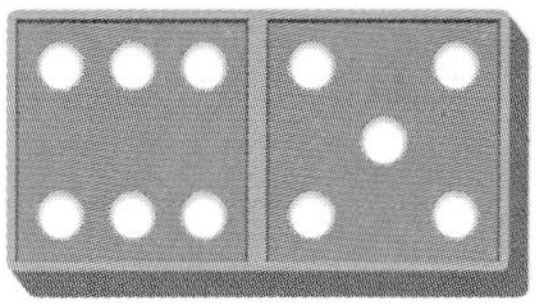

5 + 5 = ___     5 + ___ = ___     6 + ___ = ___

**Talk About It** Is 17 the sum of a doubles fact? Explain.

**Notes for Home:** Your child used double facts such as 7 + 7 = 14 to find sums for other facts such as 7 + 8 = 15. *Home Activity:* Ask your child to find 4 + 4 and 4 + 5 (8; 9).

Add.

**④** 7 + 7 = 14    7 + 8 = ___    8 + 7 = ___

**⑤** 6 + 6 = ___    6 + 7 = ___    7 + 6 = ___

**⑥**
| 8 | 8 | 9 |
| + 8 | + 9 | + 8 |

**⑦**
| 5 | 5 | 6 |
| + 5 | + 6 | + 5 |

**⑧**
| 9 | 4 | 3 | 6 | 7 | 2 | 8 |
| + 9 | + 4 | + 3 | + 6 | + 7 | + 2 | + 8 |

**⑨**
| 7 | 4 | 9 | 3 | 7 | 6 | 8 |
| + 6 | + 5 | + 8 | + 4 | + 8 | + 5 | + 9 |

**Mixed Practice** Add.

**⑩**
| 3 | 6 | 9 | 2 | 7 | 5 | 5 |
| + 8 | + 3 | + 0 | + 6 | + 2 | + 5 | + 6 |

## Problem Solving Critical Thinking

**⑪** 4 children are dancing in front of a mirror
How many legs would you see? Explain.

 **Notes for Home:** Your child solved addition facts with sums through 18. *Home Activity:* Ask your child to explain how to solve 8 + 9. (Sample answer: 8 + 8 = 16, so 8 + 9 is 1 more or 17.)

Name _____

# Name That Fact!

**Players** 2 to 4

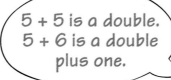

5 + 5 is a double.
5 + 6 is a double plus one.

**What You Need**

10 counters each ⬤ ⬤

**How to Play**

1.  Put all the counters in one pile. Take turns tossing a counter onto the gameboard.
2.  Tell a fact with a sum that matches the number.
3.  Take a counter each time you are correct.
4.  Take an extra counter if you named a doubles or doubles plus one fact.
5.  The player who gets 10 counters first, wins.

| 18 | 5 | 7 | 12 |
| 14 | 8 | 17 | 10 |
| 3 | 16 | 9 | 6 |
| 4 | 13 | 11 | 15 |

**Notes for Home:** Your child used addition facts to play a game. *Home Activity:* Ask your child to name two facts with the sum of 16. (Sample answers: 8 + 8 and 7 + 9)

PRACTICE

Name _____

Draw dots to make these doubles.
Write the number sentences.

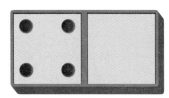

① ___4___ + ___4___ = ___8___

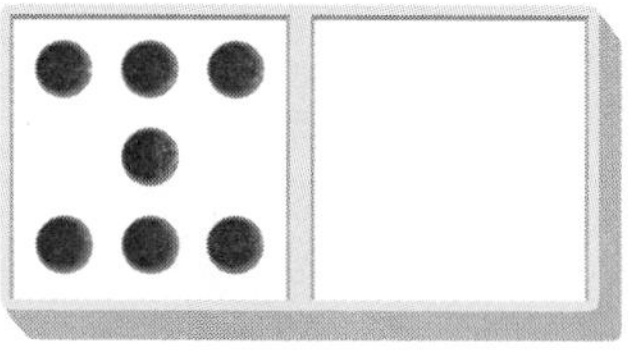

② _____ + _____ = _____

③ _____ + _____ = _____

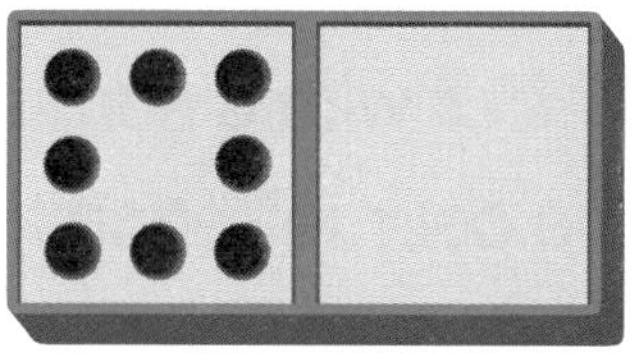

④ _____ + _____ = _____

Draw dots to make doubles plus one facts.
Write the number sentences.

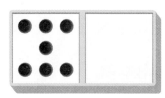

⑤ ___7___ + ___8___ = ___15___

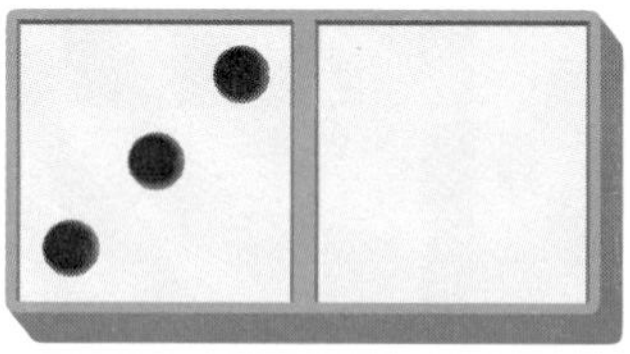

⑥ _____ + _____ = _____

⑦ _____ + _____ = _____

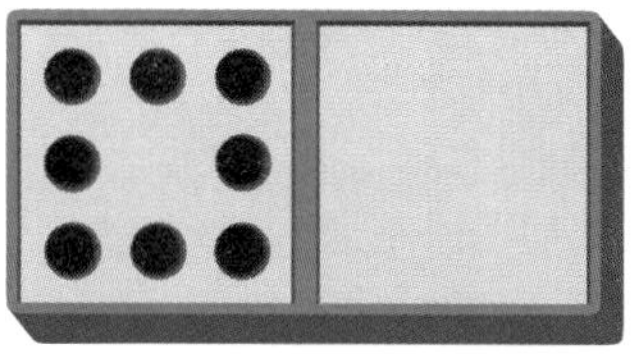

⑧ _____ + _____ = _____

**Notes for Home:** Your child practiced doubles such as 5 + 5 = 10 and doubles plus one facts such as 5 + 6 = 11. *Home Activity:* Ask your child to use the number 7 to make a doubles plus one fact. (7 + 8 = 15)

PRACTICE

Name _____

**Explore** • • • • • • • • • • • • • • • • • • • • • • • • • • •

Draw a picture. You can use thumbprints.
Put 10 things in 2 groups. Tell fun stories.

Write a number sentence for your picture.     _____ + _____ = _____

**Share** • • • • • • • • • • • • • • • • • • • • • • • • • • •

Tell your story and your number sentence.

**Notes for Home:** Your child drew a picture of ten things and told a math story.
*Home Activity:* Ask your child to tell you a math story using his or her picture.

Put a picture in each empty box.
Complete the number sentence.

**EXPLORE**

**1**

$6 + \underline{\hspace{1cm}} = \underline{\hspace{1cm}}$

**2**

$9 + \underline{\hspace{1cm}} = \underline{\hspace{1cm}}$

**3**
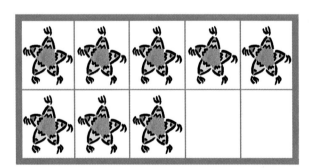

$7 + \underline{\hspace{1cm}} = \underline{\hspace{1cm}}$

**4**

$8 + \underline{\hspace{1cm}} = \underline{\hspace{1cm}}$

**Talk About It** What other number sentences
have a sum of 10?

**Notes for Home:** Your child drew pictures and wrote number sentences with the sum of 10.
*Home Activity:* Ask your child to draw a picture that shows $5 + 5 = 10$.

Name _____

**Learn** • • • • • • • • • • • • • • • • • • • • •

Find 9 + 5.
9 is close to 10.
Make a 10 to
help you add.

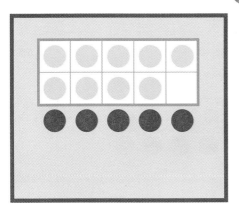

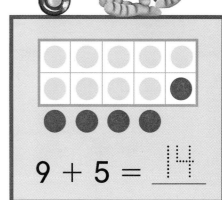

$9 + 5 = \underline{14}$

Show 9. Show 5.          Make a ten.          How many?

**Check** • • • • • • • • • • • • • • • • • • • • • • • • •

Add. Use 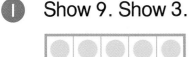 . Write the sum.

1   Show 9. Show 3.          Make a ten.          How many?

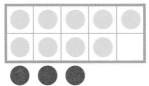

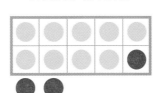

$9 + 3 = \underline{12}$

2   Show 9. Show 6.          Make a ten.          How many?

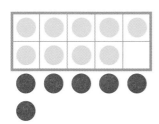

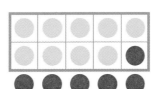

$9 + 6 = \underline{\phantom{00}}$

**Talk About It** Is it easier to add 9 + 6 or 10 + 5? Why?

**Notes for Home:** Your child added 9 to another number by first making a ten. *Home Activity:* Ask your child to explain how to add 9 + 4 by first making a ten.

Add. Write the addition sentence.

**3**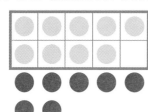

$\underline{9} + \underline{7} = \underline{16}$

**4**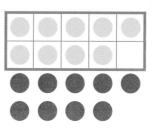

$\underline{\phantom{0}} + \underline{\phantom{0}} = \underline{\phantom{0}}$

**5**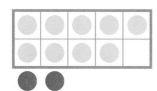

$\underline{\phantom{0}} + \underline{\phantom{0}} = \underline{\phantom{0}}$

**6**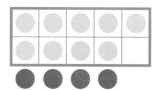

$\underline{\phantom{0}} + \underline{\phantom{0}} = \underline{\phantom{0}}$

Add.

**7**
$$\begin{array}{ccccccc} 9 & 9 & 9 & 9 & 9 & 9 & 9 \\ +7 & +6 & +4 & +8 & +3 & +5 & +9 \\ \hline \end{array}$$

**Mixed Practice** Add.

**8** $6 + 6 = \underline{\phantom{00}}$  $9 + 3 = \underline{\phantom{00}}$  $7 + 2 = \underline{\phantom{00}}$

## Problem Solving Visual Thinking

**9** Amy wants to fill this page with stickers.
Josh gives her 5 more.

How many stickers will not fit on this page? _____ stickers

How many stickers does she have in all? _____ stickers

**Notes for Home:** Your child practiced adding 9 to another number by first making a ten.
*Home Activity:* Ask your child to explain how to solve Exercise 4.

Name _____

**Learn** • • • • • • • • • • • • • • • • • • • • • • •

Find 8 + 6.
8 is close to 10.
Make a 10 to
help you add.

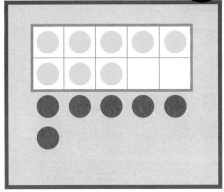

Show 8. Show 6.

Make a ten.

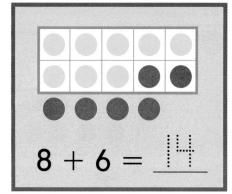

$8 + 6 = 14$

How many?

**Check** • • • • • • • • • • • • • • • • • • • • • • •

Add. Use  . Write the sum.

**1**   Show 8. Show 4.

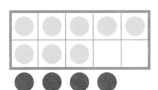

Make a ten.      How many?

$8 + 4 = 12$

---

**2**   Show 6. Show 7.

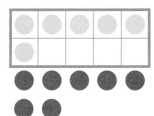

Make a ten.      How many?

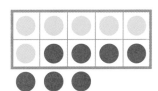

$6 + 7 = \underline{\hspace{1cm}}$

**Talk About It** Explain how to make a 10 to find 7 + 4.

**Notes for Home:** Your child added 6, 7, or 8 to another number by first making a ten.
*Home Activity:* Ask your child to explain how to make a ten when adding 7 + 4.

Add. Write the addition sentence.

**3**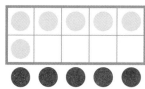

$\underset{6}{\underline{\phantom{6}}} + \underset{5}{\underline{\phantom{5}}} = \underset{11}{\underline{\phantom{11}}}$

**4**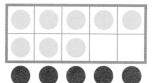

___ + ___ = ___

**5**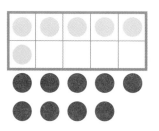

___ + ___ = ___

**6**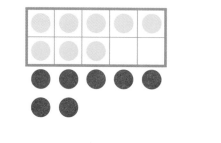

___ + ___ = ___

Add.

**7**

| 7 | 8 | 8 | 7 | 7 | 8 | 6 |
|---|---|---|---|---|---|---|
| +3 | +6 | +9 | +8 | +9 | +2 | +7 |

## Problem Solving Critical Thinking

Carlo and Sumi played Hop-Round.
They each threw two stones into the circle.
Then they added the two numbers.

**8** Carlo's score was 10. What two numbers could he have gotten?

_____ and _____

**9** Sumi's score was 11. What two numbers could he have gotten?

_____ and _____

**Notes for Home:** Your child practiced adding 7 or 8 to another number by first making a ten.
*Home Activity:* Ask your child to explain how he or she would find 8 + 4.

**For additional practice, see Skills Practice Bank, page 529, Set 1.**

© Scott Foresman Addison Wesley

Name _____

**Learn** • • • • • • • • • • • • •

**PROBLEM SOLVING GUIDE**

Understand • Plan • Solve • Look Back

Martin plays a game with stones. Find all the ways he can put 16 stones on 2 gameboards.

Use 16 . Put 15  on the red gameboard. Put 1  on the blue gameboard.

A gameboard holds up to 15 stones.

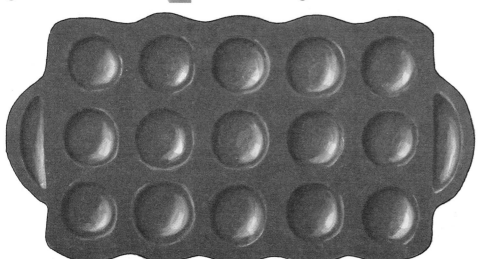

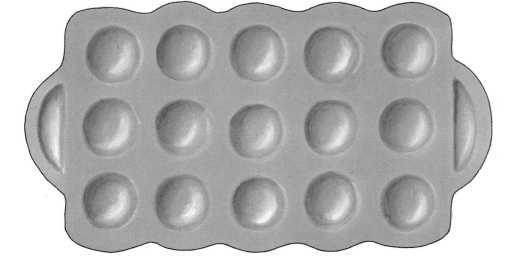

| Red | Blue |
| --- | --- |
| 15 | 1 |
| 14 | 2 |
| | |
| | |
| | |
| | |
| | |
| | |
| | |
| | |
| | |
| | |
| | |
| | |

**Check** • • • • • • • • • • • • • •

❶ Use  to find all the ways.
Write your numbers in the list.

**Talk About It** How is making a list helpful?

**Notes for Home:** Your child made a list to solve a problem. *Home Activity:* Ask your child to list all the ways 9 objects can be put into 2 groups. (1 and 8, 2 and 7, 3 and 6, 4 and 5, and so on)

**PROBLEM SOLVING**

**Chapter 3 Lesson 6**

ninety-three **93**

**Practice**

Shauna puts her toys away.
Find all the ways she can
put 13 toys into 2 toy boxes.

A toy box holds up to 12 toys.

**2** Find all the ways. You can use ▢▢.
Write your numbers in the list.

| Purple | Yellow |
|--------|--------|
| 12 | 1 |
| ___ | ___ |
| ___ | ___ |
| ___ | ___ |
| ___ | ___ |
| ___ | ___ |
| ___ | ___ |
| ___ | ___ |
| ___ | ___ |
| ___ | ___ |
| ___ | ___ |
| ___ | ___ |

**Patterns**

**3** What patterns do you see in your list?

**Notes for Home:** Your child practiced making a list to solve a problem. *Home Activity:* Ask your child to make a list to show all the ways that 11 children can sit in 2 train cars. (1 and 10, 2 and 9, 3 and 8, 4 and 7, 5 and 6, and so on)

**PROBLEM SOLVING**

94 ninety-four

**For additional practice, see Skills Practice Bank, page 529, Set 2.**

Name _____

# Mixed Practice
**Lessons 1–6**

## Concepts and Skills
Add.

❶ $9 + 9 =$ ___    $8 + 8 =$ ___    $7 + 7 =$ ___

Complete the number sentences.

❷

$5 + 5 =$ ___    $5 +$ ___ $=$ ___    $6 +$ ___ $=$ ___

Add. Write the number sentences.

❸ 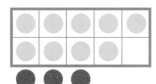        ❹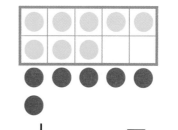

___ $+$ ___ $=$ ___        ___ $+$ ___ $=$ ___

## Problem Solving
Write a number sentence. Solve.

❺ In one week, Jim read 8 books. The next week he read 7 books. How many books did he read in two weeks?

___ $+$ ___ $=$ ___ books

❻ Kristen planted 9 daisies and 7 sunflowers. How many flowers did she plant in all?

___ $+$ ___ $=$ ___ flowers

## Journal

❼ Draw a picture to show doubles.

Write a math story about your picture.

**Notes for Home:** Your child practiced additon facts and solving word problems.
*Home Activity:* Ask your child to explain how he or she would find $9 + 6$.

MIXED PRACTICE

Name _____

# Cumulative Review
## Chapters 1–3

## Concepts and Skills

Continue the pattern.
Write the missing numbers.

Add.

**1** 3, 6, 9, ___, ___, ___

**2** 5, 10, 15, ___, ___, ___

**3**
$$8 + 3 \quad 7 + 1 \quad 4 + 2$$

## Problem Solving

Solve. Write a number sentence.

**4** Rico had 8 crayons. Lin gave her 3 more.
How many crayons did she have then?

___ + ___ = ___ crayons

### Test Prep

Favorite Outdoor Games

| Hide and Seek | 🧍🧍🧍🧍 |
| Jump Rope | 🧍🧍🧍🧍🧍🧍🧍🧍 |
| Kickball | 🧍🧍🧍🧍🧍🧍 |
| Tag | 🧍🧍 |

Each 🧍 means 1 child.

Fill in the ○ to show the correct answer.

**5** Which game did most children choose?

Hide and Seek ○   Jump Rope ○   Kickball ○   Tag ○

**6** How many more children chose **Kickball** than **Tag**?

2 ○   4 ○   6 ○   8 ○

 **Notes for Home:** Your child reviewed number patterns, addition and subtraction facts to 12, and picture graphs. *Home Activity:* Ask your child to tell you what the next three numbers would be in Exercise 2. (35, 40, 45)

Name _____

# Use Doubles to Subtract

**Learn** • • • • • • • • • • • • • • • • • • • • • • • • • • • • • •

$$6 \qquad 12$$
$$+6 \qquad -6$$
$$\overline{12} \qquad \overline{6}$$

When I subtract, I can use doubles to help.

**Check** • • • • • • • • • • • • • • • • • • • • • • • • • • • • • •

Add. Then use doubles to subtract.

 **1**

$$7 \qquad 14$$
$$+7 \qquad -7$$
$$\overline{14} \qquad \overline{7}$$

**2**

$$5 \qquad 10$$
$$+5 \qquad -5$$

 **3**

$$8 \qquad 16$$
$$+8 \qquad -8$$

**4**

$$9 \qquad 18$$
$$+9 \qquad -9$$

**Talk About It** How can you use doubles to help you subtract?

**Notes for Home:** Your child used doubles facts such as 5 + 5 = 10 to subtract. *Home Activity:* Ask your child how to use 6 + 6 = 12 to find 12 − 6.

**Chapter 3 Lesson 7** ninety-seven **97**

## Practice

Add or subtract.

Match each subtraction fact with a doubles fact.

**5**   14 − 7 = _7_

**6**   8 − 4 = ____

**7**   12 − 6 = ____

**8**   6 − 3 = ____

6 + 6 = ____

3 + 3 = ____

7 + 7 = _14_

4 + 4 = ____

Subtract. Write the double that helps.

**9**   18 − 9 = _9_     _9_ + _9_ = _18_

**10**   16 − 8 = ____     ___ + ___ = ___

**11**   12 − 6 = ____     ___ + ___ = ___

## Mental Math

Eric and his friends play kickball. Each team has the same number of players. Write the number of children on each team.

**12**   12 children play in all.

_____ are on one team.

_____ are on the other team.

**13**   10 children play in all.

_____ are on one team.

_____ are on the other team.

**Notes for Home:** Your child identified related addition and subtraction facts. *Home Activity:* Ask your child what doubles fact helps to find 14 − 7. (7 + 7 = 14)

Name _____

# Use Addition Facts to Subtract

**Learn**  • • • • • • • • • • • • • • • • • • • • • • • • •

$$\begin{array}{r} 6 \\ + 5 \\ \hline 11 \end{array}$$

$$\begin{array}{r} 11 \\ - 5 \\ \hline 6 \end{array}$$

If you know the addition fact, it's easy to subtract. These are related facts!

**Check**  • • • • • • • • • • • • • • • • • • • • • • • • •

Add. Then use the addition fact to subtract.

**1**

$$\begin{array}{r} 8 \\ + 5 \\ \hline 13 \end{array}$$

$$\begin{array}{r} 13 \\ - 5 \\ \hline 8 \end{array}$$

**2**

$$\begin{array}{r} 9 \\ + 6 \\ \hline \end{array}$$

$$\begin{array}{r} 15 \\ - 6 \\ \hline \end{array}$$

**3**

$$\begin{array}{r} 6 \\ + 8 \\ \hline \end{array}$$

$$\begin{array}{r} 14 \\ - 8 \\ \hline \end{array}$$

**4**

$$\begin{array}{r} 8 \\ + 9 \\ \hline \end{array}$$

$$\begin{array}{r} 17 \\ - 9 \\ \hline \end{array}$$

**Talk About It** What addition fact could you use to help you find $16 - 9$?

**Notes for Home:** Your child used addition facts to subtract. *Home Activity:* Ask your child to use objects such as pennies to show $7 + 8 = 15$ and $15 - 8 = 7$.

Add or subtract. Color each addition fact and the related subtraction fact the same color. Use a different color for each set of facts.

**5**

| 13<br>− 6<br>7 | 15<br>− 9 | 16<br>− 7 | 11<br>− 2 |
|---|---|---|---|
| 14<br>− 6 | 12<br>− 8 | 17<br>− 8 | 18<br>− 9 |

**6**

| 9<br>+ 7 | 8<br>+ 6 | 9<br>+ 2 | 7<br>+ 6<br>13 |
|---|---|---|---|
| 9<br>+ 9 | 4<br>+ 8 | 6<br>+ 9 | 9<br>+ 8 |

## Tell a Math Story

**7** Tell an addition story and a related subtraction story for the picture.

**Notes for Home:** Your child practiced using addition facts to subtract. *Home Activity:* Ask your child to explain how 7 + 5 = 12 helps to find 12 − 5.

Name _____

# Relate Addition and Subtraction

**Learn** • • • • • • • • • • • • • • • • • • • • • • • • • • • • • • •

I can tell an addition story and a subtraction story about the people dancing!

At the party, 9 people were dancing. 5 more joined them. How many people were dancing then?

$$9 + 5 = 14$$

14 people were dancing. 5 sat down to rest. How many people were still dancing?

$$14 - 5 = 9$$

**Check** • • • • • • • • • • • • • • • • • • • • • • • • • • • • • • •

Write a number sentence. Solve.

**1** Marcus and Ida made 13 tacos for the party. 6 people each ate a taco. How many tacos were left?

**2** Marcus made 7 tacos. Ida made 6 tacos. How many tacos were there in all?

_____    _____

**Talk About It** How are the stories about tacos the same? How are they different?

**Notes for Home:** Your child wrote related addition and subtraction facts for math stories.
*Home Activity:* Ask your child to tell you the related subtraction fact for 9 + 5 = 14.
(Answer: 14 − 5 = 9 or 14 − 9 = 5.)

Write a number sentence. Solve.

**3** There were 8 gifts on the table. Friends brought 4 more. How many gifts were there in all?

$$8 + 4 = 12$$

**4** At the party, Alex had 12 gifts. He opened 4 of them. How many were left?

_____

## Write About It

**5** Use the numbers 6, 9, and 15. Write an addition story and a related subtraction story. Write number sentences for your stories.

My Addition Story

_____

_____

_____

My Number Sentence:

_____

My Subtraction Story

_____

_____

_____

My Number Sentence:

_____

 **Notes for Home:** Your child practiced writing and solving story problems with related facts. *Home Activity:* Ask your child to write related addition and subtraction facts using these numbers: 7, 5, 12. (7 + 5 = 12 or 5 + 7 = 12 and 12 − 5 = 7 or 12 − 7 = 5)

**102** one hundred two          **For additional practice, see Skills Practice Bank, page 529, Set 3.**

Name _____

# Graphic Aids: Bar Graphs

You read this graph left to right.

## Our Favorite Stories

| Stories | | 1 | 2 | 3 | 4 | 5 | 6 | 7 | 8 | 9 | 10 | 11 | 12 |
|---------|---|---|---|---|---|---|---|---|---|---|----|----|----|
| Arthur's Tooth | | ■ | ■ | ■ | ■ | | | | | | | | |
| Stone Soup | | ■ | ■ | ■ | ■ | ■ | ■ | ■ | ■ | ■ | | | |
| Caps for Sale | | ■ | ■ | ■ | ■ | ■ | ■ | ■ | ■ | ■ | ■ | ■ | ■ |
| Tikki Tikki Tembo | | ■ | ■ | ■ | ■ | ■ | ■ | ■ | | | | | |

**Number of Votes**

**1** What is the title of the graph? _____

**2** How many rows are there? _____

**3** What is at the start of each row? _____

**4** What do the numbers tell you? _____

**5** How many votes did **Stone Soup** get? _____

**Talk About It** How do you know which story got 7 votes?

**Notes for Home:** Your child read a bar graph. *Home Activity:* Ask your child to name the stories on the graph.

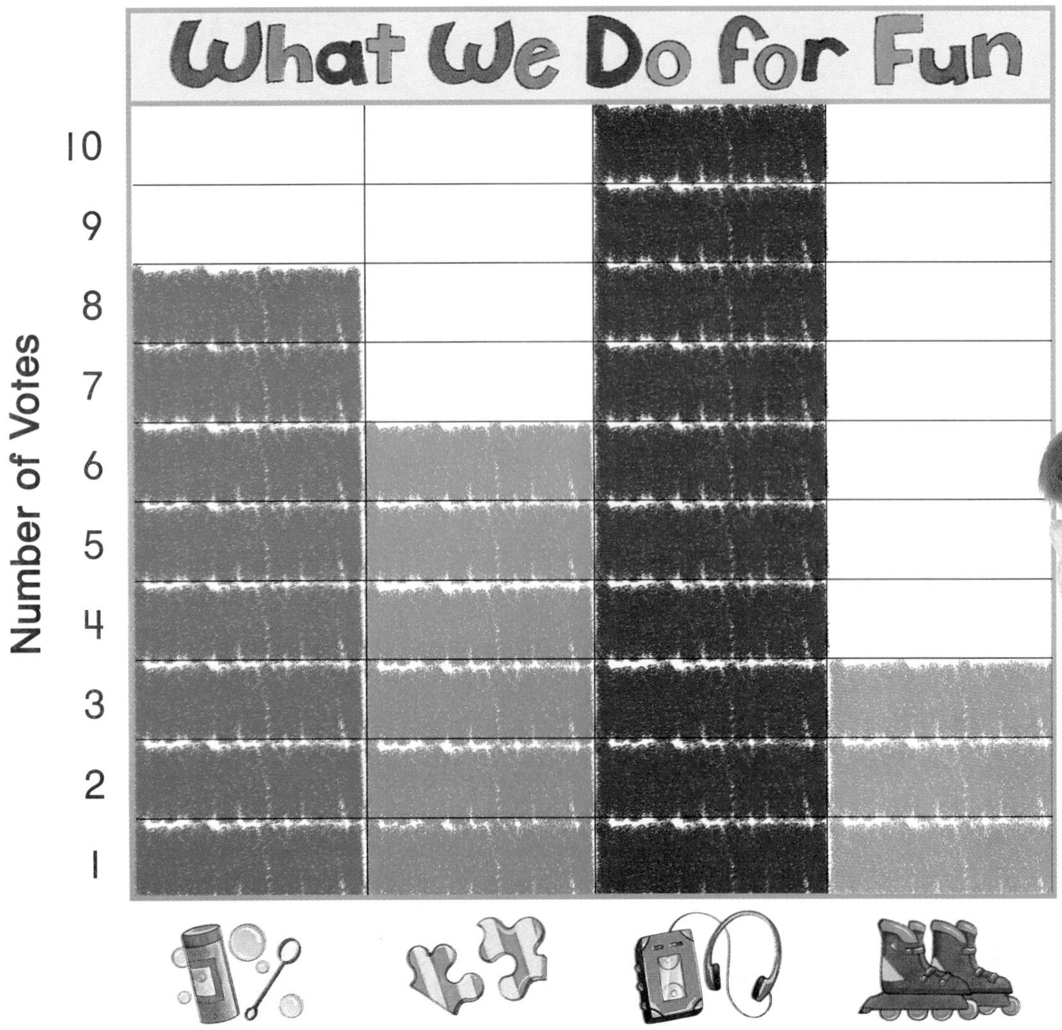

## What We Do for Fun

Number of Votes

10
9
8
7
6
5
4
3
2
1

You read this graph from bottom to top.

**6** What is the title of the graph? _____

**7** How many columns are there? _____

**8** What is at the bottom of each column? _____

**9** What do the numbers tell you? _____

**10** How many votes did 🧩 get? _____

## Visual Thinking

**11** Without counting, how can you tell which activity got the fewest votes?

**Notes for Home:** Your child practiced reading a bar graph. *Home Activity:* Ask your child which activity got the most votes. (listening to tapes)

# Problem Solving: Group Decision Making

**Learn** • • • • • • • • • • • •

**PROBLEM SOLVING GUIDE**
Understand • Plan • Solve • Look Back

I showed the favorite games of my class with tally marks.

I made a bar graph.

**Check** • • • • • • • • • • • • • • • • • • • • • • •

Find out about a favorite topic in your class.

① Choose a topic. Your group can use one of these topics or choose another topic.

② Write your group's topic on the chart. Think of four choices for that topic. Ask your class to vote.

| Our Topic: | How many? |
|---|---|
| Choice 1: | |
| Choice 2: | |
| Choice 3: | |
| Choice 4: | |

**Talk About It** How did your group decide on the 4 choices for your topic?

**Notes for Home:** Your child worked in a group to take a survey. *Home Activity:* Ask your child which choice he or she voted for.

PROBLEM SOLVING

Use your information to make a bar graph.

### Our Favorite _____

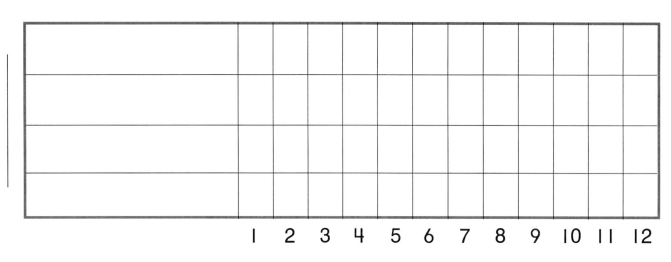

| | | | | | | | | | | | | |
|---|---|---|---|---|---|---|---|---|---|---|---|

1   2   3   4   5   6   7   8   9   10   11   12

_____

**PROBLEM SOLVING**

③ Write the title of your graph at the top.

④ Put a choice at the start of each row.

⑤ Label the side and bottom of your graph.

⑥ Color to show how many votes for each choice.

### 😊 **Write your own.**

With your group, decide on 2 questions that can be
answered by your graph. Write your questions.

⑦ _____

_____

⑧ _____

_____

**Journal**

⑨ What was the easiest part about working in a group?

What was the hardest part?

**Notes for Home:** Your child made a bar graph. *Home Activity:* Ask your child to tell you the total
number of votes for two choices.

Name _____

# Mixed Practice
### Lessons 7–10

## Concepts and Skills
Add or subtract.

**①**    7     14     **②**    6     15     **③**    5     13
     + 7   − 7        + 9   − 9        + 8   − 8

**④**   16     7     9     11     8     18     15
     − 8   + 6   + 8   − 6   + 7   − 9   − 8

## Problem Solving
Write a number sentence. Solve.

**⑤** Malinda had 9 colors of paint. Joe gave her 8 more. How many colors did she have then?

_____ colors

**⑥** Malinda had 17 colors of paint. She gave Joe 8. How many colors did she have left?

_____ colors

Use the graph to answer the questions.

**⑦** Which activity got the most votes?

_____

**⑧** How many more votes did **Reading** get than **Painting**?

_____ more votes

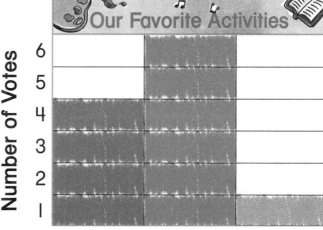

Our Favorite Activities

Number of Votes: 6 5 4 3 2 1

Reading    Singing    Painting

Activities

## Journal

**⑨** Draw a picture to show these related facts: $5 + 6 = 11$   $11 − 6 = 5$

**Notes for Home:** Your child practiced adding and subtracting related facts, reading a graph, and solving problems. *Home Activity:* Ask your child to tell you a related subtraction fact for $6 + 8 = 14$. ($14 − 8 = 6$ or $14 − 6 = 8$)

MIXED PRACTICE

Name _____

# Cumulative Review
## Chapters 1–3

## Concepts and Skills

Write the number sentence. Then write the turnaround fact.

**1**

_____

_____

**2**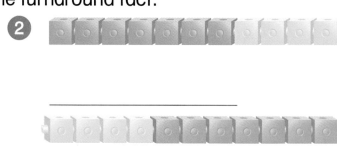

_____

_____

## Problem Solving

Write a number sentence. Solve.

**3** Dave has 5 paper planes.

He makes 5 more.

How many does he have in all?

_____ planes

**4** Camille makes 10 paper birds.

Then she gives 5 away.

How many does she have then?

_____ birds

### Test Prep

Fill in the ○ for the correct answer.

Which fact matches each picture?

**5**

     $9+2$     $9-2$     $6+4$     $6-3$
      ○       ○       ○       ○

**6**

    $12-5$    $12+5$    $8+3$    $8-3$
     ○      ○      ○      ○

 **Notes for Home:** Your child reviewed addition and subtraction facts to 12 and solved word problems. *Home Activity:* Ask your child to tell you the turnaround fact for $8 + 3 = 11$. ($3 + 8 = 11$)

**108**  one hundred eight

# Chapter 3 Review

## Vocabulary

**1** Complete the number sentence to show doubles.

$8 + \underline{\quad} = \underline{\quad}$

Write the doubles plus one fact.

$\underline{\quad} + \underline{\quad} = \underline{\quad}$

**2** Add. Use the addition fact to write a related fact.

$5 + 9 = \underline{\quad}$

$\underline{\quad} - \underline{\quad} = \underline{\quad}$

## Concepts and Skills

Add or subtract.

**3**

| 9 | 15 | 13 | 7 | 18 | 8 | 14 |
|---|---|---|---|---|---|---|
| + 8 | − 6 | − 5 | + 7 | − 9 | + 3 | − 8 |

## Problem Solving

Write a number sentence. Solve.

**4** Jesse had 9 marbles. Louisa had 7 marbles. How many marbles did they have in all?

_____ marbles

**5** Jesse and Louisa had 16 marbles. Louisa took away 7 marbles. How many were left?

_____ marbles

Solve.

**6** Make a list.
Show all the ways 6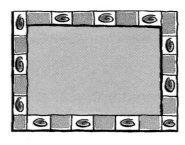
can go on 2 gameboards.
A gameboard
can hold up to 5 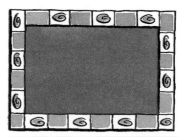.

| Yellow | Red |
|---|---|
| _____ | _____ |
| _____ | _____ |
| _____ | _____ |
| _____ | _____ |
| _____ | _____ |

 **Notes for Home:** Your child reviewed the vocabulary, concepts, skills, and problem solving taught in Chapter 3. *Home Activity:* Ask your child to tell you how he or she found the double plus one fact for 8 + 8.

CHAPTER REVIEW

Name _____

# Chapter 3 Test

Add.

**1**   8 + 8 = ____      8 + 9 = ____      9 + 8 = ____

Add or subtract.

**2**
$$\begin{array}{r} 9 \\ + 5 \\ \hline \end{array} \qquad \begin{array}{r} 13 \\ - 6 \\ \hline \end{array} \qquad \begin{array}{r} 18 \\ - 9 \\ \hline \end{array}$$

$$\begin{array}{r} 8 \\ + 7 \\ \hline \end{array} \qquad \begin{array}{r} 15 \\ - 7 \\ \hline \end{array} \qquad \begin{array}{r} 6 \\ + 4 \\ \hline \end{array}$$

**3**   Make a list. Show all the ways
5 children can sit in 2 boats
A boat can hold up to 4 children.

Write the number sentence. Solve.

**4**   Randy had 7 crayons.
Tasha had 9 crayons.
How many crayons did they
have in all?

_____ crayons

**5**   Randy and Tasha had
16 crayons.
Tasha took away 9.
How many were left?

_____ crayons

Solve.

**6**   Which season got the most votes?

_____

**7**   How many votes did **Winter** get?

_____ votes

**Notes for Home:** Your child was tested on Chapter 3 concepts, skills, and problem solving.
*Home Activity:* Ask your child to tell you three new things he or she learned in this chapter.

**CHAPTER TEST**

Name _____

# Performance Assessment
## Chapter 3

Put two sets of cards numbered 5 through 9 in a bag.

Pick 2 cards.

Write an addition fact. Write a related subtraction fact.

| | Numbers Picked | Addition Fact | Related Subtraction Fact |
|---|---|---|---|
| 1 | _____ and _____ | | |
| 2 | _____ and _____ | | |
| 3 | _____ and _____ | | |
| 4 | _____ and _____ | | |
| 5 | _____ and _____ | | |

## Problem Solving

6  Think of a number between 11 and 17.

Write an addition fact with that sum. _____

Write a related subtraction fact. _____

Tell an addition story and a subtraction story for your related facts.

**Notes for Home:** Your child did an activity that tested Chapter 3 skills, concepts, and problem solving. *Home Activity:* Ask your child to tell the related subtraction fact for 5 + 6 = 11. (11 − 6 = 5 or 11 − 5 = 6)

Name _____

Explore with a COMPUTER

## Double Up!

### Computer Skills You Will Need

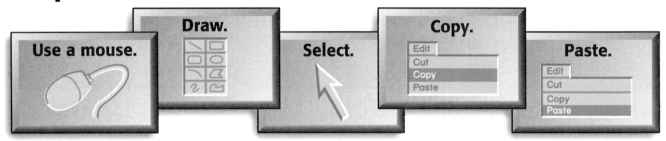

Use a mouse.

Draw.

Select.

Copy.
Edit
Cut
Copy
Paste

Paste.
Edit
Cut
Copy
Paste

① Draw a shape using your computer's drawing program.

② Select your drawing. Copy and paste to make two shapes.

**Select all** your shapes. Copy and paste. Write the double your drawing shows. To complete the chart, copy and paste all the shapes each time.

| | First Group | | Second Group | | Total |
|---|---|---|---|---|---|
| ③ | 2 | + | 2 | = | 4 |
| ④ | | + | | = | |
| ⑤ | | + | | = | |
| ⑥ | | + | | = | |

**Tech Talk** Explain how you made 8 identical shapes.

💻⇄💻 **Visit our Web site. www.parent.mathsurf.com**

# Double Trouble

1 Look around your home for things that show two matching groups or doubles. Ask a family member to help you.

2 Make a doubles list for sums to 18. List the things you find and draw a picture of them.

3 Tell the family member how each group shows a double.

2 _____
4 paws ꟙꟙꟙꟙ _____ 10 _____
6 _____ 12 eggs _____
8 _____ 14 _____
16 _____
18 _____

Visit our Web site. www.parent.mathsurf.com

Fold down

---

Scott Foresman - Addison Wesley    My Math Magazine    No. 3

# MathSoup

## Meet the Champ!

| | |
|---|---|
| 5 五 | 10 十 |
| 6 六 | 9 九 |
| 7 七 | 8 八 |
| 8 八 | 7 七 |
| 9 九 | 6 六 |
| 10 十 | 5 五 |
| 15 | 20 |
| 16 | 19 |
| 17 | 18 |
| 18 | 17 |
| 19 | 16 |
| 20 | 15 |

Now compare the Chinese numbers for

6 and 16.

7 and 17.

8 and 18.

How are all the pairs of numbers alike?

| 15 |
|---|

| 5 | 3 |
|---|---|

**Notes for Home:** Your child wrote and compared Chinese numbers. *Home Activity:* Ask your child to tell you how the Chinese numbers for 9 and 19 are alike.

# Math in Your World

# Be a Mibster*

**Target** is one game you can play with marbles.

**What You Need**

2 marbles

shoe box

**How to Play**

1 Play with your friends.

2 Each player shoots marbles until two marbles go into any of the openings. Add the scores above the openings.

3 The player with the highest score wins!

**Cat's-eyes marbles are very popular. Can you see why they're called cat's-eyes?**

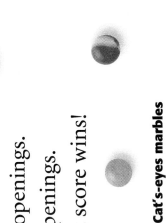

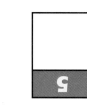

| Name | Roll 1 | + | Roll 2 | = | Score |
|---|---|---|---|---|---|
| Chris | 3 | + | 6 | = | 9 |
| Kim | | + | | = | |

**\* Marble players are called mibsters.**

**Notes for Home:** Your child played a marble game to practice facts. *Home Activity:* Ask your child to tell you the score for 9 + 5. (14)

# A World of Numbers

People around the world write numbers in lots of different ways.
These are the Chinese numbers from 1 to 20.

Write the following
numbers in Chinese.

1 | **3** |

**13**

2 | **4** |

**14**

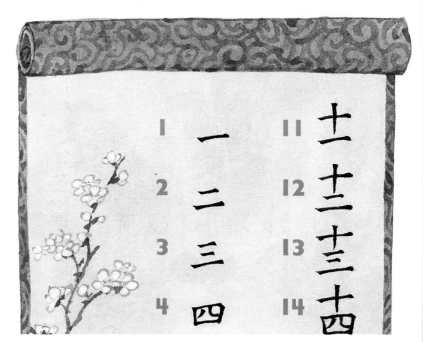

| 1 | 一 | 11 | 十一 |
| 2 | 二 | 12 | 十二 |
| 3 | 三 | 13 | 十三 |
| 4 | 四 | 14 | 十四 |

## How to Make the Target

1 Cut five openings in a cardboard box.

2 Make openings widest at the ends, narrower next to the ends, and narrowest in the middle.

3 Give the openings the scores shown above.

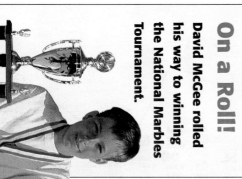

**On a Roll!**
David McGee rolled his way to winning the National Marbles Tournament.

# Go Figure!

**Math Fun**

2. Why was 6 afraid of 7?

1. What kind of snake knows its numbers?

## Number Noodles

Find the number words. Look across and down. How many can you find?

**one**
**two**
**three**
**four**
**five**
**six**
**seven**
**eight**
**nine**
**ten**

Break the Code

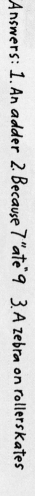

5

4

Answers: 1. An adder 2. Because 7 "ate" 9 3. A zebra on rollerskates

**Notes for Home:** Your child found number words in a puzzle and used coded numbers to write addition sentences. *Home Activity:* Ask your child to write a coded number sentence. (Example: ▬ + ▲ = 7)

# CHAPTER 4

## Using Addition and Subtraction

### Fun at the Fair

Tell an addition story and a subtraction story about one part of the picture.

**Notes for Home:** Your child told stories using addition and subtraction. *Home Activity:* Ask your child to tell an addition and a subtraction story about a different part of the picture.

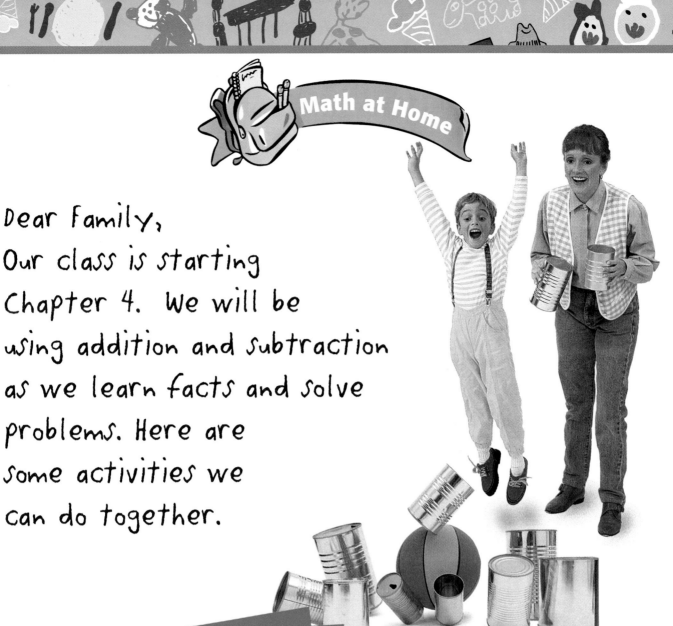

## Math at Home

Dear Family,
Our class is starting Chapter 4. We will be using addition and subtraction as we learn facts and solve problems. Here are some activities we can do together.

### Bean Counters
Use 12 to 18 objects, such as dried beans. Ask your child to count them. Put some into a cup. Show your child the remaining beans. Ask your child what number they would add to the remaining beans to equal the original number.

### Knock Them Down
Use a ball and 12 to 18 empty cans. Set up the cans like bowling pins. Roll the ball at the "pins." Ask how many were knocked down and how many are left. Use the numbers to write a subtraction sentence.

**Community Connection**
Help your child find numbers between 12 and 18 on billboards, street signs, and in other parts of the community. Ask your child to subtract a number between 5 and 9 from the number they found.

**Visit our Web site. www.parent.mathsurf.com**

Name _____

**Explore** • • • • • • • • • • • • • • • • • • • • • • • • • • • • • •

Use 7  and 5  .

Tell addition and subtraction stories using 7, 5, and 12.

Draw one of your stories.

**Share** • • • • • • • • • • • • • • • • • • • • • • • • • • • •

Compare your stories with a friend.

How are they the same? How are they different?

**Notes for Home:** Your child explored telling addition and subtraction stories about 12 objects. *Home Activity:* Ask your child to use 12 objects, such as marbles or pennies, to show you two of the stories he or she told.

EXPLORE

$$8 + 6 = 14$$

$$14 - 6 = 8$$

$$6 + 8 = 14$$

$$14 - 8 = 6$$

*The facts use the same numbers: 8, 6, and 14.*

*These four facts form a fact family.*

**EXPLORE**

Complete each fact family.

Add or subtract.

**1**

$$6 + 7 = \underline{13}$$

$$13 - 7 = \underline{6}$$

$$7 + 6 = \underline{\phantom{00}}$$

$$13 - 6 = \underline{\phantom{00}}$$

**2**

$$9 + 5 = \underline{\phantom{00}}$$

$$14 - 5 = \underline{\phantom{00}}$$

$$5 + 9 = \underline{\phantom{00}}$$

$$14 - 9 = \underline{\phantom{00}}$$

**Talk About It** Tell the fact family for the numbers 4, 9, and 13.

**Notes for Home:** Your child added and subtracted using fact families. *Home Activity:* Give your child 17 objects, such as pennies. Ask your child to write or say number sentences for 7, 8, and 15. ($7 + 8 = 15$; $8 + 7 = 15$; $15 - 8 = 7$; $15 - 7 = 8$)

Name _____

# Fact Families

**Learn** • • • • • • • • • • • • • • • • • • • • • • • • • • • • • •

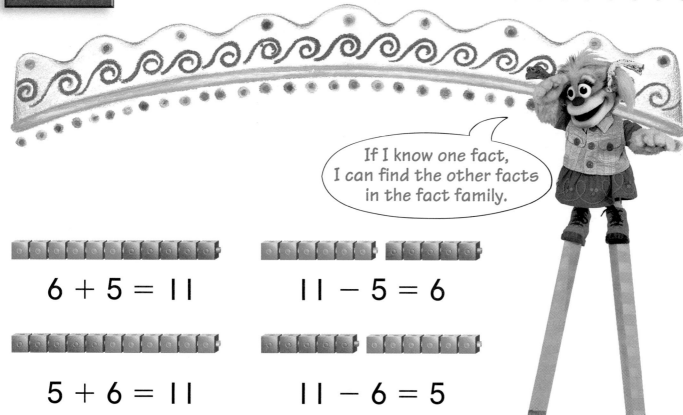

If I know one fact,
I can find the other facts
in the fact family.

6 + 5 = 11          11 − 5 = 6

5 + 6 = 11          11 − 6 = 5

**Check** • • • • • • • • • • • • • • • • • • • • • • • • • • • • •

Use 🔲.

Complete each fact family.

❶  7 + 9 = _16_

   9 + 7 = ___

   16 − 9 = _7_

   16 − 7 = ___

❷
| 8 | 5 | 13 | 13 |
|---|---|----|----|
| + 5 | + 8 | − 5 | − 8 |

❸
| 9 | 5 | 14 | 14 |
|---|---|----|----|
| + 5 | + 9 | − 5 | − 9 |

**Talk About It** How many facts would be in

the fact family for 6, 6, and 12? Explain your answer.

**Notes for Home:** Your child wrote number sentences for fact families. *Home Activity:* Ask your child
to write the fact family for the numbers 7, 7, and 14. (7 + 7 = 14, 14 − 7 = 7)

## Practice

Complete each fact family. Add or subtract.

4. $6 + 9 = 15$

$9 + 6 = ___$

$15 - 9 = 6$

$15 - 6 = ___$

5. $8 + 7 = ___$

$7 + 8 = ___$

$15 - 7 = ___$

$15 - 8 = ___$

6. $9 + 8 = ___$

$8 + 9 = ___$

$17 - 8 = ___$

$17 - 9 = ___$

7. $4 + 8 = ___$

$8 + 4 = ___$

$12 - 8 = ___$

$12 - 4 = ___$

8. $7 + 7 = ___$ $\quad 14 - 7 = ___$

9. $9 + 9 = ___$ $\quad 18 - 9 = ___$

### Problem Solving Critical Thinking

10. Write two different fact families using the number 13.

______________________________

______________________________

**Notes for Home:** Your child added and subtracted using fact families. *Home Activity:* Ask your child to tell how fact families with doubles are different from other fact families. (A fact family with doubles has only 2 facts; others have 4.)

PRACTICE



**For additional practice, see Skills Practice Bank, page 530, Set 1.**

# Fun with Facts!

This game is fun!
See if you can be
the last one!

**Players** 2

**What You Need**

paper clip

pencil

crayon | purple |

**How to Play**

1. Spin the spinner 2 times. Use the numbers you spin to write an addition sentence.

2. Write the other facts that are in that family.

3. If you write all the facts correctly, color in the space on the gameboard that shows the sum of your addition sentence from Step 1.

4. Have a friend do Steps 1–3.

5. If a space is already colored, that player's turn is over.

6. The player that colors in the last space on the gameboard, wins!

**Spinner**

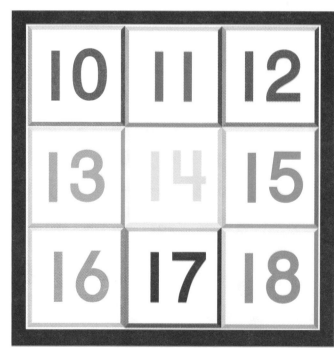

**Gameboard**

**PRACTICE**

**Notes for Home:** Your child played a game to practice writing fact families. *Home Activity:* Ask your child to write a family of facts using the sum of 15. (Sample answer: 9 + 6 = 15; 6 + 9 = 15; 15 − 6 = 9; 15 − 9 = 6)

Name _____

STOP and Practice

Complete the fact families. Circle the
extra fact that does not belong in each
family. Use the letter next to each
extra fact to solve the riddle below.

**①** 8 + 5 = ___ T

13 − 5 = ___ L

8 − 3 = ___ A

5 + 8 = ___ R

13 − 8 = ___ G

**②** 6 + 9 = ___ F

8 + 7 = ___ M

15 − 6 = ___ O

9 + 6 = ___ U

15 − 9 = ___ I

**③** 15 − 8 = ___ P

15 − 7 = ___ Q

7 + 8 = ___ N

8 + 8 = ___ I

8 + 7 = ___ L

**④** 7 + 6 = ___ Y

13 − 4 = ___ E

4 + 9 = ___ U

13 − 9 = ___ A

9 + 4 = ___ O

What did 6 and 4 say to 10?

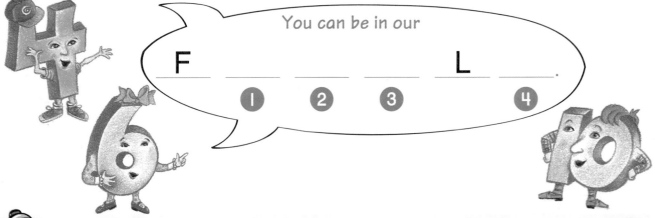

You can be in our

F ___ ___ ___ L ___ .
   ①   ②   ③    ④

**Notes for Home:** Your child practiced addition and subtraction. *Home Activity:* Ask your child what
facts would be in the fact family for the riddle on this page.
(6 + 4 = 10; 4 + 6 = 10; 10 − 4 = 6; 10 − 6 = 4)

# Use Addition to Check Subtraction

**Learn** • • • • • • • • • • • • • • • • • • • • • • • • • • • • • • • • • • •

Put cards with the numbers 7 to 12 in a bag. Pick 2 cards.

Make a subtraction fact. Write the difference on a third card.

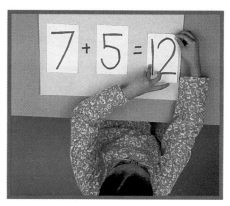

What addition fact can you make with these same numbers?

*Hmm...If we can do this...*

*...then we can do this.*

**Check** • • • • • • • • • • • • • • • • • • • • • • • • • • • • • • • • •

| | Cards Picked | Subtraction Fact | Addition Fact |
|---|---|---|---|
| 1 | ____ and ____ | ___ − ___ = ___ | ___ + ___ = ___ |
| 2 | ____ and ____ | ___ − ___ = ___ | ___ + ___ = ___ |
| 3 | ____ and ____ | ___ − ___ = ___ | ___ + ___ = ___ |

Subtract. Write a related addition sentence to check your answer.

4  $14 - 6 =$ ___     ___ + ___ = ___

5  $13 - 9 =$ ___     ___ + ___ = ___

**Talk About It** Tell a friend a subtraction fact.

Ask your friend to tell you a related addition fact.

**Notes for Home:** Your child subtracted and checked answers by using addition. *Home Activity:* Ask your child to explain how he or she would use addition to check $10 - 6 = 4$.

Use these numbers. Write a subtraction fact.
Write an addition fact to check.

6 15   8

```
  15        7
-  8    +   8
 -----    -----
   7       15
```

7   5   14

```
         
-       +
-----   -----
         
```

8   9   17

```
         
-       +
-----   -----
         
```

9   13   7

```
         
-       +
-----   -----
         
```

10   16   9

```
         
-       +
-----   -----
         
```

11   8   14

```
         
-       +
-----   -----
         
```

## Problem Solving

12  Complete the number sentence.

$17 - 8 = \underline{\hspace{1cm}}$

13  Write two related addition
    facts that you can use
    to check your answer.

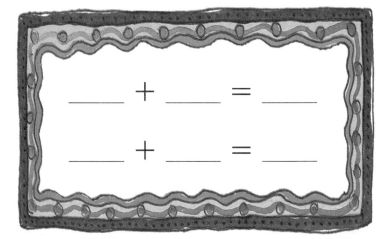

___ + ___ = ___

___ + ___ = ___

**Notes for Home:** Your child practiced checking subtraction using addition. *Home Activity:* Ask your
child to find 14 − 9 and check the answer by adding. (14 − 9 = 5; 5 + 9 = 14 or 9 + 5 = 14)

Name _____

# Problem Solving: Draw a Picture

**Learn**

There were 14 cans in the game. Jasmine knocked over 5 cans. On her next throw she knocked over 4 cans. How many cans were left standing?

_5_ cans

You can draw a picture to solve the problem.

**Check**

Draw a picture to solve the problem.

1. Nora's family brought 12 sandwiches to the fair. They ate 5 sandwiches for lunch. They ate 3 more sandwiches later. How many sandwiches were left?

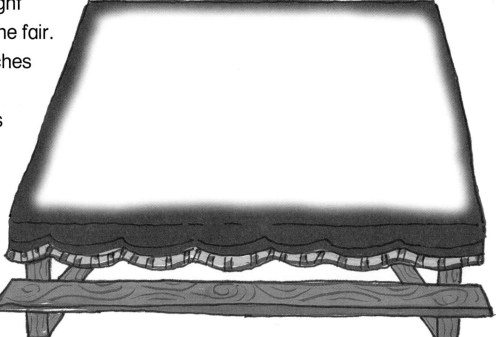

_____ sandwiches

**Talk About It** Tell how you solved the problem about sandwiches.

**Notes for Home:** Your child solved problems by drawing pictures. *Home Activity:* Draw a picture of 12 objects. Ask your child to tell a math story about your picture.

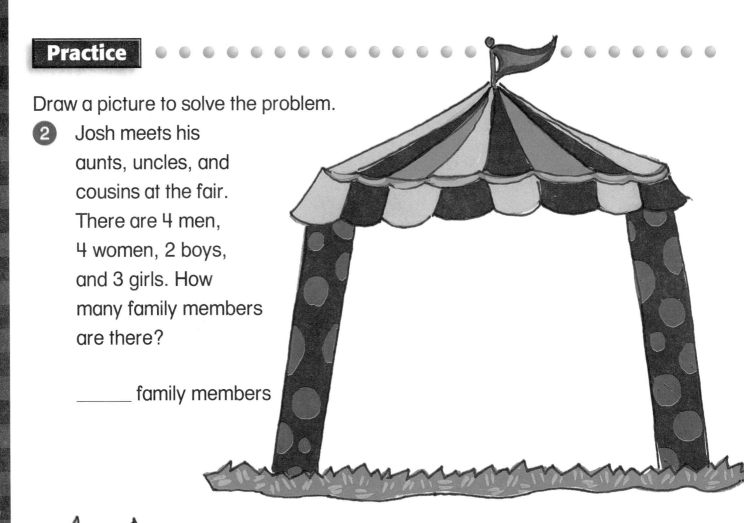

Draw a picture to solve the problem.

**2** Josh meets his aunts, uncles, and cousins at the fair. There are 4 men, 4 women, 2 boys, and 3 girls. How many family members are there?

_____ family members

PROBLEM SOLVING

## Write About It

**3** Write a problem about the fair.
Ask a friend to draw a picture to solve it.

_____

_____

_____

_____

_____

**Notes for Home:** Your child practiced drawing pictures to solve problems. *Home Activity:* Place 15 objects, such as buttons, in a cup. Remove 6 buttons, then remove 2 more. Ask your child to draw a picture to show how many buttons remain in the cup.

# Mixed Practice
### Lessons 1–4

## Concepts and Skills

Write the number sentences to make a fact family.

**1**

___ + ___ = ___         ___ − ___ = ___

___ + ___ = ___         ___ − ___ = ___

Subtract. Then write a related addition fact.

**2**  13 − 6 = ___    ___ + ___ = ___

**3**  15 − 9 = ___    ___ + ___ = ___

## Problem Solving

Draw a picture to solve the problem.

**4**  Andre has 15 tickets for rides.

He gives 6 to his sister.

He gives 3 to his brother.

How many are left?

_____ tickets

## Journal

**5**  Draw a picture that shows 2 groups.

Write the fact family that your picture shows.

**Notes for Home:** Your child practiced addition and subtraction facts and solving problems.
*Home Activity:* Ask your child to write a related addition fact for 18 − 9 = 9. (9 + 9 = 18)

# Cumulative Review
## Chapters 1–4

## Concepts and Skills

Add.

**1**
$$
\begin{array}{r} 7 \\ +7 \\ \hline \end{array}
\qquad
\begin{array}{r} 8 \\ +7 \\ \hline \end{array}
\qquad
\begin{array}{r} 9 \\ +9 \\ \hline \end{array}
\qquad
\begin{array}{r} 7 \\ +6 \\ \hline \end{array}
\qquad
\begin{array}{r} 6 \\ +6 \\ \hline \end{array}
\qquad
\begin{array}{r} 8 \\ +9 \\ \hline \end{array}
\qquad
\begin{array}{r} 8 \\ +8 \\ \hline \end{array}
$$

## Problem Solving

Use the graph to answer the questions.

**2** How many children like the Ferris Wheel best?

_____ children

**3** How many more children picked the Kiddie Coaster than the Ferris Wheel?

_____ more children

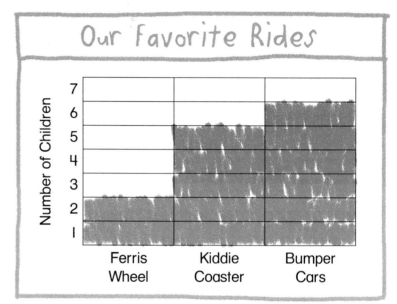

Our Favorite Rides

## Test Prep

Fill in the ○ for the correct answer.

Solve each problem.

**4** Mrs. Kim's class has 9 girls and 7 boys. How many children are in the class?

17    16    15    2
○     ○     ○     ○

**5** Mr. Roy's class has 17 children. 9 are boys. How many are girls?

6    7    8    9
○    ○    ○    ○

**Notes for Home:** Your child reviewed addition facts, reading a graph, and solving word problems. *Home Activity:* Ask your child how many fewer children picked the Kiddie Coaster than the Bumper Cars in the graph. (1)

# Missing Addends

**Learn** • • • • • • • • • • • • • • • • • • • • • • • • • •

The ring toss game gives toy bears for prizes. At the end of the day, there are 4 bears left on the shelf. The shelf holds 12 bears. How many bears are needed to fill the shelf?

$$4 + \underline{?} = 12$$

*You can use the fact family to help find the missing number!*

$$\underline{8} + 4 = 12$$

$$12 - \underline{8} = 4$$

$$12 - 4 = \underline{8}$$

8 bears are needed to fill the shelf.

**Check** • • • • • • • • • • • • • • • • • • • • • • • • • •

Find the missing numbers. Use fact families to help you.

**1**

16

9 | ___

$$9 + \underline{\phantom{0}} = 16$$

$$16 - 9 = \underline{\phantom{0}}$$

$$\underline{\phantom{0}} + 9 = 16$$

$$16 - \underline{\phantom{0}} = 9$$

**2**

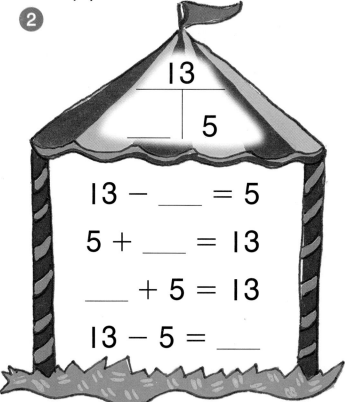

13

___ | 5

$$13 - \underline{\phantom{0}} = 5$$

$$5 + \underline{\phantom{0}} = 13$$

$$\underline{\phantom{0}} + 5 = 13$$

$$13 - 5 = \underline{\phantom{0}}$$

**Talk About It** How would you find the missing number in $5 + \underline{\phantom{0}} = 14$?

**Notes for Home:** Your child used fact families to find missing numbers. *Home Activity:* Ask your child to describe the fact family they could use to solve $6 + \underline{\phantom{0}} = 15$. ($15 - 6 = 9$; $15 - 9 = 6$; $9 + 6 = 15$; $6 + 9 = 15$)

Find the missing numbers.
Use the fact families to help you.

**3**

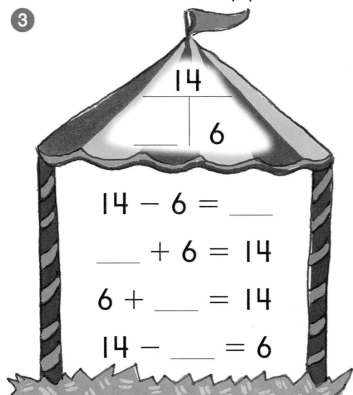

14
___ | 6

$14 - 6 = \underline{\quad}$

$\underline{\quad} + 6 = 14$

$6 + \underline{\quad} = 14$

$14 - \underline{\quad} = 6$

**4**

17
8 | ___

$\underline{\quad} + 8 = 17$

$17 - 8 = \underline{\quad}$

$8 + \underline{\quad} = 17$

$17 - \underline{\quad} = 8$

**5** Ella won 11 prizes in all at the fair. She won 4 of the prizes in the morning. How many prizes did she win in the afternoon?

_____ prizes

**6** John had 7 tickets for rides. He bought more tickets. Then he had 15. How many tickets did he buy?

_____ tickets

## Problem Solving Patterns

**7** Find the missing numbers. Find the pattern.
Write the next fact.

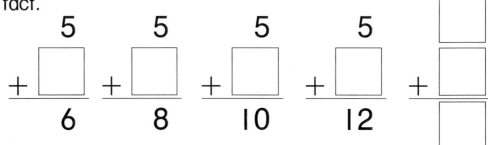

$$5 \quad\quad 5 \quad\quad 5 \quad\quad 5$$
$$+ \square \quad + \square \quad + \square \quad + \square \quad + \square$$
$$\overline{6} \quad\quad \overline{8} \quad\quad \overline{10} \quad\quad \overline{12}$$

**Notes for Home:** Your child practiced using fact families to find missing numbers.
*Home Activity:* Ask your child to solve 4 + ___ = 13. (9)

# Addition Tic-Tac-Toe

**Players** 2

**What You Need**

9 counters

paper clip

pencil

Spinner 1

**How to Play**

1. Spin Spinner 1. This is your target number.

2. Spin Spinner 2. What number would you add to this number to reach your target number?

3. Use a yellow counter. Cover the square on the gameboard that shows the number you added.

4. Have a friend do Steps 1–3. They should use a red counter.

5. If a number is already covered, the player's turn is over.

6. The first player with 3 in a row, wins!

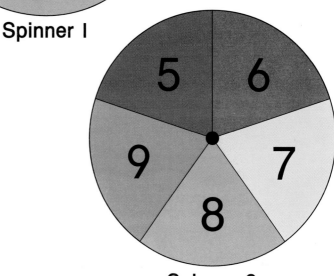

Spinner 2

Gameboard

**PRACTICE**

**Notes for Home:** Your child played a game to practice adding numbers with sums through 15. *Home Activity:* Ask your child what number he or she would add to 9 to get a sum of 15. (6)

STOP and Practice

Write a fact family for each group of numbers.

**1**

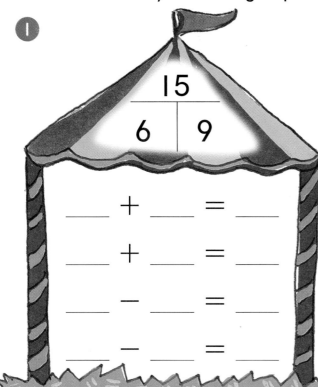

15
6 | 9

___ + ___ = ___

___ + ___ = ___

___ − ___ = ___

___ − ___ = ___

**2**

12
7 | 5

___ + ___ = ___

___ + ___ = ___

___ − ___ = ___

___ − ___ = ___

Find the missing numbers. Finish the fact families.

**3**

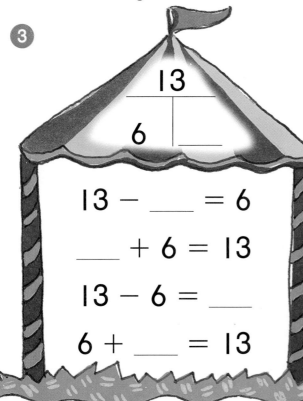

13
6 | ___

13 − ___ = 6

___ + 6 = 13

13 − 6 = ___

6 + ___ = 13

**4**

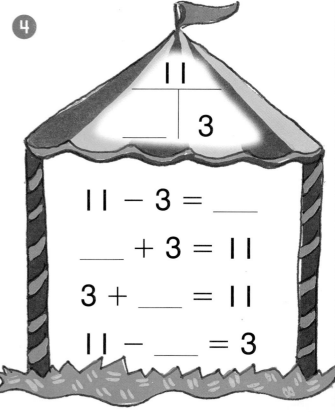

11
___ | 3

11 − 3 = ___

___ + 3 = 11

3 + ___ = 11

11 − ___ = 3

**Notes for Home:** Your child practiced addition and subtraction. *Home Activity:* Ask your child to tell you the fact family for 9, 6, and 3. (6 + 3 = 9; 3 + 6 = 9; 9 − 3 = 6; 9 − 6 = 3)

PRACTICE

# Three Addends

**Learn** • • • • • • • • • • • • • • • • • • • • • • • • • • • •

You can add in different ways.

$2 + 3 = 5$
$5 + 7 = 12$

Add the numbers in order.

$3 + 3 = 6$
$6 + 5 = 11$

Add the doubles first and then add the other number.

$6 + 4 = 10$
$10 + 3 = 13$

Make a ten first and then add the other number.

**Check** • • • • • • • • • • • • • • • • • • • • • • • • • • • •

Circle the numbers you would add first. Then add.

**1**

| 2 | 9 | 4 | 5 | 6 | 2 | 3 |
|---|---|---|---|---|---|---|
| 1 | 1 | 2 | 5 | 4 | 7 | 4 |
| + 8 | + 1 | + 6 | + 3 | + 1 | + 2 | + 5 |

**2** $1 + 7 + 3 =$ ____

**3** $3 + 4 + 3 =$ ____

**4** $5 + 4 + 4 =$ ____

**5** $2 + 6 + 2 =$ ____

**Talk About It** Explain two ways to find $3 + 7 + 3$.

**Notes for Home:** Your child added three numbers to find sums through 18. *Home Activity:* Ask your child to explain how he or she would add $6 + 4 + 4$. (Sample answers: Find $4 + 4 = 8$ and then $8 + 6 = 14$; or find $6 + 4 = 10$ and then $10 + 4 = 14$.)

Add across.
Add down.

I add across!
5 + 4 + 3 = 12

I add down!
3
5
+ 2
10

**6**

| 3 | 4 | 6 | |
|---|---|---|---|
| 5 | 4 | 3 | 12 |
| 2 | 3 | 4 | |
| 10 | | | |

**7**

| 6 | 2 | 1 | |
|---|---|---|---|
| 4 | 3 | 2 | |
| 2 | 3 | 7 | |
| | | | |

**8**

| 7 | 0 | 2 | |
|---|---|---|---|
| 3 | 8 | 6 | |
| 1 | 2 | 1 | |
| | | | |

**9**

| 1 | 3 | 4 | |
|---|---|---|---|
| 5 | 0 | 4 | |
| 1 | 6 | 4 | |
| | | | |

## Problem Solving

**10** A player needs at least 12 points to win a prize. Find each person's total score. Circle the names of the winners.

| | First Toss | Second Toss | Third Toss | Total Score |
|---|---|---|---|---|
| Adam | 5 | 3 | 5 | _____ points |
| Iris | 6 | 4 | 1 | _____ points |
| Vern | 2 | 3 | 7 | _____ points |
| Jody | 8 | 2 | 2 | _____ points |

**Notes for Home:** Your child practiced adding three numbers. *Home Activity:* Ask your child which children in the Problem–Solving chart scored exactly 12 points. (Vern, Jody)

For additional practice, see Skills Practice Bank, page 530, Set 2.

# Use Addition and Subtraction Rules

**Learn** ● ● ● ● ● ● ● ● ● ● ● ● ● ● ● ● ● ● ● ● ● ● ● ● ●

Follow the rule to finish the table.

| Add 3. | |
|:---:|:---:|
| 4 | 7 |
| 8 | 11 |
| 6 | 9 |

**Check** ● ● ● ● ● ● ● ● ● ● ● ● ● ● ● ● ● ● ● ● ● ● ● ● ●

Follow the rule. Add or subtract.

**1**

| Subtract 2. | |
|:---:|:---:|
| 18 | 16 |
| 10 | |
| 15 | |

**2**

| Add 5. | |
|:---:|:---:|
| 9 | |
| 4 | |
| 6 | |

**3**

| Subtract 4. | |
|:---:|:---:|
| 12 | |
| 9 | |
| 11 | |

Add the numbers in the first column.
Then follow the rule.

**4**

| Add 6. | |
|:---:|:---:|
| 2 + 3 | 11 |
| 4 + 3 | |
| 1 + 2 | |

**5**

| Add 4. | |
|:---:|:---:|
| 3 + 3 | |
| 6 + 1 | |
| 5 + 3 | |

**Talk About It** How do you use the rule to complete the first table on this page?

**Notes for Home:** Your child practiced adding and subtracting. *Home Activity:* Ask your child to explain how he or she completed the table in Exercise 4.

Follow the rule. Add or subtract.

**6**

| Add 6. | |
|---|---|
| 6 | 12 |
| 4 | |
| 9 | |

**7**

| Subtract 3. | |
|---|---|
| 10 | |
| 6 | |
| 7 | |

**8**

| Subtract 5. | |
|---|---|
| 10 | |
| 5 | |
| 8 | |

Add the numbers in the first column.
Then follow the rule.

**9**

| Add 5. | |
|---|---|
| 5 + 4 | 14 |
| 2 + 3 | |
| 1 + 2 | |

**10**

| Add 3. | |
|---|---|
| 2 + 2 | |
| 7 + 3 | |
| 8 + 1 | |

## Problem Solving

 **Write your own** rule for each chart.
Then follow the rule. Add or subtract.

**11**

| Add _____. | |
|---|---|
| 9 | |
| 6 | |
| 8 | |

**12**

| Add _____. | |
|---|---|
| 5 | |
| 4 | |
| 7 | |

**13**

| Subtract _____. | |
|---|---|
| 12 | |
| 10 | |
| 6 | |

**Notes for Home:** Your child practiced adding and subtracting. *Home Activity:* Ask your child to choose three numbers less than 16 and then add 2 to each of them.

Name _____

# What's My Rule?

## Learn

How can you find the rule?

I got it! You add 2 each time. That's the rule!

| Add 2. | |
|---|---|
| 2 | 4 |
| 1 | 3 |
| 3 | 5 |

What do you do to 2 to get 4?

What do you do to 1 to get 3?

What do you do to 3 to get 5?

## Check

Write the rule. Write the missing number.

**1**

| Subtract 1. | |
|---|---|
| 9 | 8 |
| 4 | 3 |
| 3 | |

**2**

| | |
|---|---|
| 3 | 6 |
| 9 | 12 |
| 2 | |

**3**

| | |
|---|---|
| 2 | 7 |
| 1 | 6 |
| 4 | |

**4**

| | |
|---|---|
| 9 | 4 |
| 5 | 0 |
| 6 | |

**5**

| | |
|---|---|
| 3 + 6 | 11 |
| 1 + 2 | 5 |
| 4 + 4 | |

**Talk About It** In the fourth problem, compare the numbers in each row. How do you know that you need to subtract?

**Notes for Home:** Your child found the rule (such as <u>add 5</u> or <u>subtract 5</u>) for addition and subtraction tables. *Home Activity:* Have your child explain how he or she found the rule for Exercise 3.

Write the rule. Write the missing number.

**6**

| 9 | 5 |
|---|---|
| 8 | 4 |
| 6 | 2 |
| 4 |   |

**7**

| 2 + 3 | 10 |
|-------|----|
| 1 + 1 | 7  |
| 5 + 3 | 13 |
| 5 + 1 |    |

 ## Write your own.

Write numbers
on each table
that follow a rule.
Ask a friend to
find each rule.

**8**

|  |  |
|--|--|
|  |  |
|  |  |
|  |  |

**9**

|  |  |
|--|--|
|  |  |
|  |  |
|  |  |

## Problem Solving Patterns

Complete the tables.
Continue the patterns.

**10**

| Number of Cars | Number of Wheels |
|----------------|------------------|
| 1 | 4 |
| 2 | 8 |
| 3 |   |
| 4 |   |

**11**

| Number of Starfish | Number of Arms |
|--------------------|----------------|
| 1 | 5 |
| 2 | 10 |
| 3 |    |
| 4 |    |

 **Notes for Home:** Your child practiced finding the rule (such as <u>add 5</u> or <u>subtract 4</u>) for addition and subtraction tables. *Home Activity:* Ask your child to explain how he or she made the tables in Exercises 8 and 9.

**Reading for Math**

## Sequencing

At the school fair, Dana won 4 goldfish.

She won 2 posters.

Then she won 1 puzzle.

How many prizes

did she win in all?

*This math story has a beginning part, two middle parts, and an end part.*

Draw pictures to show the parts of the math story.

**Talk About It** How does knowing the beginning, middle, and end parts of a math story help you solve the problem?

**Notes for Home:** Your children drew the beginning, middle, and end parts of a math story.
*Home Activity:* Ask your child to tell the two things that happened in the middle of the story.

For the bake sale, one child bakes 6 cupcakes.

Another child bakes 4 loaves of bread.

A parent bakes 3 cakes.

How many items are there?

Draw pictures to show the parts of the math story.

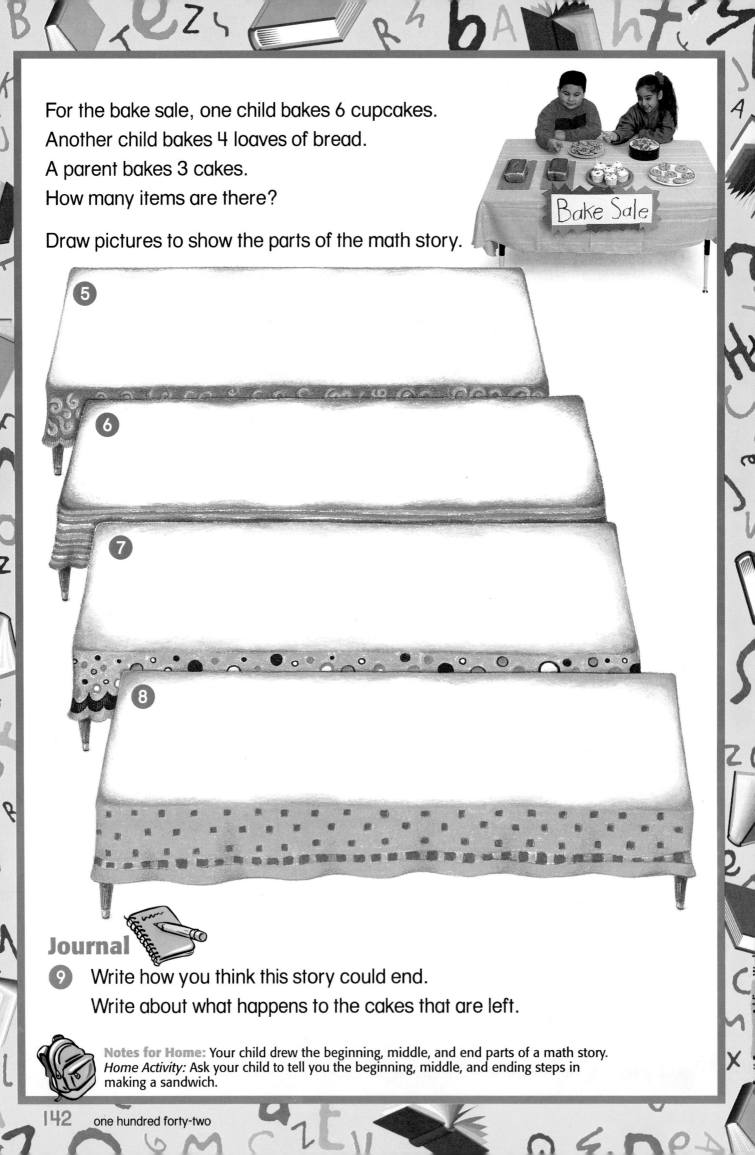

**5**

**6**

**7**

**8**

**Journal**

**9** Write how you think this story could end.

Write about what happens to the cakes that are left.

**Notes for Home:** Your child drew the beginning, middle, and end parts of a math story.
*Home Activity:* Ask your child to tell you the beginning, middle, and ending steps in
making a sandwich.

# Problem Solving: Multiple-Step Problems

**Learn** • • • • • • • • • • • • • • •

Use  .

12 children are on the merry-go-round. 5 children get off.

Step 1: Write a number sentence. Subtract since 5 got off.

$12 - 5 = 7$ children

3 children get on. How many children are on the merry-go-round now?

Step 2: Write a number sentence. Add since 3 got on.

$7 + 3 = 10$ children

**Check** • • • • • • • • • • • • • • •

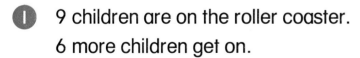

Use  .
Write each number sentence.
Solve.

1. 9 children are on the roller coaster.
6 more children get on.

$\underline{9 + 6 = 15}$ children

7 children get off. How many children are on the roller coaster now?

_____ children

**Talk About It** Use $3 + 5 = 8$ and $8 - 2 = 6$ to tell a math story.

**Notes for Home:** Your child solved word problems. *Home Activity:* Ask your child to make up his or her own math story using $13 - 4 = 9$ and $9 + 7 = 16$.

Use ⬤ ◯ .

Write each number sentence. Solve.

**2** At the fair, Kari bought
6 balloons. 4 flew away.

_6 − 4 = 2_ balloons

She bought 6 more balloons.
How many does she have now?

_____ balloons

**3** Jared bought 14 tickets for rides.
He used 9 tickets.

_____ tickets

He bought 7 more. How many tickets
does Jared have now?

_____ tickets

**4** 8 friends rode rides at the fair.
5 more friends joined them.

_____ friends

6 friends left. How many friends
are there now?

_____ friends

## Tell a Math Story

**5** Tell a story problem. Include addition and subtraction in your story.
Ask a friend to solve your problem.

**Notes for Home:** Your child practiced solving word problems. *Home Activity:* Ask your child to tell you
the word problem he or she made up for Tell a Math Story.

**For additional practice, see Skills Practice Bank, page 530, Set 3.**

PROBLEM SOLVING

# Mixed Practice
**Lessons 5–9**

## Concepts and Skills

**1** Find the missing number in the fact family.

$9 + \underline{\quad} = 17$

$\underline{\quad} + 9 = 17$

$17 - 9 = \underline{\quad}$

$17 - \underline{\quad} = 9$

**2** Add.

| 7 | 5 | 3 |
|---|---|---|
| 2 | 4 | 4 |
| + 3 | + 5 | + 6 |

**3** Follow the rule.
Write the missing numbers.

| Subtract 6. | |
|---|---|
| 12 | |
| 10 | |

**4** Find the rule.
Write the rule.

| | |
|---|---|
| 9 | 15 |
| 7 | 13 |

## Problem Solving

Write each number sentence. Solve.

**5** Tammy bought 10 tickets.
She gave 6 to Don.

_____ tickets

She bought 3 more tickets.
How many tickets
does Tammy have now?

_____ tickets

## Journal

**6** Write all the ways you can solve $2 + 3 + 7$.

**Notes for Home:** Your child practiced finding missing numbers, adding three numbers, and solving problems. *Home Activity:* Ask your child to tell you how to find the rule in Exercise 4.

Name _____

## Concepts and Skills

Add. Write the number sentence.

 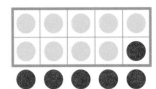

____ + ____ = ____

 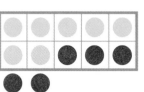

____ + ____ = ____

## Problem Solving

Use the graph to answer the questions.

**3** How many people visited the fair on Saturday?

_____ people

**4** On which day did the fewest people visit?

_____

| Number of People at the Fair | |
|---|---|
| Friday | 🯅 🯅 🯅 |
| Saturday | 🯅 🯅 🯅 🯅 🯅 |
| Sunday | 🯅 🯅 🯅 🯅 |

Each 🯅 means 10 people.

### Test Prep

Fill in the ○ for the correct answer.

**5** Which fact is shown by the picture?

| 6 + 5 | 6 + 6 | 6 + 7 | 6 − 6 |
|---|---|---|---|
| ○ | ○ | ○ | ○ |

**6** Add 8 more. How many in all?

○ 15
○ 16
○ 17
○ 18

 **Notes for Home:** Your child reviewed numbers, used graphs to solve problems, and practiced addition facts. *Home Activity:* Ask your child to use the graph on this page to find how many people visited the fair on Sunday. (40)

Name _____

## Vocabulary

**1** Complete the fact family.

$7 + 5 =$ ___         $12 - 5 =$ ___

$5 + 7 =$ ___         $12 - 7 =$ ___

## Concepts and Skills

**2** Find the missing numbers in the fact family.

$8 +$ ___ $= 14$

___ $+ 8 = 14$

$14 - 8 =$ ___

$14 -$ ___ $= 8$

**3** Find the rule. Write the rule.

| | |
|---|---|
| 10 | 4 |
| 7 | 1 |
| 13 | 7 |

**4** Subtract. Write a related addition sentence.

$16 - 9 =$ ___

___ $+$ ___ $=$ ___

**5** Add.

$$\begin{array}{r} 6 \\ 4 \\ +\,4 \\ \hline \end{array} \qquad \begin{array}{r} 7 \\ 3 \\ +\,2 \\ \hline \end{array} \qquad \begin{array}{r} 5 \\ 3 \\ +\,5 \\ \hline \end{array}$$

## Problem Solving

Write each number sentence. Solve.

**6** 7 children are on the boat ride.
8 more children get on.                    _____ children

6 children get off. How many
children are on the boat ride now?    _____ children

**Notes for Home:** Your child reviewed Chapter 4 vocabulary, concepts, skills, and problem solving.
*Home Activity:* Ask your child to tell you how he or she solved Exercise 4.

CHAPTER REVIEW

Name _____

# Chapter 4 Test

**1** Find the missing number in the fact family.

$$4 + \underline{\quad} = 13$$

$$\underline{\quad} + 4 = 13$$

$$13 - 4 = \underline{\quad}$$

$$13 - \underline{\quad} = 4$$

**2** Add.

$$\begin{array}{r} 6 \\ 4 \\ + 3 \\ \hline \end{array} \qquad \begin{array}{r} 5 \\ 2 \\ + 5 \\ \hline \end{array} \qquad \begin{array}{r} 2 \\ 4 \\ + 4 \\ \hline \end{array}$$

**3** Follow the rule.
Write the missing numbers.

| Subtract 6. | |
|---|---|
| 15 | |
| 14 | |

**4** Subtract.
Write a related addition sentence.

$$16 - 8 = \underline{\quad}$$

$$\underline{\quad} + \underline{\quad} = \underline{\quad}$$

**5** Draw a picture. Solve the problem.

12 prizes are on the shelf.
4 children win prizes.
3 more children win prizes.
How many prizes are left?

_____ prizes

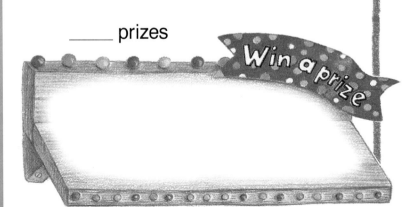

**6** Write each number sentence. Solve.

Toni bought 14 tickets for rides. She used 7 for the Ferris wheel.

_____ tickets

She bought 3 more. How many tickets does she have now?

_____ tickets

**Notes for Home:** Your child was tested on Chapter 4 concepts, skills, and problem solving.
*Home Activity:* Change the rule in Exercise 3 to <u>Subtract 7</u>. Ask your child to give the answers using this rule.

CHAPTER TEST

Name _____

# Performance Assessment
## Chapter 4

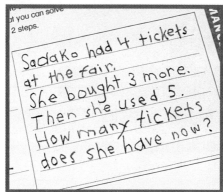

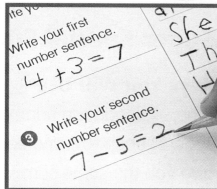

Put three sets of cards numbered 3 to 5 in a bag. Pick three cards from the bag.

Use the numbers to write a math story that you can solve in 2 steps.

Write both of the number sentences for your story. Solve.

1. Write your math story.

2. Write your first number sentence.

   _____

3. Write your second number sentence.

   _____

## Problem Solving Critical Thinking

4. Write a fact family using your first number sentence.

   _____        _____

   _____        _____

**Notes for Home:** Your child did an activity that tested Chapter 4 skills, concepts, and problem solving. *Home Activity:* Ask your child to write a different math story and different number sentences using the numbers picked.

Name _____

# Super Special Sums!

**Keys You Will Use** `ON/C` `+` `−` `=`

When you add the numbers in this special square, each row and each column will always give you the same sum.

| | | | |
|---|---|---|---|
| 12 | 3 | 3 | 18 |
| 1 | 11 | 6 | 18 |
| 5 | 4 | 9 | 18 |
| 18 | 18 | 18 | |

Find the missing numbers. To find the missing number for the first row,

Press `ON/C` `1` `2` `+` `3` `=` `15.`

Then press `1` `8` `−` `1` `5` `=` `3.`

> I can use the number I found for the first row to help me find the other missing numbers.

Now try these special squares!

**1**

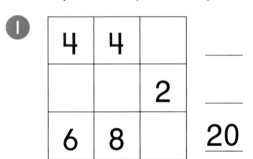

| 4 | 4 | | ___ |
|---|---|---|---|
| | | 2 | ___ |
| 6 | 8 | | 20 |

___ ___ ___

**2**

| 12 | 8 | | 30 |
|---|---|---|---|
| | | 15 | ___ |
| 9 | 16 | | ___ |

___ ___ ___

**3**

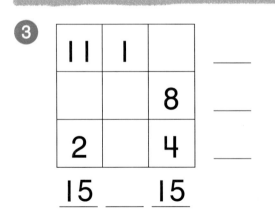

| 11 | 1 | | ___ |
|---|---|---|---|
| | | 8 | ___ |
| 2 | | 4 | ___ |
| 15 | | 15 | |

**4**

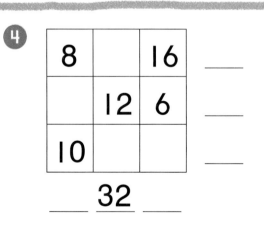

| 8 | | 16 | ___ |
|---|---|---|---|
| | 12 | 6 | ___ |
| 10 | | | ___ |
| | 32 | | |

**Tech Talk** How does using a calculator help you to solve these special squares?

🖳 **Visit our Web site.** www.parent.mathsurf.com

# Math Path

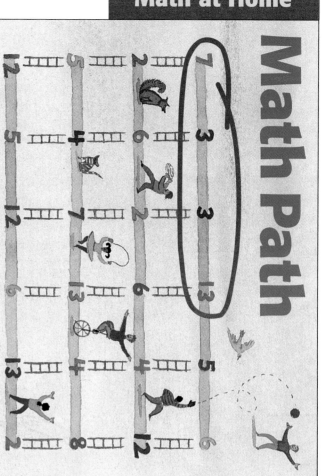

## Draw the Math Path!

1 Find four numbers in a row. Add the first three numbers.

2 If the fourth number is the sum, circle all four numbers.

3 The first one is done for you. Find all the sums. There are 2 more going across. There are 2 going down.

Visit our Web site. www.parent.mathsurf.com

**Fold down**

Fun at the Fair!

# MathSurf

Scott Foresman - Addison Wesley    My Math Magazine    No. 4

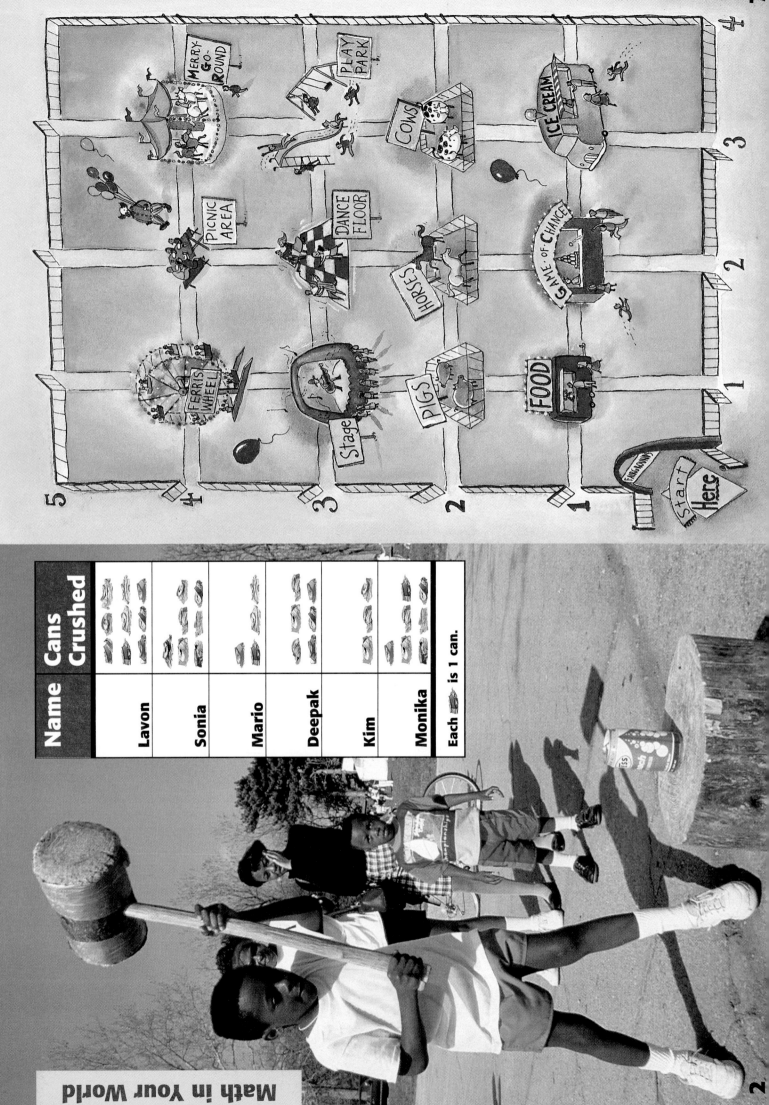

Math in Your World

| Name | Cans Crushed |
|------|--------------|
| Lavon | |
| Sonia | |
| Mario | |
| Deepak | |
| Kim | |
| Monika | |

Each ⬜ is 1 can.

# Where at the Fair?

Where do you want to go at the fair?
The map shows you different places to go.
Follow these directions using the map. Always begin at **Start**. First go over and then go up.
Where are you?

**1** Go over 1.
Go up 4.
Where are you?

**2** Go over 3.
Go up 2.
Where are you?

_____

**3** Pick a place on the map. Tell how to get there from the point marked **Start Here.**

_____

**Notes for Home:** Your child solved problems using a map. *Home Activity:* Ask your child to use the map to make up a problem for you to solve.

---

# Crushed!

Earth Day is celebrated every year in April. In St. Louis, Missouri, there was a big Earth Day Fair. People went on nature hikes. They learned about plants and animals.

Some children at the fair recycled cans. They crushed cans with a huge hammer. The children had fun and helped keep their city clean.

The pictograph shows how many cans some children crushed. Use the graph to answer the questions.

**1** Sonia and Monika are sisters. How many cans did they crush in all?

**2** How many cans did Mario, Deepak, and Kim crush in all?

**3** Which two children crushed a total of 15 cans?

**Notes for Home:** Your child practiced adding numbers using a pictograph. *Home Activity:* Ask your child how many cans Lavon, Kim, and Mario crushed in all. (9 + 3 + 4 = 16)

# Make 15

## How to Play

**1** Play with a friend. Try to make the numbers in each row and column add up to 15.

**2** Choose a number between 1 and 9. Write the number in a box.

**3** Have your friend write a number between 1 and 9 in another box.

**4** Continue playing. You can use a number more than once. Make sure rows and columns add up to 15.

**5** If a player writes a number so a row or column does not equal 15, that player loses and the other player wins.

**Helpful Hint**
If *all* the rows and columns equal 15, both players win!

**Notes for Home:** Your child played a game to practice adding three numbers. *Home Activity:* Ask your child to tell you three numbers that have a sum of 15. (Sample: 8 + 2 + 5)

## Test Your Skill!

Make 15

# Place Value and Patterns to 100

Colorful Collections

What do you
like to collect?

**Notes for Home:** Your child talked about collections. *Home Activity:* Help your child start a collection of small objects, such as buttons or pennies.

Dear Family,
Our class is starting Chapter 5. We will learn about tens and ones, number patterns, and numbers up to 100. Here are some activities we can do together.

### Numbers, Numbers, Everywhere!
Help your child find ways that numbers up to 100 are used in the home. For example, count all the silverware or find numbers in newspapers and magazines. Keep track of when and how numbers are used in daily life.

### What's My Number?
Fill a jar with less than 100 small items, such as beans or pennies. Ask your child to guess how many are in the jar, then help him or her count to find out.

**Community Connection**

Look for ways that large numbers are used around your community.

💻💻 **Visit our Web site. www.parent.mathsurf.com**

Name _____

Explore Estimation

**Explore** ● ● ● ● ● ● ● ● ● ● ● ● ● ● ● ● ● ● ● ● ● ● ● ● ●

Estimate. Try to take 50 .
Find out how many you have.
Draw what you did.

You can use groups to help.

**EXPLORE**

**Share** ● ● ● ● ● ● ● ● ● ● ● ● ● ● ● ● ● ● ● ● ● ● ● ●

How did you find out how many  you had?

 **Notes for Home:** Your child put items in groups to count them. *Home Activity:* Ask your child to take a handful of small objects, such as pennies, estimate how many there are, and put them into groups to count them.

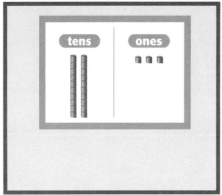

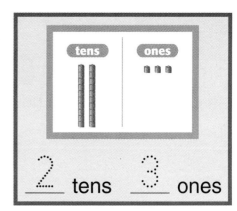

_____ tens _____ ones

Estimate. Try to take
50 .

Use your ☐☐.
Make tens and ones.

Write how many
tens and ones.

**EXPLORE**

| Try to take this many. | Write how many you took. |
|---|---|
| ❶ 20 | _____ tens _____ ones |
| ❷ 30 | _____ tens _____ ones |
| ❸ 40 | _____ tens _____ ones |
| ❹ 50 | _____ tens _____ ones |
| ❺ 60 | _____ tens _____ ones |
| ❻ 70 | _____ tens _____ ones |
| ❼ 80 | _____ tens _____ ones |

**Talk About It** How close did you get to your estimates?

Did you get closer each time?

**Notes for Home:** Your child used grouping by tens to estimate and count. *Home Activity:* Put some popcorn or other small items into a pile. Ask your child to try to take 20. Then have him or her put them into groups of tens and ones and count how many there are.

Name _____

# Record Numbers

**Learn**

*These both show 2 tens and 4 ones.*

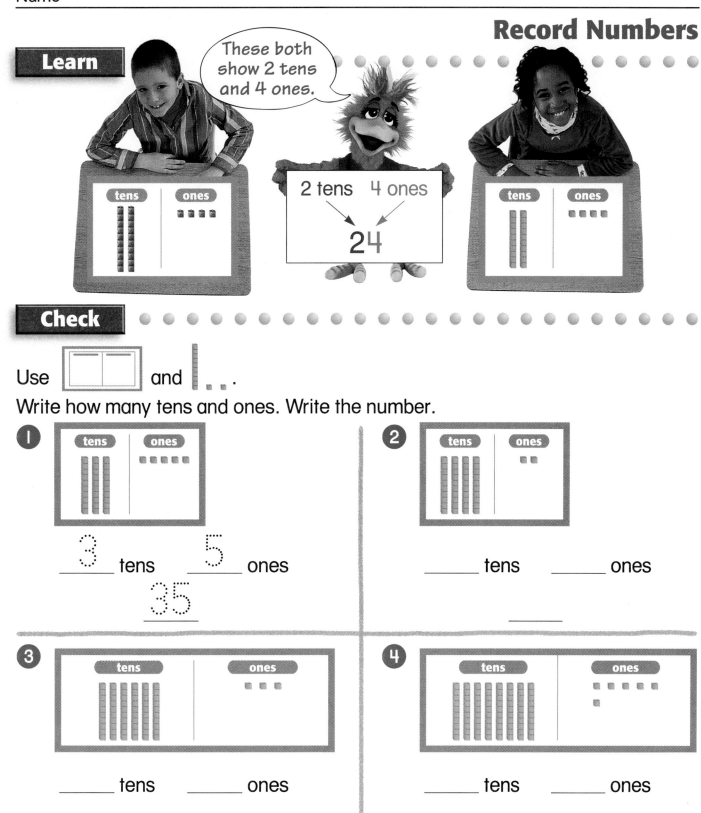

| tens | ones |
|------|------|

2 tens   4 ones

24

| tens | ones |
|------|------|

**Check**

Use [ ] and | .

Write how many tens and ones. Write the number.

**1**

| tens | ones |
|------|------|

___3___ tens ___5___ ones

35

**2**

| tens | ones |
|------|------|

_____ tens _____ ones

_____

**3**

| tens | ones |
|------|------|

_____ tens _____ ones

_____

**4**

| tens | ones |
|------|------|

_____ tens _____ ones

_____

**Talk About It** How are these alike?
How are they different?

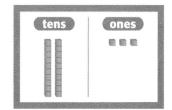

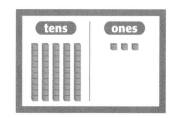

**Notes for Home:** Your child used tens and ones to write numbers. *Home Activity:* Ask your child to write the number that has 5 tens and 7 ones. (57)

**Chapter 5 Lesson 2**

one hundred fifty-nine   **159**

Write how many tens and ones. Write the number.

You can use 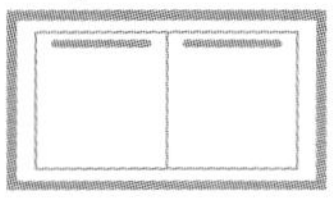  and  .

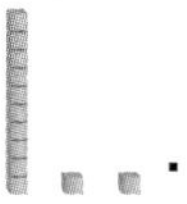

**5**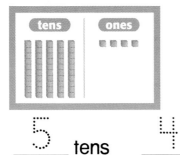

_5_ tens _4_ ones

_54_

**6**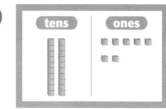

_____ tens _____ ones

_____

**7**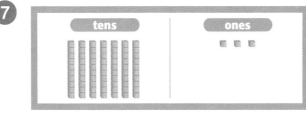

_____ tens _____ ones

_____

**8**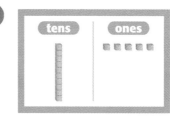

_____ ten _____ ones

_____

Write the number.

**9** 8 tens 7 ones

_87_

**10** 4 tens 6 ones

_____

**11** 9 tens 2 ones

_____

**12** 2 tens 9 ones

_____

## Problem Solving Critical Thinking

**13** How are these numbers alike? How are they different?

35     53

**Notes for Home:** Your child wrote numbers as tens and ones and as 2-digit numbers. _Home Activity:_ Ask your child to think of a number that is less than 100 and tell you how many tens and ones it has.

Name _____

**Learn** • • • • • • • • • • • • • • • •

You can write numbers as words! 48 is forty-eight.

| | | | | | |
|---|---|---|---|---|---|
| 1 one | 10 ten | 19 nineteen |
| 2 two | 11 eleven | 20 twenty |
| 3 three | 12 twelve | 30 thirty |
| 4 four | 13 thirteen | 40 forty |
| 5 five | 14 fourteen | 50 fifty |
| 6 six | 15 fifteen | 60 sixty |
| 7 seven | 16 sixteen | 70 seventy |
| 8 eight | 17 seventeen | 80 eighty |
| 9 nine | 18 eighteen | 90 ninety |

**Check** • • • • • • • • • • • • • • • • • • • • • • • • •

Write the number.

1. three _3_

2. thirteen _____

3. nineteen _____

4. forty-two _____

5. fifty-eight _____

6. fifteen _____

Write the word.

7. 4 _four_____

8. 16 _____

9. 36 _____

10. 91 _____

**Talk About It** What do you need to know
to write the word for 61?

**Notes for Home:** Your child learned to read and write words for numbers up to 99. *Home Activity:*
Ask your child to write the word for 62. (sixty-two) Repeat with other numbers between 20 and 99.

Write the number.

11 ninety-four _94_    12 eighty-three _____    13 sixty-six _____

14 seventy _____    15 twenty-six _____    16 thirty-seven _____

17 Use the clues to write each word.
   Fill in the puzzle.

| Across | Down |
|--------|------|
| 1. 4 | 1. 50 |
| 5. 70 | 2. 2 |
| 8. 9 | 3. 40 |
| 10. 90 | 4. 5 |
| | 5. 7 |
| | 6. 10 |
| | 7. 60 |
| | 9. 1 |

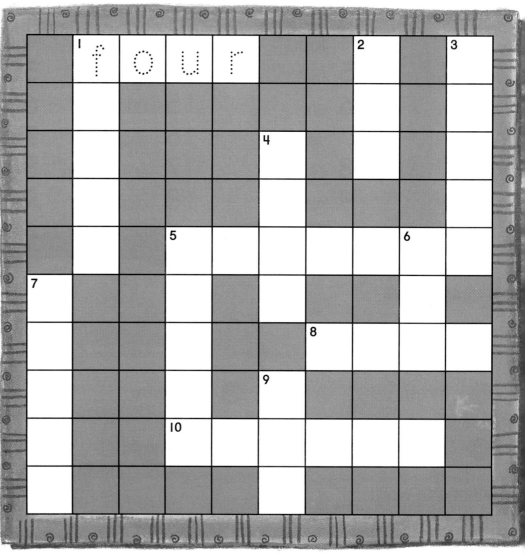

## Problem Solving **Critical Thinking**

18 Pick a number between 20 and 99.
   What are some ways you can show it?

**Notes for Home:** Your child practiced writing number words. *Home Activity:* Have your child think of a number between 20 and 99 and write the number word for it. (Sample answer: 37; thirty-seven)

Name _____

# Tell About 100

**Learn** • • • • • • • • • • • • • • • • • • • • • • • •

_5_ tens and _5_ tens is 10 tens.

_50_ and _50_ is 100.

_10_ tens is 100.

**Check** • • • • • • • • • • • • • • • • • • • • • • • •

Write how many tens. Write the numbers.

 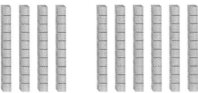

_____ tens and _____ tens is 10 tens.

_____ and _____ is 100.

2 

_____ tens and _____ tens is 10 tens.

_____ and _____ is 100.

_____ ten and _____ tens is 10 tens.

_____ and _____ is 100.

**Talk About It** How are these alike?

How are they different?

4 tens and 6 tens is 10 tens.      40 and 60 is 100.

 **Notes for Home:** Your child combined groups of tens to make 100. *Home Activity:* Ask your child how many tens would be added to 7 tens to make 100. (3 tens)

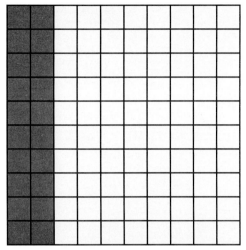

20 red and 80 yellow

Both of these show 10 tens. Both of these show 100.

**PRACTICE**

(4) Color 60 red.
Color 40 yellow.
Write how many.

$\underline{60}$ and $\underline{40}$ is $\underline{\phantom{00}}$.

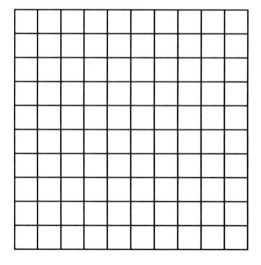

---

🙂 **Write your own.**

(5) Color some tens red.
Color the rest of the tens yellow.
Write how many.

$\underline{\phantom{00}}$ and $\underline{\phantom{00}}$ is 100.

## Problem Solving Critical Thinking

(6) How could you use 3 colors to show 100?

**Notes for Home:** Your child used a grid to show combinations of numbers that make 100.
*Home Activity:* Ask your child to tell you two numbers that can be added to make 100.

Name _____

# Problem Solving: Use Data from a Graph

How many marbles did Rachel collect?

| Marble Collections | |
|---|---|
| Rachel | 🟤🟤🟤🟤🟤 |
| Kelly | 🟤🟤🟤🟤🟤🟤 |
| Tony | 🟤🟤🟤 |

Each 🟤 means 10 marbles.

There are 5 🟤 next to Rachel's name.

Count by tens.  10  20  30  40  50

Rachel collected __50__ marbles.

**Check** ● ● ● ● ● ● ● ● ● ● ● ● ● ● ● ● ● ● ● ● ● ● ● ● ● ● ● ● ● ● ●

Use the graph to answer the questions.

**1** How many marbles
did Kelly collect?

_____ marbles

**2** How many marbles
did Tony collect?

_____ marbles

**3** How many marbles did Rachel
and Tony collect in all?

_____ marbles

**4** How many more marbles did
Kelly collect than Tony?

_____ more

**Talk About It** How many marbles would Rachel have if each
picture on the graph meant 2 marbles? Explain how you know.

**Notes for Home:** Your child used a graph to solve problems. *Home Activity:* Ask your child to
compare two of the collections in the graph. (Sample answer: Kelly has 60. Tony has 30. Kelly
has 30 more than Tony.)

**Stamp Collections**

| Jerome | 🌷 🌷 |
| Ella | 🌷 🌷 🌷 🌷 |
| Jay | 🌷 |
| Paula | 🌷 🌷 🌷 |

Each 🌷 means 5 stamps.

Be careful! Remember to count by 5s.

**PROBLEM SOLVING**

Use the graph to solve.

**5** How many stamps did Jerome collect?

__10__ stamps

**6** How many stamps did Jay collect?

_____ stamps

**7** How many stamps did Ella and Paula collect in all?

_____ stamps

**8** How many more stamps did Ella collect than Paula?

_____ more

## Visual Thinking

**9** Paula adds 10 more stamps to her collection.
What would you add to the graph? Explain.

**Notes for Home:** Your child used a graph to answer questions. *Home Activity:* Ask your child to show you how to count the stamps in the graph. (Sample answer: Each picture stands for 5. Count: 5, 10, 15)

**For additional practice, see Skills Practice Bank, page 531, Set 2.**

Name _____

# Mixed Practice
### Lessons 1–5

## Concepts and Skills

Write how many tens and ones.
Write the number.

**1**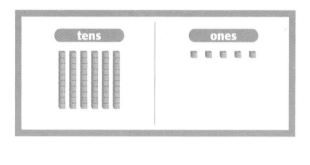

_____ tens  _____ ones

_____

Write the number.

**2** thirty-six  **3** fifteen

_____  _____

**4** fifty-two  **5** seventy-nine

_____  _____

## Problem Solving

Use the graph to answer the questions.

**6** How many more shells does Ruth have than Jules?

_____ more

**7** How many total shells do Jules and Sadie have?

_____ shells

**8** How many fewer shells does Sadie have than Ruth?

_____ fewer

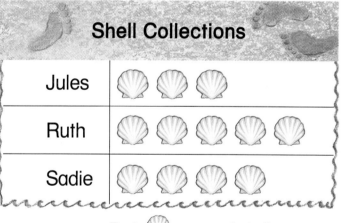

Each 🐚 means 10 shells.

**Journal**

**9** Pick a number between 10 and 100. Draw a picture of tens and ones to show your number.

**Notes for Home:** Your child counted by tens and ones, wrote numbers, and read graphs.
*Home Activity:* Ask your child to write a number sentence about the graph.

# Cumulative Review
### Chapters 1–5

## Concepts and Skills
Add or subtract.

**1**

| 12 | 5 | 7 | 18 | 13 | 5 | 10 |
|---|---|---|---|---|---|---|
| − 6 | + 4 | + 3 | − 9 | − 8 | + 5 | − 5 |

**2**

| 14 | 9 | 15 | 16 | 6 | 17 | 2 |
|---|---|---|---|---|---|---|
| − 7 | + 6 | − 6 | − 8 | + 4 | − 9 | + 8 |

## Problem Solving
Solve.

**3** Jamie has 9 stickers.
Alex gives her 7 more.
How many stickers does
Jamie have now?

_____ stickers

**4** Jamie has 16 stickers.
She gives 7 to Alex.
How many stickers
does Jamie have now?

_____ stickers

---

### Test Prep

Fill in the ○ for the correct answer.

**5** $5 + 4 + 5 =$ _____

| 9 | 14 | 6 | 10 |
|---|---|---|---|
| ○ | ○ | ○ | ○ |

**6** $3 + 7 + 2 =$ _____

| 10 | 9 | 12 | 11 |
|---|---|---|---|
| ○ | ○ | ○ | ○ |

---

**Notes for Home:** Your child reviewed addition and subtraction facts and problem solving.
*Home Activity:* Ask your child how many tens and ones are in the number 63. (6 tens and 3 ones)

CUMULATIVE REVIEW

# Hundred Chart and Skip Counting Patterns

**Learn**

| 1 | 2 | 3 | 4 | 5 | 6 | 7 | 8 | 9 | 10 |
|---|---|---|---|---|---|---|---|---|---|
| 11 | 12 | 13 | 14 | 15 | 16 | 17 | 18 | 19 | 20 |
| 21 | 22 | 23 | 24 | 25 | 26 | 27 | 28 | 29 | 30 |
| 31 | 32 | 33 | 34 | 35 | 36 | 37 | 38 | 39 | 40 |
| 41 | 42 | 43 | 44 | 45 | 46 | 47 | 48 | 49 | 50 |
| 51 | 52 | 53 | 54 | 55 | 56 | 57 | 58 | 59 | 60 |
| 61 | 62 | 63 | 64 | 65 | 66 | 67 | 68 | 69 | 70 |
| 71 | 72 | 73 | 74 | 75 | 76 | 77 | 78 | 79 | 80 |
| 81 | 82 | 83 | 84 | 85 | 86 | 87 | 88 | 89 | 90 |
| 91 | 92 | 93 | 94 | 95 | 96 | 97 | 98 | 99 | 100 |

Counting by 2s

| 1 | 2 | 3 | 4 | 5 | 6 | 7 | 8 | 9 | 10 |
|---|---|---|---|---|---|---|---|---|---|
| 11 | 12 | 13 | 14 | 15 | 16 | 17 | 18 | 19 | 20 |
| 21 | 22 | 23 | 24 | 25 | 26 | 27 | 28 | 29 | 30 |
| 31 | 32 | 33 | 34 | 35 | 36 | 37 | 38 | 39 | 40 |
| 41 | 42 | 43 | 44 | 45 | 46 | 47 | 48 | 49 | 50 |
| 51 | 52 | 53 | 54 | 55 | 56 | 57 | 58 | 59 | 60 |
| 61 | 62 | 63 | 64 | 65 | 66 | 67 | 68 | 69 | 70 |
| 71 | 72 | 73 | 74 | 75 | 76 | 77 | 78 | 79 | 80 |
| 81 | 82 | 83 | 84 | 85 | 86 | 87 | 88 | 89 | 90 |
| 91 | 92 | 93 | 94 | 95 | 96 | 97 | 98 | 99 | 100 |

Counting by 5s

| 1 | 2 | 3 | 4 | 5 | 6 | 7 | 8 | 9 | 10 |
|---|---|---|---|---|---|---|---|---|---|
| 11 | 12 | 13 | 14 | 15 | 16 | 17 | 18 | 19 | 20 |
| 21 | 22 | 23 | 24 | 25 | 26 | 27 | 28 | 29 | 30 |
| 31 | 32 | 33 | 34 | 35 | 36 | 37 | 38 | 39 | 40 |
| 41 | 42 | 43 | 44 | 45 | 46 | 47 | 48 | 49 | 50 |
| 51 | 52 | 53 | 54 | 55 | 56 | 57 | 58 | 59 | 60 |
| 61 | 62 | 63 | 64 | 65 | 66 | 67 | 68 | 69 | 70 |
| 71 | 72 | 73 | 74 | 75 | 76 | 77 | 78 | 79 | 80 |
| 81 | 82 | 83 | 84 | 85 | 86 | 87 | 88 | 89 | 90 |
| 91 | 92 | 93 | 94 | 95 | 96 | 97 | 98 | 99 | 100 |

Counting by 3s

**Check**

1  Finish counting by 4s on the chart.
Shade each number.

There are lots of patterns on a hundred chart!

| 1 | 2 | 3 | 4 | 5 | 6 | 7 | 8 | 9 | 10 |
|---|---|---|---|---|---|---|---|---|---|
| 11 | 12 | 13 | 14 | 15 | 16 | 17 | 18 | 19 | 20 |
| 21 | 22 | 23 | 24 | 25 | 26 | 27 | 28 | 29 | 30 |
| 31 | 32 | 33 | 34 | 35 | 36 | 37 | 38 | 39 | 40 |
| 41 | 42 | 43 | 44 | 45 | 46 | 47 | 48 | 49 | 50 |
| 51 | 52 | 53 | 54 | 55 | 56 | 57 | 58 | 59 | 60 |
| 61 | 62 | 63 | 64 | 65 | 66 | 67 | 68 | 69 | 70 |
| 71 | 72 | 73 | 74 | 75 | 76 | 77 | 78 | 79 | 80 |
| 81 | 82 | 83 | 84 | 85 | 86 | 87 | 88 | 89 | 90 |
| 91 | 92 | 93 | 94 | 95 | 96 | 97 | 98 | 99 | 100 |

**Talk About It** If you counted by 8s
on the chart, what pattern would you see?

  **Notes for Home:** Your child counted by 4s to 100. *Home Activity:* Ask your child to show you how to count by 2s using the chart.

**2** Complete the hundred chart. Then finish
counting by 6s on the chart. Shade each number.

| 1 | 2 | 3 | 4 | 5 | 6 | 7 | 8 | 9 | 10 |
|---|---|---|---|---|---|---|---|---|---|
| 11 | 12 | 13 | 14 | 15 | 16 | 17 | 18 | 19 | 20 |
|  |  |  |  |  |  |  |  |  |  |
|  |  |  |  |  |  |  |  |  | 40 |
|  |  |  |  |  |  |  | 48 |  |  |
|  |  |  |  |  |  |  |  |  | 60 |
|  |  |  |  | 65 |  |  |  |  |  |
| 71 |  |  |  |  |  |  |  |  | 80 |
|  |  | 83 |  |  |  |  |  |  |  |
|  |  |  |  |  |  |  | 98 | 99 | 100 |

**3** What patterns do you see?

_____

_____

_____

## Mental Math

**4** Steve has 5 toy cars in his collection.
Each car has 4 wheels.
How many wheels are there in all?

_____ wheels

**Notes for Home:** Your child counted by 6s to 100. *Home Activity:* Ask your child to count by 3s and by 5s using the chart.

Name _____

**Learn**

11 comes before 12.
13 is between 12 and 14.
15 comes after 14.

**Check**

Write the number that comes before.

**1**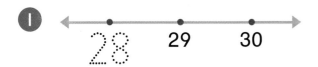
28   29   30

**2**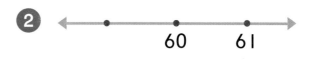
____   60   61

Write the number that comes between.

**3**
75   ____   77

**4**
49   ____   51

Write the number that comes after.

**5**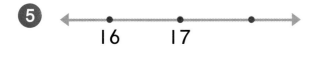
16   17   ____

**6**
34   35   ____

**Talk About It** Tell about 32 using the words before, between, and after.

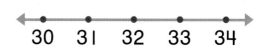
30   31   32   33   34

**Notes for Home:** Your child told which numbers come before, between, and after other numbers.
*Home Activity:* Ask your child to tell you about the number 53 using <u>before</u>, <u>between</u>, or <u>after</u>.
(Sample answer: 53 is between 52 and 54.)

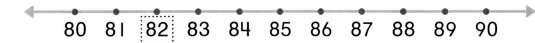

Use the number line. Answer each question.

80  81  :82:  83  84  85  86  87  88  89  90

**7** Draw a box around the number that is one before 83.

**8** Put a line under the number that is one after 89.

**9** Circle the number that is between 85 and 87.

**10** Put an X on all the numbers that are between 86 and 90.

Answer each question.

**11** What number is one before 65?

_____

**12** What number is one after 52?

_____

**13** What number is between 24 and 26?

_____

**14** What number is one before 40?

_____

## Problem Solving Critical Thinking

**15** Solve the riddle.

I am between 28 and 32.
I have 2 tens.
What number am I? _____

Make up your own riddles for a friend to solve.

**Notes for Home:** Your child answered questions about numbers. *Home Activity:* Ask your child to pick a number from the number line on this page and describe it using <u>before</u>, <u>between</u>, or <u>after</u>. (Sample answer: 83 is before 84.)

# Find the Nearest Ten

**Learn**

Is 17 closer to 10 or 20?

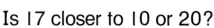

10  11  12  13  14  15  16  17  18  19  20

*The blue bar is shorter. 17 is closer to 20.*

**Check**

Draw bars to find the nearest ten.
Write the number.

1. Is 23 closer to 20 or 30?

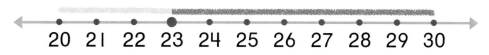

20  21  22  23  24  25  26  27  28  29  30

23 is closer to _____.

2. Is 76 closer to 70 or 80?

70  71  72  73  74  75  76  77  78  79  80

76 is closer to _____.

**Talk About It** Describe the location of 35 on the number line.

30      35      40

**Notes for Home:** Your child used number lines to solve problems. *Home Activity:* Ask your child to draw a number line and tell you if 48 is closer to 40 or 50. (50)

##  Write your own.

Pick a number on the number line.

Put a dot above that number.

Write your answer.

**3**

40 41 42 43 44 45 46 47 48 49 50

Is your number closer to 40 or 50? _____

**4**

30 31 32 33 34 35 36 37 38 39 40

Is your number closer to 30 or 40? _____

**5**

60 61 62 63 64 65 66 67 68 69 70

Is your number closer to 60 or 70? _____

For each number, write the nearest ten.

**6** 42         **7** 68 _____        **8** 33 _____

**9** 51 _____        **10** 79 _____        **11** 26 _____

## Problem Solving Estimation

**12** About how many shells in all?

Circle your estimate.

**About 20      About 70**

 **Notes for Home:** Your child practiced finding the nearest ten. (For example, 30 is the nearest ten for 33.) *Home Activity:* Ask your child to think of a number that is less than 100 and then tell you the nearest ten for that number.

Name _____

# Compare Numbers

**Learn** • • • • • • • • • • • • • • • • • • • • • • • • • •

These numbers are in order from least to greatest.

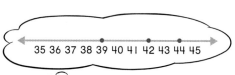

35 36 37 38 39 40 41 42 43 44 45

39 42 44

I think of tens and ones.

I think of a number line.

39 is less than 42.

44 is greater than 42.

**Check** • • • • • • • • • • • • • • • • • • • • • • • • • •

Circle the number that is greater.

① (43) 36    ② 58 64    ③ 66 76

④ 20 41    ⑤ 63 39    ⑥ 92 29

Circle the number that is less.

⑦ 52 (17)    ⑧ 28 79    ⑨ 19 63

⑩ 80 77    ⑪ 41 27    ⑫ 50 85

**Talk About It** Which number is greatest?
Which number is least? How do you know?    34 37 31

**Notes for Home:** Your child used tens to compare numbers. *Home Activity:* Ask your child to think of two numbers between 10 and 100 and tell which is greater and which is less.

Circle the number that is least.

**13**  47    62    (25)

**14**  87    31    65

**15**  59    83    94

**16**  26    12    38

Circle the number that is greatest.

**17**  (67)    42    17

**18**  29    36    74

**19**  71    93    52

**20**  56    19    28

Write the numbers in order from least to greatest.

**21**  36    85    27        27    36    85

**22**  61    99    94        ___    ___    ___

**23**  48    42    57        ___    ___    ___

## Problem Solving

Three children collected cans for recycling.

Emma collected 38 cans.

Leon collected 47 cans.

Iris collected the greatest number of cans.

How many cans could Iris have collected?

Find three possible answers.

**24** ___ cans    **25** ___ cans    **26** ___ cans

**Notes for Home:** Your child compared numbers using <u>least</u> and <u>greatest</u> and put numbers in order.
*Home Activity:* Ask your child to think of three numbers less than 100 and put them in order from least to greatest.

          **For additional practice, see Skills Practice Bank, page 531, Set 3.**

Name _____

# The Great Toss Up

**Players** 2

**What You Need**

50 🔲

Paper clip ⬭

Pencil ✏️

**How to Play**

1. Take 2 handfuls of 🔲.
   Make tens and ones.
   Write your number.

2. When your partner has had a turn,
   write his or her number.

3. Spin the spinner to see which
   number wins.

4. Circle **Greater** or **Less**.

5. Circle the winning number.

Greater Wins | Less Wins

| My Number | My Partner's Number | Which Number Wins? |
|-----------|---------------------|---------------------|
| _____ | _____ | Greater    Less |
| _____ | _____ | Greater    Less |
| _____ | _____ | Greater    Less |
| _____ | _____ | Greater    Less |

**Notes for Home:** Your child played a number game. *Home Activity:* Ask your child to tell you a number greater than 30 and a number less than 30. Repeat with other numbers.

Name _____

1  Count by 3s on the chart. Shade each number.

| 1 | 2 | 3 | 4 | 5 | 6 | 7 | 8 | 9 | 10 |
|---|---|---|---|---|---|---|---|---|---|
| 11 | 12 | 13 | 14 | 15 | 16 | 17 | 18 | 19 | 20 |
| 21 | 22 | 23 | 24 | 25 | 26 | 27 | 28 | 29 | 30 |
| 31 | 32 | 33 | 34 | 35 | 36 | 37 | 38 | 39 | 40 |
| 41 | 42 | 43 | 44 | 45 | 46 | 47 | 48 | 49 | 50 |

Write the number that comes between.

2  ←——•———•———•———→
        32          34
         _____

3  ←——•———•———•———→
        65          67
         _____

Write the numbers in order from least to greatest.

4  27     62     54          _____  _____  _____

For each number, write the nearest ten.

5  39  _____       6  52  _____       7  34  _____

8  26  _____       9  68  _____       10  77  _____

**Number Sense**

11  I am a number between 20 and 30.
    I am greater than 23.
    I am less than 26.
    I am not 24.

    What number am I? _____

**Notes for Home:** Your child practiced showing number patterns and comparing numbers.
*Home Activity:* Ask your child to pick 3 numbers and put them in order from least to greatest.

Name _____

**Learn**

first  second  third  fourth  fifth  sixth  seventh  eighth  ninth  tenth

**Check**

Circle your answer to each question.

① What is on the 3rd shelf?

② What is on the 7th shelf?

③ What is on the 17th shelf?

④ What is on the 6th shelf?

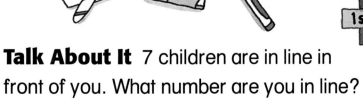

**Talk About It** 7 children are in line in front of you. What number are you in line?

 **Notes for Home:** Your child used ordinal numbers from 1st through 20th. *Home Activity:* Ask your child to put four small items, such as toys, in a line and tell which is first, second, third, and fourth.

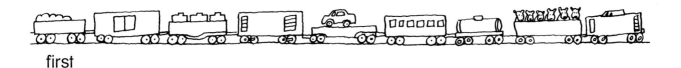

first

**5** Color the third car red.

**6** Color the 6th car purple.

**7** Color the 5th car blue.

**8** Color the ninth car yellow.

**9** Color the 2nd car green.

**10** Color the eighth car orange.

Answer each question.

**11** How many cars are in front of the 8th car?

_____

**12** How many cars are in front of the fourth car?

_____

**13** How many cars are behind the fourth car?

_____

**14** How many cars are behind the 3rd car?

_____

## Problem Solving

**15** Solve the riddle.

I am not 1st in line.
I am not 4th in line.
I am a boy.
What color is my shirt?

_____

**Notes for Home:** Your child used ordinal numbers from 1st through 20th. *Home Activity:* Ask your child to make up a riddle using the picture at the bottom of this page.

180   one hundred eighty

PRACTICE

# Odd and Even Numbers

**Learn**

You can break 10 cubes into 2 equal parts.

10 is an even number.

You cannot break 11 cubes into 2 equal parts.

11 is an odd number.

**Check**

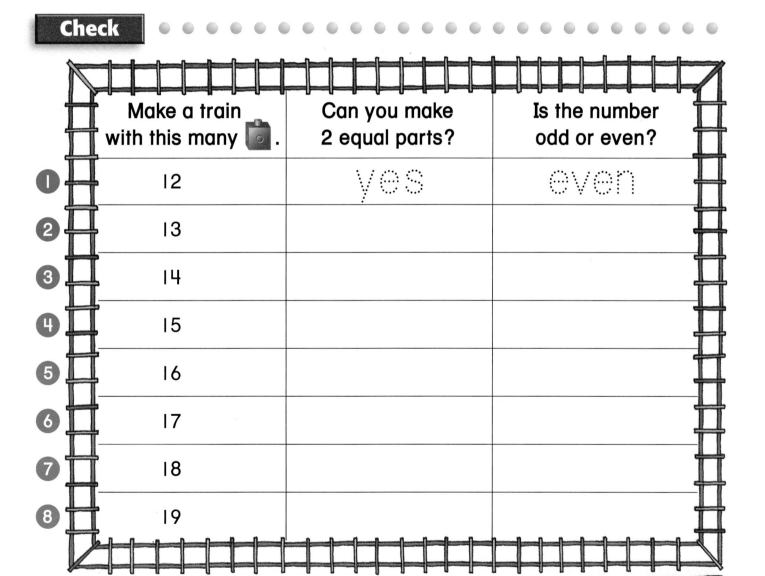

| | Make a train with this many. | Can you make 2 equal parts? | Is the number odd or even? |
|---|---|---|---|
| 1 | 12 | yes | even |
| 2 | 13 | | |
| 3 | 14 | | |
| 4 | 15 | | |
| 5 | 16 | | |
| 6 | 17 | | |
| 7 | 18 | | |
| 8 | 19 | | |

**Talk About It** Is 65 odd or even?

How do you know?

**Notes for Home:** Your child learned about odd and even numbers. *Home Activity:* Ask your child to take some objects, such as pennies, count them, and tell if the number is odd or even.

Write how many in all.
Then write **even** or **odd.**

**9**

_____    _____

**10**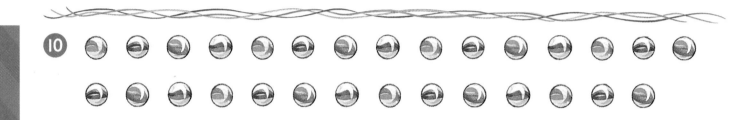

_____    _____

Write **even** or **odd.**

**11**  75  ⌂ odd ⌂ _____   **12**  32  _____

**13**  98  _____   **14**  61  _____

**Write your own.** Write three even numbers.
Then write three odd numbers.

**15**  Even numbers:  _____   _____   _____

**16**  Odd numbers:  _____   _____   _____

## Problem Solving  Patterns

**17**  Is the number 6,852 odd or even?
How do you know?

 **Notes for Home:** Your child worked with odd and even numbers. *Home Activity:* Ask your child to think of a number and tell you if it is odd or even.

Name _____

## Classification

1. Tara has 15 mugs in her collection.
   She wants to sort them by their designs.
   Finish the chart to sort the mugs into three groups.

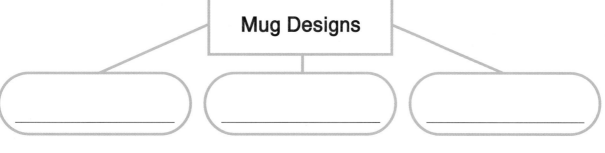

**Mug Designs**

2. What other way can you sort Tara's mugs?

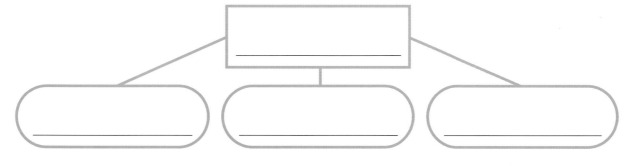

**Talk About It** What are some other ways
you could sort Tara's mugs?

**Notes for Home:** Your child learned many ways to sort items. *Home Activity:* Ask your child to find two different ways to sort some coins. (Sample answers: by size, by color, by value)

**3** Martin likes to collect banks.

How can Martin sort his banks?

Finish the chart to sort the banks into three groups.

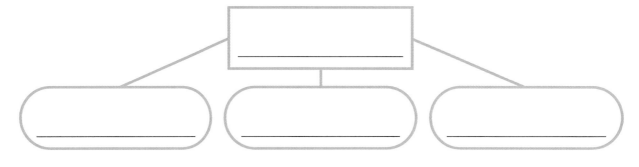

**4** Find a new way to sort Martin's banks.

Finish the chart.

## Critical Thinking

**5** How would you sort the beads? Explain your reason.

**Notes for Home:** Your child sorted items in different ways. *Home Activity:* Ask your child to tell you different ways to sort his or her clothing. (Sample answers: by color, by type, by weather)

Name _____

# Problem Solving: Group Decision Making

**Learn** • • • • • • • • • • • • • • •

**PROBLEM SOLVING GUIDE**

Understand • Plan • Solve • Look Back

I need to sort these things!

**Check** • • • • • • • • • • • • • • • • • • • • • • • • •

Work with your group.

Take items out of your desk.

**1** What items did you find?

_____     _____

_____     _____

_____     _____

**2** How many ways could you sort your group's items?

_____     _____

_____     _____

_____     _____

**3** Decide as a group which way you like best. Circle it.

**Talk About It** How did your group decide the best way
to sort the items?

**Notes for Home:** Your child made decisions with a group about how to sort items. *Home Activity:* Have your child gather a variety of small items and find many different ways to sort them.

**PROBLEM SOLVING**

**PROBLEM SOLVING**

4 As a group, sort your items the way you liked best.
Decide as a group how to show your sorted items.
Draw how you sorted them.

**Journal**

5 What was easy about working with your group?
What was hard?

**Notes for Home:** Your child sorted items and made decisions with a group. *Home Activity:* Help your child think of situations in daily life when groups must make decisions together. (Sample answers: what to have for dinner, what game to play at recess)

Name _____

# Mixed Practice
**Lessons 6–12**

## Concepts and Skills

Count by 4s. Write the numbers. You can use a hundred chart.

**1** 4, 8, 12, ____, ____, ____, ____, ____, ____, ____

Write the missing numbers.

**2**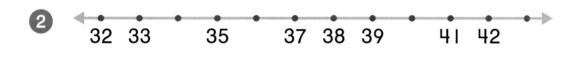

32  33  ____  35  ____  37  38  39  ____  41  42  ____

For each number, write the nearest ten.

**3** 53 ____        **4** 78 ____        **5** 37 ____

Write these numbers in order from least to greatest.

**6** 91   28   74        ____  ____  ____

## Problem Solving

Use the picture to answer the questions.

**7** What color is the second car? _____

**8** What color is the fourth car? _____

**Journal**

**9** Are these numbers even or odd?   17   9   11   3
How do you know?

**Notes for Home:** Your child practiced counting by 4s, finding the nearest 10, putting numbers in order from least to greatest, and identifying the order of cars in a picture. *Home Activity:* Ask your child to think of two even numbers under 100 and tell you how he or she knows they are even.

*MIXED PRACTICE*

Name _____

# Cumulative Review
## Chapters 1–5

## Concepts and Skills

Add or subtract.

1.

| 12 | 8 | 14 | 9 | 8 | 7 | 8 |
|---|---|---|---|---|---|---|
| − 9 | + 5 | − 6 | − 5 | + 9 | + 7 | + 4 |

## Problem Solving

Write the number sentences. Solve.

2. Milton has 10 beads.
Patti has 6 beads.
How many more beads does
Milton have than Patti?

_____ − _____ = _____ beads

3. Joan has 15 seashells.
Rob has 9 seashells.
How many more seashells
does Joan have than Rob?

_____ − _____ = _____ seashells

---

### Test Prep

Fill in the ○ for the correct answer.

4. Nikki has 12 storybooks.
She gives away 2.
How many storybooks
does she have now?

○ 12 + 2 = 14
○ 12 − 0 = 12
○ 12 − 12 = 0
○ 12 − 2 = 10

5. Mercedes has 9 toy horses.
Pablo gives her 4 more.
How many toy horses does
Mercedes have now?

○ 9 − 4 = 5
○ 9 + 4 = 13
○ 13 − 4 = 9
○ 13 + 0 = 13

---

**Notes for Home:** Your child reviewed addition and subtraction facts and problem solving.
*Home Activity:* Ask your child to tell you an addition fact with the sum of 14.

**188** one hundred eighty-eight

Name _____

# Chapter 5 Review

## Vocabulary

**1** Circle the number that is greater.

45    38

**2** Circle the number that is less.

82    79

**3** Circle the odd numbers.

21    63    54

**4** Circle the even numbers.

34    57    46

## Concepts and Skills

Write how many tens and ones.

**5** 38 _____ tens _____ ones

**6** 74 _____ tens _____ ones

Write each number.

**7** twenty-three _____

**8** forty-nine _____

**9** eighteen _____

## Problem Solving

Use the graph to answer the questions.

**10** How many books did Rosa collect? _____

**11** How many more books did Rosa have than Chris? _____

**12** How many books did Chris, Rosa, and Randy have in all? _____

Our Book Collection

| Chris | |
| Rosa | |
| Randy | |

Each 📖 means 5 books.

**Notes for Home:** Your child reviewed vocabulary, concepts, skills, and problem solving from Chapter 5. *Home Activity:* Ask your child to pick a number and tell about it using <u>before</u>, <u>between</u>, or <u>after</u>. (Sample answer: 37 is between 36 and 38.)

one hundred eighty-nine    189

Name _____

# Chapter 5 Test

Write the number.

**1** 2 tens   8 ones   _____

**2** fifty-one _____

---

**3** Complete.

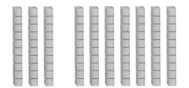

_____ and _____ is 100.

---

**4** Write the number that comes before.

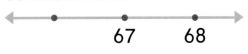

67   68

_____

**5** Is 46 closer to 40 or 50?

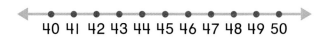

40 41 42 43 44 45 46 47 48 49 50

46 is closer to _____.

---

**6** Write the numbers in order from least to greatest.

**28   42   25**   _____   _____   _____

---

**7** Circle the animal that is fourth.

**8** Write **odd** or **even**.

**59** _____

**9** Use the graph. How many more cards does Max have than Lucas?

_____

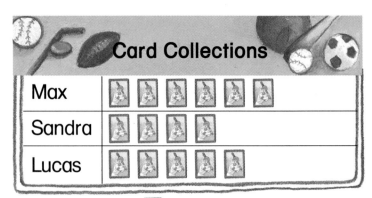

Card Collections

| Max | |
| Sandra | |
| Lucas | |

Each 🐾 means 10 cards.

**Notes for Home:** Your child was tested on Chapter 5 skills, concepts, and problem solving. *Home Activity:* Ask your child to think of combinations of tens that make 100. (Sample answers: 2 tens and 8 tens; 7 tens and 3 tens; 6 tens and 3 tens and 1 ten)

Name _____

# Performance Assessment
## Chapter 5

Choose 4 numbers between 30 and 60.

Tell about each of your numbers.

Fill in the chart.

| | Write your numbers. | How many tens? How many ones? | Write the nearest ten. | Is your number odd or even? |
|---|---|---|---|---|
| **1** | 31 | __3__ tens __1__ ones | 30 | odd |
| **2** | | _____ tens _____ ones | | |
| **3** | | _____ tens _____ ones | | |
| **4** | | _____ tens _____ ones | | |
| **5** | | _____ tens _____ ones | | |

**6** Write the numbers you chose in order from least to greatest.

31 _____ _____ _____ _____

## Critical Thinking

**7** Write sentences about some of your numbers.

Use these words: **before, after, between.**

**Notes for Home:** Your child did an activity that tested Chapter 5 skills and concepts.
*Home Activity:* Ask your child to choose a new number and answer the questions in the chart.

**PERFORMANCE ASSESSMENT**

Name _____

# Hit the Target!

**Keys You Will Use** [ON/C] [ + ] [ = ]

You can use your  to count by any number.

Press these keys to count by 3s.

[ON/C] [ 3 ] [ + ] [ 3 ] [ = ]

[ = ] [ = ] [ = ] [ 15. ]

*To add the same number again, I can press [ = ] !*

| 1 | 2 | 3 | 4 | 5 | 6 | 7 | 8 | 9 | 10 |
|---|---|---|---|---|---|---|---|---|---|
| 11 | 12 | 13 | 14 | 15 | 16 | 17 | 18 | 19 | 20 |
| 21 | 22 | 23 | 24 | 25 | 26 | 27 | 28 | 29 | 30 |
| 31 | 32 | 33 | 34 | 35 | 36 | 37 | 38 | 39 | 40 |
| 41 | 42 | 43 | 44 | 45 | 46 | 47 | 48 | 49 | 50 |
| 51 | 52 | 53 | 54 | 55 | 56 | 57 | 58 | 59 | 60 |
| 61 | 62 | 63 | 64 | 65 | 66 | 67 | 68 | 69 | 70 |
| 71 | 72 | 73 | 74 | 75 | 76 | 77 | 78 | 79 | 80 |
| 81 | 82 | 83 | 84 | 85 | 86 | 87 | 88 | 89 | 90 |
| 91 | 92 | 93 | 94 | 95 | 96 | 97 | 98 | 99 | 100 |

## How to Play

1. Player One chooses a target number between 30 and 100.

2. Player Two counts by 3s, 4s, 5s, or 10s to try and hit the target number. Use the chart to decide what number to count by.

3. If Player Two hits the target number exactly, he or she takes another turn. If Player Two misses, then Player One takes a turn. Pick a different target number each time.

4. Record your turns in this chart.

5. The first player to hit the target number 5 times wins!

| Target Number | 15 | | | | | | |
|---|---|---|---|---|---|---|---|
| Skip Count by: | 3 | | | | | | |
| Hit Target? | | | | | | | |

**Tech Talk** How would you use a calculator to count by 12s?

🖳 **Visit our Web site.** www.parent.mathsurf.com

## Math at Home

# The Winner Is…

One school held a contest and awarded prizes for unusual collections. Use the clues, then write each child's name on the correct line below.

First Place

Second Place

Third Place

Jesse did not come in first place. His ribbon is not yellow.

Helen did not come in third place.

Duane's ribbon is not blue.

**Fold down**

---

# Math Soup

Scott Foresman - Addison Wesley

My Math Magazine

No. 5

## Collections

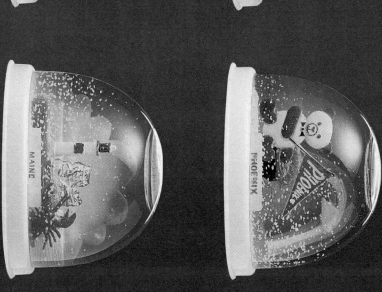

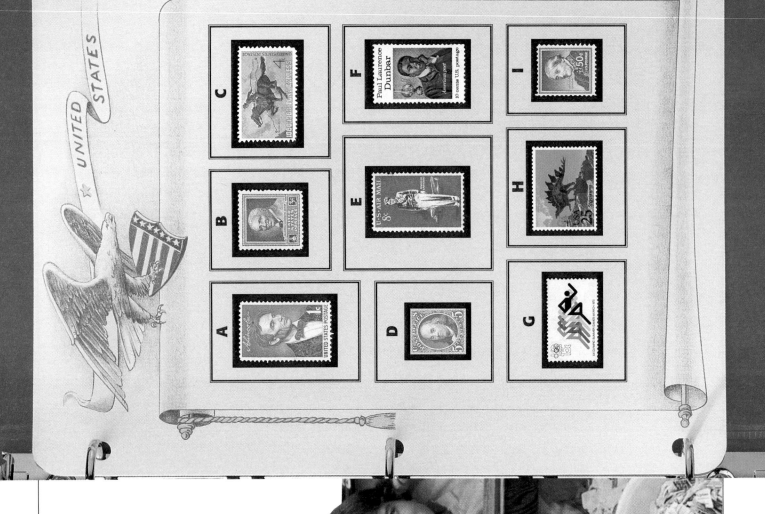

# Math in Your World

# How Many Is a Million?

Rosanne Ponchick's second grade class in Teaneck, New Jersey, wanted to collect one million things. They collected tea tags — the little tags attached to tea bags. They began in 1982. Each year, a new class added more. Now they have more than 4 million tea tags!

The graph shows how many tags the class collected in one week. Use the graph to answer the questions.

1 How many tags were collected on Monday?

2 Which two days add up to 100 tags?

**Notes for Home:** Your child used a graph to find out information and counted by tens. *Home Activity:* Ask your child how many tags were

# Stampers*

Many people collect different types of stamps. Every stamp has a price printed on it. Use the stamp collection. Answer these questions by writing the letters of the stamps.

1. Find 2 stamps that equal sixty cents together.

____ and ____

2. Find 3 stamps that equal thirteen cents together.

____, ____, and ____

What did the stamp say to the letter?

I'm stuck on you.

* Stamp collectors are called stampers.

Notes for Home: Your child read number words and found sums.
Home Activity: Ask your child to find 3 stamps that equal fifteen cents

## Tags Collected in One Week

| Day | Tags |
|---|---|
| Monday | TEA TEA TEA TEA TEA |
| Tuesday | TEA TEA TEA |
| Wednesday | TEA TEA TEA TEA |
| Thursday | TEA TEA TEA TEA |
| Friday | TEA TEA TEA TEA TEA TEA |

Each TEA means 10 tags.

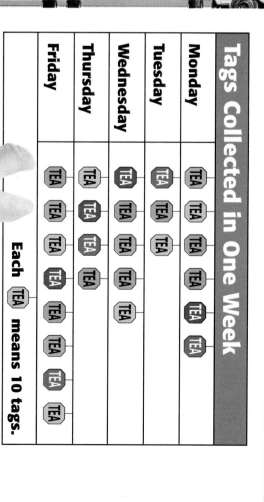

3

Robert McMath collects products that didn't sell.

Tracy has a collection of nutcrackers.

Max Watson, a boy in California, collects snow domes!

Louise Mesa collects anything shaped like a frog!

# Clever Collections

People collect all kinds of things. What do you and your friends collect?

Ask at least 10 people you know what they collect. Ask how many things are in their collections. If you have a collection, include yourself. Use tallies to fill in the chart.

## How Many Things Are in Collections

| Number of People with More Than 50 | Number of People with Fewer Than 50 |
| --- | --- |
|  |  |

What is the strangest thing someone collected?

**Notes for Home:** Your child surveyed people about their collections.
*Home Activity:* Ask your child how many people had more than 50 items in their collections and how many people had less than 50 items.

What's for Sale?

**Notes for Home:** Your child used this picture to talk about different amounts of money.
*Home Activity:* Ask your child to tell you the value for three of the groups of coins.

## Math at Home

Dear Family,
Our class is starting Chapter 6. We will be learning about amounts of money through $1.00. Here are some activities we can do at home.

### Coin Count
Put some coins, such as pennies, nickels, and dimes, into a bag. Have your child take out 3 coins. Count to find the total value of the coins.

### Sell, Sell, Sell!
Help your child set up a make-believe store. Pick items at home to pretend to sell. Make price tags and sale signs showing amounts less than $1.00.

### Community Connection
After making a purchase at a store, help your child count to find the total value of the coins you received as change.

**Visit our Web site. www.parent.mathsurf.com**

Name _____

# Explore Counting Dimes, Nickels, and Pennies

I penny

or
I cent
I ¢

I nickel

or
5 cents
5¢

I dime

or
10 cents
10¢

1 Pick an item you would like to buy. Write the amount. _____

Use coins. Show the amount in different ways. Draw the coins.

2

3

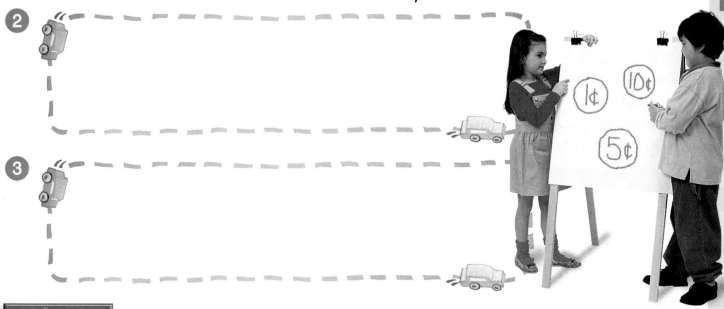

**Share**

Do you think there are more ways to show the same amount? Why or why not?

**Notes for Home:** Your child explored how to use coins to show amounts to 42¢.
*Home Activity:* Ask your child to choose a new item from the picture and draw the coins he or she would use to show the amount.

| Count by 10s. | Count on by 5s. | Count on by ones. |
|---|---|---|
|    |   |  |
| 10     20     30 | 35     40 | 41     42     43 |

**43¢** in all

Use these coins. Count the money. Write the total amount.

**4**

36¢

**5**

Use these coins. Draw the coins. Write the total amount.

**6** I dime, 2 nickels, and 3 pennies

**7** I dime, I nickel, and 4 pennies

**Talk About It** Tell how you ordered the coins to help you count them.

 **Notes for Home:** Your child counted groups of dimes, nickels, and pennies. *Home Activity:* Ask your child to draw 2 dimes, 2 nickels, and 2 pennies. Have your child count the total amount. (32¢)

**200** two hundred

Name _____

# Quarters

**Learn** ● ● ● ● ● ● ● ● ● ● ● ● ● ● ● ● ● ● ● ● ● ● ● ● ● ● ● ●

I quarter

or

25 cents
25¢

Count
by 25s.

25  50  75

Count on
by 10.

85

Count on
by 5s.

90  95

**95¢** in all

**Check** ● ● ● ● ● ● ● ● ● ● ● ● ● ● ● ● ● ● ● ● ● ● ● ● ● ● ● ●

Use these coins. Count the money. Write the total amount.

1.                                                    67¢

2.

**Talk About It** Count to find the total amount in each group.

Which group was easier to count? Why?

**Notes for Home:** Your child counted groups of coins that included quarters. *Home Activity:* Ask your child to show you how he or she would count a group of 3 or more coins. Use quarters, dimes, nickels, and pennies.

Use coins. Count the money. Write the total amount.

**3**

88¢

**4**

Use these coins. Draw the coins. Write the total amount.

**5**  2 quarters, 1 dime, and 1 penny

 **Write your own.** Draw 4 coins. Write the total amount.

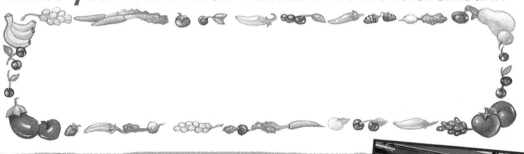

## Problem Solving Visual Thinking

**6**  Would you like to have the
stack of pennies or the
stack of dimes to spend at
the grocery store? Explain.

 **Notes for Home:** Your child practiced counting groups of coins that included quarters.
*Home Activity:* Ask your child to tell you the total value for 1 quarter, 1 dime, and 1 nickel. (40¢)

Name _____

## Coin Bingo

**Players** 2 to 4

**What You Need**

Coins

Crayon ▭ green

Paper clip ⬭

Pencil ✏

**How to Play**

① Complete the bingo card below.
Use the amounts on the tags.

② Spin 3 times. Take the coin shown by each spin.

③ Count your coins. Color the box showing that amount.

④ The first player to fill in his or her gameboard wins!

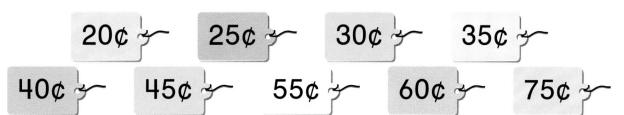

| 20¢ | 25¢ | 30¢ | 35¢ |
| --- | --- | --- | --- |

| 40¢ | 45¢ | 55¢ | 60¢ | 75¢ |
| --- | --- | --- | --- | --- |

| 15¢ |  |  |
| --- | --- | --- |
|  | free |  |
|  |  |  |

Bingo! I win!

**Notes for Home:** Your child played a game with quarters, dimes, and nickels.
*Home Activity:* Have your child practice counting quarters, dimes, nickels, and pennies in different combinations up to a total of $1.00.

Name _____

STOP and Practice

Use coins to show each amount.
Draw the coins.

①
35¢

②
58¢

③
42¢

④
67¢

⑤
75¢

⑥
29¢

## Number Sense

⑦ What other coins could you use to show 75¢?
Compare your answer with a friend's.

# Half Dollars

## Learn

I half dollar

or

50 cents

50¢

Start at 50.

Count on by 10s.

Count on by ones.

50       60   70      71   72

**72¢** in all

## Check

Use coins. Count the money. Write the total amount.

1.

    90¢

2.

Use these coins. Draw the coins. Write the total amount.

3. I half dollar, I dime, 3 nickels

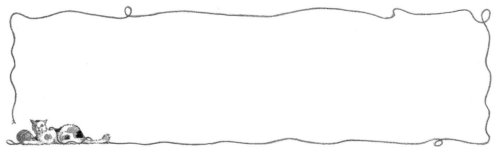 

**Talk About It** What other coins could you use to show 90¢?

 **Notes for Home:** Your child counted groups of coins that included half dollars. *Home Activity:* Ask your child to choose an exercise and use a different combination of coins to make that amount.

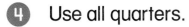

Find different ways to make 50¢.
Draw the coins. Write how many.

**4** Use all quarters.

There are _____ quarters in 50¢.

**5** Use all dimes.

There are _____ dimes in 50¢.

## Problem Solving

**6** How much could this cost?
Choose a price between 50¢ and 99¢.
Draw coins. Write the price.

 **Notes for Home:** Your child used coins to show 50¢. *Home Activity:* Ask your child how many nickels he or she would use to show 50¢. (10)

**For additional practice, see Skills Practice Bank, page 532, Set 1.**

## Problem Solving: Make a List

**Learn** ● ● ● ● ● ● ● ● ● ● ● ●

Dave needs 45¢ to buy juice from a vending machine. Use coins. Find all the ways to make 45¢ using quarters, dimes, and nickels. Finish the list.

| (quarter) | (dime) | (nickel) |
|---|---|---|
| 1 | 2 | 0 |
| 1 | 1 | 2 |
| 1 | 0 | 4 |
| 0 | 4 | 1 |
| 0 | 3 | |
| | | |
| | | |
| | | |

Try 2 dimes.

Try 1 dime.

Try 0 dimes.

**Check** ● ● ● ● ● ● ● ● ● ● ● ● ● ● ● ● ● ● ● ● ● ● ● ● ● ●

**1** Kim needs 40¢ to buy crackers from a vending machine. She only has dimes and nickels. Find all the ways she can make 40¢. Finish the list.

| (dime) | (nickel) |
|---|---|
| 4 | 0 |
| | |
| | |
| | |
| | |
| | |

**Talk About It** How does the list help you know that you have found all the ways?

**Notes for Home:** Your child used coins to make an organized list. *Home Activity:* Use dimes and nickels. Ask your child to show you all the ways to make 30¢. (3 dimes, 2 dimes and 2 nickels, 1 dime and 4 nickels, 0 dimes and 6 nickels)

**2** Mrs. Evans needs 35¢ for a phone call.
Use coins. Find all the ways to make 35¢
using quarters, dimes, and nickels.
Make a list.

Use 1 quarter.

Use 1 quarter again.

| | | |
|---|---|---|
| 1 | 1 | 0 |
| 1 | | |
| | | |
| | | |
| | | |
| | | |

## Critical Thinking

Rachel has these coins in her hand.
She has 65¢ in all. What coins
could she have in her pocket?

Show 2 ways. Draw the coins.

**3**

**4**

**Notes for Home:** Your child found ways to make 35¢ and put the information into an organized list.
*Home Activity:* Use quarters, dimes, and nickels. Ask your child to show you all the ways to make 40¢.
(1 quarter and 1 dime and 1 nickel, 1 quarter and 3 nickels, and so on)

**For additional practice, see Skills Practice Bank, page 532, Set 2.**

Name _____

# Mixed Practice

## Lessons 1–4

## Concepts and Skills

Use these coins. Count the money. Write the total amount.

1

Use these coins. Draw the coins. Write the total amount.

2   1 quarter, 3 dimes, 2 nickels

## Problem Solving

3   Sara needs 25¢ for a phone call.

Use coins. Find all the ways to make
25¢ using quarters, dimes, and nickels.
Make a list.

## Journal

4   Choose an amount between 56¢ and 99¢. Write the amount.

Use coins. Show the amount 2 different ways. Draw the coins.

**Notes for Home:** Your child practiced making a list and counting half dollars, quarters, dimes, nickels, and pennies. *Home Activity:* Ask your child to show you a group of coins and find the total amount.

# Cumulative Review
## Chapters 1–6

## Concepts and Skills

Count by ones, 5s, or 10s.
Write the numbers.

**1** 5, 6, 7, ____, ____, ____

**2** 30, 40, 50, ____, ____, ____

**3** 5, 10, 15, ____, ____, ____

**4** 35, 40, 45, ____, ____, ____

## Problem Solving

Use the graph to answer the questions.

**5** How many more Pencils than Notebooks were sold?

_____ more pencils

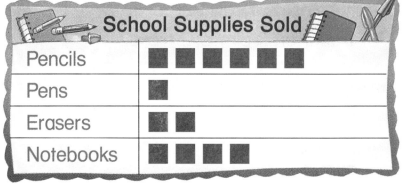

Each ■ stands for 10 things.

**6** How many Notebooks were sold?

_____ notebooks

**7** How many more Erasers than Pens were sold?

_____ more erasers

---

### Test Prep

Fill in the ○ for the correct answer.

**8** Which word is the same as this number?

42
- ○ twenty-four
- ○ four
- ○ forty-two
- ○ forty-four

**9** Which number is the same as this word?

fifty

| 60 | 5 | 50 | 15 |
| ○ | ○ | ○ | ○ |

**Notes for Home:** Your child reviewed skip counting, pictographs, and number words.
*Home Activity:* Ask your child to read the graph and tell you how many pencils were sold. (60)

Name _____

**Learn** • • • • • • • • • • • • • • • • • • • • • •

How can you pay for the jacket
using the fewest coins?

*A half dollar is too much. I can start with a quarter.*

Sidewalk Sale

46¢

**Check** • • • • • • • • • • • • • • • • • • • • • •

Use the fewest coins to show each amount. Draw the coins.

1. 41¢     25¢  10¢  5¢  1¢

2. 55¢

3. 72¢

**Talk About It** How did you know you had used the fewest coins?

**Notes for Home:** Your child learned how to show amounts of money using the fewest coins.
*Home Activity:* Ask your child to show 16¢ with the fewest coins. (one dime, one nickel, and one penny)

**Practice**

Use the fewest coins to show each amount.
Draw the coins.

4  66¢    50¢  10¢  5¢  1¢

5 27¢

6 80¢

7 75¢

## Problem Solving

8 Draw the same amount of money
using the fewest coins.

**PRACTICE**

 **Notes for Home:** Your child practiced showing amounts of money using the fewest coins.
*Home Activity:* Ask your child to think of an amount less than $1.00 and show it using the fewest coins.

# Dollar Bill

**Learn**

"The dollar sign comes first."

I dollar
100 cents
$1.00

"The decimal point separates dollars from cents."

or

**Check**

Use coins to show $1.00. Draw the coins. Write how many.

**1** Use all quarters.

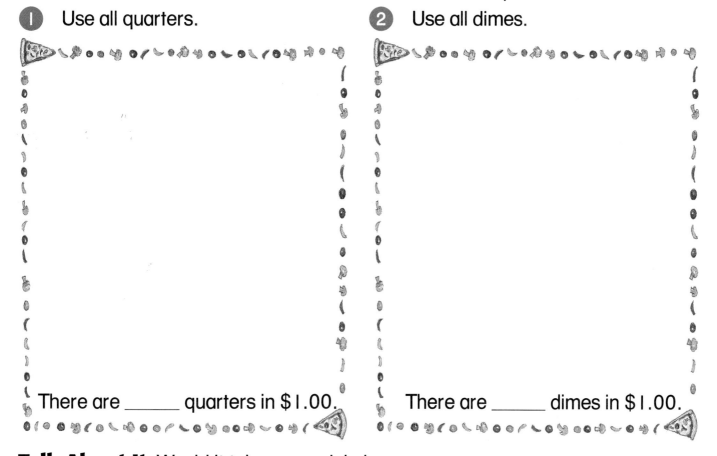

There are _____ quarters in $1.00.

**2** Use all dimes.

There are _____ dimes in $1.00.

**Talk About It** Would it take more nickels

or more dimes to make $1.00? How do you know?

**Notes for Home:** Your child learned some coin combinations that total $1.00.
*Home Activity:* Ask your child to show $1.00 using all nickels. (20 nickels)

Use half dollars, quarters, dimes, and nickels.
Find different ways to make $1.00.
Draw your coins.

3

50¢   50¢

4

5

6

7

8

**Journal**

9 Some children earn money by doing chores.
What are some ways children could earn $1.00?

**Notes for Home:** Your child made different coin combinations for $1.00. *Home Activity:* Ask your child how many pennies it takes to make $1.00. (100)

      **For additional practice, see Skills Practice Bank, page 532, Set 3.**

Name _____

# Race to $1.00

**Players** 2 to 4

## What You Need

Number cube

Coins

## How to Play

1. Each player gets 5 turns.
2. Toss the number cube, and take that many coins.
   You must take all dimes or all nickels or all pennies.
3. For each turn, record the value of the coins you took.
4. After each turn, count your total amount of money.
   If your total goes over $1.00, you are out of the game.
5. The person with the total closest to $1.00 wins!

| Number Tossed | Coins Taken | Amount of Money for this Turn | Total Amount of Money |
|---|---|---|---|
|  |  |  |  |
|  |  |  |  |
|  |  |  |  |
|  |  |  |  |
|  |  |  |  |

 **Notes for Home:** Your child played a game using coins up to $1.00. *Home Activity:* Give your child some coins to count. Keep the total amount less than $1.00.

Name _____

STOP and Practice

Draw the coins in each bank to solve
the riddle. You can use coins to help.

**① ** I have 3 coins. The total amount is 27¢.

**② ** I have 2 coins. The total amount is 55¢.

**③ ** I have 4 coins. The total amount is 62¢.

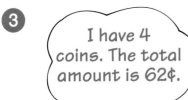

**④ ** I have 3 coins. The total amount is 76¢.

## Riddle

**⑤** Make up a riddle for a friend to solve.

**Notes for Home:** Your child used coin combinations to solve the riddles on this page.
*Home Activity:* Ask your child what 3 coins make 12¢. (1 dime, 2 pennies)

**216** two hundred sixteen

Name _____

## Retell the Story

Read the story.

### The Choice

Sean could hardly wait until Saturday. That was the day of the big garage sale. He had 7 dimes and wanted to buy a great toy. On Saturday, Sean got to the sale early. He saw a soccer ball for 69¢ and a sled for 67¢. He wanted both of them, but he had money for only one. While he was trying to decide which toy to buy, a girl came and bought the ball. Sean quickly bought the sled and got 3¢ change. That afternoon, it began to snow. "I'm sure glad I bought the sled!" Sean said.

Work with a partner.
Retell the story. Use coins to act it out.

Fill in the blanks.

**1** Sean wanted to buy a soccer ball and a _____.

**2** He bought the sled for _____ cents.

**3** Sean paid with _____ dimes.

**4** He got _____ cents change.

**5** Sean was glad he bought the sled because it _____.

**Notes for Home:** Your child retold a story about buying a toy and used coins to act it out. He or she made a book about the story. *Home Activity:* Ask your child to read the book to you.

**6** Cut on the purple line. Fold your paper to make a book.
Draw pictures or write sentences to retell the story.

## Problem Solving: Act It Out

**Learn** • • • • • • • • • • • • • •

**PROBLEM SOLVING GUIDE**

Understand • Plan • Solve • Look Back

**Check** • • • • • • • • • • • • • • • • • • • • • • • • •

Take turns buying and selling. Use dimes to
pay for items. Use pennies to make change.

| | Cost | Amount Paid | Change |
|---|---|---|---|
| 1 | 68¢ | 7 dimes | 2¢ |
| 2 | | | |
| 3 | | | |
| 4 | | | |

**Talk About It** Nancy buys this toy. She pays
with a quarter. How can you find the change?

 **Notes for Home:** Your child used coins to make change. *Home Activity:* Use pennies and dimes.
Ask your child to show you how to make change for an item in the picture.

PROBLEM SOLVING

Take turns buying and selling. Use dimes to pay for items.

Use pennies to make change.

| | Cost | Amount Paid | Change |
|---|---|---|---|
| 5 | 25¢ | 3 dimes | 5¢ |
| 6 | | | |
| 7 | | | |
| 8 | | | |
| 9 | | | |

## Critical Thinking

10   Use the picture. Name 2 items you could buy with 9 dimes.

How do you know you could buy them?

**Notes for Home:** Your child practiced using coins to make change. *Home Activity:* Ask your child to point out the highest priced item in the picture and tell how many dimes he or she would need to pay for it. (teddy bear; 10 dimes)

Name _____

# Mixed Practice
**Lessons 5–7**

## Concepts and Skills

Use the fewest coins to show this amount.
Draw the coins.

**1**

37¢

Use half dollars, quarters, dimes, and nickels.
Show 2 ways to make $1.00.
Draw the coins.

**2**

**3**

## Problem Solving

**4** Calvin has 6 dimes. He buys
a ball at the flea market
for 56¢. How much change
does he get back?

56¢
_____

## Journal

**5** What coins could you use to
pay for a book that costs 78¢?
What change would
you get back?
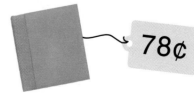
78¢

**Notes for Home:** Your child practiced choosing coins to show amounts of money and making change
to solve problems. *Home Activity:* Ask your child to draw another way to make $1.00.

MIXED PRACTICE

Name _____

# Cumulative Review
### Chapters 1–6

## Concepts and Skills

For each number, write the nearest ten.

**1** Is 78 closer to 70 or 80?

78 is closer to _____.

**2** Is 43 closer to 40 or 50?

43 is closer to _____.

Write the numbers in order
from least to greatest.

**3** 97 39 62

_____ _____ _____

**4** 73 96 44

_____ _____ _____

## Problem Solving

Solve the riddles.

**5** I am between 48 and 55.
I have 4 ones.

What number am I? _____

**6** I am greater than 78.
I have 7 tens.

What number am I? _____

| Test Prep |
| --- |

Fill in the ○ for the correct answer.

**7** Which sentence tells about the picture?

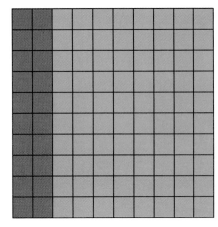

○ 50 and 50 is 100.
○ 25 and 75 is 100.
○ 20 and 80 is 100.
○ 95 and 5 is 100.

**Notes for Home:** Your child reviewed ordering numbers, finding the nearest ten for a number, and solving problems. *Home Activity:* Ask your child to put 72, 46, and 53 in order from least to greatest. (46, 53, 72)

CUMULATIVE REVIEW

Name _____

# Chapter 6 Review

## Vocabulary

Use half dollars, quarters, dimes, and nickels
to make 1 dollar. Show 2 ways.
Draw the coins.

**1**

**2**

## Concepts and Skills

Count the money. You can use coins. Write the total amount.

**3**

**4**

## Problem Solving

Solve.

**5** Kendra buys a pencil. She pays with 3 dimes. How much change does she get back?

25¢

_____

**6** Webster buys a notebook. He pays with 5 dimes. How much change does he get back?

47¢

_____

**Notes for Home:** Your child reviewed Chapter 6 vocabulary, concepts, skills, and problem solving.
*Home Activity:* Ask your child to name the coins that are worth 1¢, 5¢, 10¢, and 25¢.
(penny, nickel, dime, and quarter)

two hundred twenty-three  **223**

# Chapter 6 Test

Count the money. You can use coins. Write the total amount.

**1**

Use the fewest coins to show this amount. Draw the coins.

**2**

$1.00

**CHAPTER TEST**

Solve. You can use coins.

**3** Ina has 9 dimes. She buys a puppet at the flea market for 85¢. How much change does she get back?

_____

**4** Jay has 7 dimes. He buys a kite for 68¢. How much change does he get back?

_____

**5** Damir has 20¢ in his bank. He has no pennies.

Find all the ways to make 20¢ using dimes and nickels. Make a list.

|  |  |
|---|---|
|  |  |
|  |  |
|  |  |

 **Notes for Home:** Your child was assessed on Chapter 6 concepts, skills, and problem solving. *Home Activity:* Ask your child to tell you how many dimes he or she would need to pay for something that costs 27¢. (3 dimes)

Name _____

# Performance Assessment

## Chapter 6

Put these coins in a bag:

I

I

5

5

5

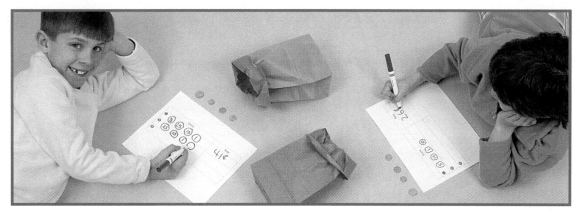

Take 4 coins. Draw your coins. Write the total amount. Repeat the activity.

| | Coins | Total |
|---|---|---|
| **1** | | |
| **2** | | |
| **3** | | |

Choose one of your totals from the table above. Use coins to find

2 new ways to show that amount. Draw your coins.

| | |
|---|---|
| **4** | |
| **5** | |

## Problem Solving Critical Thinking

Use coins from the bag.

**6** What is the greatest amount you

can make if you use 4 different coins? the least amount?

 **Notes for Home:** Your child did an activity that tested Chapter 6 skills, concepts, and problem solving. *Home Activity:* Have your child think of an amount less than $1.00 and show it using many different combinations of coins.

Name _____

Explore with a
**CALCULATOR**

# Calculate Your Costs!

**Keys You Will Use** `ON/C` `+` `·` `=`

79¢ is the same as $.79, so I press `·` `7` `9`

You can use your 🖩 to find the total cost of all the items you are buying.

How much would it cost to buy a bear, a tablet, and bubbles?

Find 79¢ + 47¢ + 25¢. Press these keys.

`ON/C` `·` `7` `9` `+` `·` `4` `7` `+` `·` `2` `5`

`=` `1.51`

The total cost of all three items is $1.51.

Use a sale flyer and your 🖩.

Choose items to buy. Find the total cost.

| | Cost of First Item | Cost of Second Item | Cost of Third Item | Total Cost |
|---|---|---|---|---|
| 1 | | | | |
| 2 | | | | |
| 3 | | | | |
| 4 | | | | |
| 5 | | | | |

**Tech Talk** Your calculator displays `34.15`. How many dollars and how many cents does this show? How do you know?

🖥 **Visit our Web site.** www.parent.mathsurf.com

# Penny Power

Different machines use different amounts of electricity. The chart below shows about how much it costs to run these machines for one hour.

| Machine | Electricity Cost (1 hour) |
|---|---|
| **Microwave**  |  |
| **Television** | |
| **Computer** | |

1 How would you spend 25¢ on electricity? Pick different machines from the chart. Tell how long you would use them.

2 Ask another person how they would spend 25¢ on electricity. Compare your answers.

**Fold down**

# MathSurf

Scott Foresman - Addison Wesley    My Math Magazine    No. 6

## Be a Dough Maker

CHAMP!
CHOCOLATE CHIP COOKIES
The Original &

Draw your own "money" using objects such as paper clips, rubber bands, or marbles. Decide how much each object stands for.

|  |  |  |
|---|---|---|
| _____ cents | _____ cents | _____ cents |

**1** Show a friend your money. Ask your friend to choose any two objects. How much are they worth in all?

_____

**2** Pick an item you would like to buy. Decide how much it should cost. Show how you would pay for it using your money.

---

# Making Dough

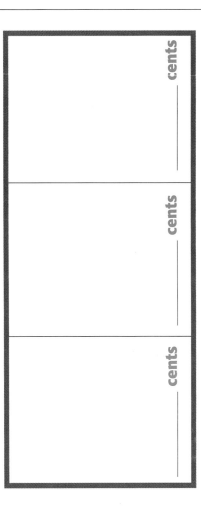

| Number of Cookies | Price |
|---|---|
|  | 10¢ |
|  | 25¢ |
|  | 50¢ |

The chart above shows prices for different packages of cookies. Find how many cookies you could buy with

**1** 40¢. _____ cookies

**2** 60¢. _____ cookies

**3** Choose an amount of money between 20¢ and 80¢. Ask a friend how many cookies he or she could buy.

**Notes for Home:** Your child learned about quantities available at different prices. *Home Activity:* Ask your child how many cookies could be purchased for 35¢. (7)

2

# Making Money

Long ago, many people did not use coins. They used other kinds of money to get things that they needed.

In China, people used shells.

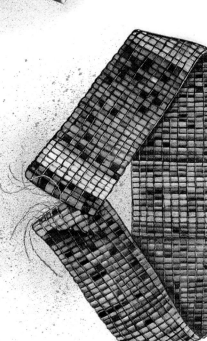

Many Native Americans and settlers used wampum.*

Some people in Ethiopia used bars of salt.

* Wampum is made of beads strung together.

**Notes for Home:** Your child learned about some items that early civilizations used as money. *Home Activity:* Ask your child to tell you the value of the three objects he or she drew.

A teacher in Washington, D.C. and his students began a company called Champ Cookies & Things. The children learned to run a business as they had fun!

The students at Champ Cookies & Things bought supplies, made cookie dough, baked cookies, and then sold them!

# Making Cents

Use the triangle of nickels on the next page to answer the following questions.

**1** How much is the triangle worth?

_____

**2** Suppose you used dimes instead of nickels. How much would the triangle be worth?

_____

**3** Suppose you added a row of 4 nickels to the bottom of the triangle. How much would the triangle be worth?

_____

**4** Suppose you made the triangle out of four rows of dimes. How much would it be worth?

_____

**Notes for Home:** Your child learned about the values of coins arranged in different patterns. *Home Activity:* Ask your child to find the value of 3 nickels and the value of 3 dimes. (15¢, 30¢)

4

**Notes for Home:** Your child shared stories about time. *Home Activity:* Ask your child to tell about the ways he or she uses time every day.

# Math at Home

Dear Family,
Our class is starting Chapter 7. We will learn to tell time and solve problems about time. Together we can do these activities.

**Saturday Schedule**

8:00  Eat breakfast.

10:30  Go to park.

12:00  Eat lunch.

1:30  Go to library to return books.

3:00  Go to store.

## It's Story Time
Create story problems about things you do as a family. For example: It is 12:00. Lunch will be ready in 30 minutes. At what time will we eat? Work with your child to solve the problem.

## Table Talk
Make a list of things to do for a weekend day. Make a schedule, listing the activities along with their starting times. As you go about the day together, talk about the schedule.

## Community Connection
Look for examples of how time is used in the community. Talk about clocks that you see and signs that show time, for example, store hours and parking signs.

💻➡️💻 **Visit our Web site. www.parent.mathsurf.com**

Name _____

**Explore**

Wait one minute while I put on my coat.

1 minute

Have you ever wondered how long one minute is?

What could you do that
takes about one minute?
Your teacher will time you as you try it.
Write and draw what you could do.

1

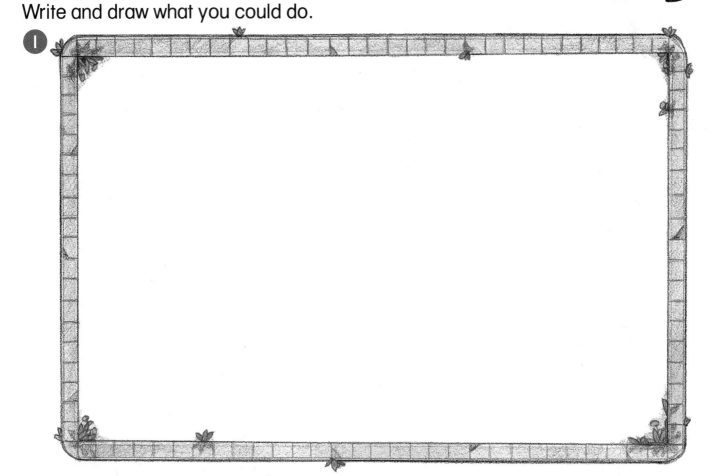

EXPLORE

**Share**

Did your activity take more than, less than, or about one minute?

**Notes for Home:** Your child explored what can be done in about one minute. *Home Activity:* Ask your child what activities he or she does at home that take about one minute.

How many times can you do each activity in one minute?
Estimate. Then do the activity. Write how many.

**2** Write your first name.

Estimate: _____ times

How many? _____ times

**3** Draw happy faces.

Estimate: _____ times

How many? _____ times

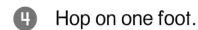

**4** Hop on one foot.

Estimate: _____ times

How many? _____ times

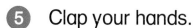

**5** Clap your hands.

Estimate: _____ times

How many? _____ times

**Talk About It** What activity did you do the most times? the fewest times?
Compare your answers with a friend.

**Notes for Home:** Your child estimated how many times he or she could do an activity in one minute. Then your child timed the activity to check. *Home Activity:* Ask your child to do one of the activities again as you time the activity.

EXPLORE

# Estimate Time

**Learn**

It takes less than one minute to pour juice.

It takes more than one minute to eat lunch.

**Check**

Estimate whether the activity takes **more** or **less**
than one minute. Then try it to check.
Complete the table.

| | Activity | Estimate | Check |
|---|---|---|---|
| **1** | Say this sentence. Tim tickled the turtle's toes. | _____ than one minute | _____ than one minute |
| **2** | Read a story. | _____ than one minute | _____ than one minute |
| **3** | Sharpen a pencil. | _____ than one minute | _____ than one minute |

**Talk About It** Name an activity that you do that takes less than one minute.

Name an activity that takes more than one minute.

**Notes for Home:** Your child estimated whether an activity would take less than one minute or more than one minute. *Home Activity:* Ask your child to tell you daily activities that take less than one minute and more than one minute.

Draw or write an activity you can do in each amount of time.

**4** Less than one minute

**5** About one minute

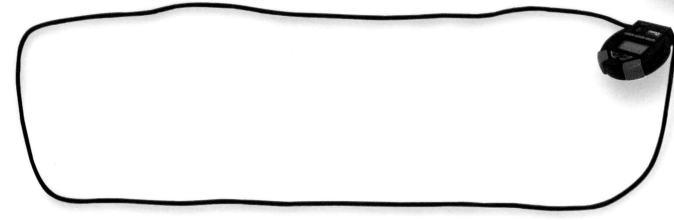

**6** More than one minute

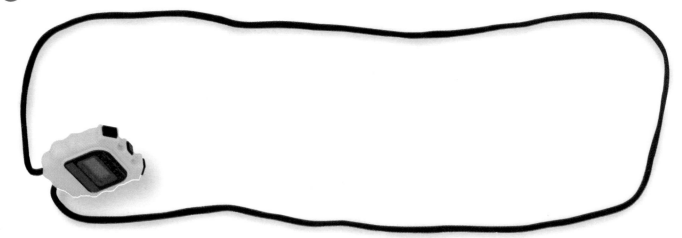

## Tell a Math Story

**7** You have one minute to tell someone about yourself.

What would you say?

**Notes for Home:** Your child drew a picture of an activity that would take less than, more than, and about one minute. *Home Activity:* Ask your child to name daily activities that take about a minute.

# Time to the Hour

## Learn

7 o'clock

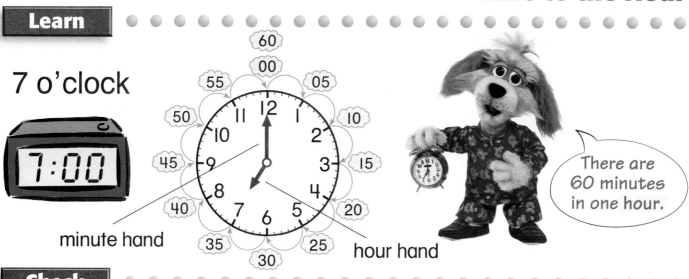

7:00

minute hand

hour hand

There are 60 minutes in one hour.

## Check

Write each time in two different ways. You can use a clock.

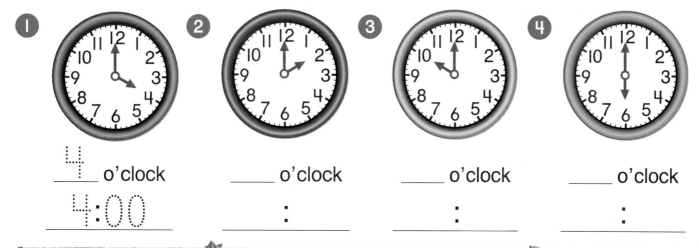

**1** __4__ o'clock

4:00

**2** _____ o'clock

____ : ____

**3** _____ o'clock

____ : ____

**4** _____ o'clock

____ : ____

**5** _____ o'clock

____ : ____

**6** _____ o'clock

____ : ____

**7** _____ o'clock

____ : ____

**8** _____ o'clock

____ : ____

**Talk About It** Tell something you do at one of the times shown on this page.

**Notes for Home:** Your child learned about telling time to the hour. *Home Activity:* Ask your child to look around your home for different kinds of clocks.

**Practice**

Draw the clock hands to show each time. You can use a clock.

**9**

**10**

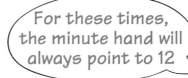
For these times, the minute hand will always point to 12

 8:00

 3:00

 **Write your own.** Choose your own time.

Draw the clock hands. Write the time. You can use a clock.

**11**

**12**

**13**

**14**

____ :00     ____ :00     ____ :00     ____ :00

## Problem Solving  Visual Thinking

Look at the picture. What time do you think it is?
Circle the time. Explain.

**15**

7:00          3:00

**16**

6:00          2:00

 **Notes for Home:** Your child practiced showing time to the hour. *Home Activity:* Ask your child to tell where the hour hand and minute hand would be at 9:00.

# Elapsed Time

**Learn**

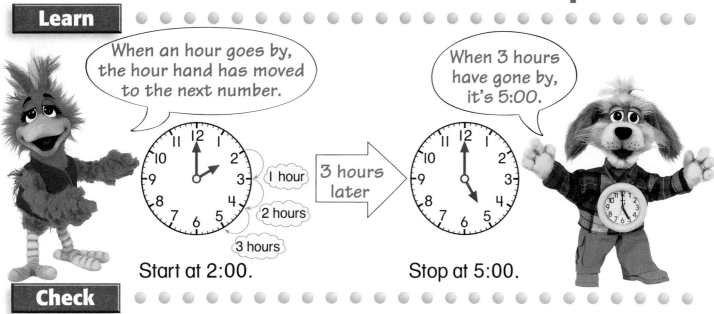

When an hour goes by, the hour hand has moved to the next number.

When 3 hours have gone by, it's 5:00.

1 hour
2 hours
3 hours

3 hours later

Start at 2:00.

Stop at 5:00.

**Check**

Draw the clock hands. Write the ending times. You can use a clock.

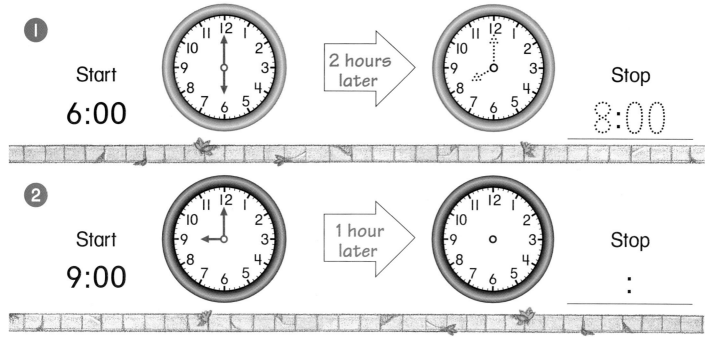

**1** Start **6:00**

2 hours later

Stop 8:00

**2** Start **9:00**

1 hour later

Stop :

Read both clocks. How many hours have gone by?

**3**

_____ hours

**Talk About It** Tell how you can look at the clock and know when it will be 2 hours later.

**Notes for Home:** Your child learned how to tell the number of hours that have gone by. *Home Activity:* Point out the clock when it shows time to the hour. Ask your child to explain how a clock shows that an hour has gone by.

Draw the clock hands. Write the ending times.
You can use a clock.

**4**

Start

**4:00**

3 hours later

Stop

**7:00**

**5**

Start

**2:00**

2 hours later

Stop

**:**
_____

When will each activity end? Write the ending time.
You can use a clock.

**6** Dena went to a movie at 7:00. The movie was 2 hours long. What time was the movie over?

:
_____

**7** Juan left home at 11:00. He met a friend 1 hour later. They played in the park for 2 more hours. What time was it then?

:
_____

## Problem Solving Critical Thinking

**8** Tina stopped fishing at 8:00. She fished for 2 hours.

What time did she start fishing? _____ : _____

**Notes for Home:** Your child solved problems involving the passing of time. *Home Activity:* Ask your child to tell you how many hours have gone by between 1:00 and 3:00 in the afternoon. (2 hours)

240 two hundred forty

For additional practice, see Skills Practice Bank, page 533 Set 1.

PRACTICE

Name _____

# Tic-Tac-Time

Make a clock spinner.

**Players** 2

## What You Need

2 paper clips

pencil

2 crayons — orange

**Spinner 1**

## How to Play

1. Player One spins both spinners.

2. Use the paper clips as hour hands. Find the hour that each paper clip is closest to. Read each time.

3. Find how many hours passed from the time on Spinner 1 to the time on Spinner 2.

4. Color in the matching space on the gameboard.

5. Player Two completes Steps 1–4 using a different color. If a space on the gameboard is already colored in, a player's turn is over.

6. Continue taking turns. The first player to complete a row or column wins!

**Spinner 2**

| 1 hour | 2 hours | 3 hours | 4 hours |
|--------|---------|---------|---------|
| 5 hours | 6 hours | 7 hours | 8 hours |
| 9 hours | 10 hours | 11 hours | 12 hours |

**Gameboard**

PRACTICE

Name _____

**STOP** and **Practice**

Does the activity take more or less than one minute?

Estimate. Then try it to check.

Complete the table. Write **more** or **less**.

| | Activity | Estimate | Check |
|---|---|---|---|
| ① | Write number words from 1 to 5. | _____ than one minute | _____ than one minute |
| ② | Count backward from 50 to 0. | _____ than one minute | _____ than one minute |

**PRACTICE**

③ Write the time in two different ways.

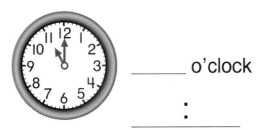

_____ o'clock

___ : ___

④ Draw the clock hands to show the time.

6:00

Draw the clock hands. Write the ending times.

⑤

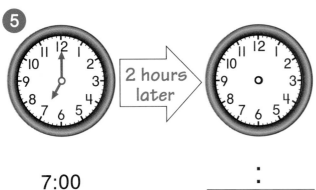

2 hours later

7:00     ___ : ___

⑥

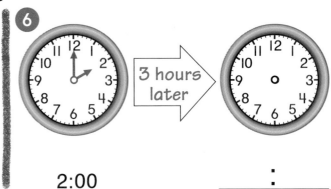

3 hours later

2:00     ___ : ___

## Number Sense

⑦ Would you ever use the number 61 to tell time? Explain your answer.

**Notes for Home:** Your child practiced estimating time, telling time to the hour, and calculating elapsed time. *Home Activity:* Ask your child what the time will be 3 hours after 9:00. (12:00)

Name _____

# Problem Solving: Use Data from a Table

**Learn**  • • • • • • • • • • • • • • •

**PROBLEM SOLVING GUIDE**
Understand • Plan • Solve • Look Back

## Saturday Classes

| Class | Starts | Ends |
|---|---|---|
| Arts and Crafts | 1:00 | 4:00 |
| Basketball | 1:00 | 3:00 |
| Bike Safety | 10:00 | 11:00 |
| Cooking | 10:00 | 12:00 |
| Sing Along | 3:00 | 5:00 |
| Puppets and Plays | 9:00 | 11:00 |

**Check**  • • • • • • • • • • • • • • • • • • • • • • • • • • • • •

Use the table to answer the questions.

1 What class starts at 9:00? _Puppets and Plays_

2 How long does **Arts and Crafts** last? _____ hours

3 What class starts 2 hours later than **Basketball**? _____

4 What class ends after 1 hour? _____

5 What class ends at the same time as **Puppets and Plays**? _____

**Talk About It** Tell how you can look at the table and know which class lasts 3 hours.

**Notes for Home:** Your child used a table to solve problems about time. *Home Activity:* Ask your child to tell you what time the cooking class shown in the table ends. (12:00)

**Chapter 7 Lesson 5**

two hundred forty-three **243**

PROBLEM SOLVING

## After-School Classes

| Class | Starts | Ends |
|---|---|---|
| Book Club | 4:00 | 5:00 |
| Clay Play | 4:00 | 6:00 |
| Computer | 5:00 | 6:00 |
| Sports | 4:00 | 6:00 |

Use the table. Solve the problems.
Write each answer.

**6** Miles gets out of school
1 hour before Sports starts.
At what time does he get
out of school?

3:00

**7** Felipe takes Clay Play.
How long is he in class?

_____ hours

**8** Tran eats dinner 1 hour after
the Book Club ends. At what
time does he eat dinner?

____ : ____

**9** Keisha takes another class
after the Book Club ends.
What class starts at this time?

_____

**Journal**

**10** What class would you add to the table?
What time would it start? How long would it last?

**Notes for Home:** Your child practiced using a table to solve problems. *Home Activity:* Ask your child
to tell what class starts 1 hour after Clay Play starts. (Computer)

**For additional practice, see Skills Practice Bank, page 533, Set 2.**

**PROBLEM SOLVING**

Name _____

# Mixed Practice
**Lessons 1–5**

## Concepts and Skills

 **1** Estimate how many times you can count to ten in one minute. Then do the activity. Write how many times.

Estimate: _____ times

How many? _____ times

---

Write the time shown on each clock.

 **2**

 **3**

___ : ___

___ : ___

Read both clocks. How many hours have gone by?

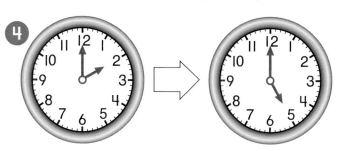 **4**

_____ hours

## Problem Solving

Use the table.
Answer the questions.

**5** Which class ends at 5:00?

_____

**6** How long does each class last?

_____ hours

**7** What time does **Painting** begin?

___ : ___

### Community Center Classes

| Class | Starts | Ends |
|---|---|---|
| Swimming | 3:00 | 5:00 |
| Painting | 4:00 | 6:00 |

**Journal**

**8** Draw two clocks. Show 4 o'clock on one. Show 3 hours later on the other.

 **Notes for Home:** Your child practiced showing and telling time. *Home Activity:* Ask your child to look at the clock in Exercise 2 and tell what time it is 4 hours later. (11:00)

two hundred forty-five **245**

Name _____

# Cumulative Review
### Chapters 1–7

## Concepts and Skills

Count by 5s. Write the numbers.

**1** 5, 10, _____, _____, _____, _____, _____, _____, _____

Count by 10s. Write the numbers.

**2** 10, 20, _____, _____, _____, _____, _____, _____, _____

Add or subtract.

**3**
$$9 + 2 \qquad 11 - 6 \qquad 7 + 6 \qquad 5 + 8 \qquad 16 - 9 \qquad 7 + 9 \qquad 11 - 8$$

**4**
$$12 - 6 \qquad 7 + 7 \qquad 14 - 8 \qquad 9 + 4 \qquad 14 - 9 \qquad 18 - 9 \qquad 8 + 7$$

## Test Prep

Fill in the ○ for the correct answer.

Count the money. How much money in all?

**5**

97¢        92¢        82¢        77¢
 ○          ○          ○          ○

**Notes for Home:** Your child reviewed counting by 5s and 10s, addition and subtraction facts, and counting groups of coins. *Home Activity:* Ask your child to count by 2s to 30.

Name _____

**Learn**  ● ● ● ● ● ● ● ● ● ● ● ● ● ● ● ● ● ● ● ● ● ● ● ●

*What time is it? I have to be home at 6:30.*

*It is 6:20. 20 minutes after 6.*

First, look at the hour hand. Then find the number of minutes after the hour. Count by 5s.

**Check**  ● ● ● ● ● ● ● ● ● ● ● ● ● ● ● ● ● ● ● ● ● ● ● ●

Write the time for each clock. You can use a clock.

**1**   8:25

**2** :

**3** :

**4** :

Draw the minute hand to show the time. You can use a clock.

**5**   10:35

**6**   1:10

**7**   7:45

**8**   9:55

**Talk About It** At 8:55, is the hour hand closer to 8 or 9? Explain.

**Notes for Home:** Your child learned how to tell time to 5 minutes. *Home Activity:* Ask your child to count from 8:00 to 9:00 using 5–minute intervals. (8:00, 8:05, 8:10, and so on)

Write the time for each clock. You can use a clock.

**9**  **10**  **11**  **12**

4:05 ___   : ___   : ___   : ___

Draw the minute hand to show the time. You can use a clock.

**13**  **14** **15**  **16**

7:55   5:20   2:35   8:10

## Problem Solving

**17** Shauna's soccer practice ended at 20 minutes before 6. What is another way to write the time that practice ended?

 5: ___

**18** Lindsey started walking to school at 10 minutes before 8. What is another way to write the time she started walking?

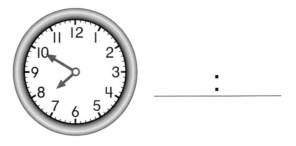 : ___

 **Notes for Home:** Your child practiced telling time to 5-minute intervals. *Home Activity:* Ask your child to tell where the minute hand would point at 9:25. (5)

**For additional practice, see Skills Practice Bank, page 533, Set 3.**

# Tell Time to the Half Hour

## Learn

Shante gets on the bus at 8:00.

The bus arrives at school at 8:30. A half hour has gone by.

After a half hour, the minute hand moves from the 12 to the 6. The hour hand moves between the 8 and the 9.

There are 30 minutes in a half hour.

The minute hand has moved halfway around the clock. It is half past 8.

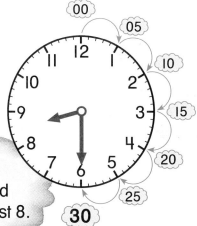

## Check

Write the time shown on each clock. You can use a clock.

❶

2:30

half past _____

❷

___:___

half past _____

❸

___:___

half past _____

❹

___:___

half past _____

**Talk About It** What activities do you do that take about a half hour?

**Notes for Home:** Your child learned how to tell time to the half hour. *Home Activity:* Ask your child to tell the time when a clock shows time to the half hour.

Write the time shown on each clock. You can use a clock.

**5**

1:30
_____

half past _____

**6**

___ : ___
_____

half past _____

**7**

___ : ___
_____

**8**

___ : ___
_____

half past _____

**9**

___ : ___
_____

half past _____

**10**

___ : ___
_____

**11**

___ : ___
_____

half past _____

**12**

___ : ___
_____

**Write your own.**

Write a time using a half hour.
Draw a picture showing
what you do at that time.

___ : ___
_____

half past _____

## Problem Solving Patterns

**13** Write the times to continue the pattern.

12:00, 12:30, 1:00, ____ : ____, ____ : ____, ____ : ____

 **Notes for Home:** Your child practiced telling time to the half hour. *Home Activity:* Ask your child where the minute hand and the hour hand point at 4:30. (The minute hand points at the 6; the hour hand points between the 4 and 5.)

# Tell Time to the Quarter Hour

**Learn** • • • • • • • • • • • • • • • • • • • • • • • • • • • •

In gym class, Laura does different activities.
She spends 15 minutes doing each.

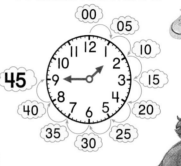

*Count by 5s to find the number of minutes.*

### 1:15
15 minutes after 1

### 1:30
Half past 1

### 1:45
45 minutes after 1
15 minutes before 2

**Check** • • • • • • • • • • • • • • • • • • • • • • • • • • • •

Write the time for each clock. You can use a clock.

**1**

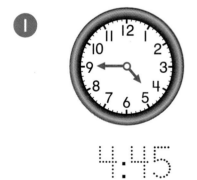

4:45

45 minutes after 4

15 minutes before 5

**2**

____ : ____

____ minutes after ____

**3**

____ : ____

____ minutes after ____

____ minutes before ____

**Talk About It** Suppose the time is 2:45.

Tell what time it will be 15 minutes later.

**Notes for Home:** Your child learned how to tell time to 15 minutes. *Home Activity:* Ask your child to describe 12:45 in two different ways. (45 minutes after 12; 15 minutes before 1)

Write the time for each clock. You can use a clock.

**4**

__10:15__

__15__ minutes after __10__

**5**

____ : ____

half past ____

**6**

____ : ____

____ minutes after ____

**7**

____ : ____

____ minutes after ____

____ minutes before ____

**8**

____ : ____

____ minutes after ____

____ minutes before ____

**9**

____ : ____

half past ____

## Problem Solving Visual Thinking

**10** Many watches do not show all the numbers.
Write the time shown on this watch.

____ : ____

**11** What time would the watch show 2 hours later?

____ : ____

 **Notes for Home:** Your child learned how to tell time in 15–minute intervals. *Home Activity:* Ask your child to tell you the time for each 15–minute interval from 2:00 to 3:00. (2:00, 2:15, 2:30, 2:45, 3:00)

Name _____

## Organize Information

This table shows the order we do things in my class.

### A Day at School

| Subject | Time |
|---|---|
| Reading | 8:30–9:30 |
| Art | 9:30–10:00 |
| Math | 10:00–11:00 |
| Lunch | 11:00–11:30 |
| Language Arts | 11:30–12:30 |
| Recess | 12:30–1:00 |
| Science | 1:00–2:00 |

Use the rows and columns to find each answer.

**1** How many subjects come before lunch?

3
____

**2** How many subjects come after lunch?

____

**3** Which subjects last for one hour? Write two of them.

_____

**4** What are children doing at 10:45?

_____

**Talk About It** Why are tables useful?

**Notes for Home:** Your child learned how to read a table. *Home Activity:* Ask your child which subject ends at 10:00 and which subject begins at 10:00. (Art ends; Math begins.)

two hundred fifty-three **253**

I can't wait to go to the park at 12:00!

## Saturday Activities

| Activity | Time |
|---|---|
| Breakfast | 9:30-10:00 |
| Library | 10:00-11:00 |
| Haircut | 11:00-11:30 |
| Lunch | 11:30-12:00 |
| Park | 12:00-1:00 |
| Movie | 1:00-3:00 |
| Shopping | 3:00-4:00 |

This table shows the order of activities for a Saturday.

**5** How much time is spent at the library?

_I hour_

**6** How long does the movie last?

_____

**7** Which activities last for a half hour? Write two of them.

_____

_____

**8** How many hours pass from the beginning of breakfast until the beginning of lunch?

_____ hours

**Journal**

**9** What would you like to do after school?

Make your own table. Include your favorite activities.

Name _____

# Problem Solving: Make a Table

**Learn** • • • • • • • • • • • • • • •

## PROBLEM SOLVING GUIDE
**Understand • Plan • Solve • Look Back**

Complete the calendar to show this month.

| This Month: _____ | | | | | | |
|---|---|---|---|---|---|---|
| Sunday | Monday | Tuesday | Wednesday | Thursday | Friday | Saturday |
| | | | | | | |
| | | | | | | |
| | | | | | | |
| | | | | | | |
| | | | | | | |

**Check** • • • • • • • • • • • • • • • • • • • • • • • • • • • • • • •

Use the calendar to answer the questions.

A calendar is a kind of table.

① How many days are in one week? __7__

② How many days are in this month? _____

③ Write one date that is on a Tuesday. _____

④ Which day of the week is the last day of this month? _____

**Talk About It** Find the 5th day of the month.

Which day of the week is that? Explain how you can tell.

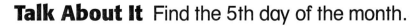
**Notes for Home:** Your child learned how to read a calendar. *Home Activity:* Ask your child to point to a date on the calendar and tell you the day of the week.

PROBLEM SOLVING

**Chapter 7 Lesson 9**

two hundred fifty-five **255**

(5) The calendar shows all the months and days in a year.

Circle your birthday.

Circle your favorite month and holiday.

**January**

| S | M | T | W | T | F | S |
|---|---|---|---|---|---|---|
| 1 | 2 | 3 | 4 | 5 | 6 | 7 |
| 8 | 9 | 10 | 11 | 12 | 13 | 14 |
| 15 | 16 | 17 | 18 | 19 | 20 | 21 |
| 22 | 23 | 24 | 25 | 26 | 27 | 28 |
| 29 | 30 | 31 | | | | |

**February**

| S | M | T | W | T | F | S |
|---|---|---|---|---|---|---|
| | | | 1 | 2 | 3 | 4 |
| 5 | 6 | 7 | 8 | 9 | 10 | 11 |
| 12 | 13 | 14 | 15 | 16 | 17 | 18 |
| 19 | 20 | 21 | 22 | 23 | 24 | 25 |
| 26 | 27 | 28 | | | | |

**March**

| S | M | T | W | T | F | S |
|---|---|---|---|---|---|---|
| | | | 1 | 2 | 3 | 4 |
| 5 | 6 | 7 | 8 | 9 | 10 | 11 |
| 12 | 13 | 14 | 15 | 16 | 17 | 18 |
| 19 | 20 | 21 | 22 | 23 | 24 | 25 |
| 26 | 27 | 28 | 29 | 30 | 31 | |

**April**

| S | M | T | W | T | F | S |
|---|---|---|---|---|---|---|
| | | | | | | 1 |
| 2 | 3 | 4 | 5 | 6 | 7 | 8 |
| 9 | 10 | 11 | 12 | 13 | 14 | 15 |
| 16 | 17 | 18 | 19 | 20 | 21 | 22 |
| 23/30 | 24 | 25 | 26 | 27 | 28 | 29 |

**May**

| S | M | T | W | T | F | S |
|---|---|---|---|---|---|---|
| | 1 | 2 | 3 | 4 | 5 | 6 |
| 7 | 8 | 9 | 10 | 11 | 12 | 13 |
| 14 | 15 | 16 | 17 | 18 | 19 | 20 |
| 21 | 22 | 23 | 24 | 25 | 26 | 27 |
| 28 | 29 | 30 | 31 | | | |

**June**

| S | M | T | W | T | F | S |
|---|---|---|---|---|---|---|
| | | | | 1 | 2 | 3 |
| 4 | 5 | 6 | 7 | 8 | 9 | 10 |
| 11 | 12 | 13 | 14 | 15 | 16 | 17 |
| 18 | 19 | 20 | 21 | 22 | 23 | 24 |
| 25 | 26 | 27 | 28 | 29 | 30 | |

**July**

| S | M | T | W | T | F | S |
|---|---|---|---|---|---|---|
| | | | | | | 1 |
| 2 | 3 | 4 | 5 | 6 | 7 | 8 |
| 9 | 10 | 11 | 12 | 13 | 14 | 15 |
| 16 | 17 | 18 | 19 | 20 | 21 | 22 |
| 23/30 | 24/31 | 25 | 26 | 27 | 28 | 29 |

**August**

| S | M | T | W | T | F | S |
|---|---|---|---|---|---|---|
| | | 1 | 2 | 3 | 4 | 5 |
| 6 | 7 | 8 | 9 | 10 | 11 | 12 |
| 13 | 14 | 15 | 16 | 17 | 18 | 19 |
| 20 | 21 | 22 | 23 | 24 | 25 | 26 |
| 27 | 28 | 29 | 30 | 31 | | |

**September**

| S | M | T | W | T | F | S |
|---|---|---|---|---|---|---|
| | | | | | 1 | 2 |
| 3 | 4 | 5 | 6 | 7 | 8 | 9 |
| 10 | 11 | 12 | 13 | 14 | 15 | 16 |
| 17 | 18 | 19 | 20 | 21 | 22 | 23 |
| 24 | 25 | 26 | 27 | 28 | 29 | 30 |

**October**

| S | M | T | W | T | F | S |
|---|---|---|---|---|---|---|
| 1 | 2 | 3 | 4 | 5 | 6 | 7 |
| 8 | 9 | 10 | 11 | 12 | 13 | 14 |
| 15 | 16 | 17 | 18 | 19 | 20 | 21 |
| 22 | 23 | 24 | 25 | 26 | 27 | 28 |
| 29 | 30 | 31 | | | | |

**November**

| S | M | T | W | T | F | S |
|---|---|---|---|---|---|---|
| | | | 1 | 2 | 3 | 4 |
| 5 | 6 | 7 | 8 | 9 | 10 | 11 |
| 12 | 13 | 14 | 15 | 16 | 17 | 18 |
| 19 | 20 | 21 | 22 | 23 | 24 | 25 |
| 26 | 27 | 28 | 29 | 30 | | |

**December**

| S | M | T | W | T | F | S |
|---|---|---|---|---|---|---|
| | | | | | 1 | 2 |
| 3 | 4 | 5 | 6 | 7 | 8 | 9 |
| 10 | 11 | 12 | 13 | 14 | 15 | 16 |
| 17 | 18 | 19 | 20 | 21 | 22 | 23 |
| 24/31 | 25 | 26 | 27 | 28 | 29 | 30 |

(6) Use tallies to show how many months
have a total of 28, 30, and 31 days.

| Months with 28 days total | Months with 30 days total | Months with 31 days total |
|---|---|---|
| | | |

**Journal**

(7) Look at this year's calendar. Make a table using tallies
to show how many months have their first date on
Sunday, Monday, and the other days of the week.

**Notes for Home:** Your child practiced using a calendar. *Home Activity:* Ask your child to show you the date and the day of the week of each family member's birthday.

**PROBLEM SOLVING**

# Mixed Practice
**Lessons 6–9**

## Concepts and Skills

Write each time in two different ways. You can use a clock.

**1**

_____ : _____

half past _____

**2**

_____ : _____

_____ minutes after _____

**3**

_____ : _____

_____ minutes after _____

_____ minutes before _____

Write the time for each clock. You can use a clock.

**4** 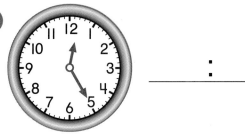  _____ : _____

**5**   _____ : _____

## Problem Solving

Use the calendar to answer the questions.

**6** How many Sundays are in November? _____

**7** On what day of the week is
the tenth day of November? _____

| November | | | | | | |
|---|---|---|---|---|---|---|
| S | M | T | W | T | F | S |
| | | | 1 | 2 | 3 | 4 |
| 5 | 6 | 7 | 8 | 9 | 10 | 11 |
| 12 | 13 | 14 | 15 | 16 | 17 | 18 |
| 19 | 20 | 21 | 22 | 23 | 24 | 25 |
| 26 | 27 | 28 | 29 | 30 | | |

## Journal

**8** Draw two clocks. Show 3:45 on one clock.

Show 15 minutes later on the other clock.

Tell how the clock hands moved during that time.

**Notes for Home:** Your child practiced telling time and using a calendar. *Home Activity:* Ask your child to show you today's date on a calendar.

MIXED PRACTICE

# Cumulative Review
### Chapters 1–7

## Concepts and Skills

Use the graph.
Answer the questions.

| Favorite Activity | | | | | | | | | |
|---|---|---|---|---|---|---|---|---|---|
| Crafts | | | | | | | | | |
| Singing | | | | | | | | | |
| Sports | | | | | | | | | |
| Reading | | | | | | | | | |
| | 1 | 2 | 3 | 4 | 5 | 6 | 7 | 8 | 9 |

**1** Which activity do most of these children like best?

_____

**2** Which activity do 4 children like best?

_____

Add or subtract.

**3**

$$\begin{array}{r} 8 \\ + 7 \\ \hline \end{array} \qquad \begin{array}{r} 18 \\ - 9 \\ \hline \end{array} \qquad \begin{array}{r} 7 \\ + 6 \\ \hline \end{array} \qquad \begin{array}{r} 13 \\ - 5 \\ \hline \end{array} \qquad \begin{array}{r} 12 \\ - 8 \\ \hline \end{array} \qquad \begin{array}{r} 9 \\ + 6 \\ \hline \end{array} \qquad \begin{array}{r} 16 \\ - 7 \\ \hline \end{array}$$

## Test Prep

Fill in the ○ for the correct answer.

**4** What is the missing number in the Nickels column?

| 7 | 8 | 10 | 1 |
|---|---|---|---|
| ○ | ○ | ○ | ○ |

**5** What is the missing number in the Dimes column?

| 3 | 5 | 4 | 2 |
|---|---|---|---|
| ○ | ○ | ○ | ○ |

| Ways to Show 40¢ | |
|---|---|
| Dimes | Nickels |
| 4 | 0 |
| 3 | 2 |
| | 4 |
| 1 | 6 |
| 0 | |

**Notes for Home:** Your child reviewed using a graph, addition and subtraction facts, and making an organized list. *Home Activity:* Ask your child which activity in the graph did 5 children like best. (Sports)

Name _____

# Chapter 7 Review

## Vocabulary

Choose from these words
to solve the riddles.

| hour | minute | half hour |
|------|--------|-----------|

 There are 60 of me in one hour.

I am one _____.

 I am 30 minutes long.

I am a _____.

## Concepts and Skills

Write the time shown on each clock. You can use a clock.

___ : ___

___ : ___

___ : ___

___ : ___

**7** Does it take **more** or **less**
than one minute to close a door? _____

## Problem Solving

Use the table.
Write the answer.

**8** Travis leaves school one
hour after gym class ends.
At what time does he
leave school?

___ : ___

### Class Schedule

| Class | Starts | Ends |
|-------|--------|------|
| Music | 8:00 | 9:00 |
| Art | 10:00 | 11:00 |
| Gym | 1:00 | 2:00 |

 **Notes for Home:** Your child reviewed the vocabulary, skills, concepts, and problem solving taught in Chapter 7. *Home Activity:* Ask your child to look at a clock, tell the time, and then tell what the time will be one hour later.

# Chapter 7 Test

Write each time in two different ways. You can use a clock.

**①**

\_\_\_\_\_ : \_\_\_\_\_

half past \_\_\_\_\_

**②**

\_\_\_\_\_ : \_\_\_\_\_

\_\_\_\_\_ minutes after \_\_\_\_\_

**③**

\_\_\_\_\_ : \_\_\_\_\_

\_\_\_\_\_ minutes after \_\_\_\_\_

**CHAPTER TEST**

**④** Draw the clock hands.
Write the ending time.

8:00                    \_\_\_\_\_ : \_\_\_\_\_

**⑤** Circle the activity that takes more than one minute.

**baking muffins**

**counting to 10**

**⑥** Use the calendar to complete the table. Find how many dates are in the column below each day of the week. Make tallies to show the number of dates.

| January | | | | | | |
|---|---|---|---|---|---|---|
| S | M | T | W | T | F | S |
| 1 | 2 | 3 | 4 | 5 | 6 | 7 |
| 8 | 9 | 10 | 11 | 12 | 13 | 14 |
| 15 | 16 | 17 | 18 | 19 | 20 | 21 |
| 22 | 23 | 24 | 25 | 26 | 27 | 28 |
| 29 | 30 | 31 | | | | |

| Sunday | Monday | Tuesday | Wednesday | Thursday | Friday | Saturday |
|---|---|---|---|---|---|---|
| | | | | | | |

**Notes for Home:** Your child was assessed on Chapter 7 concepts, skills, and problem solving.
*Home Activity:* Ask your child to look at the calendar and tell you the date of the third Sunday in the month. (15)

Name _____

# Performance Assessment
## Chapter 7

Show What You Know

Pick one card
from each bag.

Draw the clock hands to
show the time.

Write the time. Then write
the time one hour later.

| | Draw the clock hands to show the time. | Write the time. | Write the time one hour later. |
|---|---|---|---|
| 1 | | ___:___ | ___:___ |
| 2 | | ___:___ | ___:___ |

3  What are two things this calendar tells you?

_____

_____

| May | | | | | | |
|---|---|---|---|---|---|---|
| S | M | T | W | T | F | S |
| | 1 | 2 | 3 | 4 | 5 | 6 |
| 7 | 8 | 9 | 10 | 11 | 12 | 13 |
| 14 | 15 | 16 | 17 | 18 | 19 | 20 |
| 21 | 22 | 23 | 24 | 25 | 26 | 27 |
| 28 | 29 | 30 | 31 | | | |

## Problem Solving Critical Thinking

4  Look at a calendar for this month.

How is it like this calendar for May? How is it different?

**Notes for Home:** Your child did an activity that assessed Chapter 7 skills, concepts, and problem solving. *Home Activity:* Ask your child to tell you the earliest time that they wrote for Exercises 1–2.

PERFORMANCE ASSESSMENT

Name _____

# Add Again and Again!

**Keys You Will Use** `ON/C` `+` `=`

*Is it quicker to use a calculator or pencil and paper?*

How many 2s can you add in one minute using paper and pencil?

1. Write the sums for 2 + 2, 4 + 2, 6 + 2, and 8 + 2.

2. Predict what your sum will be if you continue the pattern for one minute. _____

3. Start over. Have your partner time you. What is your final sum? _____

4. Compare your prediction to your final sum. Was your prediction **greater** or **less** than your final sum?

_____

How many 2s can you add in one minute using your  ?

5. Press these keys.

`ON/C` `2` `+` `2` `=` `=` `=` `=` `10.`

6. Think about how many times in one minute you could add 2. Predict your final sum. _____

7. Start over. Have your partner time you. What is your final sum? _____

8. Compare your prediction to your final sum. Was your prediction **greater** or **less** than your final sum?

_____

**Tech Talk** Repeat the activity by adding 5s. Do you think your sum will be greater or less than when you added 2s? Explain.

💻÷💻 **Visit our Web site.** www.parent.mathsurf.com

# Fun Time!

What if you could do anything you wanted to do for one day?

Make a table to show the activities you would like to do most.

| Time | Activity |
|------|----------|
| 12:00–1:00 | Lunch |
|  |  |
|  |  |
|  |  |
|  |  |
|  |  |
|  |  |

1. Which activity would take longest?

2. How much time would you spend doing that activity?

Visit our Web site. www.parent.mathsurf.com

8

**Fold down**

Scott Foresman - Addison Wesley    My Math Magazine    No. 7

# MathSoup

## It's About Time!

Use the diagram to answer the questions.

**1** How many hours later is it in New York than in San Francisco?

_____ hours

**2** How many hours earlier is it in Chicago than in Cairo?

_____ hours

## Make a Move

How do you spend your time on a rainy day? One seven-year-old from Oregon, Joshua White, spent a rainy day inventing a board game! He created Dinomite, a board game about dinosaurs. A company decided to make his game and sold it in stores all over the United States!

**Math in Your World**

2

# Time Travels

When you are getting out of school, children in England may be fast asleep in bed! When it is 3:00 in the afternoon in your town, it's a different time in other parts of the United States and the world! The diagram shows different times for some cities.

**1** Suppose you played a game of Dinomite. Look at the clocks to find how long it took to play.

Start    End

It took _____ hours.

**2** Suppose you were staying inside on a rainy day. Make a schedule to show what you would do.

| Time | Activity |
|------|----------|
|      |          |
|      |          |
|      |          |

**Notes for Home:** Your child learned about different times in cities around the world. *Home Activity:* Ask your child what time it is in London when it is 6:00 in New York. (11:00)

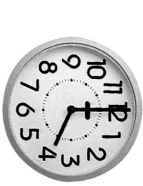

1 Record the time. Was your time more than one minute or less than one minute?

2 Repeat the activity. How can you make the time closer to one minute?

**Notes for Home:** Your child learned to make a sand clock and practiced estimating time. *Home Activity: Ask your child to do the activity at home, using water rather than sand. Do the activity over a sink to avoid spills.*

# Sands of Time

Make your own time machine!

## What You Need

2 paper cups    clock with a second hand
pencil    piece of paper    sand

## What You Do

Poke a hole through the bottom of one paper cup.

Fill the other paper cup with sand.

Pour sand into the cup with the hole, over the paper.

Time how long it takes for the cup to empty.

# Two-Digit Addition

What a Ride!

Train Station

Airport

50 miles to airport

60 miles to toy store

10 miles to train station

30 miles to airport

30 miles to train station

50 miles to train station

School

30 miles to airport

Toys Are Here

40 miles to school

Park

20 miles to school

How far away is one place from another? Tell addition stories to find out.

**Notes for Home:** Your child told addition stories to find out the distance between two places on the map. *Home Activity:* Ask your child to find the distance between the school and the airport.

## Math at Home

Dear Family,
Our class is starting Chapter 8. We will be learning about adding two-digit numbers. You can help me practice addition at home. Together we can have fun doing these activities.

### Backward Fun!

Play a game called *What's My Question?* Begin the game by saying the answer. For example: The sum is 33. Have your child say the question. For example: What is 10 plus 23? Repeat using other numbers.

### Adding to Meals

Tell stories about mealtimes. For example: It took 10 minutes to fix lunch. It took us 15 minutes to eat lunch. How much time did it take altogether?

### Community Connection

Take your child to the grocery store. Point out an item that costs less than 50¢. Ask your child how much two of the items would cost.

  **Visit our Web site. www.parent.mathsurf.com**

Name _____

**Explore** • • • • • • • • • • • • • • • • • • • • • • • • •

Use ▭▭▭ to find different ways to load the truck.
Do not go over 100 pounds. Draw one of your ways.

**Share** • • • • • • • • • • • • • • • • • • • • • • • •

Compare your ways with those of your classmates.

 **Notes for Home:** Your child explored ways to add tens. *Home Activity:* Ask your child to explain how to use tens to show 60. (Sample answer: 2 tens and 4 tens)

Adding tens is easy when you use these!

How many in all?

_2_ tens + _3_ tens = _5_ tens

_20_ + _30_ = _50_

Use  to find how many in all.

 ①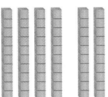

___ tens + ___ tens = ___ tens

___ + ___ = ___

②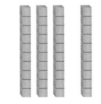

___ tens + ___ ten = ___ tens

___ + ___ = ___

 **Write your own** problems about adding tens.

Draw the  you use.

③

___ tens + ___ tens = ___ tens

___ + ___ = ___

④

___ tens + ___ tens = ___ tens

___ + ___ = ___

**Talk About It** How is 5 + 3 like 50 + 30?

How is it different?

 **Notes for Home:** Your child used materials to add tens. *Home Activity:* Ask your child to explain how to find 3 tens + 5 tens. (3 tens + 5 tens = 8 tens; 8 tens = 80)

# Add Tens with a Hundred Chart

**Learn**

There are 24 people with bikes on the path. 30 more people with bikes join them. How many bikes are on the path now?

$$24 + 30 = 54$$

There are 54 bikes on the path.

*Use a hundred chart to add tens. Move down 3 rows because each row is 10.*

| 1 | 2 | 3 | 4 | 5 | 6 | 7 | 8 | 9 | 10 |
|---|---|---|---|---|---|---|---|---|----|
| 11 | 12 | 13 | 14 | 15 | 16 | 17 | 18 | 19 | 20 |
| 21 | 22 | 23 | 24 | 25 | 26 | 27 | 28 | 29 | 30 |
| 31 | 32 | 33 | 34 | 35 | 36 | 37 | 38 | 39 | 40 |
| 41 | 42 | 43 | 44 | 45 | 46 | 47 | 48 | 49 | 50 |
| 51 | 52 | 53 | 54 | 55 | 56 | 57 | 58 | 59 | 60 |
| 61 | 62 | 63 | 64 | 65 | 66 | 67 | 68 | 69 | 70 |
| 71 | 72 | 73 | 74 | 75 | 76 | 77 | 78 | 79 | 80 |
| 81 | 82 | 83 | 84 | 85 | 86 | 87 | 88 | 89 | 90 |
| 91 | 92 | 93 | 94 | 95 | 96 | 97 | 98 | 99 | 100 |

**Check**

Use the hundred chart to add.

1. $24 + 10 = 34$

2. $56 + 30 = \underline{\phantom{00}}$

3. $60 + 20 = \underline{\phantom{00}}$

4. $73 + 20 = \underline{\phantom{00}}$

5.
$$\begin{array}{ccccccc} 49 & 80 & 32 & 45 & 50 & 11 & 34 \\ +10 & +10 & +30 & +20 & +20 & +40 & +60 \\ \end{array}$$

**Talk About It** Explain how you would use the hundred chart to find $53 + 10 + 20$.

**Notes for Home:** Your child used a hundred chart to add tens. *Home Activity:* Ask your child how he or she would add 37 + 40 using the chart.

**Practice** • • • • • • • • • • • • •

> The hundred chart can help you add!

Add. You can use the hundred chart.

| 1 | 2 | 3 | 4 | 5 | 6 | 7 | 8 | 9 | 10 |
|---|---|---|---|---|---|---|---|---|---|
| 11 | 12 | 13 | 14 | 15 | 16 | 17 | 18 | 19 | 20 |
| 21 | 22 | 23 | 24 | 25 | 26 | 27 | 28 | 29 | 30 |
| 31 | 32 | 33 | 34 | 35 | 36 | 37 | 38 | 39 | 40 |
| 41 | 42 | 43 | 44 | 45 | 46 | 47 | 48 | 49 | 50 |
| 51 | 52 | 53 | 54 | 55 | 56 | 57 | 58 | 59 | 60 |
| 61 | 62 | 63 | 64 | 65 | 66 | 67 | 68 | 69 | 70 |
| 71 | 72 | 73 | 74 | 75 | 76 | 77 | 78 | 79 | 80 |
| 81 | 82 | 83 | 84 | 85 | 86 | 87 | 88 | 89 | 90 |
| 91 | 92 | 93 | 94 | 95 | 96 | 97 | 98 | 99 | 100 |

**6**
$$\begin{array}{r} 54 \\ + 30 \\ \hline 84 \end{array} \qquad \begin{array}{r} 68 \\ + 20 \\ \hline \end{array}$$

**7**
$$\begin{array}{r} 71 \\ + 20 \\ \hline \end{array} \qquad \begin{array}{r} 59 \\ + 40 \\ \hline \end{array}$$

**8**
$$\begin{array}{r} 23 \\ + 40 \\ \hline \end{array} \qquad \begin{array}{r} 39 \\ + 50 \\ \hline \end{array}$$

**9**
$$\begin{array}{r} 62 \\ + 10 \\ \hline \end{array} \quad \begin{array}{r} 26 \\ + 30 \\ \hline \end{array} \quad \begin{array}{r} 60 \\ + 10 \\ \hline \end{array} \quad \begin{array}{r} 57 \\ + 40 \\ \hline \end{array} \quad \begin{array}{r} 33 \\ + 20 \\ \hline \end{array} \quad \begin{array}{r} 74 \\ + 20 \\ \hline \end{array} \quad \begin{array}{r} 41 \\ + 10 \\ \hline \end{array}$$

## Problem Solving Patterns

**10** Add. What patterns do you see?

$50 + 20 = $ \_\_\_\_

$51 + 20 = $ \_\_\_\_

$52 + 20 = $ \_\_\_\_

$53 + 20 = $ \_\_\_\_

$54 + 20 = $ \_\_\_\_

**Write your own** number sentences to make a pattern.

\_\_\_\_ + \_\_\_\_ = \_\_\_\_

\_\_\_\_ + \_\_\_\_ = \_\_\_\_

\_\_\_\_ + \_\_\_\_ = \_\_\_\_

\_\_\_\_ + \_\_\_\_ = \_\_\_\_

\_\_\_\_ + \_\_\_\_ = \_\_\_\_

**Notes for Home:** Your child practiced adding tens. *Home Activity:* Ask your child to show you how to add 53 + 30, 54 + 30, and 55 + 30.

**PRACTICE**

# Add Using Mental Math

**Learn** • • • • • • • • • • • • • • • • • • • • • • • • • • • •

The bicycle costs $53. The skateboard costs $20. What is the total cost of the bicycle and the skateboard? Find 53 + 20.

> Think: Add the tens.
> **50 + 20 = 70**
> Then add the ones.
> **70 + 3 = 73**

$53

$20

I don't have paper and pencil, so I will use mental math.

53 + 20 = $73

**Check** • • • • • • • • •

Add. Use mental math.

**1** 44 + 20 = 64

Think:

40 + 20 = 60
60 + 4 = 64

**2** 36 + 40 = ___

Think:

___ + ___ = ___
___ + ___ = ___

**3** 52 + 30 = ___

Think:

___ + ___ = ___
___ + ___ = ___

**4** 29 + 30 = ___

Think:

___ + ___ = ___
___ + ___ = ___

**Talk About It** What other ways can you add 53 + 20 in your head?

**Notes for Home:** Your child used mental math to add. *Home Activity:* Ask your child how he or she would find 70 + 20 using mental math.

Use mental math to add.

**5** $18 + 40 = \underline{58}$    $53 + 30 = \underline{\phantom{00}}$    $72 + 20 = \underline{\phantom{00}}$

**6** $46 + 20 = \underline{\phantom{00}}$    $27 + 40 = \underline{\phantom{00}}$    $56 + 30 = \underline{\phantom{00}}$

**7** $24 + 30 = \underline{\phantom{00}}$    $64 + 30 = \underline{\phantom{00}}$    $42 + 50 = \underline{\phantom{00}}$

## Problem Solving Patterns

Add. Use mental math. Then write the number
sentences to continue the patterns.

**8**  $11 + 20 = \underline{\phantom{00}}$

$11 + 30 = \underline{\phantom{00}}$

$11 + 40 = \underline{\phantom{00}}$

$\underline{\phantom{00}} + \underline{\phantom{00}} = \underline{\phantom{00}}$

$\underline{\phantom{00}} + \underline{\phantom{00}} = \underline{\phantom{00}}$

**9**  $37 + 10 = \underline{\phantom{00}}$

$37 + 20 = \underline{\phantom{00}}$

$37 + 30 = \underline{\phantom{00}}$

$\underline{\phantom{00}} + \underline{\phantom{00}} = \underline{\phantom{00}}$

$\underline{\phantom{00}} + \underline{\phantom{00}} = \underline{\phantom{00}}$

**10**  Describe the patterns you see.

_____

_____

**Notes for Home:** Your child practiced using mental math to add. *Home Activity:* Ask your child to choose a number less than 50 and add 30 to it.

Name _____

# Estimate Two-Digit Sums

**Learn** • • • • • • • • • • • • • • • • • • • • • • • • • • • • • •

The bus for a field trip holds 60 children.
One class has 27 children. Another class has
21 children. Can all the children fit on one bus?

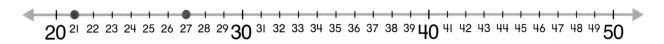

20 21 22 23 24 25 26 27 28 29 **30** 31 32 33 34 35 36 37 38 39 **40** 41 42 43 44 45 46 47 48 49 **50**

27
+ 21

27 is closer to _30_.

21 is closer to _20_.

Think:
30
+ 20
50

27 + 21 is about _50_.

There are about _50_ children.

They ___can___ fit on one bus.

I don't need an exact answer. I can use the nearest ten to estimate!

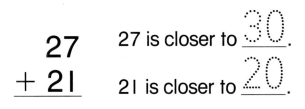

**Check** • • • • • • • • • • • • • •

Find the nearest ten. Estimate the sum.

51
+ 28

51 is closer to ____.

28 is closer to ____.

Think:

☐
+ ☐
☐

51 + 28 is about ____.

**Talk About It** Explain how you would
estimate the sum for this problem.

25
+ 42

 **Notes for Home:** Your child estimated sums. *Home Activity:* Ask your child to estimate 52 + 19. (70)

**Chapter 8 Lesson 4**

two hundred seventy-five **275**

Find the nearest ten. Estimate the sum.

**2**

Think:

43
+ 29

$+$ 40
30

70

70

43 + 29 is about ___70___.

**3**

Think:

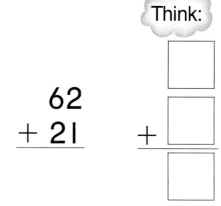

62
+ 21

$+$

62 + 21 is about _____.

**4**

Think:

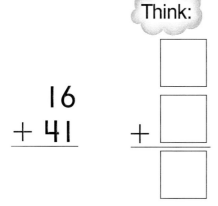

16
+ 41

$+$

16 + 41 is about _____.

**5**

Think:

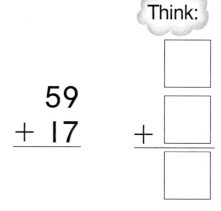

59
+ 17

$+$

59 + 17 is about _____.

## Problem Solving **Estimation**

**6** Mrs. Borke's class went to the museum. Mr. Reed's class saw a play. About how many children went on the two field trips?

about _____ children

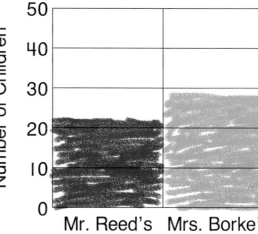

**Field Trips**

Number of Children / Mr. Reed's Class / Mrs. Borke's Class

**Notes for Home:** Your child estimated sums by finding the nearest ten. *Home Activity:* Ask your child to explain how he or she solved Exercise 6.

© Scott Foresman Addison Wesley

**276** two hundred seventy-six

Name ______________________________

Reading for Math

## Make Predictions

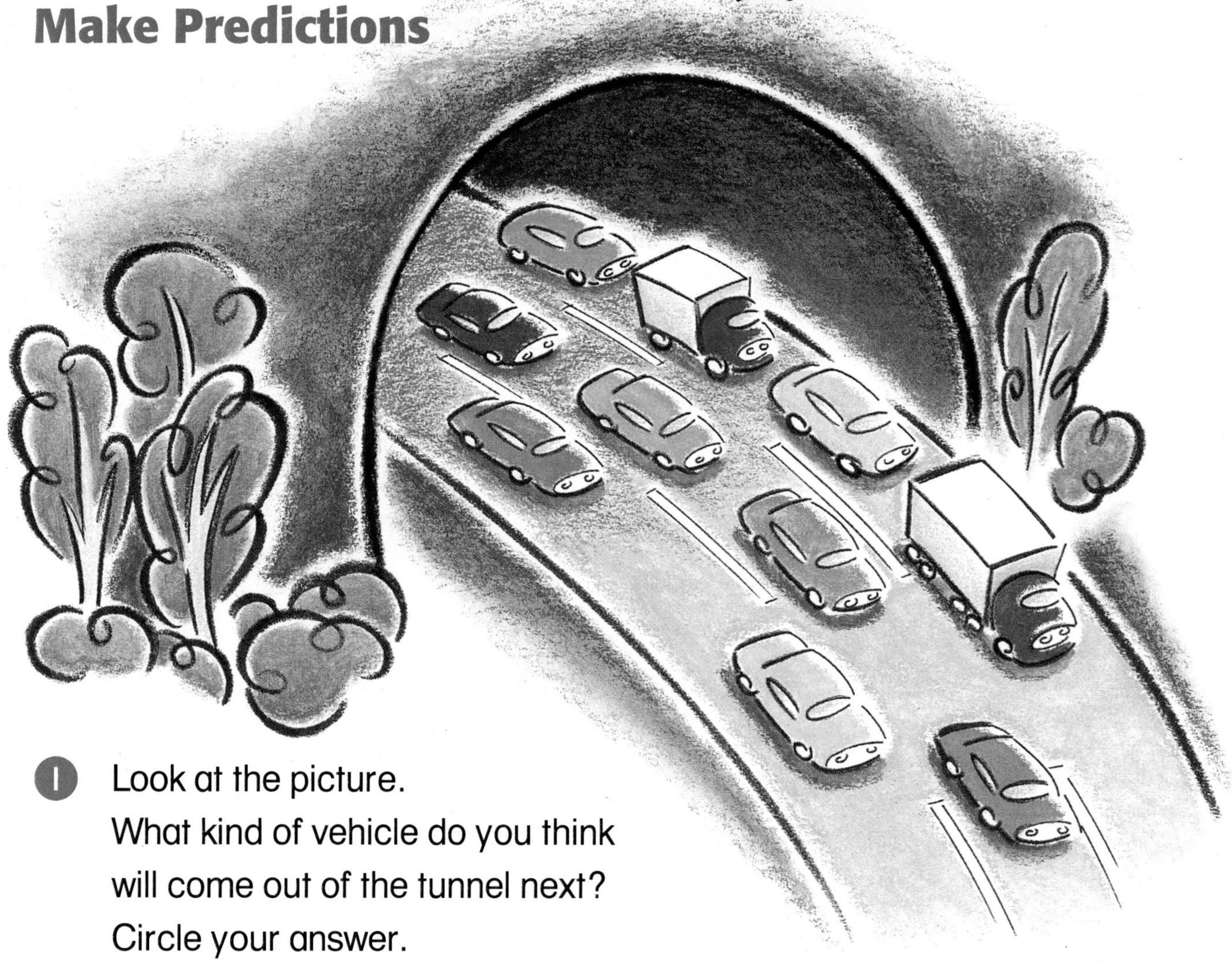

1. Look at the picture.
What kind of vehicle do you think
will come out of the tunnel next?
Circle your answer.

**a car** **a truck** **a train**

2. Why do you think so?

______________________________

______________________________

______________________________

**Talk About It** How did the picture help you to predict?

**Notes for Home:** Your child used a picture to make a prediction. *Home Activity:* Ask your child to make a prediction about what they will eat for breakfast tomorrow.

**3** Look at the picture.
Who do you think will get on next?
Circle your answer.

      an adult      a child         a dog

**4** Why do you think so?

_____

_____

_____

## Critical Thinking

**5** Can you think of a place where a dog would be next?

**Notes for Home:** Your child used a picture to predict who would get on a bus next.
*Home Activity:* Ask your child to predict what color clothes he or she will wear tomorrow.

# Problem Solving: Make Predictions

**Learn** ● ● ● ● ● ● ● ● ● ● ● ● ● ●

**PROBLEM SOLVING GUIDE**
Understand ● Plan ● Solve ● Look Back

Think of a car that someone you know has.

What color is it? _____
Share what color you wrote with your class.
Fill in the chart for your class.

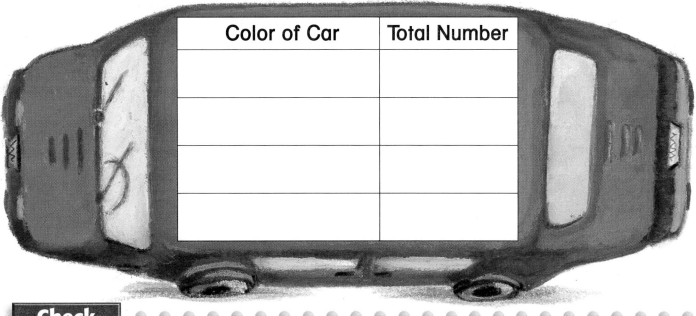

| Color of Car | Total Number |
|---|---|
|  |  |
|  |  |
|  |  |
|  |  |

**Check** ● ● ● ● ● ● ● ● ● ● ● ● ● ● ● ● ● ● ● ● ● ● ● ● ● ● ● ● ●

① Predict. On your way home from school today,
   what color car do you think you will see most often?

   _____

② Why do you think so?

   _____

   _____

   _____

**Talk About It** How does using what we know

help us to predict?

**Notes for Home:** Your child made predictions about the color of car they would see going home from school. *Home Activity:* Ask your child to predict what time he or she will eat dinner tomorrow.

PROBLEM SOLVING

**PROBLEM SOLVING**

③ Predict. If you watched the cars that go by, which color car would you see most often?

_____

④ Why do you think so?

_____

_____

⑤ Watch cars go by for 5 minutes. Record the results.

| Color of Car | Tally | Total |
|---|---|---|
| | | |
| | | |
| | | |
| | | |
| | | |
| | | |

⑥ Was your prediction close? _____

## Critical Thinking

⑦ If you did this activity again on another day, would you make the same prediction? Why or why not?

**Notes for Home:** Your child predicted the color of car they would see most often, and then did an activity to check that prediction. *Home Activity:* Ask your child to tell you the order in which the colors of the cars were seen most often.

# Explore Addition With or Without Regrouping

**Explore** ● ● ● ● ● ● ● ● ● ● ● ● ● ● ● ● ● ● ● ● ● ● ● ● ● ● ● ●

Do this activity with a partner.

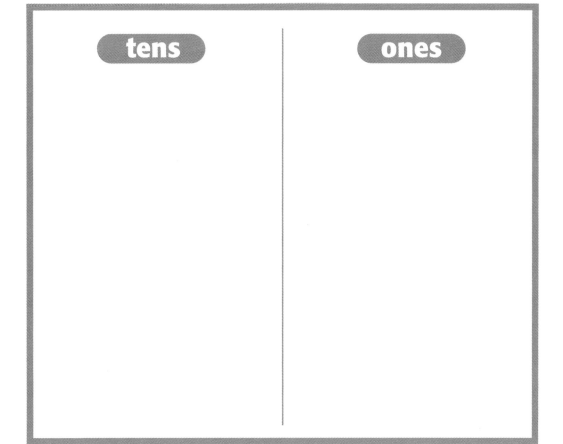

1.  Use cards numbered 1–9. Put the cards facedown.

2.  Take turns. Draw a card and take that many ▪ .
    Then put the number card back.

3.  Continue taking turns.
    Trade for a ▬▬▬ whenever you can.
    Keep your ▬▬▬ and ▪ on the chart.

4.  The first player to get 100 wins!

| tens | ones |
|------|------|
|      |      |

**Share** ● ● ● ● ● ● ● ● ● ● ● ● ● ● ● ● ● ● ● ● ● ● ● ● ● ● ●

How did you know when to trade ▪ for ▬▬▬ ?

**Notes for Home:** Your child did an activity to group tens and ones. *Home Activity:* Ask your child how to group 7 ones and 5 ones as tens and ones. (1 ten 2 ones)

18 children ride the bus to school.

6 children ride their bikes.

How many children ride to school in all?

Add 6 to 18.

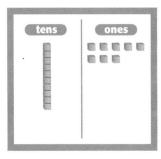

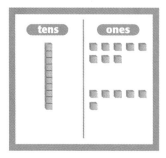

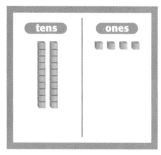

Start with 18.          Add 6.          Regroup 10 ones as 1 ten.

Regroup means changing the way you group your tens and ones.

24 in all

**EXPLORE**

Use  , 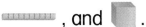 , and ⬛ .

**5** Show 39. Add 4.
How many in all?

_____ tens _____ ones

_____ in all

**6** Show 46. Add 7.
How many in all?

_____ tens _____ ones

_____ in all

**7** Show 14. Add 6.
How many in all?

_____ tens _____ ones

_____ in all

**8** Show 24. Add 8.
How many in all?

_____ tens _____ ones

_____ in all

**Talk About It** Why is it helpful to regroup?

**Notes for Home:** Your child added two numbers and wrote the answer as tens and ones.
*Home Activity:* Ask your child to explain how he or she did Exercise 6.

Name _____

# Add With or Without Regrouping

**Learn** • • • • • • • • • • • • • • • • • • • • • • • • • • • • • • • •

Do you need to regroup to add?

$$24 + 8 = \underline{32}$$

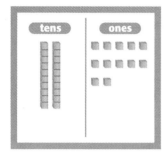 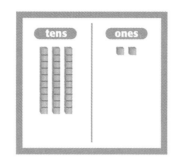

Start with 24.
Add 8. You have
more than 10 ones.

You need to regroup.

$$23 + 3 = \underline{26}$$

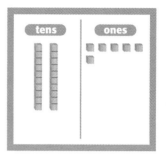

You have less than 10 ones.
You do not need to regroup.

**Check** • • • • • • • • • • • • • • • • • • • • • • • • • • • • • • •

Use ▭ , ▭▭▭ , and ◻ .

| | Show this many. | Add this many. | Do you need to regroup? | Add. |
|---|---|---|---|---|
| **1** | 36 | 7 | yes | $36 + 7 = \underline{43}$ |
| **2** | 23 | 4 | | $23 + 4 = \underline{\quad}$ |
| **3** | 19 | 5 | | $19 + 5 = \underline{\quad}$ |

**Talk About It** Start with 17. Tell an addition problem.

Explain how you would solve your problem.

**Notes for Home:** Your child determined if regrouping was needed to add two numbers.
*Home Activity:* Ask your child if regrouping is needed to do these problems: 49 + 15; 67 + 11. (yes, no)

**Chapter 8 Lesson 7**

two hundred eighty-three **283**

Use ▭ , ▬ , and ▪ .

| Show this many. | Add this many. | Do you need to regroup? | Solve. |
|---|---|---|---|
| ④ 22 | 4 | no | 22 + 4 = 26 |
| ⑤ 43 | 9 | | 43 + 9 = ___ |
| ⑥ 56 | 5 | | 56 + 5 = ___ |
| ⑦ 34 | 6 | | 34 + 6 = ___ |
| ⑧ 12 | 7 | | 12 + 7 = ___ |
| ⑨ 21 | 7 | | 21 + 7 = ___ |
| ⑩ 37 | 5 | | 37 + 5 = ___ |

## Problem Solving Critical Thinking

⑪ What numbers less than 10 can you add to the number 16 without needing to regroup? How do you know?

**Notes for Home:** Your child decided if regrouping was needed before adding two numbers.
*Home Activity:* Ask your child to tell you an addition problem that requires regrouping and one that does not.

Name _____

**Learn** · · · · · · · · · · · · · · · · · · · · · · · · · · · · · · · · ·

Find 27 + 8.

Add the ones.
7 ones + 8 ones = 15 ones.
Regroup before you
add the tens.

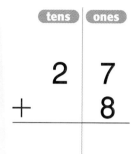
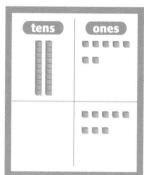

```
     tens | ones
       2  |  7
    +     |  8
```

Regroup 15 ones
as 1 ten and 5 ones.
Write 5 ones.
Write 1 to show 1 ten.

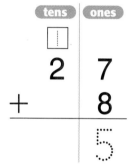
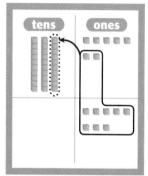

```
     tens | ones
      [1] |
       2  |  7
    +     |  8
          |  5
```

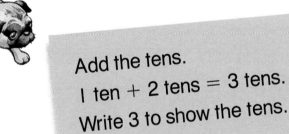

Add the tens.
1 ten + 2 tens = 3 tens.
Write 3 to show the tens.
The sum is 35.

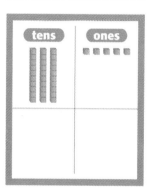

```
     tens | ones
      [1] |
       2  |  7
    +     |  8
       3  |  5
```

**Check** · · · · · · · · · · · · · · · · · · · · · · · · · · · · · · · · ·

Use   , ▭▭▭▭▭ , and ◼ . Add.

**1.**

```
 tens | ones        tens | ones        tens | ones        tens | ones
  [ ] |              [ ] |              [ ] |              [ ] |
   2  |  5            3  |  7            7  |  4            8  |  2
 +    |  9          +    |  5          +    |  3          +    |  9
   3  |  4
```

**Talk About It** How do you show regrouping 10 ones as 1 ten?

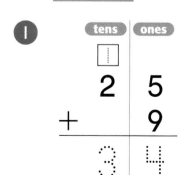 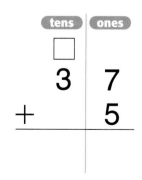 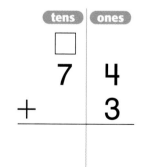

**Notes for Home:** Your child recorded sums to addition problems which involved regrouping.
*Home Activity:* Ask your child to explain the steps he or she would do to find 67 + 19.

**Practice** • • • • • • • • • • • • • • • • • • • • • • • •

Add. Then circle the sum if you regrouped.

You can use  , ▭▭▭▭▭ , and ◼ .

**2** | tens | ones |

3 4
+   6
(4 0)

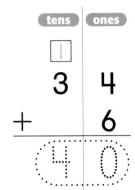

**3** | tens | ones |

2 2
+   7

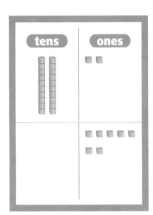

**4** | tens | ones |

7 3
+   9

  | tens | ones |

6 3
+   5

  | tens | ones |

4 7
+   5

  | tens | ones |

5 7
+   3

**5** | tens | ones |

5 9
+   7

  | tens | ones |

1 2
+   5

  | tens | ones |

2 8
+   2

  | tens | ones |

3 8
+   6

## Problem Solving Critical Thinking

**6**   Leon's dog walked on his math paper.
Now Leon can't read some of the numbers.
What could the missing numbers be?
How do you know?

42
+ 🐾
5🐾

**Notes for Home:** Your child added two numbers and identified sums which involved regrouping.
*Home Activity:* Ask your child to explain why he circled three of the sums in the exercises.

For additional practice, see Skills Practice Bank, page 534, Set 1.

Name _____

# Mixed Practice
## Lessons 1–8

## Concepts and Skills

**1** Estimate the sum.

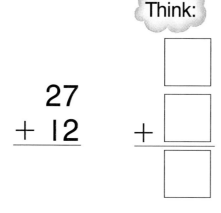

Think:

27
+ 12

+ ☐ ☐ ☐

27 + 12 is about _____.

**2** Add. Use mental math.

$27 + 40 = $ ___

$47 + 30 = $ ___

$56 + 20 = $ ___

$73 + 20 = $ ___

## Problem Solving

**3** Complete the chart. Fill in the totals.

| Color of Socks | Tally | Totals |
|---|---|---|
| red | ‖‖‖ | |
| blue | ‖‖‖ ‖‖ | |
| green | ‖ | |

Use the chart to predict.

**4** Mrs. Jacob's second-grade class made a chart to show the color of socks worn by the students. What color of socks would you predict to see most often in Mrs. Jacob's second-grade class? _____

## Journal

**5** Write two addition problems. Explain how you would estimate to find each sum.

**Notes for Home:** Your child practiced adding tens, using mental math, estimating sums, and solving problems. *Home Activity:* Ask your child to explain how to find 54 + 30 using mental math.

Name _____

## Concepts and Skills

Add or subtract.

**1**    7      14     **2**    9      18     **3**    5      10
     + 7    − 7        + 9    − 9        + 5    − 5

**4**    6      12     **5**    8      16     **6**    4      8
     + 6    − 6        + 8    − 8        + 4    − 4

Write how many. Then write **even** or **odd**.

**7**

**8**

_____         _____

---

## Test Prep

Fill in the ○ for the correct answer.

Use the picture to answer the questions.

**9** Which car is blue?

   ○ first
   ○ second
   ○ third
   ○ fourth

**10** Which car is red?

   ○ second
   ○ fifth
   ○ third
   ○ first

**11** Which car is yellow?

   ○ fourth
   ○ fifth
   ○ second
   ○ first

**Notes for Home:** Your child reviewed related addition and subtraction facts, even and odd numbers, and ordinal numbers. *Home Activity:* Ask your child which color car in the picture is second. (yellow)

**CUMULATIVE REVIEW**

# Add Two-Digit Numbers With or Without Regrouping

**Learn** ● ● ● ● ● ● ● ● ● ● ● ● ● ● ● ● ● ● ● ● ● ● ●

Knowing how to find 28 + 5 helps you find 28 + 35.

**Check** ● ● ● ● ● ● ● ● ● ● ● ● ● ● ● ● ● ● ● ● ● ● ●

Add. Use ▢, ▭, and ▪.
Regroup if you need to.

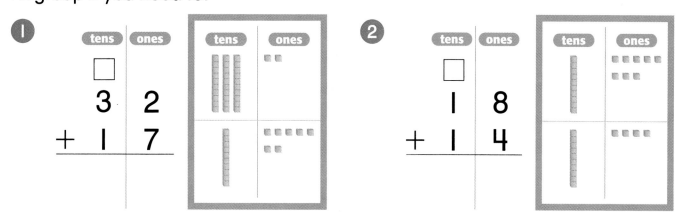

**Talk About It** How are these problems alike?
How are they different?

46
+ 2

46
+ 12

**Notes for Home:** Your child added two numbers involving regrouping. *Home Activity:* Ask your child to explain how the two problems in the Learn section are alike and how they are different.

Add. Use  , ▭▭▭▭▭▭ , and ◼ .
Regroup if you need to.

**3**

| tens | ones |
|------|------|
| □ | |
| 3 | 7 |
| + 1 | 6 |
| 5 | 3 |

| tens | ones |
|------|------|
| □ | |
| 5 | 6 |
| + 2 | 0 |

| tens | ones |
|------|------|
| □ | |
| 2 | 4 |
| + 1 | 7 |

| tens | ones |
|------|------|
| □ | |
| 2 | 5 |
| + 3 | 5 |

**4**

| tens | ones |
|------|------|
| □ | |
| 4 | 9 |
| + 2 | 3 |

| tens | ones |
|------|------|
| □ | |
| 3 | 8 |
| + 2 | 7 |

| tens | ones |
|------|------|
| □ | |
| 7 | 5 |
| + 1 | 4 |

| tens | ones |
|------|------|
| □ | |
| 7 | 7 |
| + 1 | 4 |

**5**

| tens | ones |
|------|------|
| □ | |
| 4 | 1 |
| + 3 | 8 |

| tens | ones |
|------|------|
| □ | |
| 5 | 6 |
| + 1 | 2 |

| tens | ones |
|------|------|
| □ | |
| 6 | 2 |
| + 1 | 9 |

| tens | ones |
|------|------|
| □ | |
| 6 | 8 |
| + 2 | 1 |

## Problem Solving Visual Thinking

**6** We started with this:   Now we have this:   Draw what was added.

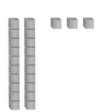    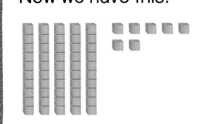

**Notes for Home:** Your child added two numbers. *Home Activity:* Ask your child to identify two problems in Exercise 3 which involved regrouping. (the first, third, or fourth exercise)

Name _____

**Learn** • • • • • • • • • • • • • • •

Find 28 + 25.

Don't forget to add the ten you made!

| tens | ones |
|------|------|
| ☐ | |
| 2 | 8 |
| + 2 | 5 |
| | 3 |

Add the ones.
Regroup if you need to.

| tens | ones |
|------|------|
| I | |
| 2 | 8 |
| + 2 | 5 |
| 5 | 3 |

Add the tens.

**Check** • • • • • • • • • • • • • • • • • • • • •

Add. Regroup if you need to.

**1**

| tens | ones |
|------|------|
| ☐ | |
| 4 | 6 |
| + I | 3 |
| 5 | 9 |

| tens | ones |
|------|------|
| ☐ | |
| 5 | 8 |
| + 2 | 3 |
| | |

| tens | ones |
|------|------|
| ☐ | |
| 3 | 7 |
| + 2 | 9 |
| | |

| tens | ones |
|------|------|
| ☐ | |
| 2 | 5 |
| + 4 | 5 |
| | |

**Talk About It** Use the nearest ten to estimate:

27 + 39 is about _____.

Now add to find the exact sum.

How close was your estimate to your exact answer?

27
+ 39
____

42 + 33 is about _____.

Now add to find the exact sum.

How close was your estimate to your exact answer?

42
+ 33
____

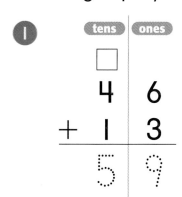

**Notes for Home:** Your child used regrouping to add two numbers. *Home Activity:* Ask your child to estimate 27 + 32 and then find the exact sum. (30 + 30 = 60; 59)

Add. Regroup if you need to.

**2**
$$\begin{array}{r} 51 \\ + 17 \\ \hline 68 \end{array}$$

$$\begin{array}{r} 59 \\ + 32 \\ \hline \end{array}$$

$$\begin{array}{r} 39 \\ + 15 \\ \hline \end{array}$$

$$\begin{array}{r} 47 \\ + 21 \\ \hline \end{array}$$

$$\begin{array}{r} 28 \\ + \ 6 \\ \hline \end{array}$$

$$\begin{array}{r} 43 \\ + 32 \\ \hline \end{array}$$

**3**
$$\begin{array}{r} 52 \\ + 21 \\ \hline \end{array}$$

$$\begin{array}{r} 63 \\ + 17 \\ \hline \end{array}$$

$$\begin{array}{r} 45 \\ + 38 \\ \hline \end{array}$$

$$\begin{array}{r} 37 \\ + 21 \\ \hline \end{array}$$

$$\begin{array}{r} 29 \\ + 23 \\ \hline \end{array}$$

$$\begin{array}{r} 38 \\ + 41 \\ \hline \end{array}$$

**4**
$$\begin{array}{r} 81 \\ + 15 \\ \hline \end{array}$$

$$\begin{array}{r} 74 \\ + 18 \\ \hline \end{array}$$

$$\begin{array}{r} 68 \\ + 23 \\ \hline \end{array}$$

$$\begin{array}{r} 62 \\ + 14 \\ \hline \end{array}$$

$$\begin{array}{r} 27 \\ + 31 \\ \hline \end{array}$$

$$\begin{array}{r} 19 \\ + 18 \\ \hline \end{array}$$

**PRACTICE**

## Problem Solving

**5** Kate's luggage weighs 35 pounds. Circle her two pieces of luggage.

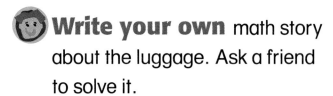 **Write your own** math story about the luggage. Ask a friend to solve it.

_____

_____

_____

_____

_____

 **Notes for Home:** Your child found sums for addition problems. _Home Activity:_ Ask your child to show you two pieces of luggage in Exercise 5 that have a total weight of 33 pounds. (the red suitcase and the blue suitcase)

Name _____

# Sum It Up!

**Players** 2–4

## What You Need

Paper clip ⌾

Pencil ✐

## How to Play

① Take turns. Spin each spinner two times.

② Record the numbers you spin in the squares below. Add.

③ The player with the highest sum wins!

④ Play again.

Tens                  Ones

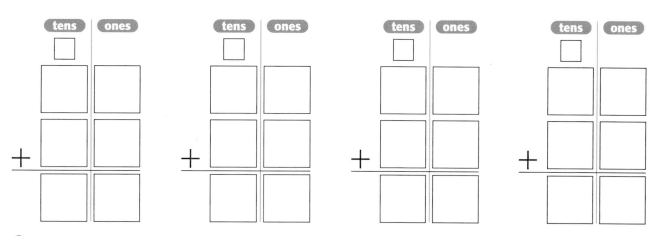

Name _____

Add. Use mental math.

① 20 + 60 = _____          ② 40 + 30 = _____

③ 50 + 40 = _____          ④ 38 + 20 = _____

⑤ 56 + 10 = _____          ⑥ 29 + 20 = _____

Estimate. Use the nearest ten to help.

⑦ 59 + 28 is about _____.          ⑧ 21 + 68 is about _____.

⑨ 42 + 41 is about _____.          ⑩ 79 + 11 is about _____.

⑪ 39 + 12 is about _____.          ⑫ 19 + 33 is about _____.

Add.

⑬
$$
\begin{array}{cccccc}
24 & 47 & 52 & 64 & 39 & 18 \\
+35 & +\phantom{0}6 & +29 & +12 & +41 & +\phantom{0}4 \\
\end{array}
$$

## Riddle

⑭ I have two missing numbers.
Each missing number
is greater than 10.
The sum is 87.
What could the
missing numbers be?

_____ and _____

**Notes for Home:** Your child practiced finding estimates and adding numbers. *Home Activity:* Ask your child to tell you a second pair of numbers that could solve the riddle.

Name _____

**Learn** • • • • • • • • • • •

Joey bought a toy car and a toy boat.
How much money did he spend?

39¢
+ 45¢
84¢

Sam's Store

55¢    39¢    45¢

Don't forget the cents sign!

Joey spent 84¢ .

**Check** • • • • • • • • • • • • • • • • •

Add.

❶
14¢      27¢      31¢      42¢      69¢      14¢
+ 59¢    + 5¢    + 47¢    + 6¢    + 25¢    + 6¢
73¢

❷
59¢      28¢      31¢      11¢      19¢      36¢
+ 35¢    + 44¢    + 7¢    + 33¢    + 79¢    + 9¢

**Talk About It** How are these problems alike?
How are they different?

23        23¢
+ 19      + 19¢

**Notes for Home:** Your child added money amounts up to 99¢. *Home Activity:* Ask your child to add 29¢ and 26¢. (55¢)

Add.

**3**

| 16¢ | 18¢ | 27¢ | 55¢ | 45¢ | 27¢ |
|---|---|---|---|---|---|
| + 18¢ | + 31¢ | + 9¢ | + 36¢ | + 3¢ | + 53¢ |
| 34¢ | | | | | |

**4**

| 28¢ | 32¢ | 25¢ | 17¢ | 54¢ | 29¢ |
|---|---|---|---|---|---|
| + 49¢ | + 37¢ | + 4¢ | + 68¢ | + 25¢ | + 61¢ |

**Mixed Practice** Add.

**5**

| 21¢ | 45¢ | 42 | 37 | 18¢ | 63 |
|---|---|---|---|---|---|
| + 36¢ | + 25¢ | + 7 | + 28 | + 11¢ | + 9 |

**6**

| 53 | 12¢ | 73 | 41¢ | 65 | 14¢ |
|---|---|---|---|---|---|
| + 26 | + 9¢ | + 18 | + 35¢ | + 28 | + 13¢ |

## Problem Solving Critical Thinking

**7** Malinda has 43¢. Which two items could she buy?

_____ and _____

Meg's Market

Pencils 8¢    Erasers 21¢    Notebooks 34¢

**Notes for Home:** Your child added amounts of money up to 99 cents. *Home Activity:* Ask your child to use coins to show you one of the sums on this page.

# Add Three Numbers

**Learn** • • • • • • • • • • • • • • • • • • • • • • • • •

You can add three numbers in different ways.

*I look for numbers that make a ten.*

27
14
+ 13
54

*I look for doubles.*

16
21
+ 26
63

*I add the top two numbers first.*

42
13
+ 16
71

**Check** • • • • • • • • • • • • • • • • • • • • • • • • •

Add. Circle the numbers that you added first.

1.
| 51 | 27 | 16 | 24 | 48 | 12 |
| 23 | 48 | 20 | 32 | 21 | 25 |
| + 13 | + 13 | + 6 | + 13 | + 2 | + 51 |
| 87 | | | | | |

2.
| 32 | 56 | 63 | 30 | 34 | 29 |
| 15 | 27 | 12 | 24 | 13 | 23 |
| + 42 | + 4 | + 14 | + 20 | + 5 | + 11 |

**Talk About It** How is adding three numbers different from adding two numbers? How is it the same?

**Notes for Home:** Your child added three numbers. *Home Activity:* Ask your child to show you the steps he or she used to add one of the exercises on this page.

Add.

**3**

| 34 | 54 | 13 | 22 | 15 | 43 |
| 13 | 12 | 10 | 13 | 24 | 10 |
| + 44 | + 16 | + 6 | + 42 | + 13 | + 23 |

91

**4**

| 35 | 28 | 47 | 38 | 54 | 46 |
| 21 | 11 | 12 | 23 | 11 | 21 |
| + 25 | + 30 | + 7 | + 12 | + 14 | + 2 |

**5**

| 62 | 26 | 18 | 32 | 27 | 32 |
| 14 | 31 | 21 | 41 | 32 | 13 |
| + 3 | + 16 | + 4 | + 22 | + 3 | + 42 |

## Problem Solving Critical Thinking

**6** The engine cannot pull more than 70 tons.
How many tons could be in the first car of the train?

18 tons    17 tons    22 tons    _____ tons

**Notes for Home:** Your child found the sum of three numbers. *Home Activity:* Ask your child to explain how he or she solved the Problem Solving exercise.

PRACTICE

Name _____

# Problem Solving: Guess and Check

**Learn** ● ● ● ● ● ● ● ● ● ● ● ● ● ●

**PROBLEM SOLVING GUIDE**
Understand ● Plan ● Solve ● Look Back

Chen has 93¢. Which two toys could he buy?

40¢   45¢   48¢   49¢

I'm closer, but it is still too much. I'll try a toy that costs even less.

These toys cost too much. I'll try a toy that costs less.

I did it! I have enough to buy two toys.

$$49¢ + 48¢ = 97¢$$

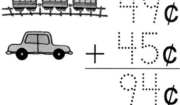
$$49¢ + 45¢ = 94¢$$

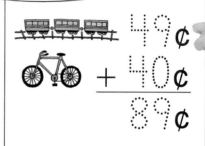
$$49¢ + 40¢ = 89¢$$

Chen can buy the ___train___ and the ___bike___.

**Check** ● ● ● ● ● ● ● ● ● ● ● ● ● ● ● ● ● ● ● ● ● ● ● ● ●

Solve. Show and check each guess.

**1** Sofia has 86¢.

She wants to buy two toys.

What can she buy?

Sofia can buy the _____ and the _____.

**Talk About It** Which other two toys can

Chen buy with 93¢?

**Notes for Home:** Your child solved problems by guessing possible solutions and then checking them. *Home Activity:* Ask your child to find two toys that could be bought with 90¢. (bike and car, bike and truck, bike and train)

PROBLEM SOLVING

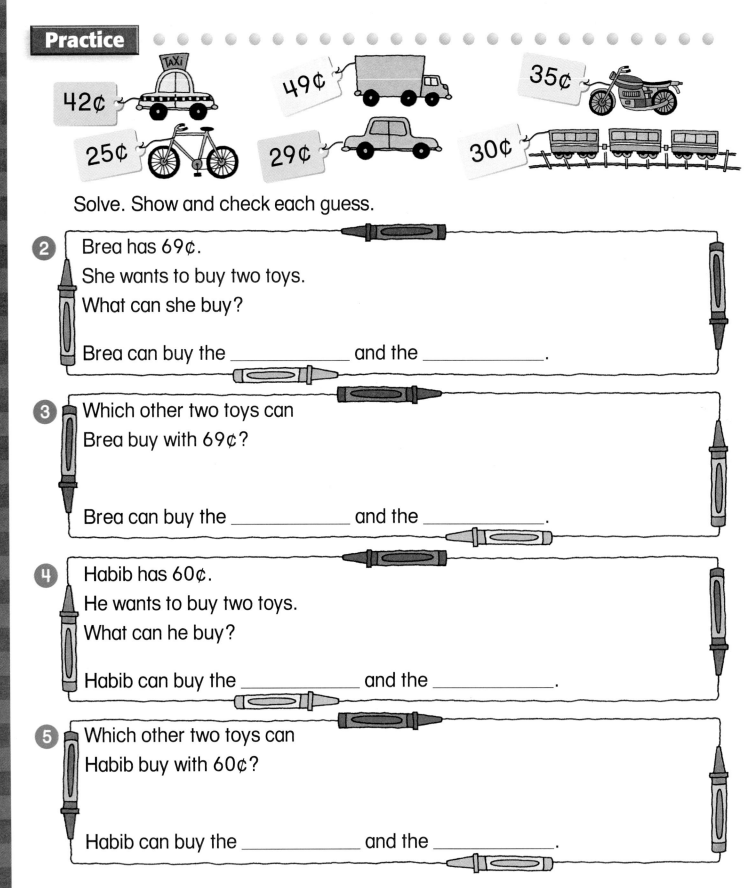

## Practice

Solve. Show and check each guess.

**2** Brea has 69¢.
She wants to buy two toys.
What can she buy?

Brea can buy the _____ and the _____.

**3** Which other two toys can
Brea buy with 69¢?

Brea can buy the _____ and the _____.

**4** Habib has 60¢.
He wants to buy two toys.
What can he buy?

Habib can buy the _____ and the _____.

**5** Which other two toys can
Habib buy with 60¢?

Habib can buy the _____ and the _____.

## Estimation

**6** Brea wants to buy three toys. Does she have
enough money? How do you know?

**Notes for Home:** Your child solved problems by guessing possible solutions and then checking those solutions. *Home Activity:* Ask your child if it is possible to buy 3 of the toys pictured with 90 cents. (Yes; the bike, the motorcycle, and the train; or the bike, the car, and the train)

**For additional practice, see Skills Practice Bank, page 534, Set 3.**

**PROBLEM SOLVING**

Name _____

# Mixed Practice
**Lessons 9–13**

## Concepts and Skills

Add. Regroup if you need to.

**1**
| 43 | 38¢ | 52 | 21 | 64¢ | 75 |
|---|---|---|---|---|---|
| + 25 | + 16¢ | + 19 | + 62 | + 17¢ | + 12 |

**2**
| 36 | 19¢ | 24¢ | 15 | 62 | 75¢ |
|---|---|---|---|---|---|
| + 21 | + 65¢ | + 6¢ | + 37 | + 8 | + 13¢ |

**3**
| 24 | 37 | 49 | 13 | 52 | 48 |
|---|---|---|---|---|---|
| 10 | 25 | 12 | 36 | 15 | 26 |
| + 34 | + 23 | + 11 | + 23 | + 12 | + 12 |

## Problem Solving

Solve. Show and check each guess.

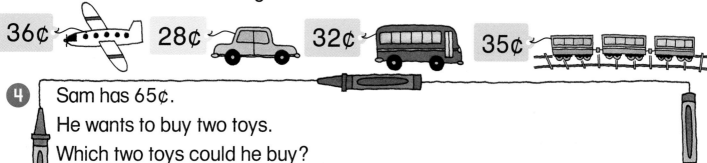

36¢    28¢    32¢    35¢

**4** Sam has 65¢.

He wants to buy two toys.

Which two toys could he buy?

He can buy the _____ and the _____.

## Journal

**5** How did you decide which numbers to

try in the problem about toys? Explain.

**Notes for Home:** Your child practiced adding numbers with and without regrouping, adding three numbers, and solving problems. *Home Activity:* Ask your child how much money would be needed to buy the two most expensive toys in Exercise 4. (35¢ + 36¢ = 71¢)

Name _____

# Cumulative Review
## Chapters 1–8

**Concepts and Skills**

Circle the numbers you would add first. Look for
doubles and numbers that make ten. Add.

| 4 | 3 | 5 | 2 | 7 | 6 |
|---|---|---|---|---|---|
| 2 | 4 | 5 | 1 | 8 | 8 |
| + 6 | + 4 | + 3 | + 8 | + 3 | + 6 |

Draw coins. Show two different ways to make $1.00.

Draw coins. Show two different ways to make 50¢.

---

## Test Prep

Fill in the ○ for the correct answer.

Which group of numbers is in order from the least to the greatest?

**6**
- ○ 65, 42, 37, 19
- ○ 10, 24, 39, 52
- ○ 23, 47, 15, 32
- ○ 36, 71, 49, 83

**7**
- ○ 62, 43, 16, 50
- ○ 97, 23, 46, 17
- ○ 18, 32, 71, 60
- ○ 39, 57, 83, 94

**Notes for Home:** Your child reviewed adding three numbers, finding coin combinations that equal 50¢
and $1.00, and putting numbers in order from least to greatest. *Home Activity:* Ask your child to think
of four numbers between 10 and 100 and put them in order from least to greatest.

# Chapter 8 Review

## Vocabulary

Add. Then circle the sum if you regrouped.

**1**

| 23 | 18 | 46 | 17 | 35 | 63 | 24 |
|---|---|---|---|---|---|---|
| + 14 | + 7 | + 25 | + 2 | + 27 | 12 | 12 |
| | | | | | + 23 | + 36 |

## Concepts and Skills

Add. Use mental math.

**2**  20 + 30 = ____

**3**  52 + 20 = ____

Use the nearest ten to estimate.

**4**  31 + 42 is about ____.

**5**  9 + 21 is about ____.

## Problem Solving

Use the chart.

**6**  Which color bike do you think you would see most often next Monday?

_____

**7**  Why do you think so?

_____

_____

### Bikes at School on Monday

| Bike colors | Tally | Totals |
|---|---|---|
| Blue | 卌 IIII | 9 |
| Red | IIII | 4 |
| Green | II | 2 |

**Notes for Home:** Your child reviewed Chapter 8 vocabulary, concepts, skills, and problem solving. *Home Activity:* Ask your child to explain how he or she regrouped to solve one of the problems in Exercise 1.

# Chapter 8 Test

Add. Use mental math.

**1** 40 + 30 = ___   20 + 70 = ___   50 + 10 = ___

**2** 56 + 20 = ___   39 + 10 = ___   42 + 40 = ___

Estimate.

**3** 63 + 21 is about _____.     **4** 38 + 41 is about _____.

Add. Regroup if you need to.

**5**
```
        12        24        38
14   37  52   48  64   27   24
+23  +6  +29  +3  +11  +34  +32
```

**CHAPTER TEST**

## Problem Solving

Use the chart.

**6** Which vehicle do you think you would see most in the parking lot next Monday?

_____

**7** Why do you think so?

_____

_____

| Vehicles in Parking Lot on Monday | | |
|---|---|---|
| **Vehicles** | **Tally** | **Totals** |
| Cars | 卌 卌 IIII | 14 |
| Trucks | 卌 | 5 |
| Motorcycles | 卌 I | 6 |

**Notes for Home:** Your child was tested on Chapter 8 skills, concepts, and problem solving. *Home Activity:* Ask your child to use the chart to tell you how many more cars were seen than motorcycles. (8)

# Performance Assessment
## Chapter 8

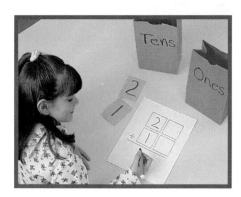

Pick 2 cards from
the tens bag.
Write the numbers
in the tens place.

Pick 2 cards from
the ones bag.
Write the numbers
in the ones place.

Add the numbers.

Repeat the activity. Circle your answer
if you needed to regroup.

**1**
$$+$$

**2**
$$+$$

**3**
$$+$$

**4**
$$+$$

**5**
$$+$$

**6**
$$+$$

## Problem Solving Critical Thinking

**7** Cecelia found 3 pairs of numbers that each have a sum
of 99. What 3 pairs of numbers could she have found?

**Notes for Home:** Your child did an activity that tested Chapter 8 skills, concepts, and problem solving.
*Home Activity:* Ask your child to tell you the greatest and the least sum on the page.

PERFORMANCE ASSESSMENT

Name _____

# Use the World Wide Web

## Computer Skills You Will Need

You can use the Internet to get different kinds of information.

1  Go to: **www.mathsurf.com/2** **Click** on Chapter 8.
This activity can tell you about different forms
of transportation used by second graders.

2  **Click** **Forward** and **Backward** to get from screen to screen.

3  What did you learn from this activity?

_____

Use the information you found on the Internet.
Write 2 questions that you could ask about different
forms of transportation.

4  _____

_____

5  _____

_____

6  Exchange your questions with a friend.
Answer each other's questions.

**Tech Talk** Do you think the information at this Web site will always be
the same? Why or why not?

Visit our Web site. **www.parent.mathsurf.com**

# Keep on Truckin'

## What You Need

2 players    2 game pieces    9 cards

## How to Play

1 Place each player's game piece on a truck labeled "Start."

2 Number the cards by 10s from 10 through 90.

3 Place the cards facedown. Turn over 3 cards. Try to make an addition sentence using the cards.

4 If you can make an addition sentence, move your game piece forward one space. Put the cards back, facedown.

5 Take turns. The first player to reach **End**, wins!

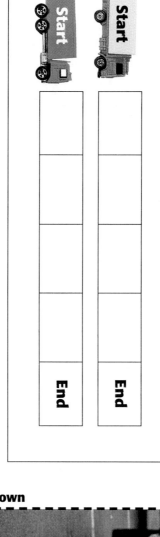

Start ... End

Start ... End

**Fold down**

Ride the Fun Bus!

Scott Foresman – Addison Wesley

MathSurf

My Math Magazine    No. 8

## Math in Your World

# Buckle Up

Since he was 8 years old, Aaron Gordon has been trying to get seat belts installed on school buses. Aaron is currently studying the safety of different belts.

**1** One school wants to install seat belts on its 2 buses. One bus holds 22 children. The other bus holds 72 children. How many seat belts should they install?

_____ seat belts

**2** Two classes are going on a field trip. One class has 34 children. The other class has 27 children. How many children in all will ride the bus to the field trip?

_____ children

 **Notes for Home:** Your child practiced two-digit addition.
*Home Activity:* Ask your child to add 57 + 39. (96)

**2**

---

## How Fast Did They Go?

| Machine | Speed (mph) |
| --- | --- |
| Steamboat | 5 |
| Airplane | |
| Model T car | |
| Airship | |

▲ The Model T car's top speed was about 15 miles per hour faster than the first airplane.

▲ Giant airships used to carry people. They went about 23 miles per hour faster than the Model T.

**Notes for Home:** Your child practiced addition and completed a table.
*Home Activity:* Ask your child to explain how he or she found the speed for each machine listed in the table.

6

# Life in the Fast Lane

For many years, people have built machines so they could travel faster and faster. Look at these pictures of different machines. Use the clues to complete the table that shows how fast they traveled.

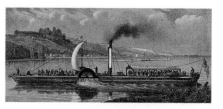

▲ **The first steamboat traveled about 5 miles per hour.**

**The first airplane traveled about 25 miles per hour faster than the steamboat.** ▼

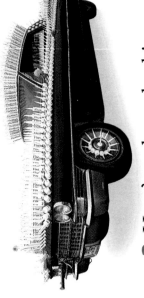

# Fun-Mobiles

Each year in Houston, Texas, there is a parade of cars. People come to see cars that are decorated with all sorts of things. Some cars are covered with toys. One car even looks like a giant shark! These "art cars" are as much fun to make as they are to watch!

**1** This car is covered with dolls! Suppose there are 34 dolls on the hood and 46 dolls on the roof. How many dolls are there in all?

_____ dolls

**2** Here's a sharp-looking car! It's covered with bottles of glue! Suppose there are 64 bottles on the front of the car and 32 on the back. How many bottles are there altogether?

_____ bottles

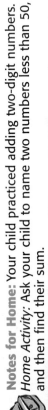

**Notes for Home:** Your child practiced adding two-digit numbers. *Home Activity:* Ask your child to name two numbers less than 50, and then find their sum.

**CHAPTER**

**9**

# Two-Digit Subtraction

**Creatures and Critters**

How much more does one animal weigh than another? Tell a subtraction story.

**Red King Crab**
about 10 pounds

**Giant Octopus**
about 50 pounds

**Commersons Dolphin**
about 90 pounds

**Bluefish**
about 30 pounds

**Hawksbill Turtle**
about 70 pounds

**Ray**
about 80 pounds

**Notes for Home:** Your child told subtraction stories using the picture. *Home Activity:* Ask your child to tell you one of his or her stories.

**Math at Home**

Dear Family,
Our class is starting Chapter 9. We will learn about subtraction with two-digit numbers. Together we can do these activities.

### Weather Watch

With your child, listen for the day's high and low temperatures on the weather report. Work with your child to find the difference between the high and low temperatures.

### Family Differences

Make a list of some family members, along with their ages. Pick out two of the family members. Help your child find the difference in their ages.

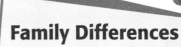

Mom      36
Dad      38
Joey     10
Grandma  61
Anita     3
me        7

### Community Connection

Look for mileage signs as you travel on roads or highways. Help your child find the distance between two locations given on one sign.

💻⇆💻 **Visit our Web site. www.parent.mathsurf.com**

# Explore Subtracting Tens

**Explore** • • • • • • • • • • • • • • • • • • • • • • • • • • • • • • • • •

The caretaker feeds the animals in the morning and in the afternoon.

Use a ▭▭▭ to stand for 10 pounds of food. Show the total number of pounds of food each group of animals will get. Take away some ▭▭▭ to show how much food each group will get in the morning. Find out how many pounds of food each group will get in the afternoon.

| | Animal | Total Food Each Day | Morning Amount | Afternoon Amount |
|---|---|---|---|---|
| 1 | Zebras | 50 pounds | | |
| 2 | Monkeys | 40 pounds | | |
| 3 | Birds | 30 pounds | | |
| 4 | Giraffes | 70 pounds | | |
| 5 | Elephants | 90 pounds | | |

**Share** • • • • • • • • • • • • • • • • • • • • • • • • • • • • • • • • •

How did you find out how much food to give the giraffe in the afternoon?

**Notes for Home:** Your child explored subtracting tens. *Home Activity:* Ask your child to explain how he or she found how much food the elephants ate in the morning and in the afternoon.

Subtract. Use  to find how many are left.

**6**

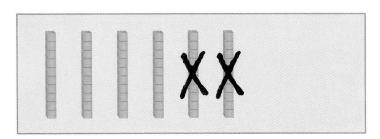

6 tens    60
− 2 tens    − 20
4 tens    40

**7**

4 tens    40
− 1 ten    − 10

**8**

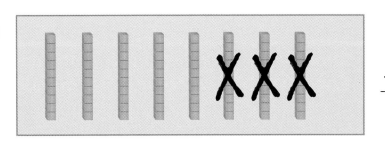

8 tens    80
− 3 tens    − 30

---

Subtract. You can use  to help.

**9**
9 tens    90
− 3 tens    − 30

**10**
7 tens    70
− 5 tens    − 50

**Talk About It** How does finding 6 − 2 help you find 60 − 20?

 **Notes for Home:** Your child subtracted tens. *Home Activity:* Ask your child to find 8 tens − 5 tens and 80 − 50. (3 tens, 30)

Name _____

## Subtract Tens with a Hundred Chart

• • • • • • • • • • • • • • • • • • • • • • • • • • • •

The caretaker has 54 pounds of bananas. The monkeys eat 20 pounds. How many pounds are left?

54 − 20 = 34 pounds

| 1 | 2 | 3 | 4 | 5 | 6 | 7 | 8 | 9 | 10 |
|---|---|---|---|---|---|---|---|---|----|
| 11 | 12 | 13 | 14 | 15 | 16 | 17 | 18 | 19 | 20 |
| 21 | 22 | 23 | 24 | 25 | 26 | 27 | 28 | 29 | 30 |
| 31 | 32 | 33 | 34 | 35 | 36 | 37 | 38 | 39 | 40 |
| 41 | 42 | 43 | 44 | 45 | 46 | 47 | 48 | 49 | 50 |
| 51 | 52 | 53 | 54 | 55 | 56 | 57 | 58 | 59 | 60 |
| 61 | 62 | 63 | 64 | 65 | 66 | 67 | 68 | 69 | 70 |
| 71 | 72 | 73 | 74 | 75 | 76 | 77 | 78 | 79 | 80 |
| 81 | 82 | 83 | 84 | 85 | 86 | 87 | 88 | 89 | 90 |
| 91 | 92 | 93 | 94 | 95 | 96 | 97 | 98 | 99 | 100 |

Use a hundred chart to subtract. Move up 2 rows because each row is a 10.

**Check** • • • • • • • • • • • • • • • • • • • • • • • • • • • •

Use the hundred chart to subtract.

1. 66 − 30 = 36

2. 37 − 20 = ___

3. 58 − 20 = ___

4. 71 − 40 = ___

5.
```
   42        83        29        32        75        62
 − 10      − 20      − 10      − 20      − 30      − 40
```

**Talk About It** Explain how you would use the hundred chart to find 88 − 20 − 10.

**Notes for Home:** Your child used a hundred chart to subtract tens. *Home Activity:* Ask your child how he or she would find 93 − 20 using the hundred chart. (Sample answer: Start at 93. Move up two rows to 73.)

The hundred chart can help you subtract!

Subtract. You can use the hundred chart.

**6** 29 − 10 = 19

**7** 68 − 30 = _____

**8** 79 − 40 = _____

**9** 47 − 20 = _____

**10** 86 − 50 = _____

**11** 97 − 80 = _____

| 1 | 2 | 3 | 4 | 5 | 6 | 7 | 8 | 9 | 10 |
|---|---|---|---|---|---|---|---|---|---|
| 11 | 12 | 13 | 14 | 15 | 16 | 17 | 18 | 19 | 20 |
| 21 | 22 | 23 | 24 | 25 | 26 | 27 | 28 | 29 | 30 |
| 31 | 32 | 33 | 34 | 35 | 36 | 37 | 38 | 39 | 40 |
| 41 | 42 | 43 | 44 | 45 | 46 | 47 | 48 | 49 | 50 |
| 51 | 52 | 53 | 54 | 55 | 56 | 57 | 58 | 59 | 60 |
| 61 | 62 | 63 | 64 | 65 | 66 | 67 | 68 | 69 | 70 |
| 71 | 72 | 73 | 74 | 75 | 76 | 77 | 78 | 79 | 80 |
| 81 | 82 | 83 | 84 | 85 | 86 | 87 | 88 | 89 | 90 |
| 91 | 92 | 93 | 94 | 95 | 96 | 97 | 98 | 99 | 100 |

**12**
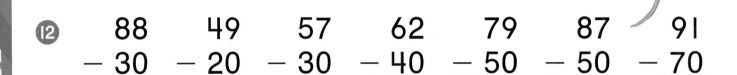
```
  88      49      57      62      79      87      91
− 30    − 20    − 30    − 40    − 50    − 50    − 70
```

**13**
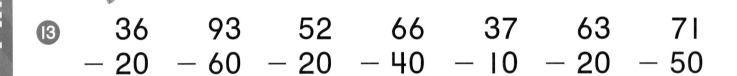
```
  36      93      52      66      37      63      71
− 20    − 60    − 20    − 40    − 10    − 20    − 50
```

**Problem Solving Patterns**

**14** Subtract. What patterns do you see?

50 − 10 = _____

50 − 20 = _____

50 − 30 = _____

50 − 40 = _____

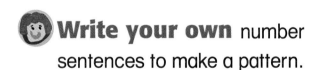**Write your own** number sentences to make a pattern.

_____ − _____ = _____

_____ − _____ = _____

_____ − _____ = _____

_____ − _____ = _____

**Notes for Home:** Your child subtracted tens by using a hundred chart. *Home Activity:* Ask your child to choose a number between 60 and 90. Then ask your child to explain how he or she would subtract 40 from that number.

PRACTICE

Name _____

# Estimate Two-Digit Differences

• • • • • • • • • • • • • • •

In a mob of 41 kangaroos, 29 of them were adults. The rest were young kangaroos. A young kangaroo is called a joey. About how many of the kangaroos were joeys?

20 21 22 23 24 25 26 27 28 29 **30** 31 32 33 34 35 36 37 38 39 **40** 41 42 43 44 45 46 47 48 49 **50** 51

41  41 is closer to __40__.
− 29  29 is closer to __30__.

Think:
40
− 30
10

41 − 29 is about __10__.
About __10__ were joeys.

**Check** • • • • • • • • • • • • • • • • • • • • • • • •

Find the nearest ten. Estimate the difference.

43  43 is closer to _____.
− 22  22 is closer to _____.

Think:
[ ]
− [ ]
[ ]

43 − 22 is about _____.

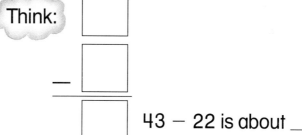

**Talk About It** Explain how would you estimate the difference.

48
− 36

 **Notes for Home:** Your child used the nearest ten to estimate differences. *Home Activity:* Ask your child to tell you the nearest ten for 72, 67, and 24. (70, 70, 20)

Find the nearest ten. Estimate the difference.

**2**

Think:

58
− 31

− ⬚60⬚
⬚30⬚
⬚30⬚

58 − 31 is about ⬚30⬚.

**3**

Think:

42
− 18

−

42 − 18 is about _____.

**4**

Think:

61
− 49

−

61 − 49 is about _____.

**5**

Think:

39
− 28

−

39 − 28 is about _____.

## Problem Solving Estimation

Find the nearest ten. Estimate the difference.

**6** An adult kangaroo weighs about 92 pounds.
A young kangaroo, called a joey, weighs
about 11 pounds. About how much more
does the adult kangaroo weigh than its joey?

About _____ pounds

**Notes for Home:** Your child estimated differences by finding the nearest ten. *Home Activity:* Ask your
child how to estimate 52 − 18. (Sample answer: 52 is closer to 50. 18 is closer to 20. 50 − 20 = 30)

# Explore Subtraction With or Without Regrouping

1 Start with 5  on your chart.

2 Take turns spinning the spinner.

3 Take away that many 🔲 .

Trade a ▭ for 10 🔲 whenever you need to.

4 The first player to get to zero wins!

| tens | ones |
|---|---|
|  |  |

**EXPLORE**

**Share**

How did you know when to trade ▭ for 🔲 ?

**Notes for Home:** Your child explored subtraction with regrouping. *Home Activity:* Ask your child how he or she would take 7 ones away from 2 tens and 4 ones. (Sample answer: Trade 1 ten for 10 ones. Take 7 ones away. You have 1 ten and 7 ones left.)

**Connect** • • • • • • • • • • •

The Senegal bush baby found
a nest of 30 bugs. It ate 6 bugs.
How many more bugs were left in the nest?

Subtract 6 from 30.

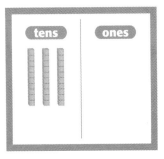
Start with 30.

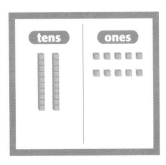
Regroup 1 ten
as 10 ones.

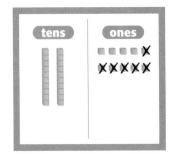
Subtract 6.

_24_ bugs were left.

Use ⬚ , ▭ , and ◼ .
Find how many are left.

5  Show 23. Subtract 5.

_1_ tens _8_ ones

_18_

6  Show 45. Subtract 8.

_____ tens _____ ones

_____

7  Show 34. Subtract 6.

_____ tens _____ ones

_____

8  Show 28. Subtract 9

_____ tens _____ ones

_____

**Talk About It** Why did you need to regroup each time?

**Notes for Home:** Your child did subtraction with regrouping. *Home Activity:* Ask your child to explain
how he or she would subtract 7 from 25.

Name _____

**Learn** • • • • • • • • • • • • • • • • • • • • • • • • • • •

Do you need to regroup to subtract?

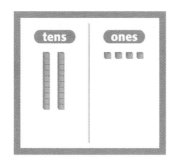

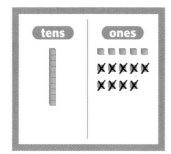

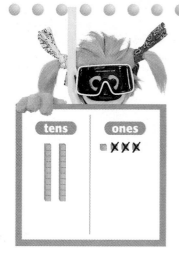

$$24 - 9 = \underline{15}$$

You need to regroup to subtract the ones.

$$24 - 3 = \underline{21}$$

You do not need to regroup to subtract the ones.

**Check** • • • • • • • • • • • • • • • • • • • • • • • • • • •

Use  , ⬛⬛⬛⬛ , and ⬛ .

| | Show this many. | Subtract this many. | Do you need to regroup? | Solve. |
|---|---|---|---|---|
| **1** | 45 | 8 | yes | $45 - 8 = \underline{37}$ |
| **2** | 27 | 5 | | $27 - 5 = \underline{\phantom{00}}$ |
| **3** | 32 | 4 | | $32 - 4 = \underline{\phantom{00}}$ |

**Talk About It** Start with 36 fish. Tell a subtraction problem. Explain how you would solve your problem.

**Notes for Home:** Your child determined if regrouping was needed before subtracting. *Home Activity:* Ask your child if regrouping is needed to find $83 - 7$ and $59 - 6$. (Yes, no)

## Practice

Use [ | ] , ▭▭▭ , and ◻ .

| | Show this many. | Subtract this many. | Do you need to regroup? | Solve. |
|---|---|---|---|---|
| **4** | 46 | 4 | no | 46 − 4 = 42 |
| **5** | 39 | 4 | | 39 − 4 = ___ |
| **6** | 44 | 8 | | 44 − 8 = ___ |
| **7** | 26 | 5 | | 26 − 5 = ___ |
| **8** | 49 | 6 | | 49 − 6 = ___ |
| **9** | 42 | 7 | | 42 − 7 = ___ |
| **10** | 23 | 7 | | 23 − 7 = ___ |
| **11** | 34 | 4 | | 34 − 4 = ___ |
| **12** | 31 | 5 | | 31 − 5 = ___ |

## Problem Solving Critical Thinking

**13** Which numbers less than ten can you subtract from 35 without needing to regroup? For which numbers would you need to regroup? How do you know?

**14** Which number less than ten can you subtract from 30 without needing to regroup? Explain.

**Notes for Home:** Your child determined if regrouping was needed before finding differences for subtraction problems. *Home Activity:* Ask your child to write one subtraction problem that uses regrouping and one problem that doesn't.

# Record Subtraction

**Learn** • • • • • • • • • • • • • • • • • • • • • • • • • • • • •

Subtract 42 − 7.

7 is more than 2.
Regroup before you
subtract the ones.

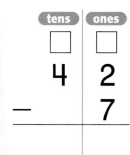

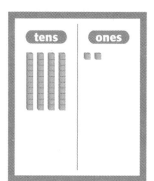

Regroup a ten as 10 ones.
Write 3 to show the tens.
Write 12 to show the ones.

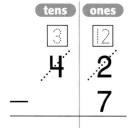

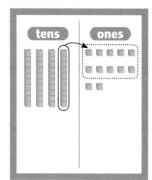

Subtract 7 ones from
12 ones. Write 5 to
show the ones. Write
3 to show the tens.

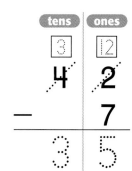

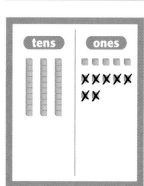

**Check** • • • • • • • • • • • • • • • • • • • • • • • • • • • • •

Use 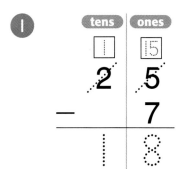 , , and . Subtract.

| | tens | ones |
|---|---|---|
| | 2 | 5 |
| − | | 7 |
| | 1 | 8 |

| | tens | ones |
|---|---|---|
| | 3 | 6 |
| − | | 4 |

| | tens | ones |
|---|---|---|
| | 5 | 2 |
| − | | 9 |

| | tens | ones |
|---|---|---|
| | 7 | 2 |
| − | | 8 |

**Talk About It** How did you decide which number to write in the tens place?

 **Notes for Home:** Your child recorded the differences for subtraction problems. *Home Activity:* Ask your child to explain what the numbers in the small boxes mean in Exercise 1. (Sample answer: The numbers show how many tens and ones after regrouping.)

Subtract. You can use  , ▭▭▭▭▭ , and ▣ to help.
Then circle the difference if you regrouped.

**2**

| tens | ones |
|------|------|
| ⁷ | ¹² |
| 8 | 2 |
| − | 6 |
| (7 | 6) |

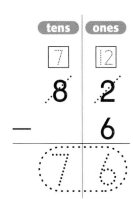

| tens | ones |
|------|------|
| □ | □ |
| 2 | 8 |
| − | 1 |

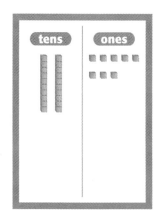

**3**

| tens | ones |
|------|------|
| □ | □ |
| 4 | 3 |
| − | 7 |

| tens | ones |
|------|------|
| □ | □ |
| 5 | 6 |
| − | 9 |

| tens | ones |
|------|------|
| □ | □ |
| 8 | 8 |
| − | 5 |

| tens | ones |
|------|------|
| □ | □ |
| 2 | 4 |
| − | 6 |

**4**

| tens | ones |
|------|------|
| □ | □ |
| 7 | 3 |
| − | 1 |

| tens | ones |
|------|------|
| □ | □ |
| 6 | 4 |
| − | 5 |

| tens | ones |
|------|------|
| □ | □ |
| 3 | 9 |
| − | 0 |

| tens | ones |
|------|------|
| □ | □ |
| 4 | 7 |
| − | 8 |

## Problem Solving Patterns

Subtract. What patterns do you see?

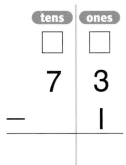

**5**

| 68 | 58 | 48 | 38 | 28 | 18 |
|----|----|----|----|----|----|
| − 9 | − 9 | − 9 | − 9 | − 9 | − 9 |

 **Notes for Home:** Your child found the differences for subtraction problems. *Home Activity:* Ask your child to describe the pattern in the Problem Solving section. (The differences decreased by ten each time.)

**For additional practice, see Skills Practice Bank, page 535, Set 1.**

Name _____

# What's the Difference?

**Players** 2

**What You Need**

2 number cubes

**How to Play**

1. Take turns.
2. Roll both number cubes. Record as tens and ones.
3. Roll one number cube. Record as ones.
4. Subtract. Regroup if you need to.
5. The player with the least difference wins!

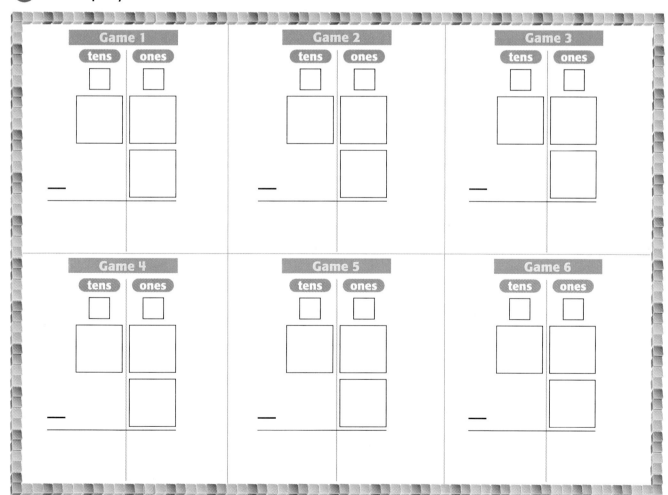

 **Notes for Home:** Your child played a game to practice subtraction. *Home Activity:* Ask your child to identify the game with the least difference.

**STOP and Practice**

Subtract.

1  40 − 30 = ___          2  90 − 70 = ___

3  50 − 10 = ___          4  74 − 20 = ___

5  82 − 30 = ___          6  61 − 10 = ___

7
| tens | ones |
|---|---|
| □ | □ |
| 4 | 6 |
| − | 5 |

| tens | ones |
|---|---|
| □ | □ |
| 7 | 3 |
| − | 8 |

| tens | ones |
|---|---|
| □ | □ |
| 5 | 4 |
| − | 3 |

| tens | ones |
|---|---|
| □ | □ |
| 2 | 5 |
| − | 6 |

8
| tens | ones |
|---|---|
| □ | □ |
| 8 | 5 |
| − | 9 |

| tens | ones |
|---|---|
| □ | □ |
| 3 | 6 |
| − | 2 |

| tens | ones |
|---|---|
| □ | □ |
| 6 | 5 |
| − | 7 |

| tens | ones |
|---|---|
| □ | □ |
| 5 | 4 |
| − | 8 |

## Riddle

Solve.

9  I am a number between 40 and 50.
My nearest ten is 40. You can subtract
one or 2 from me without regrouping.
I am not an even number.

What number am I?  _____

 **Notes for Home:** Your child practiced subtraction. *Home Activity:* Ask your child to explain how he or she found the answer to the riddle.

Name _____

# Problem Solving: Choose a Computation Method

**Learn** • • • • • • • • • • • • • • •

22 parrots fly through the jungle. 16 more parrots join them. Then 12 parrots fly away. Now how many parrots are there?

There is more than one way to solve this problem.

I drew tens and ones.

_26_ parrots

I used a calculator.

$$22 + 16 = 38$$
$$38 - 12 = 26$$

_26_ parrots

**Check** • • • • • • • • • • • • • • • • • • • • • • •

Choose a way to solve the problem. Draw the place-value blocks or write a number sentence.

Show your work here.

1. 31 Canada geese are on a lawn. 14 fly away. 8 fly back. How many Canada geese are there now?

_____ Canada geese

**Talk About It** Explain how you solved the problem about geese.

**Notes for Home:** Your child used place-value materials or a calculator to solve subtraction problems.
*Home Activity:* Ask your child to explain the two steps needed to solve the problem about parrots.
(Find 22 + 16. Then find 38 − 12.)

PROBLEM SOLVING

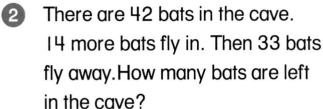

Choose a strategy to solve the problems.
Draw the blocks or write the number sentence.

**2** There are 42 bats in the cave. 14 more bats fly in. Then 33 bats fly away. How many bats are left in the cave?

_____ bats

**3** The ranger counted 17 penguins in the water. 23 more jumped in. Later, 17 more came. How many penguins were in the water?

_____ penguins

## Visual Thinking

**4** Write a story problem for the picture.

 **Notes for Home:** Your child solved subtraction problems by using place-value materials or a calculator.
*Home Activity:* Ask your child to write two number sentences for the story problem he or she made up.
$(33 + 15 = 48; 48 - 13 = 35)$

PROBLEM SOLVING

# Mixed Practice
## Lessons 1–7

## Concepts and Skills

Subtract.

**1**   8 tens     80
    − 5 tens   − 50

**2**   7 tens     70
    − 3 tens   − 30

Use the chart to subtract.

**3** 38 − 20 = ____

**4** 42 − 30 = ____

**5** 49 − 40 = ____

**6** 23 − 10 = ____

| 1 | 2 | 3 | 4 | 5 | 6 | 7 | 8 | 9 | 10 |
|---|---|---|---|---|---|---|---|---|----|
| 11 | 12 | 13 | 14 | 15 | 16 | 17 | 18 | 19 | 20 |
| 21 | 22 | 23 | 24 | 25 | 26 | 27 | 28 | 29 | 30 |
| 31 | 32 | 33 | 34 | 35 | 36 | 37 | 38 | 39 | 40 |
| 41 | 42 | 43 | 44 | 45 | 46 | 47 | 48 | 49 | 50 |

## Problem Solving

Choose a way to solve the problem.
Draw the place-value blocks
or write a number sentence.

**7**   23 meerkats guard their burrows.
     8 run away. 6 come back.
     How many meerkats are there now?

     _____ meerkats

## Journal

**8**   For each problem, do you need to
     regroup to subtract? How do you know?

     43       56
     − 9     − 5

**Notes for Home:** Your child practiced subtraction and problem solving. *Home Activity:* Ask your child to show you how to find 47 − 20 using the chart. (Sample answer: Start at 47. Move up two rows to 27.)

# Cumulative Review
## Chapter 1–9

## Concepts and Skills

Draw the clock hands.

Write the ending time.

**1** Start                Stop

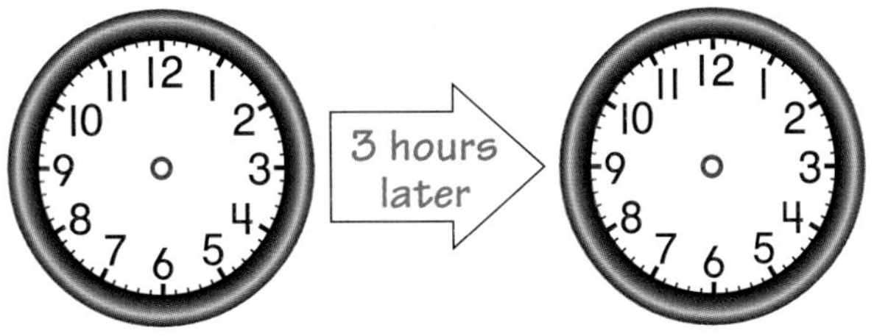

3 hours later

7:00                    ___:___

**2** Start                Stop

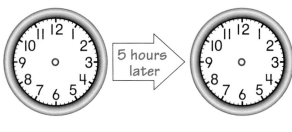

5 hours later

1:00                    ___:___

## Problem Solving

Circle **add** or **subtract**. Write a number sentence.

Solve.

**3** 6 sea lions are swimming.
5 more join them.
How many sea lions are
swimming now?

**add   subtract**

_____

_____ sea lions

**4** 9 frogs are in a pond.
4 jump out.
How many are left?

**add   subtract**

_____

_____ frogs

### Test Prep

Fill in the ○ for the correct answer.

Add. Regroup if you need to.

**5**
```
  14
+ 36
```
○ 40
○ 49
○ 50
○ 41

**6**
```
  37
+ 46
```
○ 72
○ 81
○ 73
○ 83

**7**
```
  52
+ 46
```
○ 94
○ 98
○ 97
○ 88

**Notes for Home:** Your child reviewed telling time, solving problems, and adding.
*Home Activity:* Ask your child to tell a story using the addition problem in Exercise 6.

# Explore Subtracting Two-Digit Numbers

**1** Choose a number from each box.

Use  and 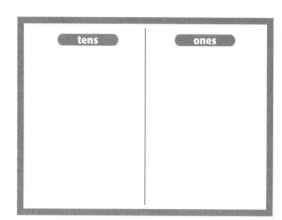 to subtract

the lesser number from the greater number.
Draw a picture to show what you did.

Write a number sentence.

_____ − _____ = _____

Choose numbers from each box to make up
two more subtraction problems. Use
and ▭▭▭ to solve. Write the number sentences.

**2** _____ − _____ = _____   | **3** _____ − _____ = _____

Using one number from each box, what subtraction
problem can you make that can be solved
without regrouping? How do you know?

 **Notes for Home:** Your child subtracted two-digit numbers using materials. *Home Activity:* Ask your child to choose another number from each box at the top of the page, write a subtraction problem using those numbers, and tell you if regrouping is needed to solve his or her problem.

Find 42 – 17.

Before I can subtract, I need to regroup.

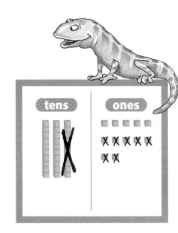

Take 42.

Regroup 1 ten as 10 ones.

Subtract 17. Write the difference.

$42 - 17 = \underline{25}$

Use ▭ and ◼ to subtract.

| | Show this many. | Subtract this many. | Solve. |
|---|---|---|---|
| 4 | 55 | 34 | $55 - 34 =$ \_\_\_\_ |
| 5 | 36 | 27 | $36 - 27 =$ \_\_\_\_ |
| 6 | 84 | 39 | $84 - 39 =$ \_\_\_\_ |
| 7 | 27 | 9 | $27 - 9 =$ \_\_\_\_ |
| 8 | 68 | 46 | $68 - 46 =$ \_\_\_\_ |

**Talk About It** How can you tell if you will need to regroup?

**Notes for Home:** Your child used place-value materials to solve subtraction problems.
*Home Activity:* Ask your child which exercises on this page required regrouping. (Exercises 5, 6, and 7)

Name _____

# Subtract Two-Digit Numbers With or Without Regrouping

**Learn** ● ● ● ● ● ● ● ● ● ● ● ● ● ● ● ● ● ●

Knowing how to find 53 − 9 helps you find 53 − 19.

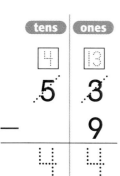
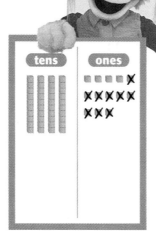

| tens | ones |
|---|---|
| 4 | 13 |
| 5 | 3 |
| − | 9 |
| 4 | 4 |

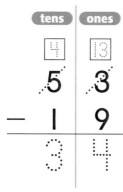
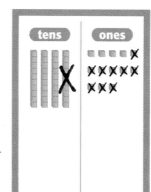

| tens | ones |
|---|---|
| 4 | 13 |
| 5 | 3 |
| − 1 | 9 |
| 3 | 4 |

**Check** ● ● ● ● ● ● ● ● ● ● ● ● ● ● ● ● ● ● ● ● ● ● ● ●

Subtract. Use  ,  , and  .
Regroup if you need to.

**①**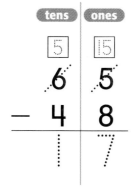

| tens | ones |
|---|---|
| 5 | 15 |
| 6 | 5 |
| − 4 | 8 |
| 1 | 7 |

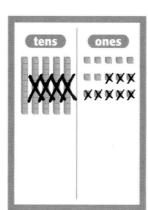

**②**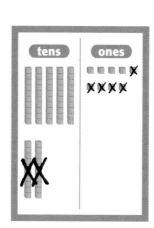

| tens | ones |
|---|---|
| □ | □ |
| 7 | 9 |
| − 2 | 5 |

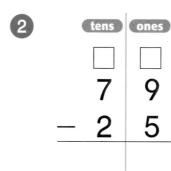

**Talk About It** How are the pairs of problems alike? How are they different?

```
  85      85        83      83
−  3    − 23      −  5    − 25
```

**Notes for Home:** Your child subtracted two-digit numbers with or without regrouping.
*Home Activity:* Ask your child to explain how to solve Exercise 2.

**Chapter 9 Lesson 9**      three hundred thirty-three   **333**

**Practice** ● ● ● ● ● ● ● ● ● ● ● ● ● ● ● ● ●

Subtract. Use , ▭▭▭▭▭, and ◼ .
Regroup if you need to.

**3**

| tens | ones |
|------|------|
| ⌐5⌐ | ⌐11⌐ |
| .6 | ./1 |
| − 3 | 7 |
| 2 | 4 |

| tens | ones |
|------|------|
| ☐ | ☐ |
| 7 | 4 |
| − 2 | 1 |

| tens | ones |
|------|------|
| ☐ | ☐ |
| 6 | 3 |
| − 4 | 8 |

| tens | ones |
|------|------|
| ☐ | ☐ |
| 2 | 8 |
| − 1 | 9 |

**4**

| tens | ones |
|------|------|
| ☐ | ☐ |
| 8 | 5 |
| − 4 | 3 |

| tens | ones |
|------|------|
| ☐ | ☐ |
| 9 | 6 |
| − 5 | 7 |

| tens | ones |
|------|------|
| ☐ | ☐ |
| 6 | 2 |
| − 1 | 5 |

| tens | ones |
|------|------|
| ☐ | ☐ |
| 4 | 5 |
| − 2 | 6 |

**5**

| tens | ones |
|------|------|
| ☐ | ☐ |
| 7 | 9 |
| − 1 | 4 |

| tens | ones |
|------|------|
| ☐ | ☐ |
| 3 | 7 |
| − 1 | 2 |

| tens | ones |
|------|------|
| ☐ | ☐ |
| 6 | 4 |
| − 3 | 9 |

| tens | ones |
|------|------|
| ☐ | ☐ |
| 5 | 2 |
| − 3 | 6 |

## Problem Solving Visual Thinking

**6** We started with this: | Now we have this: | Draw what was subtracted.

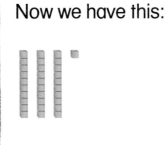

 **Notes for Home:** Your child used place-value materials to solve subtraction problems.
*Home Activity:* Ask your child to tell you which problems required regrouping in Exercise 4.
(96 − 57, 62 − 15, and 45 − 26)

## Subtract Two-Digit Numbers

**Learn** • • • • • • • • • • • • • • • • • • • • • • • • •

Looks like I need to regroup!

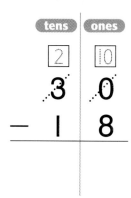

| tens | ones |
|------|------|
| 2 | 10 |
| 3 | 0 |
| − 1 | 8 |

Regroup if you need to.

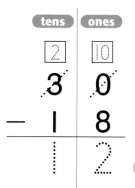

| tens | ones |
|------|------|
| 2 | 10 |
| 3 | 0 |
| − 1 | 8 |
| 1 | 2 |

Subtract the ones.
Then subtract the tens.

**Check** • • • • • • • • • • • • • • • • • • • • • • • • •

Subtract. Regroup if you need to.

**1**

| tens | ones |
|------|------|
| 3 | 15 |
| 4 | 5 |
| − 1 | 8 |
| 2 | 7 |

| tens | ones |
|------|------|
| ☐ | ☐ |
| 5 | 0 |
| − 3 | 4 |

| tens | ones |
|------|------|
| ☐ | ☐ |
| 6 | 8 |
| − 4 | 7 |

| tens | ones |
|------|------|
| ☐ | ☐ |
| 2 | 0 |
| − 1 | 4 |

**2**

| tens | ones |
|------|------|
| ☐ | ☐ |
| 7 | 3 |
| − 2 | 1 |

| tens | ones |
|------|------|
| ☐ | ☐ |
| 8 | 7 |
| − 5 | 7 |

| tens | ones |
|------|------|
| ☐ | ☐ |
| 9 | 0 |
| − 7 | 0 |

| tens | ones |
|------|------|
| ☐ | ☐ |
| 3 | 2 |
| − 1 | 4 |

**Talk About It** Do you always have to regroup when there's a zero in the ones place? Why or why not?

 **Notes for Home:** Your child found differences for subtraction problems. *Home Activity:* Ask your child to explain the two steps in the Learn section.

## Practice  • • • • • • • • • • • • • • • • • •

Subtract. Regroup if you need to.

③
```
 4 12
 52        93        54        60        85        42
-37       -61       -29       -13       -20       -19
 15
```

④
```
 83        60        39        57        20        46
-24       -40       -12       -38       -13       -25
```

⑤
```
 40        37        56        70        84        92
-25       -14       -47       -21       -39       -51
```

Follow the rule. Subtract.

⑥

| Subtract 15. | |
|---|---|
| 60 | |
| 45 | |
| 30 | |
| 15 | |

Find the rule. Write the missing number.

⑦

| Subtract ____. | |
|---|---|
| 80 | 68 |
| 60 | 48 |
| 40 | 28 |
| 20 | 8 |

## Problem Solving Critical Thinking

⑧ Julia's dog ate her math paper! This is all that was left.
What could the missing numbers be?
How do you know?

```
 3 17
 4 7
- 1
───
   2
```

**Notes for Home:** Your child solved subtraction problems. *Home Activity:* Ask your child to explain how he or she found the rule in Exercise 7.

336    three hundred thirty-six        **For additional practice, see Skills Practice Bank, page 534, Set 2.**

# Use Addition to Check Subtraction

**Learn** • • • • • • • • • • • • • • • • • • • • • • • • • • •

There are 55 frogs in the pond. 17 of the frogs are green. The rest are orange. How many frogs are orange?

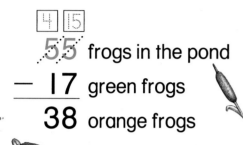

*I added to check my subtraction. These numbers are the same. My answer is correct!*

$$\begin{array}{r} {}^{4}\!\!\!\!\phantom{5}{}^{15} \\ 55 \\ -\ 17 \\ \hline 38 \end{array}$$ frogs in the pond / green frogs / orange frogs

$$\begin{array}{r} {}^{1}\phantom{3} \\ 38 \\ +\ 17 \\ \hline 55 \end{array}$$ orange frogs / green frogs / frogs in the pond

**Check** • • • • • • • • • • • • • • • • • • • • • • • • • • •

Subtract. Add to check.

**1**

$$\begin{array}{r} {}^{3}\!\!\!\!\phantom{4}{}^{13} \\ 43 \\ -\ 18 \\ \hline 25 \end{array} \qquad \begin{array}{r} 25 \\ +\ 18 \\ \hline 43 \end{array} \qquad \begin{array}{r} 61 \\ -\ 47 \\ \hline \ \end{array} + \begin{array}{r} \square \\ \square \\ \hline \square \end{array} \qquad \begin{array}{r} 38 \\ -\ 29 \\ \hline \ \end{array} + \begin{array}{r} \square \\ \square \\ \hline \square \end{array}$$

**Talk About It** Susan solved this subtraction problem and used addition to check her work. What mistake did she make?

$$\begin{array}{r} {}^{4}\phantom{5}{}^{12} \\ 5\!\!\!/2 \\ -\ 38 \\ \hline 24 \end{array} \qquad \begin{array}{r} {}^{1}\phantom{2} \\ 24 \\ +\ 38 \\ \hline 62 \end{array}$$

 **Notes for Home:** Your child used addition to check the differences for subtraction problems.
*Home Activity:* Ask your child to pick a problem in Exercise 1. Have him or her explain how the addition problem shows if the subtraction problem has been done correctly.

Subtract. Write an addition problem to check.

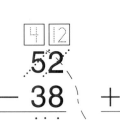

Are your numbers the same in both problems?

**2**

```
   4 12
  5̶2̶        14
 - 38   +  38
  14       52
```

```
  71
- 56   +
```

**3**

```
  80
- 40   +
```

```
  35
- 24   +
```

```
  60
- 43   +
```

**4**

```
  57
-  9   +
```

```
  99
- 62   +
```

```
  42
- 25   +
```

## Problem Solving Critical Thinking

**5** Joe did these subtraction problems.
Use addition to check his work.
Did he do both problems correctly? Explain.

```
  5 14      6 13
  6̶4̶        7̶3̶
- 29      - 38
  35        45
```

**Notes for Home:** Your child checked subtraction by adding. *Home Activity:* Ask your child to subtract and check 74 − 55. (19)

# Subtract Money

**Learn** • • • • • • • • • • • • • • • • • • • • • • • • • • • • • • •

Calvin has 63¢. At the museum he buys a toy for 55¢. How much money does he have left?

Don't forget the cents sign!

$$\begin{array}{r} \boxed{5}\ \boxed{13} \\ 63¢ \\ - 55¢ \\ \hline 8¢ \end{array}$$

Calvin has __8¢__ left.

**Check** • • • • • • • • • • • • • • • • • • • • • • • • • • • • • • •

Subtract.

**1**
$$\begin{array}{r} \boxed{4}\ \boxed{15} \\ 55¢ \\ -39¢ \\ \hline 16¢ \end{array} \qquad \begin{array}{r} 90¢ \\ -65¢ \\ \hline \end{array} \qquad \begin{array}{r} 66¢ \\ -24¢ \\ \hline \end{array} \qquad \begin{array}{r} 57¢ \\ -\ 8¢ \\ \hline \end{array} \qquad \begin{array}{r} 83¢ \\ -50¢ \\ \hline \end{array} \qquad \begin{array}{r} 35¢ \\ -\ 4¢ \\ \hline \end{array}$$

**2**
$$\begin{array}{r} 75¢ \\ -35¢ \\ \hline \end{array} \qquad \begin{array}{r} 47¢ \\ -29¢ \\ \hline \end{array} \qquad \begin{array}{r} 63¢ \\ -\ 5¢ \\ \hline \end{array} \qquad \begin{array}{r} 89¢ \\ -23¢ \\ \hline \end{array} \qquad \begin{array}{r} 57¢ \\ -\ 7¢ \\ \hline \end{array} \qquad \begin{array}{r} 48¢ \\ -29¢ \\ \hline \end{array}$$

**3**
$$\begin{array}{r} 60¢ \\ -51¢ \\ \hline \end{array} \qquad \begin{array}{r} 59¢ \\ -30¢ \\ \hline \end{array} \qquad \begin{array}{r} 40¢ \\ -\ 6¢ \\ \hline \end{array} \qquad \begin{array}{r} 72¢ \\ -43¢ \\ \hline \end{array} \qquad \begin{array}{r} 99¢ \\ -18¢ \\ \hline \end{array} \qquad \begin{array}{r} 22¢ \\ -13¢ \\ \hline \end{array}$$

**Talk About It** How are these problems alike? How are they different?

$$\begin{array}{r} 62 \\ -17 \\ \hline \end{array} \qquad \begin{array}{r} 62¢ \\ -17¢ \\ \hline \end{array}$$

**Notes for Home:** Your child subtracted two-digit numbers for amounts of money.
*Home Activity:* Ask your child to find 96¢ - 29¢. (67¢)

• • • • • • • • • • • •

Subtract.

**4**

| 2 7 | | | | | |
|---|---|---|---|---|---|
| .37¢ | 60¢ | 46¢ | 72¢ | 99¢ | 65¢ |
| − 28¢ | − 49¢ | − 4¢ | − 53¢ | − 79¢ | − 8¢ |
| 9¢ | | | | | |

**5**

| 85¢ | 58¢ | 16¢ | 43¢ | 77¢ | 86¢ |
|---|---|---|---|---|---|
| − 65¢ | − 50¢ | − 4¢ | − 14¢ | − 8¢ | − 37¢ |

---

**Mixed Practice** Add or subtract.

**6**

| 55 | 46 | 18¢ | 57 | 39 | 43¢ |
|---|---|---|---|---|---|
| + 22 | − 12 | + 9¢ | + 16 | − 6 | − 28¢ |

**7**

| 34 | 47¢ | 26 | 96¢ | 72 | 51¢ |
|---|---|---|---|---|---|
| − 6 | − 39¢ | + 8 | − 23¢ | + 9 | + 42¢ |

---

## Problem Solving

Solve.

**8** A pride of 15 lions is resting in the sun. 8 more lions join them. 11 lions leave. How many lions are there now?

_____ lions

**Notes for Home:** Your child solved addition and subtraction problems involving money. *Home Activity:* Ask your child to write a story using one of the subtraction problems in Exercise 5.

Name _____

## Main Idea and Details

Henry is writing a report about animals. In each paragraph, he writes the main idea and some details. The main idea tells what the paragraph is about. Details tell more about the main idea.

*Some animals are fast runners. A cheetah can run 70 miles an hour. A giraffe can run 32 miles an hour.*

| Some animals are fast runners. |
| :---: |
| **Main Idea** |

| A cheetah can run 70 miles an hour. | A giraffe can run 32 miles an hour. |
| :---: | :---: |
| **Detail** | **Detail** |

Henry's report got all mixed up. Help him match the sentences below with their main idea.

A lobster has 10 legs.

An alligator can live about 50 years.

A spider has 8 legs.

**1**

| Some animals have many legs. |
| :---: |
| **Main Idea** |

|  |  |
| :---: | :---: |
| **Detail** | **Detail** |

**Talk About It** Which sentence was not a detail for the main idea in Henry's report? Explain.

**Notes for Home:** Your child identified the details for a main idea. *Home Activity:* Ask your child to tell you which main idea on the page this detail tells about: Insects have 6 legs. (Some animals have many legs.)

Match the sentences below with their main ideas.

Blue whales can weigh 150 tons.

A sailfish can swim 68 miles in one hour.

African elephants can weigh 6 tons.

A giraffe can be 18 feet tall.

A seahorse can swim 1 mile in 10 hours.

**2** | Some animals weigh a lot more than we might think.

**Main Idea**

Detail                                    Detail

**3** | Some fish swim very fast and some swim very slowly.

**Main Idea**

Detail                                    Detail

## Critical Thinking

**4** These 2 sentences are details.

What could the main idea be?

African elephants can be 12 feet tall.

Grizzly bears can be 8 feet tall.

**Notes for Home:** Your child matched details with main ideas. *Home Activity:* Ask your child to tell another detail for one of the main ideas on this page.

Name _____

# Problem Solving: Too Much Information

**Learn** • • • • • • • • • • • • •

A python can be as long as 32 feet. It can weigh up to 150 pounds. An anaconda snake can be 37 feet long. How much longer can an anaconda snake be than a python?

*I don't need to know how much the python weighs. I'll cross out that sentence.*

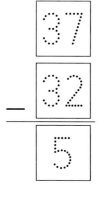

$$\begin{array}{r} 37 \\ -\ 32 \\ \hline 5 \end{array}$$

The anaconda snake can be ___5___ feet longer.

**Check** • • • • • • • • • •

Solve. Cross out the information you do not need.

**1** A bushmaster snake can be 12 feet long.
It has fangs more than 1 inch long.
A cobra can be 18 feet long.
How much longer can a cobra be than a bushmaster?

$$\begin{array}{c} \boxed{\phantom{0}} \\ -\ \boxed{\phantom{0}} \\ \hline \boxed{\phantom{0}} \end{array}\ \text{feet}$$

**2** A box turtle can live to be 120 years old.
Some snakes can live to be 30 years old.
An alligator can live to be 60 years old.
How much longer can an alligator live than a snake?

$$\begin{array}{c} \boxed{\phantom{0}} \\ -\ \boxed{\phantom{0}} \\ \hline \boxed{\phantom{0}} \end{array}\ \text{years}$$

**Talk About It** How did you decide which information you did not need?

**Notes for Home:** Your child identified unneeded information for solving problems.
*Home Activity:* Ask your child to explain why the information is unneeded in Exercises 1-2.

Solve. Cross out the information you do not need.

**3** The leatherback turtle travels 22 miles in one hour. The black mamba snake travels 7 miles in one hour. The largest reptile is 16 feet long. How much faster is the leatherback turtle than the black mamba snake?

$$\begin{array}{r} \square \\ -\ \square \\ \hline \square \end{array}$$ miles in one hour

**4** A male alligator can grow to be 12 feet long. An alligator can live to be 60 years old. A female alligator can grow to be 9 feet long. How much longer can a male alligator be than a female?

$$\begin{array}{r} \square \\ -\ \square \\ \hline \square \end{array}$$ feet

**Journal**

**5** Write a problem about pythons, turtles, or alligators with too much information. Have a friend solve it.

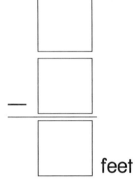

**Pythons**

Pythons are among the world's largest snakes.
An African rock python may grow to 32 feet long.
An Indian python may grow to 20 feet long.
A female python may lay up to 100 eggs.

**Turtles**

There are 7 main types of turtles.
Mud turtles may grow to be 6 inches long.
Pond turtles may grow to be 12 inches long.
Sea turtles may grow to be 28 inches long.

**Alligators**

Alligators live to be 50 or 60 years old.
Male alligators may grow to 12 feet long.
Female alligators may grow to 9 feet long.
Female alligators can lay 20 to 60 eggs.

**Notes for Home:** Your child solved problems by identifying unneeded information. *Home Activity:* Ask your child to write a different problem about pythons, turtles, or alligators with too much information.

**For additional practice, see Skills Practice Bank, page 535, Set 3.**

**PROBLEM SOLVING**

Name _____

# Mixed Practice
### Lessons 8–13

## Concepts and Skills

Subtract. Regroup if you need to.

**①**

| tens | ones |
|------|------|
| □ | □ |
| 6 | 5 |
| − 3 | 4 |

| tens | ones |
|------|------|
| □ | □ |
| 5 | 2 |
| − 2 | 9 |

| tens | ones |
|------|------|
| □ | □ |
| 4 | 0 |
| − 2 | 8 |

| tens | ones |
|------|------|
| □ | □ |
| 3 | 1 |
| − 1 | 6 |

**②**

$$87¢ - 14¢ \qquad 62¢ - 47¢ \qquad 70¢ - 23¢ \qquad 59¢ - 18¢ \qquad 90¢ - 26¢$$

Subtract. Write an addition problem to check.

**③**

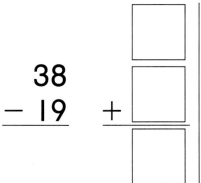    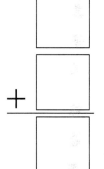    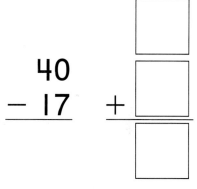

$$38 - 19 \quad + \boxed{\phantom{0}}$$
$$75 - 23 \quad + \boxed{\phantom{0}}$$
$$40 - 17 \quad + \boxed{\phantom{0}}$$

## Problem Solving

Solve. Cross out the information you do not need.

**④** An Indian python can be 20 feet long. An alligator can live to be 60 years old. A male alligator can be 12 feet long. How much longer can an Indian python be than a male alligator?

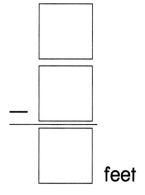

_____ feet

## Journal

**⑤** Write an addition problem to check this problem:  **57 − 8 = 39**

How do you know if the difference is correct or incorrect? Explain.

Name _____

## Concepts and Skills

Write the time.

**1**

_____ o'clock

_____ : _____

**2**

_____ : _____

**3**

_____ : _____

## Problem Solving

Use the chart to solve each problem.

**4** Which color of frogs was seen most often?

_____

**5** How many more **red** frogs than **yellow** frogs were seen?

_____ red frogs

### Frogs in the Jungle

| Frog Colors | Tally | Total |
|---|---|---|
| Blue | 卌 卌 | 10 |
| Red | 卌 || | 7 |
| Yellow | 卌 | 5 |

---

### Test Prep

Fill in the ○ for the correct answer.

Use mental math to add.

**6** 24 + 50 = _____

64    74    54    84
○     ○     ○     ○

**7** 59 + 30 = _____

59    69    89    99
○     ○     ○     ○

**Notes for Home:** Your child reviewed telling time, solving problems, and adding.
*Home Activity:* Ask your child where the hour hand and minute hand would be at 12 o'clock.
(Both hands would point at 12.)

Name _____

## Concepts and Skills

Subtract. You can use the chart.

1. $46 - 20 =$ _____

2. $34 - 10 =$ _____

3. $29 - 20 =$ _____

| 1 | 2 | 3 | 4 | 5 | 6 | 7 | 8 | 9 | 10 |
|---|---|---|---|---|---|---|---|---|----|
| 11 | 12 | 13 | 14 | 15 | 16 | 17 | 18 | 19 | 20 |
| 21 | 22 | 23 | 24 | 25 | 26 | 27 | 28 | 29 | 30 |
| 31 | 32 | 33 | 34 | 35 | 36 | 37 | 38 | 39 | 40 |
| 41 | 42 | 43 | 44 | 45 | 46 | 47 | 48 | 49 | 50 |

Find the nearest ten.
Estimate the difference.

4.  $\begin{array}{r} 73 \\ - 19 \\ \hline \end{array}$   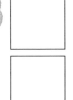 Think:  □

    □
    − □
    —
    □

73 − 19 is about _____.

Subtract.
Write an addition problem to check.

5.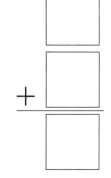

    $\begin{array}{r} 90 \\ - 38 \\ \hline \end{array}$   $+$   □ □ □

Subtract. Regroup if you need to.

6.  $\begin{array}{r} 75 \\ - 41 \\ \hline \end{array}$  $\begin{array}{r} 53¢ \\ - 6¢ \\ \hline \end{array}$  $\begin{array}{r} 40¢ \\ - 17¢ \\ \hline \end{array}$  $\begin{array}{r} 68 \\ - 31 \\ \hline \end{array}$  $\begin{array}{r} 50¢ \\ - 9¢ \\ \hline \end{array}$  $\begin{array}{r} 86 \\ - 52 \\ \hline \end{array}$

## Problem Solving

Solve. Cross out the information you do not need.

7.  On Monday, Kevin saw 14 cranes wading in
    a pond. The cranes were white and grey. On
    Wednesday, he saw 7 cranes. How many more
    cranes did he see on Monday than on Wednesday?

    □
    − □
    —
    □ cranes

**Notes for Home:** Your child reviewed Chapter 9 concepts, skills, and problem solving.
*Home Activity:* Ask your child to explain how to estimate 59 − 23. (60 − 20 = 40)

CHAPTER REVIEW

Name _____

# Chapter 9 Test

Subtract.

**1** $50 - 30 =$ ____    **2** $70 - 20 =$ ____

**3** $48 - 10 =$ ____    **4** $67 - 20 =$ ____

Find the nearest ten. Estimate the difference.

**5** $89 - 21$ is about ____.    **6** $72 - 48$ is about ____.

Subtract. Regroup if you need to.

**7**

| 60 | 37¢ | 29 | 50 | 84 | 92¢ |
|----|-----|----|----|----|-----|
| − 25 | − 6¢ | − 13 | − 19 | − 27 | − 49¢ |

Subtract. Write an addition problem to check.

**8**

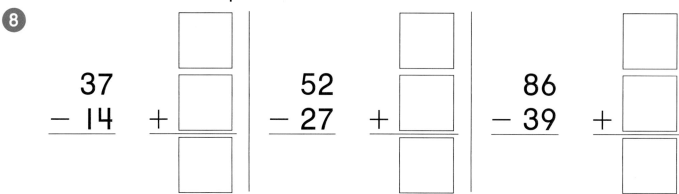

Solve. Cross out the information you do not need.

**9** An adult gorilla is about 6 feet tall. A wolf can live about 20 years. A howler monkey is only about 2 feet tall. About how much taller is an adult gorilla than a howler monkey?

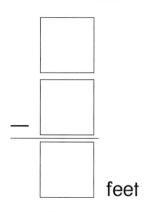

feet

**Notes for Home:** Your child was tested on two-digit subtraction concepts, skills, and problem solving. *Home Activity:* Ask your child to identify one problem in Exercise 7 which requires regrouping and one which does not. (37¢ − 6¢ and 29 − 13 do not require regrouping.)

Name _____

Mix up the number cards.
Make a stack.

Use the top two cards.
Write the numbers in the
squares in any order.

Subtract.

---

Do the activity again.

**1**    6   8
        ☐ ☐
      − ‾‾‾‾

**2**    7   2
        ☐ ☐
      − ‾‾‾‾

**3**    8   6
        ☐ ☐
      − ‾‾‾‾

**4**    8   0
        ☐ ☐
      − ‾‾‾‾

**5**    9   5
        ☐ ☐
      − ‾‾‾‾

**6**    7   0
        ☐ ☐
      − ‾‾‾‾

---

## Problem Solving  Critical Thinking

**7** Mario used four numbers from 1 through 9
to write a subtraction problem. The answer
to his problem was 47. What numbers
could he have used?

☐ ☐
− ☐ ☐
‾‾‾‾
 4  7

**Notes for Home:** Your child did an activity that tested Chapter 9 skills, concepts, and problem solving.
*Home Activity:* Ask your child to tell you another pair of numbers that could be used to solve Exercise 7.

Name _____

# Zoom to Zero!

## Keys You Will Use

You can subtract on a calculator without using [=] each time.

$100 - 24 - 35 - 18 = ?$

Press these keys.

## How to Play

**1** Play with a partner. Use counters to cover 3 or 4 numbers.

Use your [calculator] to subtract those numbers from 100.

**2** The player who gets closest to zero wins the round. He or she colors in the numbers that were covered by the counters.

**3** For the next round, players move the counters to new numbers and subtract from 100.

**4** To win, a player must color 12 numbers on his or her gameboard.

| 13 | 24 | 32 | 33 | 12 |
|----|----|----|----|----|
| 16 | 19 | 10 | 29 | 30 |
| 15 | 14 | 26 | 11 | 34 |
| 27 | 23 | 28 | 25 | 12 |
| 17 | 20 | 31 | 22 | 18 |

**Tech Talk** How can using a calculator help when you are subtracting more than one number?

💻💻 **Visit our Web site. www.parent.mathsurf.com**

# Speed Spin

The spinner below shows the speeds traveled by some fast animals. Find out how much faster some animals can travel than others.

1 Use a pencil and a paper clip to make a spinner. Then spin twice.

2 Compare the speeds of the two animals.

3 How much faster can one animal travel than the other?

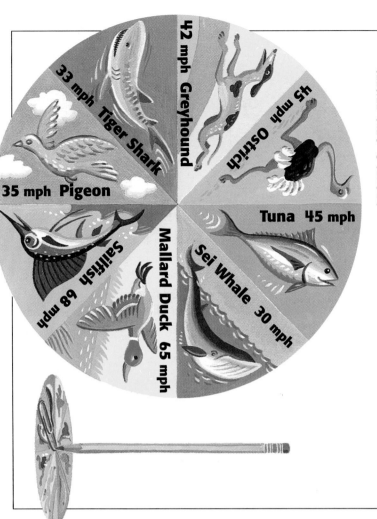

42 mph Greyhound

45 mph Ostrich

33 mph Tiger Shark

35 mph Pigeon

Tuna 45 mph

Sailfish 68 mph

Mallard Duck 65 mph

Sei Whale 30 mph

**Fold down**

# MathSoup

Scott Foresman - Addison Wesley    My Math Magazine    No. 9

Ready. Set...

# Math in Your World

## Boing!

Have you ever won a contest? Have you ever tickled a frog?

Four-year-old Cody Shilts did both. He won a frog jumping contest. His frog jumped about 19 feet in three hops.

People in the contest gave their frogs funny names. Cody called his frog Free Willy. The frog that has the record for the longest jump ever was named Rosie the Ribeter.

Complete the table to show how many hours each of these animals is asleep and awake during one day. Remember that there are 24 hours in one day.

| Animal | Hours Awake | Hours Asleep |
|---|---|---|
| Anteater | 12 | |
| Sloth | | 20 |
| Armadillo | | 19 |
| Squirrel | 10 | |
| Lemur | 8 | |

© Scott Foresman Addison Wesley

**Notes for Home:** Your child practiced subtraction and completed a table. *Home Activity:* Ask your child how many hours a koala is awake each day. (2)

**Notes for Home:** Your child practiced subtraction. *Home Activity:* Ask your child to compare the distance "jumped" by a frog on his or her chart to the distance jumped by Rosie the Ribeter.

# Snoozzzzz z z $_e$

Sleep is very important to good health. You need at least 10 hours of sleep every night. However, some animals need to sleep much more than you do. For example, a pig sleeps for about 13 hours a day.

**A koala spends more time asleep each day than any other animal–22 hours in all!**

1 Rosie the Ribeter jumped about 21 feet. About how much farther is that than Free Willy's jump?

_____ feet farther

2 Fill in the chart below with funny frog names. Roll three number cubes each with 4, 5, 6, 7, 8, and 9 on them. Add the numbers on the cubes to show how far one of the frogs on your chart "jumped." Repeat for the other names on your chart.

| Frog Name | Distance Jumped |
| --- | --- |
| | feet |
| | feet |
| | feet |

3 Write your own word problem asking how much farther one frog on your chart jumped than another.

# Create a Flap

In order to fly, birds flap their wings very fast. Some birds flap their wings faster than others.

The chart shows how many times some birds flap their wings in 10 seconds.

| Type of Bird | Flaps (in 10 seconds) |
|---|---|
| Heron 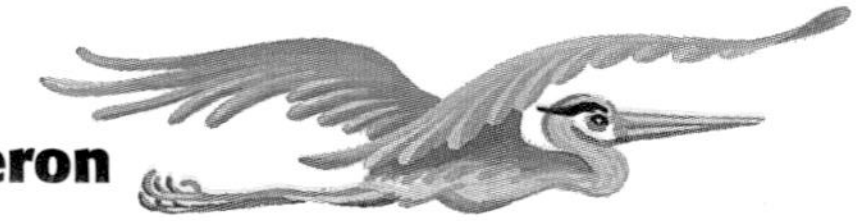 | 20 times |
| Pigeon 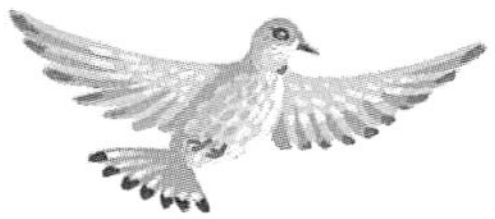 | 60 times |
| Starling 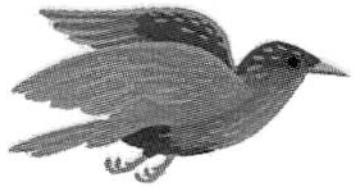 | 70 times |

**1** You try it! Count how many times you flap your arms in 10 seconds. Record your results.

_____ times

Use your data to answer the questions.

**2** Did you flap your arms **more** or **fewer** times in 10 seconds than a heron?

_____ times

**3** How many more or fewer times?

**4** How many more times can a pigeon flap its wings in 10 seconds than you flapped your arms?

_____ more times

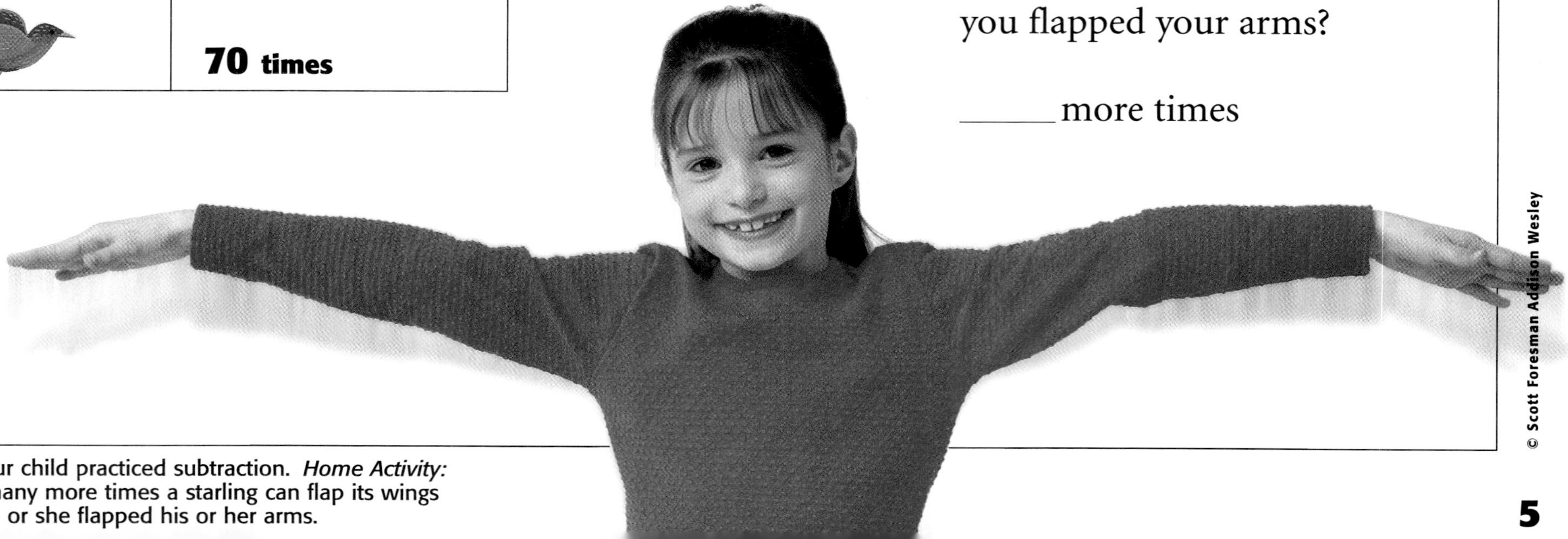

# Numbers to 1,000

## Math at Home

Dear Family,
Our class is starting Chapter 10. We will be learning about numbers up to 1,000. We will add and subtract larger numbers. Here are some activities we can do together.

### Ready, Set, Count!
Have your child find different ways to count to 100. Suggest counting by different numbers such as 10 or 25. Then help him or her count beyond 100.

### See and Say
Point out three-digit numbers, such as 592 or 327, in magazines, books, or addresses. Read the numbers aloud. Tell how many hundreds, tens, and ones. Help your child tell what number comes after each number.

### Community Connection

Look for three-digit numbers on buildings and signs. Read the numbers aloud. Then have your child tell you a number that is more or less.

**Visit our Web site. www.parent.mathsurf.com**

Name _____

**Explore** • • • • • • • • • • • • • • • • • • • • • • • •

Show 100 using ▊.

**Share** • • • • • • • • • • • • • • • • • • • • • • • •

How many ▪▪ do you need to show 100?

How many ▊ do you need to show 100?

**Notes for Home:** Your child explored making 100. *Home Activity:* Help your child explore other ways to show 100, for example, using 10 dimes to show 100 cents.

**Chapter 10 Lesson 1**                        three hundred fifty-seven  **357**

These are both 100.

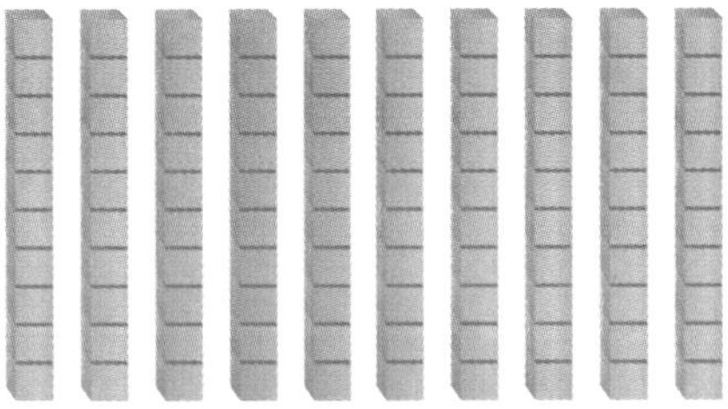

10 tens

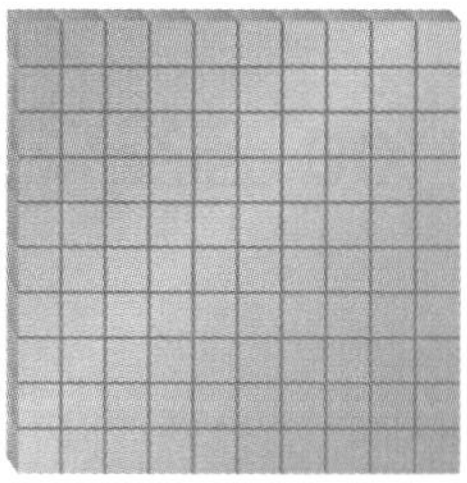

100

Write how many hundreds.
Write the number.

| | How many hundreds? | Write the number. |
|---|---|---|
| ① | 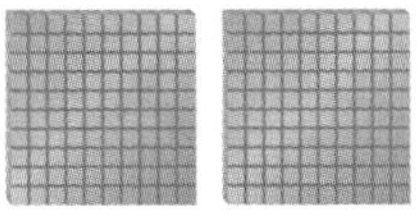 _2_ hundreds | 200 |
| ② | 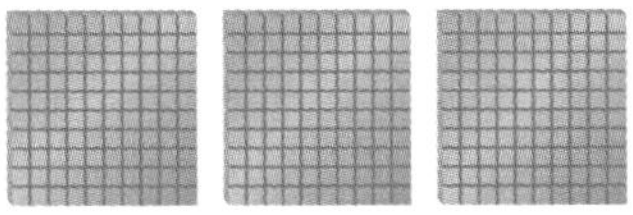 _____ hundreds | _____ |
| ③ | 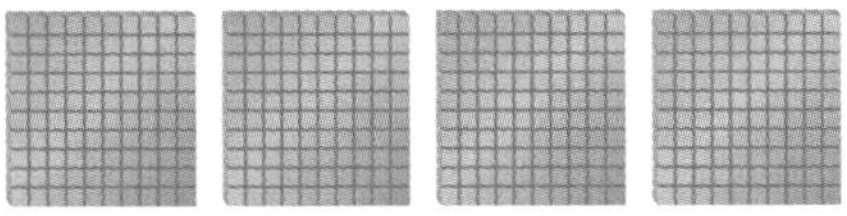 _____ hundreds | _____ |
| ④ | 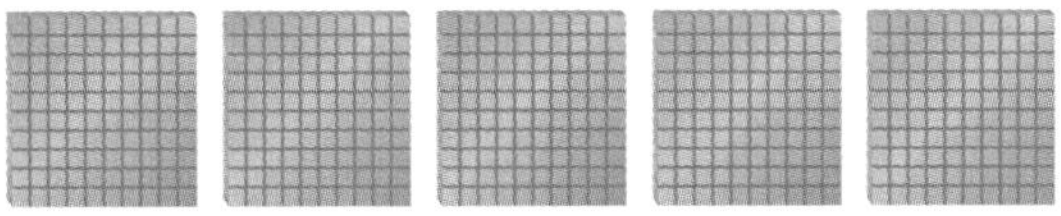 _____ hundreds | _____ |
| ⑤ | 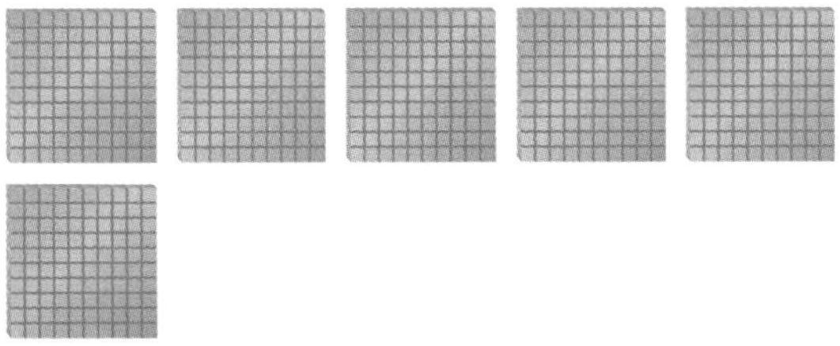 _____ hundreds | _____ |
| ⑥ | 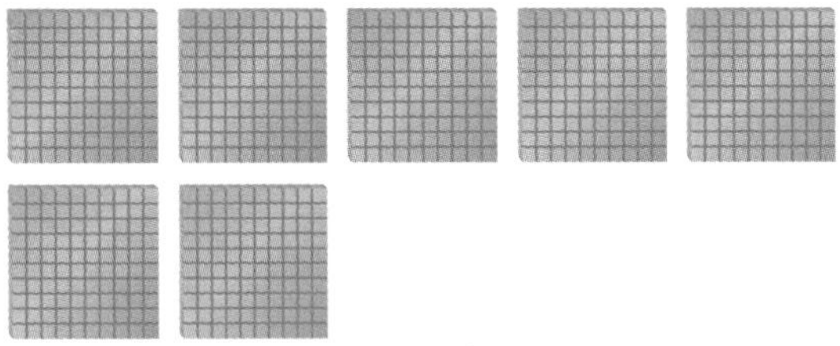 _____ hundreds | _____ |

**Journal**

⑦ Write five things you know about 100.

**Notes for Home:** Your child wrote how many hundreds and the number for different hundreds.
*Home Activity:* Ask your child how many hundreds are in 900. (9)

© Scott Foresman Addison Wesley

# Identify Hundreds

**Learn**

**Check**

Use [▦] to complete the chart.

| | Show this many. Write the number. | Show 100 less. Write the number. | Show 100 more. Write the number. |
|---|---|---|---|
| **1** | 200 | 100 | 300 |
| **2** | | _____ | _____ |
| **3** | | _____ | _____ |

**Talk About It** What pattern do you see in the chart?

**Notes for Home:** Your child showed groups of 100 and wrote the number for different hundreds.
*Home Activity:* Ask your child what numbers would be 100 less and 100 more than 500. (400, 600)

Use [grid] to complete the chart.

| | Show this many. Write the number. | Show 200 less. Write the number. | Show 200 more. Write the number. |
|---|---|---|---|
| **4** | [5 hundred-grids] 500 | 300 | 700 |
| **5** | [6 hundred-grids] _____ | _____ | _____ |
| **6** | [7 hundred-grids] _____ | _____ | _____ |

## Problem Solving Visual Thinking

**7** Gina needs 800 beads.

Circle bags to show 800.

**Notes for Home:** Your child practiced writing numbers for groups of 100. *Home Activity:* Ask your child to write the numbers that are 200 less than 700 and 200 more than 400. (500, 600)

**360** three hundred sixty

# Write Three-Digit Numbers

**Learn**

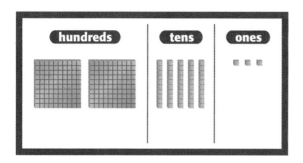

| hundreds | tens | ones |
|---|---|---|
| 2 | 5 | 3 |

253

*I count hundreds, tens, and ones. Then I write the number.*

two hundred fifty-three

**Check**

Use ⬚ and ▦ ∷ .

Write how many hundreds, tens, and ones. Then write the number.

**1**

| hundreds | tens | ones |
|---|---|---|
| 3 | 2 | 4 |

324

**2**

| hundreds | tens | ones |
|---|---|---|
|  |  |  |

_____

**3**

| hundreds | tens | ones |
|---|---|---|
|  |  |  |

_____

**4**

| hundreds | tens | ones |
|---|---|---|
|  |  |  |

_____

**Talk About It** What does the 3 stand for in each number?

386    138    423

**Notes for Home:** Your child wrote three-digit numbers. *Home Activity:* Ask your child what the 2 in 324 stands for. (2 tens)

Write how many hundreds, tens, and ones. Write the number.

You can use 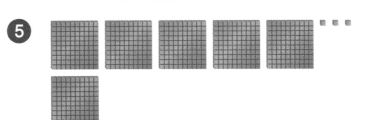 and 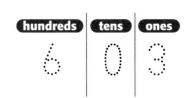  ...

**5**

| hundreds | tens | ones |
|----------|------|------|
| 6 | 0 | 3 |

603

**6**

| hundreds | tens | ones |
|----------|------|------|
| | | |

_____

**7**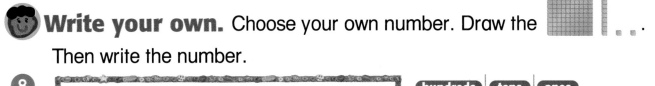

| hundreds | tens | ones |
|----------|------|------|
| | | |

_____

**Write your own.** Choose your own number. Draw the  ...
Then write the number.

**8**

| hundreds | tens | ones |
|----------|------|------|
| | | |

_____

## Problem Solving Patterns

Find each answer. What patterns do you see?

**9** How many [hundred square] in 500? _____

How many [tens bar] in 500? _____

How many [ones] in 500? _____

**10** How many [hundred square] in 700? _____

How many [tens bar] in 700? _____

How many [ones] in 700? _____

 **Notes for Home:** Your child practiced writing three-digit numbers. *Home Activity:* Help your child find a three-digit number on a package, can, or jar. Ask him or her to tell how many hundreds, tens, and ones are in the number.

**362** three hundred sixty-two

© Scott Foresman Addison Wesley

# Before, After, Between

**Learn** ● ● ● ● ● ● ● ● ● ● ● ● ● ● ● ● ● ● ● ● ● ● ● ● ● ● ● ●

Page 156 is one before page 157. Page 157 is one after page 156.

Page 157 is between pages 156 and 158.

**Check** ● ● ● ● ● ● ● ● ● ● ● ● ● ● ● ● ● ● ● ● ● ● ● ● ● ● ● ●

Write the missing numbers.

**1**

| 101 | 102 | 103 | 104 | 105 | 106 | 107 | 108 | 109 | 110 |
|-----|-----|-----|-----|-----|-----|-----|-----|-----|-----|
| 111 | 112 |     | 114 | 115 |     | 117 | 118 | 119 | 120 |
| 121 | 122 | 123 |     | 125 | 126 | 127 | 128 |     | 130 |
|     | 132 | 133 | 134 |     | 136 | 137 | 138 | 139 | 140 |
| 141 |     | 143 | 144 | 145 | 146 |     | 148 | 149 |     |
| 151 | 152 |     |     | 155 | 156 | 157 | 158 |     | 160 |
|     | 162 | 163 | 164 | 165 |     | 167 |     | 169 | 170 |
| 171 |     | 173 | 174 |     | 176 | 177 | 178 |     | 180 |
| 181 | 182 | 183 |     | 185 | 186 |     | 188 | 189 |     |
|     | 192 |     | 194 | 195 | 196 | 197 |     | 199 | 200 |

**Talk About It** What would the numbers be in the row that would come after 200? What would the numbers be in the row that would come before 101?

**Notes for Home:** Your child identified numbers that are before, after, and between other numbers. *Home Activity:* Point to a three-digit number. Ask your child to say the numbers that come one before and one after.

Write the number that comes one before.

② __184__, 185        _____, 131        _____, 116

③ _____, 243        _____, 653        _____, 500

④ _____, 524        _____, 187        _____, 469

Write the number that comes one after.

⑤ 419, __420__        721, _____        199, _____

⑥ 112, _____        578, _____        989, _____

⑦ 84, _____        344, _____        636, _____

Write the number that comes between.

⑧ 118, __119__, 120        299, _____, 301

⑨ 350, _____, 352        224, _____, 226

⑩ 541, _____, 543        695, _____, 697

## Problem Solving

⑪ Write all the even numbers between 340 and 360.

   __342, 344,__ _____

   _____

**Notes for Home:** Your child practiced identifying numbers that are one before, one after, and between other numbers. *Home Activity:* Pick a number between 100 and 200. Ask your child to say the two numbers that the number he or she picked is between.

Name _____

# Compare Numbers

**Learn** • • • • • • • • • • • • • • • • • • • • • • • • • • • •

Betty sells hundreds of beads.

She sold 250 large beads.

She sold 175 small beads.

Did she sell more large or small beads?

She sold more ⟨large⟩ beads.

*250 has more hundreds. 250 is greater than 175.*

Symbols can be used to compare numbers.

> means
is **greater than.**

< means
is **less than.**

= means
is **equal to.**

250 > 175

250 is greater than 175.

175 < 250

175 is less than 250.

250 = 250

250 is equal to 250.

**Check** • • • • • • • • • • • • • • • • • • • • • • • • • • • • •

Compare each number.

Write >, <, or =.

1. 423 ⟩ 353      501 ◯ 489      380 ◯ 380

2. 141 ◯ 241      677 ◯ 712      447 ◯ 399

3. 168 ◯ 168      750 ◯ 570      126 ◯ 216

**Talk About It** How would you compare 361 and 327?

**Notes for Home:** Your child used symbols to compare numbers. *Home Activity:* Ask your child to write the numbers 561 and 651 and then write the symbol to compare the numbers. (561 < 651)

**Chapter 10 Lesson 5**

three hundred sixty-five **365**

Compare the numbers.
Write >, <, or =.

> is greater than
< is less than
= is equal to

If the number of hundreds are the same, compare the tens. 2 tens is less than 7 tens.

4   432 < 454      631 ◯ 613

5   327 ◯ 516      823 ◯ 832

6   240 ◯ 212      409 ◯ 409

**Write your own.** Make true statements.
Use numbers between 200 and 300.

7   _____ > _____       8   _____ > _____

9   _____ < _____      10   _____ < _____

11   _____ = _____      12   _____ = _____

## Problem Solving Critical Thinking

Solve the riddle.

13   I am a number less than 345
and greater than 340.
I have 2 ones.
What number am I?

_____

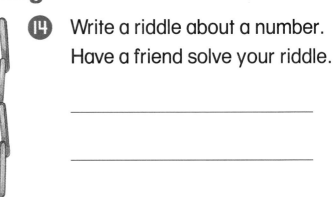

14   Write a riddle about a number.
Have a friend solve your riddle.

_____

_____

_____

**Notes for Home:** Your child practiced comparing numbers. *Home Activity:* Ask your child to pick two numbers between 100 and 999. Ask your child to write the two numbers with a "greater than" or "less than" symbol.

**For additional practice, see Skills Practice Bank, page 536, Set 1.**

# Order Numbers

**Learn** • • • • • • • • • • • • • • • • • • • • • • • • • • • • •

Table of Contents
Chapter 10

Cottonball
Caterpillar ..........312

Paper Plate
Porcupine ..........329

Standing Duck...336

Stuffed Bag
Bear ..............340

Brown Bag
Bunny ............351

A book's table of contents has numbers. The numbers tell the order of the pages.

These numbers are in order from least to greatest.

## 312, 329, 336, 340, 351

These numbers are in order from greatest to least.

## 351, 340, 336, 329, 312

**Check** • • • • • • • • • • • • • • • • • • • • • • • • • • • • •

Write the numbers in order from least to greatest.

**1**

140, 235, 318, 96, 421

_96_ , _140_ , _____ , _____ , _____

**2** 

480, 415, 453, 496, 437

_____ , _____ , _____ , _____ , _____

Write the numbers in order from greatest to least.

**3**

77, 415, 690, 152, 349

_690_ , _____ , _____ , _____ , _____

**Talk About It** Where would you put 602 in this list of numbers? Why?

202  502  702  902

**Notes for Home:** Your child put numbers in order. *Home Activity:* Ask your child to order 160, 43, 215, 189, and 300 from least to greatest. (43, 160, 189, 215, 300)

Write the numbers in order from least to greatest.

**4** 119, 93, 125, 201     _93_, _____, _____, _____

**5** 296, 228, 252, 283     _____, _____, _____, _____

Write the numbers in order from greatest to least.

**6** 348, 220, 464, 732     _732_, _____, _____, _____

**7** 605, 973, 751, 489     _____, _____, _____, _____

**8** 245, 217, 273, 229     _____, _____, _____, _____

## Write your own.

**9** List four numbers in order from least to greatest. Choose numbers between 400 and 500.

_____, _____, _____, _____

**10** List four numbers in order from greatest to least. Choose numbers between 600 and 800.

_____, _____, _____, _____

## Problem Solving Estimation

**11** These stacks of paper are for the art class. Draw lines to match each number to a stack. Then write the numbers in order from least to greatest.

150     115     50     100

_____, _____, _____, _____

**Notes for Home:** Your child practiced putting numbers in order. *Home Activity:* Ask your child where he or she would place 255 in Exercise 5. (between 252 and 283)

Name _____

## Problem Solving: Group Decision Making

**Learn** • • • • • • • • • • • • • •

**Understand** what the problem asks.

**Plan** how to solve the problem.

**Solve** the problem.

**Look back** to check your work.
"Does my answer make sense?"

*Use this guide to help you solve problems.*

**Check** • • • • • • • • • • • • • • • • • • • • • • • • • • • • • • •

Work with your group to solve the problem. Use the Problem Solving Guide.

**1**   Grove School sold 74 tickets to the craft fair.

38 people came in the front door.

27 people came in the side door.

How many people bought tickets but did not come?

**Understand** What does the problem ask?  *How many people*
*bought tickets but did not come to the fair?*

**Plan** How can you solve the problem? _____

_____

**Solve** Solve the problem. _____

_____

**Look Back** Check your work. Does your answer make sense? _____

_____

**Talk About It** How did using a Problem-Solving Guide help?

**Notes for Home:** Your child worked with a group and learned how to use the Problem Solving Guide.
*Home Activity:* Ask your child to think of another way to solve the story problem on this page.

PROBLEM SOLVING

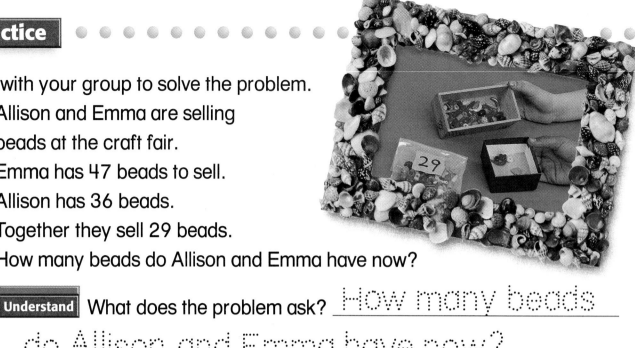

## Practice ● ● ● ● ● ● ● ● ● ● ● ● ● ●

Work with your group to solve the problem.

**2** Allison and Emma are selling
beads at the craft fair.
Emma has 47 beads to sell.
Allison has 36 beads.
Together they sell 29 beads.
How many beads do Allison and Emma have now?

**Understand** What does the problem ask? _How many beads_
_do Allison and Emma have now?_

**Plan** How can you solve the problem? _____

_____

**Solve** Solve the problem. _____

_____

**Look Back** Check your work. Does your answer make sense? _____

_____

### Write About It

**3** Explain how you know that your answer makes sense.

_____

_____

_____

**Notes for Home:** Your child practiced using the Problem Solving Guide. *Home Activity:* Ask your child how he or she can check the answer to the story problem.

**370** three hundred seventy

PROBLEM SOLVING

# Mixed Practice
## Lessons 1–7

## Concepts and Skills

Write 100 less and 100 more. You can use  .

|  | Show this many.<br>Write the number. | Show 100 less.<br>Write the number. | Show 100 more.<br>Write the number. |
|---|---|---|---|
| **1** | _____ | _____ | _____ |

Write how many hundred, tens, and ones. Then write the number.

**2**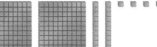

| hundreds | tens | ones |
|---|---|---|
| | | |

_____

Write the number one before, one after, or between.

**3**    _____, 132    829, _____    499, _____, 501

Compare. Write >, <, or =.

**4**  650 ◯ 610    330 ◯ 330    897 ◯ 905

## Problem Solving

Solve. Use the Problem Solving Guide to help.

**5**  Lee bought a bag of 50 colored tiles. Later he bought
30 more tiles. He used 62 tiles. How many
tiles does he have left?                    _____ tiles

## Journal

**6**  Think of another way to solve the problem. Write about it.

**Notes for Home:** Your child practiced writing and comparing three-digit numbers. *Home Activity:* Ask
your child to tell you the number one before 132 and the number one after 829. (131, 830)

# Cumulative Review
## Chapters 1-10

## Concepts and Skills

Count the money.

Write the total amount.

**1**

_____ ¢

## Problem Solving

Use the graph to answer the questions.

**2** How many more cards does Calvin have than Lamar?

_____ more

**3** How many cards do Calvin, Lamar, and Kim have together?

_____ cards

Each  means 10 cards.

| Card Collections | |
|---|---|
| Calvin | |
| Lamar | |
| Kim | |

---

### Test Prep

Fill in the ○ for the correct answer.

Subtract.

**4**
$$\begin{array}{r} 90 \\ -25 \\ \hline \end{array}$$

| 55 | 65 | 75 | 115 |
|----|----|----|-----|
| ○  | ○  | ○  | ○   |

**5**
$$\begin{array}{r} 57 \\ -30 \\ \hline \end{array}$$

| 17 | 27 | 37 | 87 |
|----|----|----|----|
| ○  | ○  | ○  | ○  |

 **Notes for Home:** Your child reviewed counting money, using a graph to solve problems, and subtracting. *Home Activity:* Ask your child to look at the graph and tell how many more cards Lamar has than Kim. (20 more)

Name _____

# Add and Subtract Mentally

**Learn**

*I can do these in my head. Can you?*

| 2 | 20 | 200 |
|---|---|---|
| + 3 | + 30 | + 300 |
| 5 | 50 | 500 |

| 9 | 90 | 900 |
|---|---|---|
| − 4 | − 40 | − 400 |
| 5 | 50 | 500 |

**Check**

Add or subtract. Use mental math.

① 
| 4 | 40 | 400 |
|---|---|---|
| + 3 | + 30 | + 300 |

② 
| 6 | 60 | 600 |
|---|---|---|
| − 2 | − 20 | − 200 |

③ 
| 5 | 50 | 500 |
|---|---|---|
| + 1 | + 10 | + 100 |

④ 
| 8 | 80 | 800 |
|---|---|---|
| − 3 | − 30 | − 300 |

⑤ 
| 7 | 70 | 700 |
|---|---|---|
| + 2 | + 20 | + 200 |

⑥ 
| 9 | 90 | 900 |
|---|---|---|
| − 6 | − 60 | − 600 |

⑦ 
| 1 | 10 | 100 |
|---|---|---|
| + 6 | + 60 | + 600 |

⑧ 
| 5 | 50 | 500 |
|---|---|---|
| − 4 | − 40 | − 400 |

**Talk About It** What patterns do you see in the problems above?

**Notes for Home:** Your child learned to add and subtract mentally. *Home Activity:* Ask your child to add 500 and 300 mentally and to tell you what basic fact he or she used. (500 + 300 = 800; 5 + 3 = 8)

**Chapter 10 Lesson 8**

three hundred seventy-three  **373**

Add or subtract. Use mental math.

(9)
```
    40        200        300        50       400
  + 20      + 100      + 200      + 30     + 500
    60
```

(10)
```
    50        900        700        40        20
  - 30      - 300      - 500      - 10      - 10
```

Follow the rule.

(11)

| Add 100. | |
|----------|------|
| 300 | 400 |
| 200 | |
| 500 | |
| 400 | |

(12)

| Subtract 10. | |
|--------------|---|
| 620 | |
| 850 | |
| 170 | |
| 210 | |

(13)

| Add 30. | |
|---------|---|
| 700 | |
| 450 | |
| 320 | |
| 570 | |

Use mental math!

## Problem Solving Patterns

Add or subtract. What patterns do you see?

(14)
```
    2        22       222
  + 4      + 44     + 444
```

(15)
```
    3        33       333
  + 4      + 44     + 444
```

(16)
```
    9        99       999
  - 7      - 77     - 777
```

(17)
```
    8        88       888
  - 5      - 55     - 555
```

**Notes for Home:** Your child practiced adding and subtracting using mental math. *Home Activity:* Ask your child to explain how to use mental math to add: 300 + 400. (3 + 4 = 7; 300 + 400 = 700)

**374** three hundred seventy-four

Name _____

# Add Three-Digit Numbers

**Learn** • • • • • • • • • • • • • • • • • • • • • • • • • • • • •

Parker School is having an art show.

247 people came on Monday.

132 people came on Tuesday.

How many people in all came to the art show?

Add the ones first. Then add the tens and the hundreds.

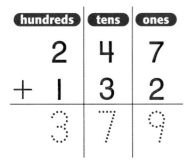

| hundreds | tens | ones |
|:---:|:---:|:---:|
| 2 | 4 | 7 |
| + 1 | 3 | 2 |
| 3 | 7 | 9 |

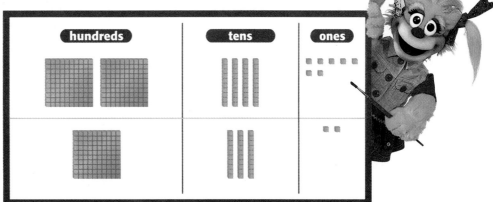

379 people came to the art show.

**Check** • • • • • • • • • • • • • • • • • • • • • • • • • • • • •

Use ▭ and ▦ . Show each number. Add.

1.

| hundreds | tens | ones |
|:---:|:---:|:---:|
| 1 | 2 | 5 |
| + 3 | 3 | 4 |

2.

| hundreds | tens | ones |
|:---:|:---:|:---:|
| 3 | 1 | 4 |
| + 1 | 2 | 2 |

| hundreds | tens | ones |
|:---:|:---:|:---:|
| 1 | 2 | 4 |
| + 7 | 5 | 1 |

| hundreds | tens | ones |
|:---:|:---:|:---:|
| 2 | 3 | 5 |
| + 4 | 5 | 2 |

**Talk About It** How is adding three-digit numbers like adding two-digit numbers?

**Notes for Home:** Your child learned how to add three-digit numbers without regrouping.
*Home Activity:* Ask your child to add 512 + 246. (758)

Show each number. Add. You can use 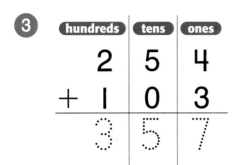 and ⬛ ▮ . . .

**3**

| hundreds | tens | ones |
|---|---|---|
| 2 | 5 | 4 |
| + 1 | 0 | 3 |
| 3 | 5 | 7 |

| hundreds | tens | ones |
|---|---|---|
| 3 | 1 | 6 |
| + 2 | 7 | 0 |

| hundreds | tens | ones |
|---|---|---|
| 1 | 2 | 8 |
| + 4 | 5 | 1 |

**4**

$$316 + 201$$  $$421 + 15$$  $$352 + 124$$  $$247 + 101$$  $$451 + 34$$

**5**

$$129 + 30$$  $$341 + 128$$  $$170 + 312$$  $$206 + 172$$  $$612 + 35$$

**6**

$$403 + 215$$  $$159 + 220$$  $$325 + 72$$  $$508 + 261$$  $$412 + 45$$

## Problem Solving

**7** Fill in the missing numbers.

| hundreds | tens | ones |
|---|---|---|
| ☐ | 1 | ☐ |
| + 1 | ☐ | 6 |
| 4 | 8 | 9 |

| hundreds | tens | ones |
|---|---|---|
| 2 | ☐ | 6 |
| + ☐ | 7 | ☐ |
| 5 | 9 | 8 |

**Notes for Home:** Your child practiced adding three-digit numbers without regrouping .
*Home Activity:* Ask your child to explain how he or she solved the problems with missing numbers.

# Add Three-Digit Numbers With or Without Regrouping

**Learn** • • • • • • • • • • • • • • • • • • • • • • • • • • •

Find 243 + 391.

Regroup 10 tens to make 100.

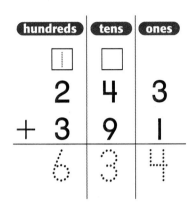

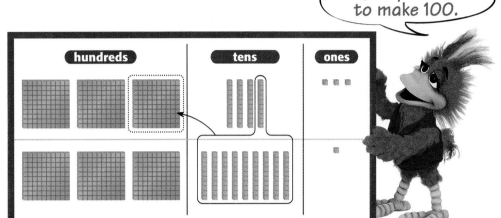

|  | hundreds | tens | ones |
|---|---|---|---|
|  | ☐ | ☐ |  |
|  | 2 | 4 | 3 |
| + | 3 | 9 | 1 |
|  | 6 | 3 | 4 |

**Check** • • • • • • • • • • • • • • • • • • • • • • • • • • •

Use 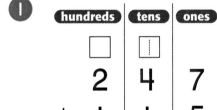 and ▦ ▪ ▪ ▪ .

Show each number.

Add. Regroup if you need to.

**1**

|  | hundreds | tens | ones |
|---|---|---|---|
|  | ☐ | ☐ |  |
|  | 2 | 4 | 7 |
| + | 1 | 1 | 5 |
|  | 3 | 6 | 2 |

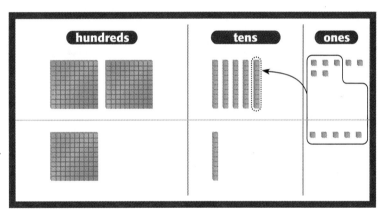

**2**

| hundreds | tens | ones |
|---|---|---|
| ☐ | ☐ |  |
| 4 | 3 | 6 |
| + 2 | 5 | 7 |

| hundreds | tens | ones |
|---|---|---|
| ☐ | ☐ |  |
| 1 | 6 | 2 |
| + 5 | 3 | 6 |

| hundreds | tens | ones |
|---|---|---|
| ☐ | ☐ |  |
| 3 | 2 | 9 |
| + 3 | 5 | 4 |

**Talk About It** How do you know when you need to regroup?

**Notes for Home:** Your child learned how to add two three-digit numbers with or without regrouping. *Home Activity:* Have your child show you how to add 136 + 283. (419)

Add. Regroup if you need to. You can use ☐☐☐ and ▦ ▮ ...

**3**

| hundreds | tens | ones |
|---|---|---|
| ☐ | ⬚ | |
| 2 | 4 | 9 |
| + 1 | 3 | 6 |
| 3 | 8 | 5 |

| hundreds | tens | ones |
|---|---|---|
| ☐ | ☐ | |
| 4 | 0 | 9 |
| + 2 | 1 | 3 |

| hundreds | tens | ones |
|---|---|---|
| ☐ | ☐ | |
| | 5 | 3 |
| + 5 | 5 | 4 |

**4**

$$453 + 512$$   $$274 + 61$$   $$548 + 425$$   $$524 + 135$$   $$347 + 72$$

**5**

$$281 + 356$$   $$402 + 315$$   $$569 + 50$$   $$216 + 312$$   $$167 + 25$$

## Problem Solving

Solve.

**6** Marco's class made 378 notecards.

Jason's class made 265 notecards.

How many notecards did the two classes make altogether?

☐
+ ☐
☐  notecards

**Notes for Home:** Your child practiced adding with and without regrouping. *Home Activity:* Ask your child to pick two numbers between 100 and 400 and find their sum. Ask if he or she needed to regroup and explain why or why not.

Name _____

# That's Sum Toss!

**Players** 2

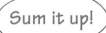
Sum it up!

**What You Need**

2 number cubes

**How to Play**

1. Toss the number cubes.

2. Use your toss to make a two–digit number. Write it on your chart.

3. Toss again. Write the number.

4. Add the numbers.

5. Take turns. For your next turns, toss the number cubes once. Write the number and add it to the last sum.

6. After 6 turns, the player with the greatest sum wins.

| hundreds | tens | ones |
|---|---|---|
| | | |
| + | | |
| | | |
| + | | |
| | | |
| + | | |
| | | |
| + | | |
| | | |
| + | | |
| | | |
| + | | |

**PRACTICE**

**Notes for Home:** Your child played an addition game. *Home Activity:* Ask your child to think of a two-digit number and add it to the last sum on this page.

Name _____

## STOP and Practice

Write how many hundreds, tens, and ones. Then write the number.

 **1**

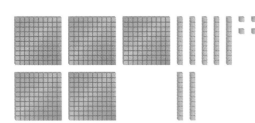

| hundreds | tens | ones |
|----------|------|------|
|          |      |      |

_____

Write the number that comes one before, one after, or between.

**2**   _____, 300     499, _____     769, _____, 771

Compare. Write >, <, or =.

**3**   736 ◯ 763     981 ◯ 918     515 ◯ 515

Add or subtract. Use mental math.

**4**
$$\begin{array}{r} 100 \\ + 600 \\ \hline \end{array} \qquad \begin{array}{r} 400 \\ + 200 \\ \hline \end{array} \qquad \begin{array}{r} 60 \\ + 20 \\ \hline \end{array} \qquad \begin{array}{r} 40 \\ - 20 \\ \hline \end{array} \qquad \begin{array}{r} 600 \\ - 100 \\ \hline \end{array}$$

Add. Regroup if you need to. You can use  and [blocks].

**5**
$$\begin{array}{r} 532 \\ + 134 \\ \hline \end{array} \qquad \begin{array}{r} 439 \\ + 22 \\ \hline \end{array} \qquad \begin{array}{r} 480 \\ + 182 \\ \hline \end{array} \qquad \begin{array}{r} 340 \\ + 430 \\ \hline \end{array} \qquad \begin{array}{r} 608 \\ + 82 \\ \hline \end{array}$$

## Riddle

**6**   Solve.

I'm less than 125 and greater than 120.

Add 100 to me and all my digits are the same.

What number am I? _____

**Notes for Home:** Your child practiced writing, comparing, adding, and subtracting numbers.
*Home Activity:* Ask your child to add 300 + 400. (700)

Name _____

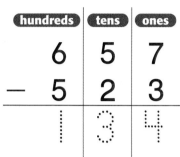

# Subtract Three-Digit Numbers

**Learn** • • • • • • • • • • • • • • • • • • • • • • • • • • • • • • •

The craft store had 657 rolls of yarn in January.

523 rolls were sold during the year.

How many rolls were left at the end of the year?

> Subtract the ones first. Then subtract the tens and the hundreds.

| hundreds | tens | ones |
|----------|------|------|
| 6 | 5 | 7 |
| − 5 | 2 | 3 |
| 1 | 3 | 4 |

134 rolls are left.

**Check** • • • • • • • • • • • • • • • • • • • • • • • • • • • • • • •

Use [ ▭ ▭ ▭ ] and ⬛ . Subtract.

**1**

| hundreds | tens | ones |
|----------|------|------|
| 3 | 8 | 6 |
| − 2 | 5 | 1 |

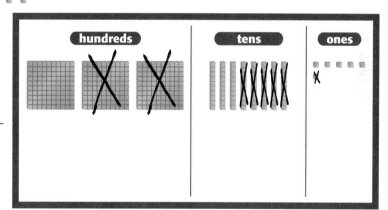

**2**

| hundreds | tens | ones |
|----------|------|------|
| 7 | 2 | 6 |
| − 1 | 1 | 4 |

| hundreds | tens | ones |
|----------|------|------|
| 5 | 8 | 9 |
| − 4 | 1 | 6 |

| hundreds | tens | ones |
|----------|------|------|
| 6 | 9 | 5 |
| − 1 | 3 | 2 |

**Talk About It** How is subtracting three-digit

numbers like subtracting two-digit numbers?

**Notes for Home:** Your child learned how to subtract two three–digit numbers without regrouping.
*Home Activity:* Ask your child to explain how to find the answer to 350-200.

Show each number. Subtract. You can use  and  .

**3**

| hundreds | tens | ones |
|---|---|---|
| 5 | 3 | 9 |
| − 2 | 3 | 5 |
| 3 | 0 | 4 |

| hundreds | tens | ones |
|---|---|---|
| 6 | 2 | 5 |
| − 4 | 1 | 3 |

| hundreds | tens | ones |
|---|---|---|
| 9 | 8 | 5 |
| − 4 | 0 | 4 |

**4**

$$679 - 151$$ $$487 - 237$$ $$389 - 64$$ $$573 - 120$$ $$759 - 52$$

**5**

$$574 - 301$$ $$215 - 102$$ $$695 - 12$$ $$728 - 315$$ $$956 - 412$$

## Write About It

**6** Use this subtraction problem to write a math story. Then solve.

$$796 - 531$$

_____

_____

_____

_____

_____

_____

**Notes for Home:** Your child practiced subtracting three-digit numbers without regrouping.
*Home Activity:* Ask your child to write another math story using the problem in Exercise 6.

Name _____

# Subtract Three-Digit Numbers With or Without Regrouping

**Learn** • • • • • • • • • • • • • • • • • • • • • • • • • • •

Subtract 427 − 173.

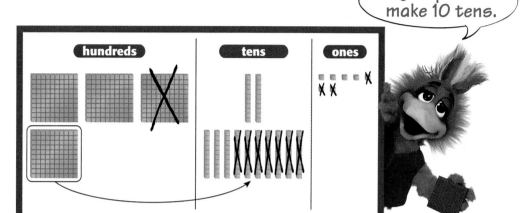

Regroup 100 to make 10 tens.

| hundreds | tens | ones |
|----------|------|------|
| 3 | 12 | |
| 4 | 2 | 7 |
| − 1 | 7 | 3 |
| 2 | 5 | 4 |

**Check** • • • • • • • • • • • • • • • • • • • • • • • • • •

Use ▭ and ▦ ▫ .
Subtract. Regroup if you need to.

**1**

| hundreds | tens | ones |
|----------|------|------|
| | 8 | 15 |
| 6 | 9 | 5 |
| − 2 | 4 | 8 |
| 4 | 4 | 7 |

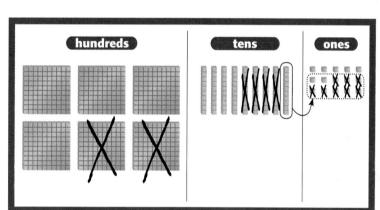

**2**

| hundreds | tens | ones |
|----------|------|------|
| □ | □ | □ |
| 7 | 4 | 5 |
| − 5 | 3 | 1 |

| hundreds | tens | ones |
|----------|------|------|
| □ | □ | □ |
| 5 | 2 | 9 |
| − 2 | 8 | 3 |

| hundreds | tens | ones |
|----------|------|------|
| □ | □ | □ |
| 4 | 6 | 1 |
| − 2 | 5 | 3 |

**Talk About It** How are these problems alike?
How are they different?

```
  374          374
− 120        − 129
```

**Notes for Home:** Your child learned how to subtract two three–digit numbers with regrouping.
*Home Activity:* Have your child show you how to find: 827 − 319. (508)

 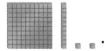
Subtract. Regroup if you need to. You can use [□□□] and [▦] ▮ · · .

**3**

| hundreds | tens | ones |
|---|---|---|
| □ | 2 | 17 |
| 5 | 3 | 7 |
| − 3 | 1 | 9 |
| 2 | 1 | 8 |

| hundreds | tens | ones |
|---|---|---|
| □ | □ | □ |
| 7 | 2 | 1 |
| − 4 | 1 | 4 |

| hundreds | tens | ones |
|---|---|---|
| □ | □ | □ |
| 4 | 2 | 9 |
| − 1 | 6 | 1 |

**4**

| 645 | 589 | 741 | 846 | 957 |
|---|---|---|---|---|
| − 218 | − 16 | − 230 | − 92 | − 427 |

**5**

| 759 | 537 | 372 | 450 | 725 |
|---|---|---|---|---|
| − 613 | − 64 | − 158 | − 310 | − 91 |

## Problem Solving Critical Thinking

**6** You need to regroup. What numbers could you write in the boxes?

| hundreds | tens | ones |
|---|---|---|
| 5 | □ | 7 |
| − 2 | 4 | □ |

**7** You do not need to regroup. What numbers could you write in the boxes?

| hundreds | tens | ones |
|---|---|---|
| 5 | □ | 7 |
| − 2 | 4 | □ |

**Notes for Home:** Your child practiced subtracting three-digit numbers with and without regrouping .
*Home Activity:* Ask your child to write a three-digit subtraction problem that needs regrouping and show you how to solve it.

**For additional practice, see Skills Practice Bank, page 536, Set 2.**

Name _____

## Use Picture Clues

James is shopping for art supplies.
Can you help him find what he needs?

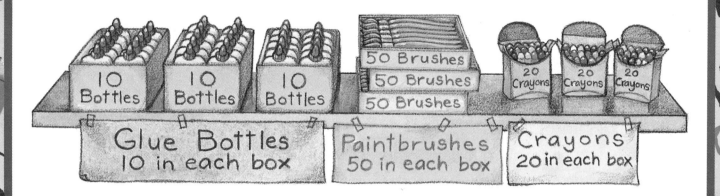

50 Brushes
50 Brushes
50 Brushes

10 Bottles    10 Bottles    10 Bottles

20 Crayons    20 Crayons    20 Crayons

Glue Bottles
10 in each box

Paintbrushes
50 in each box

Crayons
20 in each box

Use the picture to answer the questions.

1. James buys two boxes of glue. How many bottles of glue does he buy?

   _____ bottles

2. How many paint brushes are on the shelf?

   _____ paintbrushes

3. How many crayons are in the picture?

   _____ crayons

4. James needs 40 crayons. Circle 40 crayons in the picture.

5. James wants 150 paintbrushes. How many boxes does he need?

   _____ boxes

6. James buys two boxes of crayons. How many crayons are left on the shelf?

   _____ crayons

**Talk About It** How did the pictures help you find each of the answers above?

**Notes for Home:** Your child used details in a picture to answer questions. *Home Activity:* Ask your child how many bottles of glue are in 3 boxes. (30 bottles)

Carrie has 30 jars of paint. She buys 2 more boxes of paint. How many jars of paint does she have in all?

7 What information do you need from the picture to solve the problem?

_____

_____

_____

_____

8 Solve. _____ jars of paint

9 Use the above picture to write a problem. Have a friend solve it.

_____

_____

_____

_____

**Journal**

10 Write about how the picture helped you solve the problems.

**Notes for Home:** Your child solved a story problem using pictures and addition. *Home Activity:* Ask your child how many colored stones he or she would have in two bags. (400 colored stones)

Name _____

# Problem Solving: Use Data from a Picture

**Learn** • • • • • • • • • • • • •

**PROBLEM SOLVING GUIDE**
Understand • Plan • Solve • Look Back

You need 250 craft
sticks for a project.
Which bins could you use?
Circle your answer.

150 + 100 = 250
I'll circle these.
Which other bins
could I choose?

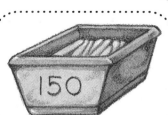
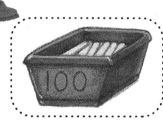

**Check** • • • • • • • • • • • • • • • • • • • • • • • •

Use the picture to answer the questions.

1. Gregory needs 270 colored
   stones for an art project.
   Which bags could he use?
   Circle them in red.

2. Luisa needs 250 stones.
   Which bags could she use?
   Circle them in blue.

3. Walt used two bags of stones that
   each had fewer than 100. How
   many stones did he use?

   _____ stones

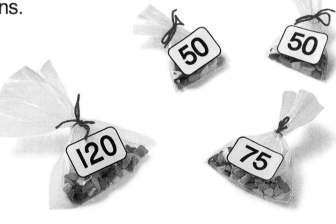

**Talk About It** Which other bags of stones could Luisa use?

**Notes for Home:** Your child used the pictures on this page to solve problems. *Home Activity:* Ask your
child to make up his or her own problem using some of the pictures on this page.

*Chapter 10 Lesson 13*

three hundred eighty-seven **387**

PROBLEM SOLVING

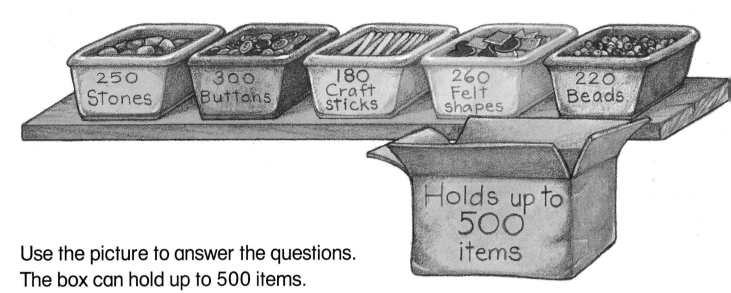

250 Stones    300 Buttons    180 Craft sticks    260 Felt shapes    220 Beads

Holds up to 500 items

Use the picture to answer the questions.
The box can hold up to 500 items.

**4** Jean puts the bin of buttons in the box. What else can she put in?

craft sticks

**5** Sam put 470 items in the box. What did he put in?

_____

**6** Elise put the felt shapes in the box. What else can she put in?

_____

**7** Lucy put 400 items in the box. What did she put in?

_____

Derrick puts 480 items in the box.
What items did he put in the box?
Give two possible combinations.

**8** _____

**9** _____

## Critical Thinking

**10** Are there 3 bins that could be put in the box together? Explain your answer.

Notes for Home: Your child used the numbers in this picture to solve problems.
*Home Activity:* Ask your child which two items add to make 560. (the buttons and the felt shapes)

**For additional practice, see Skills Practice Bank, page 536, Set 3.**

Name _____

# Mixed Practice
**Lessons 8–13**

## Concepts and Skills

Add or subtract. Use mental math.

**1**
$$300 + 200 \qquad 400 + 500 \qquad 70 - 20 \qquad 600 - 300 \qquad 33 + 44$$

Add or subtract. Regroup if you need to.

**2**
$$253 + 34 \qquad 837 - 184 \qquad 394 + 255 \qquad 754 - 34 \qquad 842 + 128$$

## Problem Solving

Use the picture to answer the questions.

**3** Wayne and his father need 375 craft sticks to build a model of a log cabin. How many boxes of craft sticks do they need?

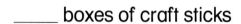

_____ boxes of craft sticks

**4** Donald has 3 boxes of craft sticks. How many more boxes of craft sticks does he need to build a model that uses 525 craft sticks?

_____ more boxes of craft sticks

## Journal

**5** How did the pictures help you answer the questions about building model log cabins? Write about it.

**Notes for Home:** Your child practiced adding and subtracting numbers and solving problems. *Home Activity:* Ask your child how many craft sticks there would be in 2 boxes. (150 craft sticks)

Name _____

# Cumulative Review
### Chapters 1–10

## Concepts and Skills

Write the number of tens and ones.

Then write the number.

**1**

_____ tens and _____ ones

_____

**2**

_____ tens and _____ ones

_____

Does the activity take more or less than one minute?

Circle **more** or **less.**

**3** taking a bath

**more**          **less**

**4** reading a book

**more**          **less**

**5** pouring milk

**more**          **less**

**6** raking leaves

**more**          **less**

## Test Prep

Fill in the ○ for the correct answer.

Add.

**7**      25¢
     + 13¢
     ____

| 38¢ | 28¢ | 12¢ | 48¢ |
| ○ | ○ | ○ | ○ |

**8**      17¢
     + 35¢
     ____

| 32¢ | 42¢ | 47¢ | 52¢ |
| ○ | ○ | ○ | ○ |

 **Notes for Home:** Your child reviewed identifying and writing tens and ones, estimating if activities take more or less than one minute, and adding amounts of money. *Home Activity:* Ask your child to think of an activity that takes less than one minute and an activity that take more than one minute.

**390**   three hundred ninety

Name _____

## Vocabulary

Choose from these words to complete each sentence.

| greater than | less than | equal to |
| --- | --- | --- |

**1** 216 is _____ 261.

**2** 425 is _____ 385.

## Concepts and Skills

Write how many hundreds, tens, and ones. Then write the number.

**3**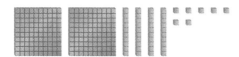

| hundreds | tens | ones |
| --- | --- | --- |
| | | |

_____

Compare the numbers. Write >, <, or =.

**4** 294 ◯ 291    83 ◯ 83    516 ◯ 519

Write the numbers in order from greatest to least.

**5** 358, 704, 129, 816    _____, _____, _____, _____

**6** Add or subtract.
Use mental math.

$$\begin{array}{r} 70 \\ -\ 30 \\ \hline \end{array} \qquad \begin{array}{r} 600 \\ +\ 100 \\ \hline \end{array} \qquad \begin{array}{r} 400 \\ +\ 200 \\ \hline \end{array}$$

**7** Add or subtract.
Regroup if you need to.

$$\begin{array}{r} 804 \\ +\ 172 \\ \hline \end{array} \qquad \begin{array}{r} 637 \\ -\ 475 \\ \hline \end{array} \qquad \begin{array}{r} 418 \\ +\ 173 \\ \hline \end{array}$$

## Problem Solving

Use the picture to answer the question.

**8** Ms. Silva's class needs exactly 450 beads for a craft project. Circle the bags they could use.

 **Notes for Home:** Your child reviewed Chapter 10 vocabulary, concepts, skills, and problem solving. *Home Activity:* Ask your child to find the bags in the picture that total 300. (Two bags of 150 each, or one bag of 125 and one bag of 175.)

Name _____

# Chapter 10 Test

Write how many hundreds, tens, and ones. Then write the number.

①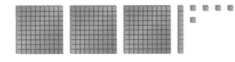

| hundreds | tens | ones |
|----------|------|------|
|          |      |      |

_____

Write the number that comes one before, one after, or between.

②  _____ , 524     839, _____     212, _____ , 214

Compare the numbers. Write >, <, or =.

③ 152 ◯ 152     734 ◯ 741     695 ◯ 692

Write the numbers in order from least to greatest.

④ 514, 827, 279, 613     _____ , _____ , _____ , _____

Add or subtract.
Use mental math.

⑤
```
  60     400     700
+ 20   − 100   − 200
```

Add or subtract.
Regroup if you need to.

⑥
```
 524     842     317
+123   − 224   + 435
```

Use the picture to answer the question.

⑦ Mr. Simon's class needs exactly
425 colored stones for a craft project.
Which bags could they use?
Circle the bags.

**Notes for Home:** Your child was tested on Chapter 10 concepts, skills, and problem solving learned in Chapter 10. *Home Activity:* Ask your child to find the bags in the picture that total 525. (Two bags of 200 and one bag of 125.)

# Performance Assessment

## Chapter 10

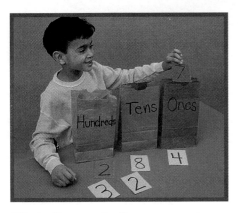

Pick 2 cards from each bag. Write your numbers.

Compare your numbers.

Write an addition problem. Solve.

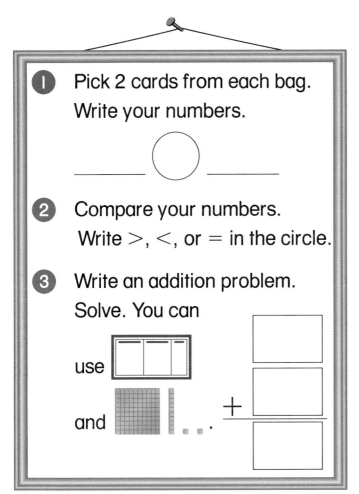

**1** Pick 2 cards from each bag. Write your numbers.

_____ ◯ _____

**2** Compare your numbers. Write >, <, or = in the circle.

**3** Write an addition problem. Solve. You can use ▭ and ▦ ▪.

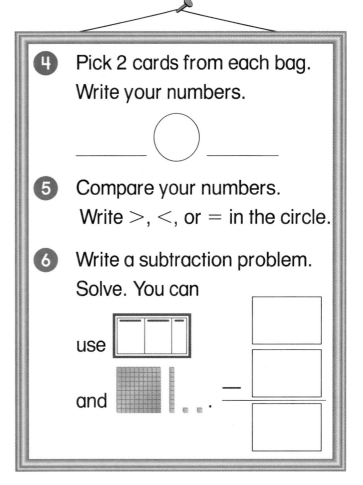

**4** Pick 2 cards from each bag. Write your numbers.

_____ ◯ _____

**5** Compare your numbers. Write >, <, or = in the circle.

**6** Write a subtraction problem. Solve. You can use ▭ and ▦ ▪.

## Critical Thinking

**7** Take all of the numbers out of the bags. Make an addition problem using 2 three-digit numbers with the greatest possible sum. Then use the numbers to make a problem with the smallest possible sum.

**Notes for Home:** Your child did an activity that tested Chapter 10 concepts, skills, and problem solving. *Home Activity:* Ask your child to think of two three-digit numbers below 500 and write an addition or subtraction problem using them.

PERFORMANCE ASSESSMENT

Name _____

**Explore with a COMPUTER**

# Picture 1,000!

## Computer Skills You Will Need

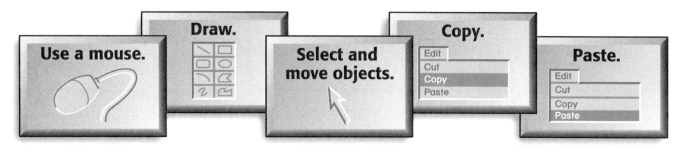

Use a mouse.

Draw.

Select and move objects.

Copy.
Edit
Cut
Copy
Paste

Paste.
Edit
Cut
Copy
Paste

**1** Draw a small shape using your computer's drawing program.

**2** Copy and paste your shape to make as many shapes as you can. Print your page.

**3** How many shapes are on your page? _____ shapes

**4** Use your [calculator]. Find the number of shapes one group in your class made.

**5** Find the number of shapes your class made.

**6** With your class, make a display of your shapes when they total 1,000.

**Tech Talk** How did you find the number of shapes your class made?

# Make a Mosaic

For many years, artists have used colored tiles to make works of art called **mosaics.**

Follow these steps to make a mosaic drawing or pattern.

**1** Use a piece of grid paper and at least 3 different colors of crayons.

**2** Color squares on the grid paper to make a picture or a pattern.

**3** Find how many total squares are in your mosaic picture. Explain how you found out.

**Fold down**

# MathSurf

Scott Foresman - Addison Wesley

My Math Magazine

No. 10

## Made by Hand

# American Arts

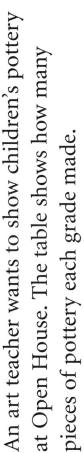

An art teacher wants to show children's pottery at Open House. The table shows how many pieces of pottery each grade made.

| Grade | Pieces Made |
|-------|-------------|
| 1 | 89 |
| 2 | 117 |
| 3 | 131 |
| 4 | 119 |
| 5 | 142 |

1 Find the three grades that made the greatest number of pieces. What is the total number of pieces made by these three grades?

_____

2 Write the numbers of pieces made in order from least to greatest.

_____ , _____ , _____ , _____ , _____

Bridget is a member of the Cherokee Nation living in Oklahoma. Bridget's grandparents demonstrate crafts and skills at the Cherokee Heritage Center.

1 Bridget's grandmother weaves baskets using dried vines. To make one basket, she uses 110 vines. To make a second basket, she uses 175 vines. How many more vines does she use for the second basket?

_____ more vines

**Notes for Home:** Your child practiced adding and subtracting three-digit numbers. *Home Activity:* Ask your child to find 415 − 290. (125)

2

# Fired Up About Clay

Travis Owens doesn't study art only at school. He makes clay pottery at home with his mother and father.

A beautiful bowl takes many hours of hard work. First, Travis uses a potter's wheel to form a bowl. Then he lets the clay dry completely. Finally, Travis "fires," or bakes, the clay twice. A coating called glaze is put on the bowl when it is fired.

**2** Bridget's grandmother also makes quilts. In January, she spent 125 hours working on a quilt. In February, she worked on the quilt for 115 more hours. How many hours did Bridget's grandmother work in 2 months?

_____ hours

**Notes for Home:** Your child practiced ordering and adding three-digit numbers. *Home Activity:* Ask your child to add to find the total number of pieces made for all the grades. (598)

6

**Math Fun**

# Patch Patterns

These quilts were made by African American quilters from small patches of cloth.

Photographs courtesy of The Kentucky Quilt Project, Inc., Louisville, KY

What patterns do you see? Use a pattern to make your own paper quilt!

**What You Need**

construction paper    scissors    glue

**What You Do**

1 Use colored construction paper to make paper patches this size.

2 Use green, blue, and red paper. Cut out 7 squares from each color.

3 Find the answer for each problem. Use the code to match each answer to a color patch. Glue the color patch on top of each square.

**Use the color patch shown for answers from:**

401-500.

501-600.

601-700.

| | | | |
|---|---|---|---|
| 464<br>+ 221 | 300<br>+ 290 | 300<br>+ 290 | 300<br>+ 290 |

| | | | |
|---|---|---|---|
| 464<br>+ 221 | 300<br>+ 290 | 100<br>+ 406 | 505<br>+ 100 |
| 300<br>+ 201 | 576<br>– 132 | 268<br>+ 220 | 400<br>+ 190 |
| 888<br>– 280 | 900<br>– 350 | 700<br>– 120 | 957<br>– 321 |

**Notes for Home:** Your child practiced adding, subtracting, and ordering three-digit numbers. *Home Activity:* Ask your child to put the following numbers in order from least to greatest: 563, 490, 679. (490, 563, 679)

## Math at Home

Dear Family,
Our class is starting
Chapter 11. We will
be learning about
measurement.
Here are some
activities we can
do together.

### Assistant Chef
When cooking or baking, ask your child to help you by measuring some of the ingredients, especially some of those that are measured with cups.

### Measure It
Help your child use a ruler to measure various small household objects. Measure spaces to find if the space can be used to store a certain object.

### Community Connection

When you are at the grocery store, help your child estimate how many pounds food items, such as apples, will weigh. Then let your child use a scale to see how much the items actually weigh.

**Visit our Web site. www.parent.mathsurf.com**

Name _____

**Explore** • • • • • • • • • • • • • • • • • • • • • • • • • • • • •

Choose an object in your classroom to measure. Measure its length.

door     desk     chair     teacher's desk     chalkboard     shelves

Choose a unit of measure.

clip     Snap Cube     pencil     eraser     shoe

Measure the same object with a different unit. Complete the chart.

| | What I Measured | Unit of Measure | Measurement |
|---|---|---|---|
| **1** | _____ | _____ | about _____ |
| | | _____ | about _____ |
| **2** | _____ | _____ | about _____ |
| | | _____ | about _____ |
| **3** | _____ | _____ | about _____ |
| | | _____ | about _____ |

**Share** • • • • • • • • • • • • • • • • • • • • • • • • • • • • •

Which units were easiest to use? Why?

**Notes for Home:** Your child used different objects to measure the lengths of objects in the classroom. *Home Activity:* Ask your child to measure the length of his or her bed with an object such as a spoon or straw.

EXPLORE

Estimate the lengths.

Use Snap Cubes to measure.

Write the numbers.

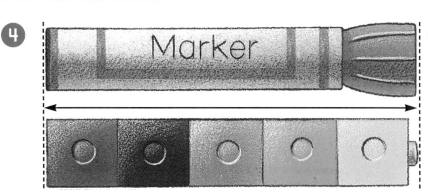

I think it looks about 5 cubes long.

**4**

Estimate: about _____ Snap Cubes          Measure: about _____ Snap Cubes

**5**

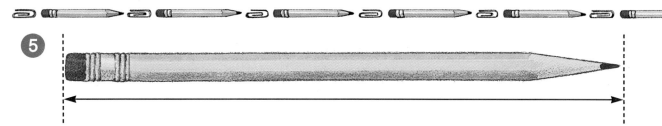

Estimate: about _____ Snap Cubes          Measure: about _____ Snap Cubes

**6**

Glue Stick

Estimate: about _____ Snap Cubes          Measure: about _____ Snap Cubes

## Problem Solving Critical Thinking

**7** Pablo measured how tall he is.

First he measured with paper clips.

Then he measured with pencils.

Did Pablo need more paper clips

or more pencils? Explain.

**Notes for Home:** Your child estimated and measured the lengths of objects using Snap Cubes.
*Home Activity:* Ask your child to use a paper clip or another similar object to measure the lengths of objects in the kitchen.

Name _____

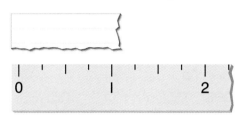

**Learn** • • • • • • • • • • • • • • • • • • • • • • • • •

The piece of paper
is about 1 inch long.

0       1       2

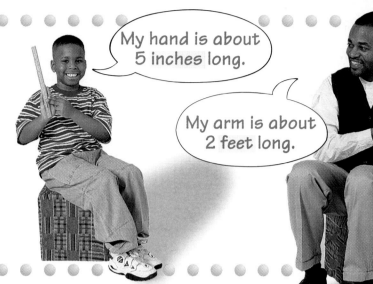

My hand is about
5 inches long.

My arm is about
2 feet long.

**Check** • • • • • • • • • • • • • • • • • • • • • •

Estimate the length in inches. Measure with your inch ruler.

| What to Measure | Estimate | Measurement |
|---|---|---|
| 1 length of your shoe | about _____ inches | about _____ inches |

Estimate the length or height in feet. Measure with your yardstick.

| What to Measure | Estimate | Measurement |
|---|---|---|
| 2 a friend's height | about _____ feet | about _____ feet |
| 3 a friend's arm span | about _____ feet | about _____ feet |

**Talk About It** What are two more objects you
would measure using inches? using feet? Explain.

**Notes for Home:** Your child learned how to measure length and height in inches and feet.
*Home Activity:* Ask your child to measure the lengths of your arm, foot, arm span, and height using
inches or feet.

**Practice** • • • • • • • • • • • • • • • • • • • • • • • • • • •

Estimate about how many inches.
Measure with your inch ruler.

④

| What to Measure | Estimate | Measurement |
|---|---|---|
| length of your finger | about _____ inches | about _____ inches |

Estimate about how many feet.
Measure with your yardstick.

⑤

| What to Measure | Estimate | Measurement |
|---|---|---|
| length of your arm | about _____ feet | about _____ feet |

 **Write your own.**

Draw or write what you will measure.

Use inches or feet to measure.

⑥

| What You Will Measure | Estimate | Measurement |
|---|---|---|
|  | about _____ | about _____ |

## Problem Solving Visual Thinking

⑦ Look at the two pieces of ribbon. Circle the piece of ribbon
you think is longer. Explain. You can use string to check.

 **Notes for Home:** Your child practiced estimating and measuring lengths in inches and feet.
*Home Activity:* Ask your child to estimate and measure the length of an object in inches or feet
and tell you the measurement.

# Inches, Feet, and Yards

Yuko just completed a jump.
She wants to find out how long it is.
She can measure length in inches,
feet, and yards.

Work with a partner. Use an inch ruler and a yardstick.

**1** Find how many inches are in 1 foot.

There are __12__ inches in 1 foot.

**2** Find how many inches are in 2 feet.

There are _____ inches in 2 feet.

**3** Find how many inches are in 3 feet.

There are _____ inches in 3 feet.

**4** Find how many feet are in 1 yard.

There are _____ feet in 1 yard.

**Talk About It** How did you find the number
of inches in 1 foot? the number of feet in 1 yard?

**Notes for Home:** Your child investigated inches, feet, and yards. *Home Activity:* Ask your child to tell
you which is longer—an inch, a foot, or a yard. (yard)

Complete the chart.

| | Estimate. Find an object about this long. | Write or draw your object. | Measure length to check. |
|---|---|---|---|
| **5** | about 1 inch | | about _____ |
| **6** | about 1 foot | | about _____ |
| **7** | about 1 yard | | about _____ |

## Problem Solving Estimation

Circle the best estimate for the length of each object.

**8**

about 1 inch

about 1 foot

about 1 yard

**9**

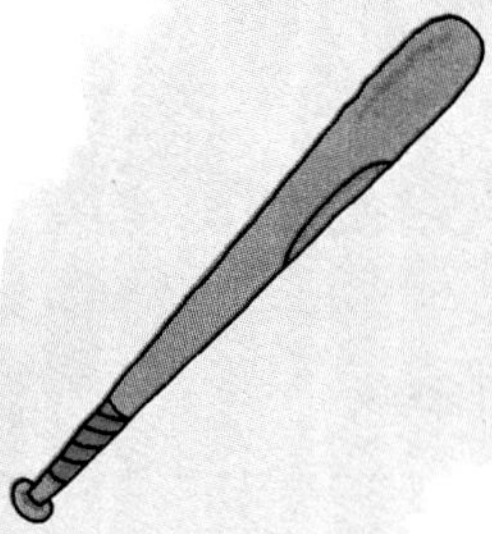

about 1 inch

about 1 foot

about 1 yard

**10**

about 1 inch

about 1 foot

about 1 yard

**Notes for Home:** Your child found and measured objects that were about 1 inch, 1 foot, and 1 yard long. *Home Activity:* Ask your child to find objects at home that are about 1 inch, 1 foot, and 1 yard long.

# Every Inch Counts

**Players** 2 – 4

## What You Need

I red beanbag for a target

I blue beanbag for each player

ruler or yardstick

## How to Play

1. One player tosses the red beanbag. This will be the target for all players.

2. Each player tosses a blue beanbag as close to the target as possible.

3. After each turn, each player measures the distance in inches from the target to his or her beanbag.

4. Record your score after each turn. Each inch from the target counts as one point.

5. Do the activity 2 more times. Find your total number of points.

6. The player with the **least** number of points, wins!

| Turn | Distance from Target | Points |
|------|---------------------|--------|
| I | _____ inches | _____ |
| 2 | _____ inches | _____ |
| 3 | _____ inches | _____ Total _____ |

**Notes for Home:** Your child practiced measuring distances using inches while playing a game.
*Home Activity:* Play the game with your child. Use small blocks or crumpled paper if beanbags are not available.

Name _____

Estimate the length of this picture.
Use Snap Cubes to measure.

**1**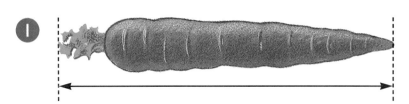

Estimate: about _____ Snap Cubes    Measure: about _____ Snap Cubes

Estimate the length of the chalkboard
in your classroom. Use a yardstick to measure.

**2**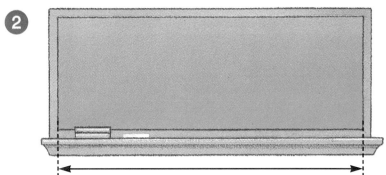

Estimate: about _____ feet

Measure: about _____ feet

Complete the chart. Use an inch ruler and a yardstick to measure.

| What to Measure | Estimate | Measure |
|---|---|---|
| **3** | about _____ inches | about _____ inches |
| **4** Write or draw your own. | about _____ | about _____ |

**Notes for Home:** Your child practiced estimating and measuring lengths. *Home Activity:* Have your child estimate the length of a favorite toy in inches. Ask your child to measure the length of the toy, then compare the actual length to his or her estimate.

# Centimeters and Meters

**Learn** • • • • • • • • • • • • • • • • • • • • • • • • • • •

A golf club is about 1 meter long.

Your finger is about 1 centimeter wide.

**Check** • • • • • • • • • • • • • • • • • • • • • • • • • • •

Estimate the length in centimeters.

Measure with a centimeter ruler. Write the numbers.

**1**

Estimate: about _____ centimeters

Measure: about _____ centimeters

**2**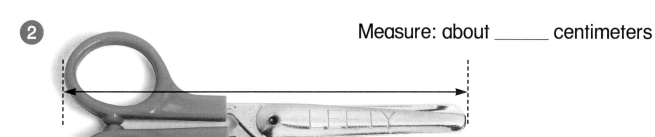

Estimate: about _____ centimeters

Measure: about _____ centimeters

**Talk About It** Estimate how many centimeters

are in a meter. Then find out how many.

Explain how you found out.

**Notes for Home:** Your child estimated and measured length using centimeters. *Home Activity:* Ask your child to use the width of his or her finger to estimate the length of a book in centimeters.

**Practice** ● ● ● ● ● ● ● ● ● ● ● ● ● ● ● ● ● ● ● ● ● ● ● ● ● ●

Estimate about how many meters.
Measure with a meter stick.

| What to Measure | Estimate | Measure |
|---|---|---|
| **3** width of the doorway | about _____ meters | about _____ meters |
| **4** length of the bulletin board | about _____ meters | about _____ meters |
| **5** distance from the doorway to the other side of your classroom | about _____ meters | about _____ meters |

**PRACTICE**

## Mental Math

**6** Solve.

Cara is 130 centimeters tall.
Maya is 115 centimeters tall.
How much taller is Cara?

_____ centimeters taller

**Notes for Home:** Your child estimated and measured length in meters. *Home Activity:* Ask your child to find something at home that is about 1 meter in length, width, or height.

# Perimeter

**Learn** ● ● ● ● ● ● ● ● ● ● ● ● ● ● ● ● ● ● ● ● ● ● ● ● ● ● ● ● ●

Mark is making a box. He wants to put
ribbon around the edge of the box.
How much ribbon does he need?

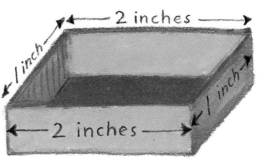

2 inches

1 inch

1 inch

2 inches

Add the lengths of all the sides.

$$\underline{\;1\;} + \underline{\;2\;} + \underline{\;1\;} + \underline{\;2\;} = \underline{\;6\;} \text{ inches around}$$

Mark needs __6__ inches of ribbon.

**Check** ● ● ● ● ● ● ● ● ● ● ● ● ● ● ● ●

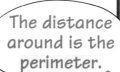
The distance
around is the
perimeter.

Pick three objects you can measure. Draw them.
Measure the lengths of all the sides with your inch ruler.
Add to find each perimeter.

| What I Measured | About how many inches around? |
| --- | --- |
| ❶ | _____ inches around |
| ❷ | _____ inches around |
| ❸ | _____ inches around |

**Talk About It** What does the perimeter tell you about an object?

**Notes for Home:** Your child found the perimeter of objects. *Home Activity:* Ask your child to find
the perimeter of an object at home, such as a box of cereal.

**4** Mark an **X** on the shape that you estimate has
the greatest perimeter. Measure the lengths
of the sides. Add to find the perimeter.
Circle the shape with the greatest perimeter.

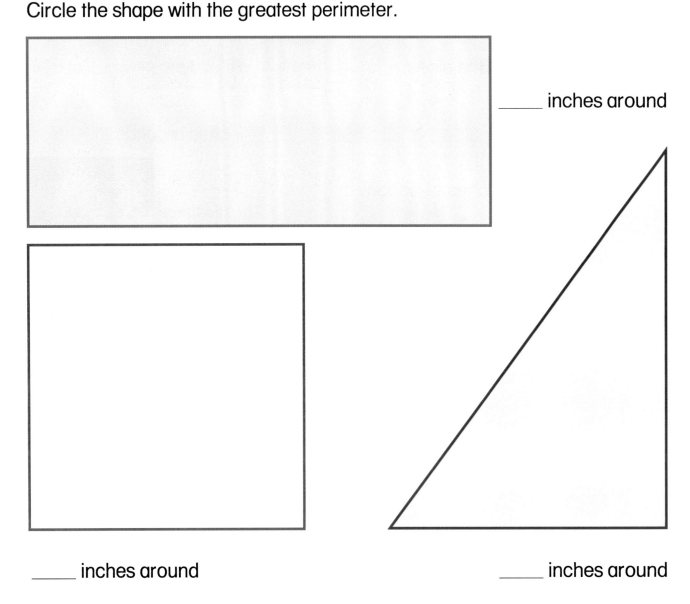

_____ inches around

_____ inches around

_____ inches around

## Problem Solving Visual Thinking

**5** Do not measure. Which has the
greater perimeter, the triangle
or the rectangle? Explain why.

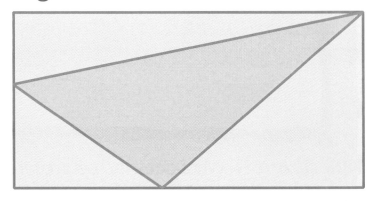

**Notes for Home:** Your child practiced finding the perimeter of different shapes. _Home Activity:_ Ask your
child to explain how he or she found each perimeter on the page.

Name _____

**Explore**

Use 6 . Cover 6 squares.

Make different shapes.

Color each shape you make.

Be sure to match up the sides of each Snap Cube.

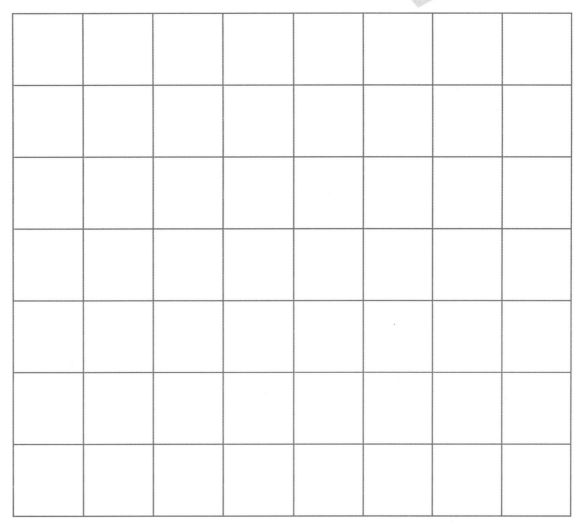

**Share**

How many shapes did you make?

Did you find all the ways?

**Notes for Home:** Your child used Snap Cubes to make shapes that covered 6 squares on a grid.
*Home Activity:* Ask your child to color a new shape on the grid that covers 6 squares.

**Connect**

I covered 8 squares with 8 Snap Cubes.

I counted 8 square units.

One Snap Cube covers one square unit.

**EXPLORE**

Estimate how many 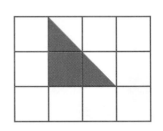 will cover each shape. Then find how many. Draw square units to show what you did.

**1**

Estimate: _____ Snap Cubes

Measure: _____ Snap Cubes

**2**

Estimate: _____ Snap Cubes

Measure: _____ Snap Cubes

**Talk About It** How could you find the number of square units inside the triangle?

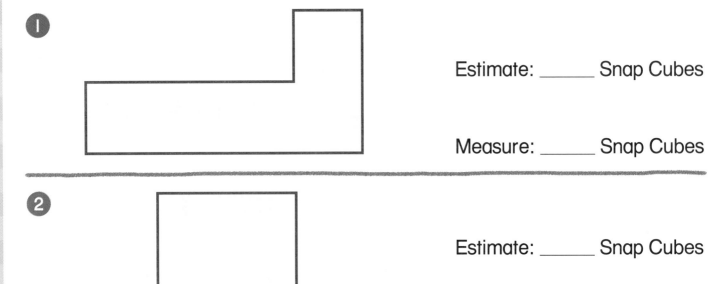

**Notes for Home:** Your child used Snap Cubes to find the number of square units inside different shapes. *Home Activity:* Ask your child to tell you how he or she found the number of square units inside each shape.

## Problem Solving: Use Objects

**Learn** • • • • • • • • • • •

When you make different
rectangles with the same number
of square units inside, does
the perimeter stay the same?

**PROBLEM SOLVING GUIDE**

**Understand • Plan • Solve • Look Back**

There are 26 units
around the outside
of this rectangle.
There are 12 square
units inside.

|← 12 UNITS →|

1 UNIT

**Check** • • • • • • • • • • • • • • • • • • • • • • • • • •

Use 12 🔲 to make different rectangles. Color the grids
to show your rectangles. Write the perimeter for each.

| **Rectangle** | **Perimeter** |
|---|---|

**1**

12 square units inside

_26_ units
around the outside

**2**

12 square units inside

_____ units
around the outside

**3**

12 square units inside

_____ units
around the outside

**Talk About It** For each of the rectangles you
made, did the perimeter stay the same? Explain.

**Notes for Home:** Your child solved problems involving perimeter and square units. *Home Activity:*
Draw a square with 4 smaller squares inside. Ask your child to tell how many square units are inside
and to find the perimeter around the outside. (4 square units inside and 8 units around the outside)

**PROBLEM SOLVING**

## Practice

● ● ● ● ● ● ● ● ● ● ● ● ● ● ● ● ● ● ● ● ● ● ● ●

Use  to make each rectangle.

Color the grids to show your rectangles.

Complete the chart.

**PROBLEM SOLVING**

| | Use this many. | Make a rectangle with this perimeter. | Color to show the rectangle. | How many square units inside? |
|---|---|---|---|---|
| 4 | 8 | 18 units around the outside | | _____ square units inside |
| 5 | 9 | 12 units around the outside | | _____ square units inside |
| 6 | 10 | 14 units around the outside | | _____ square units inside |

## Estimation

7  About how many  would you need to cover the inside space of this circle? Explain.

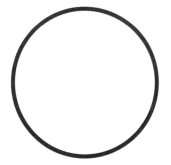

**Notes for Home:** Your child used Snap Cubes to find rectangles with a given perimeter.
*Home Activity:* Ask your child to draw a rectangle that has 2 square units inside and 6 units around the outside. (The rectangle would be made of 2 squares side by side.)

**For additional practice, see Skills Practice Bank, page 537, Set 2.**

Name _____

# Mixed Practice
## Lessons 1–7

## Concepts and Skills

Estimate the length.
Measure with a centimeter ruler.

**1**  Eraser

Estimate: about _____ centimeters long

Measure: _____ centimeters long

Estimate the perimeters.
Measure with an inch ruler.

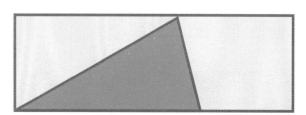

**2** **Perimeter of the rectangle**

Estimate: _____ inches around

Measure: _____ inches around

**3** **Perimeter of the triangle**

Estimate: _____ inches around

Measure: _____ inches around

## Problem Solving

Draw a different shape with the same
number of square units inside.

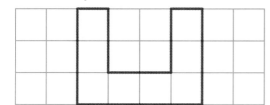
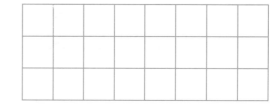

**4** _____ square units inside

Perimeter: _____ units around

**5** _____ square units inside

Perimeter: _____ units around

## Journal

**6** Draw a shape on grid paper. Estimate and measure the perimeter
and the number of square units inside. Write about how you measured.

**Notes for Home:** Your child practiced estimating and measuring length, perimeter, and square units inside a shape (area). *Home Activity:* Have your child estimate the length or the perimeter of a small object in your home. Compare the estimate with the measurement.

MIXED PRACTICE

Name _____

# Cumulative Review
### Chapters 1–11

## Concepts and Skills

Add.

**1**

| 23 | 40 | 64 | 16 | 34 | 72 |
|---|---|---|---|---|---|
| + 18 | + 37 | + 9 | + 15 | + 55 | + 27 |

Write how many hundreds, tens, and ones.
Then write the number.

**2** 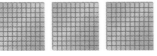         _____

**3** 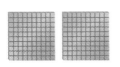         _____

## Problem Solving

Solve.

**4** The truck took 25 boxes to the grocery store. Then it took 17 boxes to the hardware store. How many boxes did the truck take?

_____ boxes

**5** 46 railroad cars stop at the train station. Another 37 railroad cars hook up to the train. How long is the train now?

_____ cars

### Test Prep

Fill in the ○ for the correct answer.

**6** Choose the number that comes one before 475.

| 476 | 447 | 474 |
|---|---|---|
| ○ | ○ | ○ |

**7** Choose the number that comes one after 356.

| 357 | 365 | 355 |
|---|---|---|
| ○ | ○ | ○ |

 **Notes for Home:** Your child reviewed two-digit addition, writing large numbers, and using addition to solve problems. *Home Activity:* Ask your child what the 6 stands for in 689. (6 hundreds)

CUMULATIVE REVIEW

Name

**Explore**

When objects weigh about the same, the scale is balanced.

Find objects you can weigh. Use a balance scale.

Make a list of objects that are lighter than 1 pound.

Make a list of objects that are heavier than 1 pound.

Lighter than 1 pound

Heavier than 1 pound

EXPLORE

**Share**

What are some objects that weigh about 1 pound?

**Notes for Home:** Your child compared the weights of objects to one pound by using a balance scale.
*Home Activity:* Look for objects in the kitchen or grocery store that weigh about 1 pound.

Is each object **heavier than, lighter than,** or **about**
1 pound? Estimate. Then use a pound weight and
a balance scale to check. Complete the chart.

| | Object | Estimate | Measure |
|---|---|---|---|
| **1** | | _____ 1 pound | _____ 1 pound |
| **2** | | _____ 1 pound | _____ 1 pound |
| **3** | | _____ 1 pound | _____ 1 pound |
| **4** | | _____ 1 pound | _____ 1 pound |
| **5** | | _____ 1 pound | _____ 1 pound |

**EXPLORE**

## Tell a Math Story

**6** Write a math story about something
you need to weigh.

**Notes for Home:** Your child estimated whether objects weigh more or less than 1 pound.
*Home Activity:* Help your child find weights on labels of food products.

# Kilograms

**Learn** ● ● ● ● ● ● ● ● ● ● ● ● ● ● ● ● ● ● ● ● ● ● ● ●

| Lighter than 1 kilogram | About 1 kilogram | Heavier than 1 kilogram |
|---|---|---|
|  | 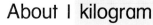 |  |

**Check** ● ● ● ● ● ● ● ● ● ● ● ● ● ● ● ● ● ● ● ● ● ● ● ●

Find each of these objects. Use a balance scale.
Circle the words that tell about the object.

**1**

lighter than 1 kilogram

about 1 kilogram

heavier than 1 kilogram

**2**

lighter than 1 kilogram

about 1 kilogram

heavier than 1 kilogram

**3**

lighter than 1 kilogram

about 1 kilogram

heavier than 1 kilogram

**4**

lighter than 1 kilogram

about 1 kilogram

heavier than 1 kilogram

**Talk About It** If one object is larger than another
object, is it always heavier?

 **Notes for Home:** Your child used a balance scale to find objects that are lighter than, heavier than, or about 1 kilogram. *Home Activity:* Ask your child to find something in your home that weighs about 1 kilogram or about 2 pounds. You can use a bathroom scale to check.

**5** Circle in **red** the objects that are lighter than 1 kilogram.

**6** Circle in **blue** the objects that are heavier than 1 kilogram.

**Write your own.** Choose an object.

**7** Is your object lighter than or heavier than 1 kilogram?

My _____ is _____ than 1 kilogram.

## Problem Solving Critical Thinking

**8** Is 1 kilogram of nails heavier than 1 kilogram of feathers? Explain.

**Notes for Home:** Your child identified objects that are lighter or heavier than 1 kilogram.
*Home Activity:* Ask your child to hold objects from your refrigerator and estimate if they are lighter or heavier than 1 kilogram.

# Cups, Pints, and Quarts

**Learn** • • • • • • • • • • • • • • • • • • • • • • • • • • •

There are 2 cups in 1 pint.

There are 2 pints in 1 quart.

**Check** • • • • • • • • • • • • • • • • • • • • • • • • • • •

Color the containers to answer each question.

**1** How many cups fill 1 pint?

**2** How many cups fill 2 pints?

**3** How many cups fill 1 quart?

**4** How many pints fill 1 quart?

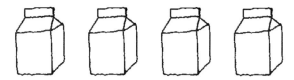

**Talk About It** What measurements did you find

that are the same as one quart?

**Notes for Home:** Your child learned about cups, pints, and quarts. *Home Activity:* Ask your child to order these units of measure from least to greatest: pint, cup, quart. (cup, pint, quart)

2 cups
fill
1 pint.

2 pints
fill
1 quart.

Solve each problem.

**5** Gina buys 3 pints of milk. Color the number of cups she could fill.

**6** Mr. Habib buys 1 quart of yogurt. Color the number of cups he could fill.

**7** Simon has 4 pints of juice. Color the number of quarts that holds the same amount.

**8** Jorge has 2 quarts of juice. Color the number of pints that holds the same amount.

## Problem Solving Visual Thinking

**9** Draw cups to solve.

Jess has 2 quarts of milk.
Ed has 6 cups of milk. Who has more?

_____ has more.

**Notes for Home:** Your child solved problems about cups, pints, and quarts. *Home Activity:* Ask your child to show you some liquids at home that could be measured in cups, pints, or quarts.

# Liters

**Learn** ● ● ● ● ● ● ● ● ● ● ● ● ● ● ● ● ● ● ● ● ● ● ●

These hold about one liter of water or juice.

**Check** ● ● ● ● ● ● ● ● ● ● ● ● ● ● ● ● ● ● ● ● ● ● ●

Use a one-liter container. Check other containers
to see if they hold **more** or **less** than one liter.

| | Draw your container. | Does it hold **more** or **less** than one liter? |
|---|---|---|
| **1** | | _____ than one liter |
| **2** | | _____ than one liter |
| **3** | | _____ than one liter |

**Talk About It** Would your class need more or less

than one liter of juice for a snack? Explain.

**Notes for Home:** Your child determined if containers hold more or less than one liter.
*Home Activity:* Ask your child to find a container at home or at the store and find out if it holds
more than one liter, less than one liter, or about one liter.

**4** Which things hold **less** than one liter?
Circle them.

**5** Which things hold **more** than one liter?
Mark an **X** on them.

## Mental Math

**6** A barrel holds ten liters of apple juice.

How many liters will ten barrels hold? _____

**Notes for Home:** Your child identified containers that hold more or less than one liter.
*Home Activity:* Ask your child to find two containers in your home that hold more than one liter and two containers that hold less than one liter.

## Use Context Clues

*The meaning of the whole sentence helps me find the missing word.*

length
yards
pounds
height
centimeter
measure
inches
perimeter
yardstick

**1** Complete the story.
Fill in the blanks with the
words that make the most sense.

Mrs. Marshall's class is putting on a play. To make the scenery, they

have to _____ carefully.

Martin's job is to make a tree. He needs to know how tall to make it. He

will measure the tree's _____. Justin wants to paint a big window.

He needs to know the distance around its outside edge. He needs to know

its _____.

Katie wants to paint a fence along the front of the stage. She needs to

measure the _____ of the stage. She will use a _____

because a ruler is too small. The stage is 15 _____ long! Katie

says, "I'm going to need a lot of paint!"

**Talk About It** How did you choose the missing word?

**Notes for Home:** Your child used math terms to complete a story. *Home Activity:* Ask your child to tell you how he or she chose each missing word.

**2** Complete the story.
Fill in the blanks with the words that make the most sense.

| equal | quarts | ruler |
| pound | length | cups |
| scale | more | |

---

Mrs. Marshall plans to give her class a surprise party after the play!

She wants to serve fruit salad. She will go to the store and buy one

_____ each of apples, bananas, and grapes. She will weigh them

on the _____ to make sure she has the right amounts.

She also wants to make fruit punch. Her recipe calls for an

_____ amount of orange juice, grape juice, and pineapple juice.

She needs to buy 3 _____ of each type of juice. She knows that

this will make 36 _____ in all.

Then all she has to do is try to keep the party secret!

---

## Critical Thinking

How do you think Mrs. Marshall found the total amount of punch?

**Notes for Home:** Your child used math terms to complete a story. *Home Activity:* Ask your child to use at least 2 of the math terms on this page to make up a sentence about measuring.

# Problem Solving: Group Decision Making

**Learn** ● ● ● ● ● ● ● ● ● ● ● ● ●

**PROBLEM SOLVING GUIDE**
Understand ● Plan ● Solve ● Look Back

How many different ways can you measure
an object? What tools will you need?

I can use
a ruler to find
how long this
squash is and a
balance scale to
find how much
it weighs.

I can use
a cup to find
how much this pail
holds inside and
a piece of string
to find how big
around it is.

**Check** ● ● ● ● ● ● ● ● ● ● ● ● ● ● ● ● ● ● ● ● ● ● ●

Choose an object. Work with your group
to find how many ways you can measure it.

My object is _____ .

Draw a picture of your object.

| | Unit of Measure | Tool | Estimate | Measurement |
|---|---|---|---|---|
| **1** | | | | |
| **2** | | | | |
| **3** | | | | |
| **4** | | | | |

**Talk About It** How many different ways did you
find to measure your object? Are there more ways?

**Notes for Home:** Your child chose the tools and measured an object in many different ways.
*Home Activity:* Ask your child to tell you which tools he or she would use to find the height and
weight of an object.

**Practice** ● ● ● ● ● ● ● ● ● ● ● ● ● ● ● ● ● ●

Compare your group's objects.
Put them in order.

I put these jars in order by height.

**PROBLEM SOLVING**

**5** Length    _____  _____  _____  _____

          shortest                                              longest

**6** Distance
Around    _____  _____  _____  _____

          shortest                                              longest

**7** Weight    _____  _____  _____  _____

          lightest                                              heaviest

**8** Amount It
Can Hold  _____  _____  _____  _____

          the least                                           the most

**Journal**

**9** Which object do you think takes up the most space?
What makes you think so?

**10** Is the largest object always the heaviest?
Explain.

**Notes for Home:** Your child worked with a group to put objects in order by length, distance around (circumference), weight, and amount it can hold (capacity). *Home Activity:* Choose several objects and ask your child to put them in order by height.

**430**  four hundred thirty

© Scott Foresman Addison Wesley

Name _____

# Temperature

**Learn**

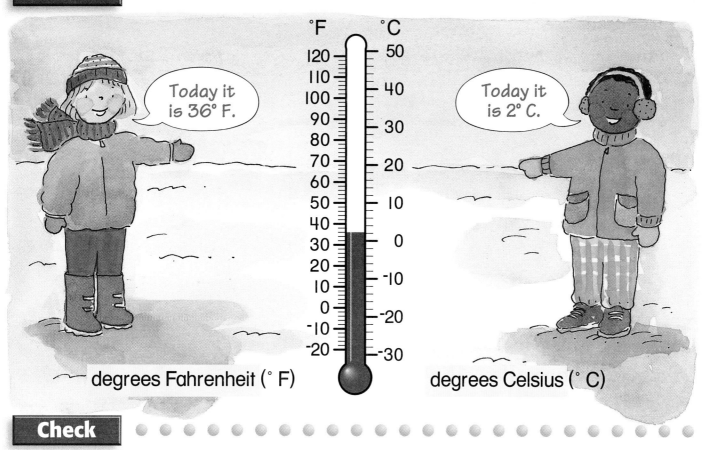

Today it is 36° F.

Today it is 2° C.

degrees Fahrenheit (° F)

degrees Celsius (° C)

**Check**

Color to show the temperature.

**1** 20° C

**2** 25° F

**Talk About It** Before school, it is 40° F. After school,

it is 65° F. How many degrees did the temperature rise?

Explain how you found out.

**Notes for Home:** Your child learned how to use a thermometer to show the temperature.
*Home Activity:* Ask your child to use a newspaper or listen to a weather forecast to find out predicted temperatures for the next few days.

Color to show the temperature.

**3** 0° C

Fahrenheit   Celsius
100 — 40
90 — 30
80
70 — 20
60
50 — 10
40
30 — 0
20
10 — -10
0
-10 — -20

**4** 82° F

Fahrenheit   Celsius
100 — 40
90 — 30
80
70 — 20
60
50 — 10
40
30 — 0
20
10 — -10
0
-10 — -20

**Write your own.**

Choose and write a temperature.
Color in the thermometer. Draw a picture to show
an activity you might do at that temperature.

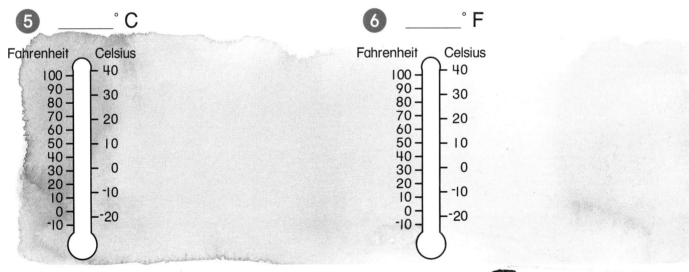

**5** _____ ° C

Fahrenheit   Celsius
100 — 40
90 — 30
80
70 — 20
60
50 — 10
40
30 — 0
20
10 — -10
0
-10 — -20

**6** _____ ° F

Fahrenheit   Celsius
100 — 40
90 — 30
80
70 — 20
60
50 — 10
40
30 — 0
20
10 — -10
0
-10 — -20

## Problem Solving Critical Thinking

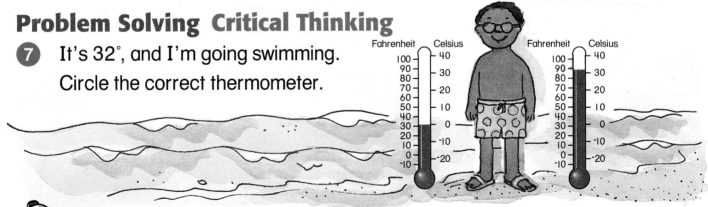

**7** It's 32°, and I'm going swimming.
Circle the correct thermometer.

Fahrenheit   Celsius
100 — 40
90 — 30
80
70 — 20
60
50 — 10
40
30 — 0
20
10 — -10
0
-10 — -20

Fahrenheit   Celsius
100 — 40
90 — 30
80
70 — 20
60
50 — 10
40
30 — 0
20
10 — -10
0
-10 — -20

**Notes for Home:** Your child practiced showing different temperatures on thermometers.
*Home Activity:* Help your child use a thermometer on the page to indicate the current temperature
in both Celsius and Fahrenheit degrees.

Name _____

# Mixed Practice
### Lessons 8–13

## Concepts and Skills

**1** Color to show the temperature.

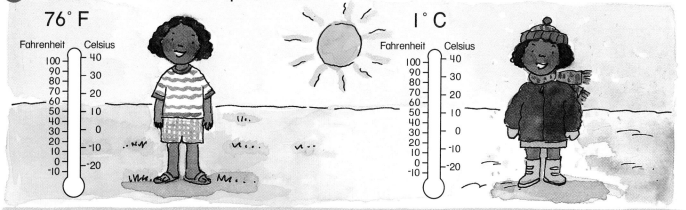

76° F

1° C

**2** Is the penny heavier or lighter than 1 kilogram? Write **heavier** or **lighter**.

A penny is _____ than 1 kilogram.

**3** Is the bowling ball heavier or lighter than 1 pound? Write **heavier** or **lighter**.

A bowling ball is _____ than 1 pound.

Circle the tool you would use to solve.

**4** Which container holds more juice?

## Journal

**5** Keep track of the temperature in the morning for 5 days. Write about what you find.

**Notes for Home:** Your child practiced showing temperatures, determining the weights of objects using kilograms and pounds, choosing measurement tools. *Home Activity:* Ask your child to estimate how much an object weighs. Weigh the object and compare the result with the estimate.

Name _____

# Cumulative Review
## Chapters 1–11

## Concepts and Skills

Use the hundred chart to subtract.

| 1 | 2 | 3 | 4 | 5 | 6 | 7 | 8 | 9 | 10 |
|---|---|---|---|---|---|---|---|---|----|
| 11 | 12 | 13 | 14 | 15 | 16 | 17 | 18 | 19 | 20 |
| 21 | 22 | 23 | 24 | 25 | 26 | 27 | 28 | 29 | 30 |
| 31 | 32 | 33 | 34 | 35 | 36 | 37 | 38 | 39 | 40 |
| 41 | 42 | 43 | 44 | 45 | 46 | 47 | 48 | 49 | 50 |
| 51 | 52 | 53 | 54 | 55 | 56 | 57 | 58 | 59 | 60 |
| 61 | 62 | 63 | 64 | 65 | 66 | 67 | 68 | 69 | 70 |
| 71 | 72 | 73 | 74 | 75 | 76 | 77 | 78 | 79 | 80 |
| 81 | 82 | 83 | 84 | 85 | 86 | 87 | 88 | 89 | 90 |
| 91 | 92 | 93 | 94 | 95 | 96 | 97 | 98 | 99 | 100 |

1. $39 - 20 = $ _____

2. $55 - 30 = $ _____

3. $77 - 40 = $ _____

4. $36 - 10 = $ _____

5. $83 - 50 = $ _____

6. $63 - 60 = $ _____

## Problem Solving

Write each number sentence. Solve.

7. 68 boxes are on the truck.

7 more boxes are loaded on. _____ boxes

At the first stop 20 boxes are unloaded.

How many boxes are on the truck now? _____ boxes

## Test Prep

Fill in the ○ for the correct answer.

8.
$$\begin{array}{r} 323 \\ + 247 \\ \hline \end{array}$$
○ 76
○ 560
○ 570
○ 670

9.
$$\begin{array}{r} 145 \\ + 194 \\ \hline \end{array}$$
○ 329
○ 331
○ 339
○ 1,243

**Notes for Home:** Your child reviewed subtracting tens, multiple-step problems, and adding and subtracting large numbers. *Home Activity:* Ask your child to find 97 − 50 and then add 6. (53)

**434** four hundred thirty-four

Name _____

# Chapter 11 Review

## Vocabulary

**1** Circle the picture that is about 1 centimeter long.

**2** Circle the object that weighs about 1 pound.

## Concepts and Skills

**3** Use an inch ruler to measure the length.

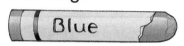

Measure: about _____ inches

**4** Color to show the temperature.

30° F

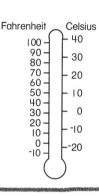

**5** Is an orange lighter or heavier than 1 kilogram?

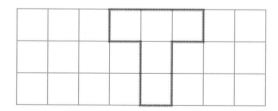

An orange is _____ than 1 kilogram.

**6** Does a juice box hold more or less than one liter?

A juice box holds _____ than one liter.

## Problem Solving

**7** Find the perimeter of this shape and the number of square units inside. Then draw a different shape with the same number of square units.

Perimeter: _____ units around

_____ square units inside

Perimeter: _____ units around

_____ square units inside

**Notes for Home:** Your child reviewed Chapter 11 vocabulary, concepts, skills, and problem solving.
*Home Activity:* Ask your child to use a ruler to compare lengths of different silverware.

Name _____

# Chapter 11 Test

How long is each candle?

**1** Measure in inches.

about _____ inches

**2** Measure in centimeters.

about _____ centimeters

**3** Color to show 27° C.

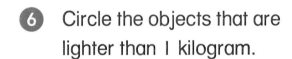

**4** Jarek has 1 quart of milk. Color to show how many cups he can fill.

**5** Circle the objects that hold less than one liter.

**6** Circle the objects that are lighter than 1 kilogram.

**7** Mark an **X** on the object that is heavier than 1 pound.

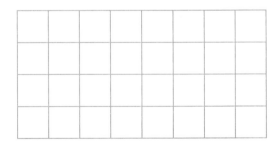

**8** Draw a rectangle with 8 square units inside. Find its perimeter.

_____ units around.

**Notes for Home:** Your child was assessed on Chapter 11 concepts, skills, and problem solving.
*Home Activity:* Ask your child to name different units that can be used to measure length.
(inch, foot, yard, centimeter, meter)

**CHAPTER TEST**

Name _____

Find a container that is shaped like a box.

**1** Draw a picture of your container.

Measure your container in different ways.
Complete the chart.

| | | |
|---|---|---|
| **2** Length | about _____ inches | |
| **3** Area of one face | about _____ square units inside | |
| **4** Perimeter | about _____ inches around | |

**5** Does your container weigh more
or less than 1 pound?                    _____ than one pound

**6** How much does your container hold?    about _____ cups

## Problem Solving Critical Thinking

**7** Describe a day that is 30° F.

Describe a day that is 30° C.

You can use a thermometer to help.

**Notes for Home:** Your child did an activity that assessed Chapter 11 skills, concepts, and problem solving. *Home Activity:* Estimate the number of small objects in a jar. Estimate how much the filled jar weighs.

**Explore with a COMPUTER**

# Shape Up!

## Computer Skills You Will Need

Use a mouse. | Draw a square. | Select and move squares. | Copy. | Paste.

Use your drawing program.

1. Draw a square. Hold down **Shift** while you use the rectangle tool.

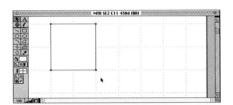

2. Copy and paste your square. Move your new square so that the sides are lined up.

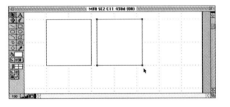

3. Paste more squares, and move them to make a shape.

4. On a separate card, write a riddle about the perimeter and the area of your shape.

5. Work in a group. Make a display of your shapes. Mix up the riddles. Ask another group to solve them.

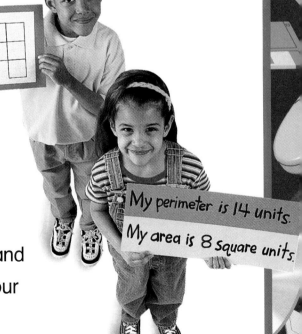

My perimeter is 14 units.
My area is 8 square units.

**Tech Talk** A shape has a perimeter of 10 units and an area of 6 square units. How would you use your computer to draw it?

**Visit our Web site. www.parent.mathsurf.com**

# Food Finds

With an adult, look through your cupboards and refrigerator at home. Find cans, bottles, and packages of food that show different measurements on the labels.

List or draw foods in the correct box below.

| Cups, Pints, Quarts | Liters |
|---|---|
| | |
| **Pounds** | **Kilograms** |
| | |

**Fold down**

# MathSoup

Scott Foresman - Addison Wesley

My Math Magazine

No. 11

**Lane 3**

**Lane 2**

**Lane 1**

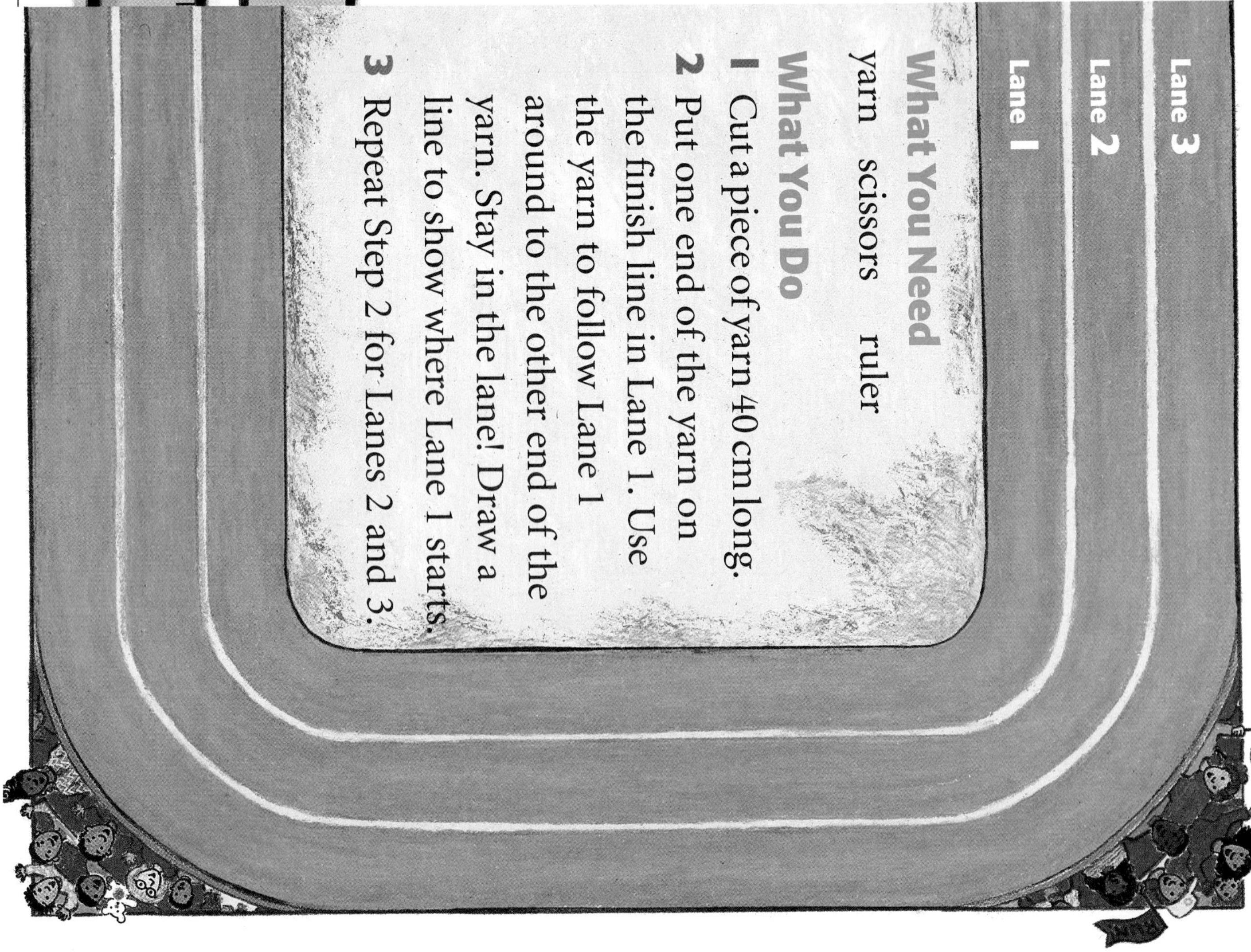

### What You Need

yarn    scissors    ruler

### What You Do

**1** Cut a piece of yarn 40 cm long.

**2** Put one end of the yarn on the finish line in Lane 1. Use the yarn to follow Lane 1 around to the other end of the yarn. Stay in the lane! Draw a line to show where Lane 1 starts.

**3** Repeat Step 2 for Lanes 2 and 3.

# Hot, Hotter, Hottest!

The temperature is different in different places. Even when it is warm where you are, it may be much warmer or cooler somewhere else. This chart shows warm temperatures in different cities.

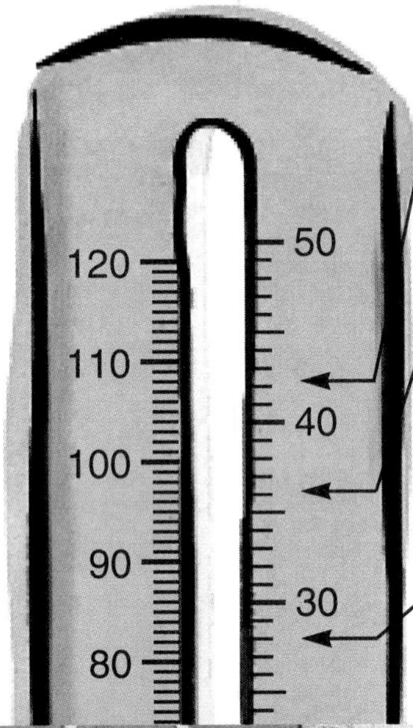

**1** Write the name of each city from the chart next to the correct line on the thermometer.

**2** What is today's temperature where you live? Circle that temperature on the thermometer.

## Stay in Your Lane!

When runners race on a track, they sometimes start at different places so they will all run the same distance and finish at the same place. Use the diagram and follow the directions to draw the starting lines for a race.

**Finish Line**

Notes for Home: Your child practiced metric measurement.
*Home Activity:* Ask your child to find an object that measures about 40 cm in length.

| City | °F | °C |
|---|---|---|
| New York City, U.S.A. | 82° | 28° |
| London, England | 73° | 23° |
| Reykjavik, Iceland | 57° | 14° |
| Khartoum, Sudan | 107° | 42° |
| Calcutta, India | 96° | 36° |

Notes for Home: Your child learned about temperatures in different cities.
*Home Activity:* Ask your child to compare the temperatures in Khartoum and Reykjavik. (Khartoum is 50°F warmer, 28°C warmer)

# Wrap It Up!

You know how to find the perimeter of rectangles. But how could you find the perimeter of these shapes? Follow these directions to find out.

## What You Need

yarn    scissors    ruler

## What You Do

1  Find the circle. Put one end of a piece of yarn on the border of the circle.

2  Curve the yarn around the border of the circle. Cut the piece of yarn when it reaches all the way around the circle.

3  Straighten out the piece of yarn. Measure it to the nearest inch. Measure it to the nearest centimeter. Record your measurements.

4  Repeat the steps for the other shapes.

Perimeter:

_____ in.

_____ cm

Perimeter:

_____ in.

_____ cm

Perimeter:

_____ in.

_____ cm

Perimeter:

_____ in.

_____ cm

inches

300

290

280

270

1 in

260

250

2

240

230

3

**Notes for Home:** Your child practiced finding perimeters. *Home Activity:* Ask your child to find the perimeter of a curved object at home using string or yarn and a ruler.

5

4

**Notes for Home:** Your child matched food containers with different kinds of solids. *Home Activity:* Ask your child to find objects in your home that are solids like those shown in the picture.

Dear Family,
Our class is starting Chapter 12. We will be learning about different shapes and using fractions. Here are some fun things we can do together.

### It's in the Bag
Put several food items into a brown grocery bag. Ask your child to reach into the bag without looking, feel an object, and describe the shape. Then ask your child to guess what the object is.

### Share Your Lunch
When serving food such as pizza, pie, or casseroles, ask your child how to share the food with four people. Help your child cut it into equal pieces.

**Community Connection**

Take your child on a shape search around your neighborhood. Look for circles, triangles, and rectangles in buildings or on street signs.

**Visit our Web site. www.parent.mathsurf.com**

Name _____

**Explore**

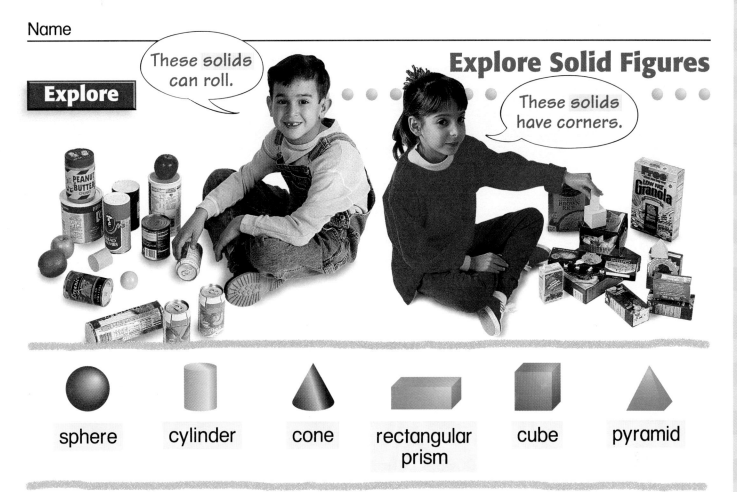

"These solids can roll."

"These solids have corners."

sphere    cylinder    cone    rectangular prism    cube    pyramid

Sort solid figures into 2 groups.

Write the names of the solids you sorted.

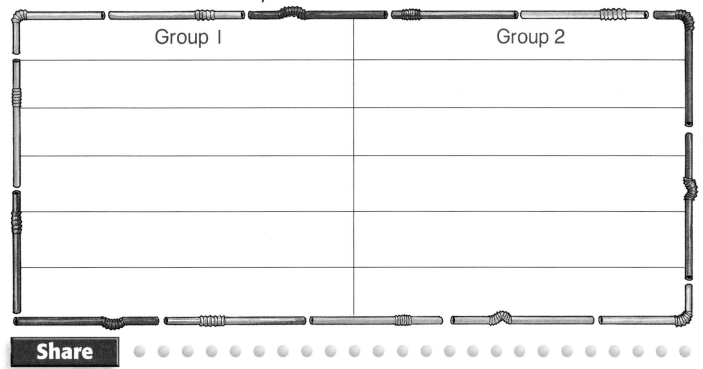

| Group 1 | Group 2 |
|---|---|
| | |
| | |
| | |
| | |
| | |

**Share**

How did you sort the solid figures?

What other ways could you sort them?

**Notes for Home:** Your child sorted solid objects into two groups. *Home Activity:* Ask your child to sort objects at home into two groups and explain how he or she sorted them.

EXPLORE

**Connect**

My juice box is a rectangular prism. It has 6 faces, 8 corners, and 12 edges.

corner

edge

face

Use solids. Find how many faces, corners, and edges.

| | Solid | Name | Faces | Corners | Edges |
|---|---|---|---|---|---|
| 1 | | cube | 6 | 8 | 12 |
| 2 | | | | | |
| 3 | | | | | |
| 4 | | | | | |
| 5 | | | | | |

## Problem Solving  Critical Thinking

6  How many faces, corners, and edges do these rectangular prisms have? Do you think this is true for all rectangular prisms? Explain.

**Notes for Home:** Your child found the number of corners, faces, and edges in different solid objects. *Home Activity:* Ask your child to find two objects in your home and tell you how many faces, corners and edges for each object.

EXPLORE

Name _____

**Explore**  • • • • • • • • • • • • • • • • • • • • • • • • •

Look around. What solids do you see?

What shapes do they have?

"I see a circle on this cylinder!"

"I see a square on this cube!"

Find objects in your classroom.

Trace faces of these solids to make a picture.

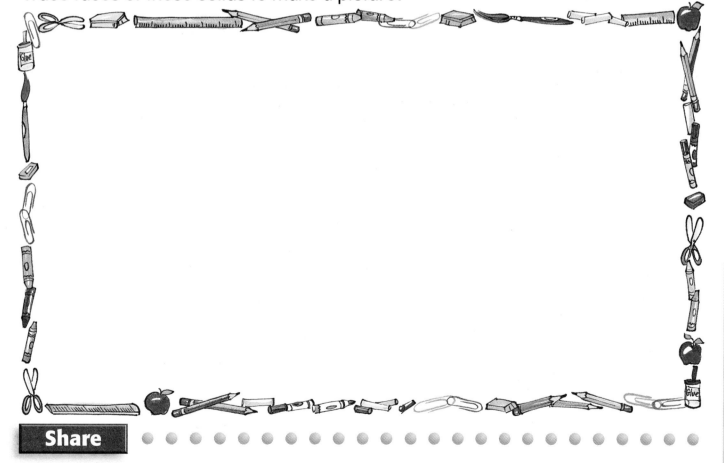

**EXPLORE**

**Share**  • • • • • • • • • • • • • • • • • • • • • • • • •

What everyday objects could you use to trace a circle?

**Notes for Home:** Your child traced objects to draw shapes. *Home Activity:* Ask your child to trace two objects in your home and describe the shapes he or she drew.

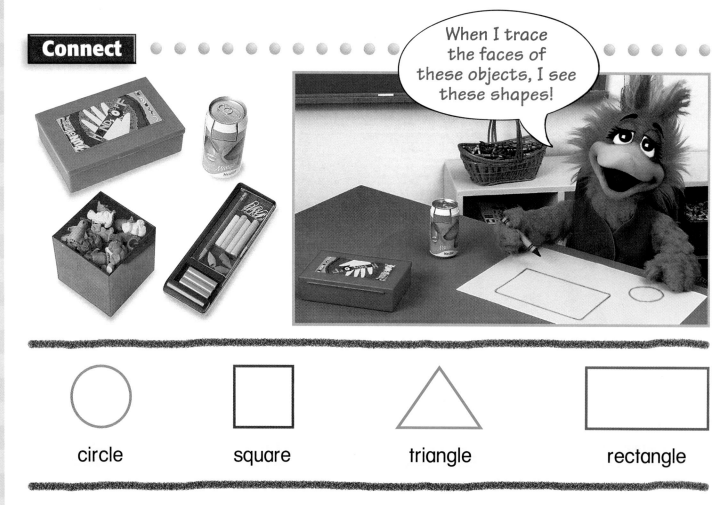

When I trace the faces of these objects, I see these shapes!

circle      square      triangle      rectangle

Circle the shape you would make if you traced the face each object is sitting on.

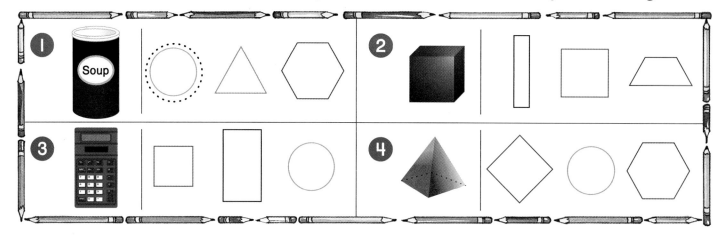

## Problem Solving Visual Thinking

5. Draw a picture of shapes you would make if you traced each object.

**Notes for Home:** Your child identified the shape that would be drawn if different objects were traced. *Home Activity:* Ask your child to tell you what shape would be drawn if he or she traced a box. (rectangle)

Name _____

**Learn** • • • • • • • • • • • • • • • • • • • • • • • • • • • • •

Put pattern blocks together. Be sure the edges match!

Trace your new shape.

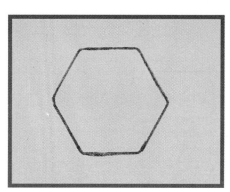

Count the sides and corners.

___6___ sides    ___6___ corners

**Check** • • • • • • • • • • • • • • • • • • • • • • • • • • • •

Use pattern blocks to make shapes. Complete the chart.

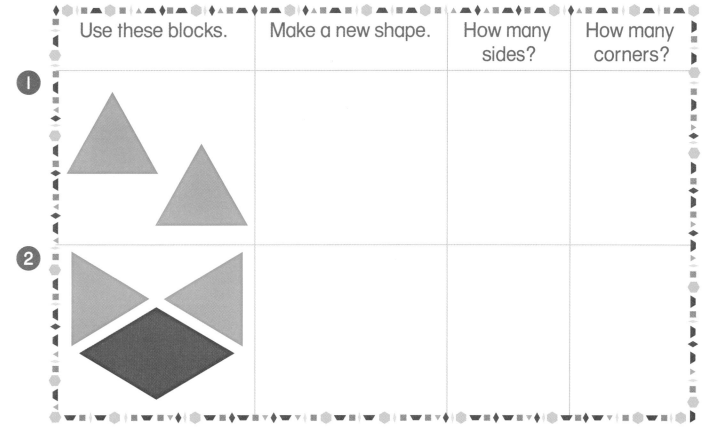

| Use these blocks. | Make a new shape. | How many sides? | How many corners? |
|---|---|---|---|
| **1** | | | |
| **2** | | | |

**Talk About It** Can you make a shape that has a

different number of sides than corners? Why or why not?

**Notes for Home:** Your child combined shapes to make other shapes. *Home Activity:* Ask your child to count the edges and corners on a table in your home.

**Write your own.** Use pattern blocks.

Make new shapes. Complete the chart.

|   | Blocks I Used | New Shape I Made | How many sides? | How many corners? |
|---|---|---|---|---|
| **3** | | | | |
| **4** | | | | |

## Problem Solving Patterns

**5** Draw what comes next.

**Notes for Home:** Your child used pattern blocks to make new shapes and found the number of sides and corners for the new shape. *Home Activity:* Ask your child to make a new shape by drawing a square and a triangle together. Ask your child how many sides and corners the new shape has.

Name _____

**Learn**

These two shapes match exactly!

They are congruent. That means they are the same size and the same shape.

**Check**

Circle the shape that is congruent to the first shape.

1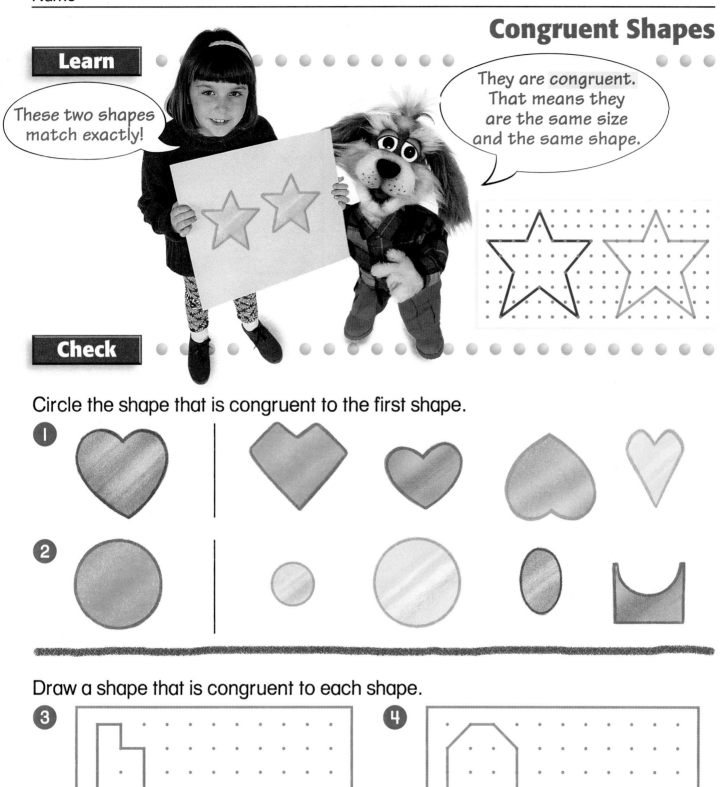

2

Draw a shape that is congruent to each shape.

3

4

**Talk About It** How do you know when two shapes are congruent?

 **Notes for Home:** Your child learned about congruent shapes, or shapes that are the same size and shape. *Home Activity:* Show your child a set of plates that are small, medium, and large. Then ask your child to find the plates that are congruent.

Draw a shape that is congruent to each shape.

**5**
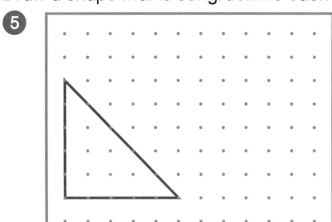

**6**
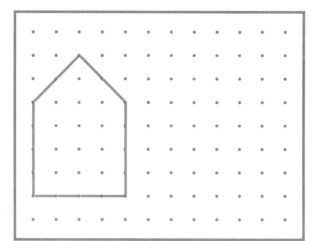

 **Write your own.** Draw a shape. Then have a friend draw a shape that is congruent to your shape.

**7**
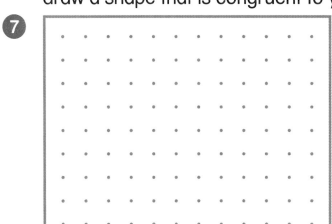

**8**
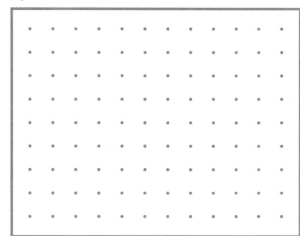

## Problem Solving Visual Thinking

Which fences will keep a pet in the yard? Explain why.
Draw a pet inside those fences.

**9**

 **Notes for Home:** Your child practiced drawing shapes that are congruent to other shapes.
*Home Activity:* Show forks, spoons, and knives that are different sizes and shapes. Ask your child to make pairs showing congruent shapes.

**For additional practice, see Skills Practice Bank, page 538, Set 1.**

# Slides, Flips, and Turns

**Learn**

You can slide, flip, and turn shapes.

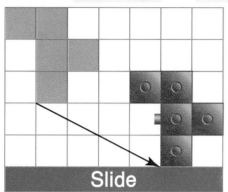

Slide

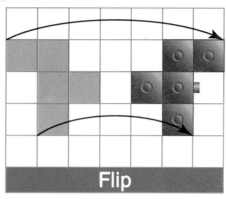

Flip

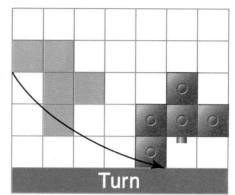

Turn

**Check**

Use 🔲 to make each shape. Slide, flip, or turn the shape. Draw to show how it was moved.

| Make this shape. | Slide it. | Flip it. | Turn it. |
|---|---|---|---|
| **1** | | | |
| **2** | | | |

**Talk About It** Tell how this shape was moved.

**Notes for Home:** Your child moved shapes by sliding, flipping, or turning them.
*Home Activity:* Ask your child to use a piece of paper to show you how to slide, flip, and turn a shape.

Write **slide**, **flip**, or **turn**. Use  to check.

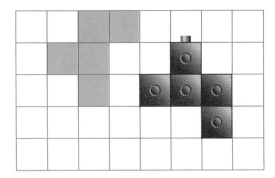

**3**

_____

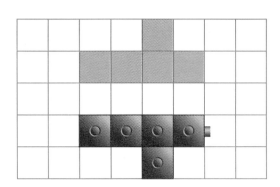

**4**

_____

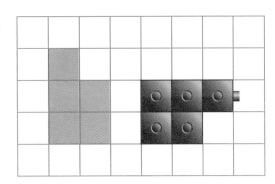

**5**

_____

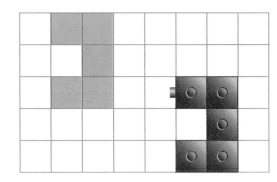

**6**

_____

## Problem Solving Patterns

Use 3 or 4  to make a shape.

Flip it several times to make a pattern.

Color to show what you did.

**7**

 **Notes for Home:** Your child used Snap Cubes to tell whether a shape had been flipped, turned, or slid. _Home Activity:_ Ask your child to draw a picture of a shape that has been slid.

# Symmetry

**Learn** • • • • • • • • • • • • • • • • • • • • • • • • •

This shape shows a line of symmetry. The parts match when the picture is folded. It looks like a flip!

This shape does not show a line of symmetry. The parts do not match when the picture is folded.

**Check** • • • • • • • • • • • • • • • • • • • • • • • • • • • • • •

Does the shape show symmetry? Circle **yes** or **no**.
Draw a line of symmetry if there is one.

**1** 　　　　　　　　 **yes**
　　　　　　　　　　　 no

**2** 　　　　　　　　 yes
　　　　　　　　　　　 no

**3** 　　　　　　　　 yes
　　　　　　　　　　　 no

**4** 　　　　　　　　 yes
　　　　　　　　　　　 no

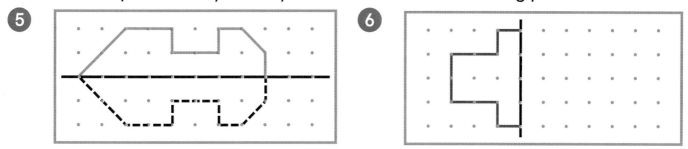

Make the shapes show symmetry. Draw to show the matching parts.

**5**

**6**

**Talk About It** What objects in your classroom show symmetry?

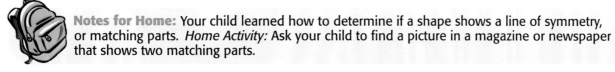

Notes for Home: Your child learned how to determine if a shape shows a line of symmetry, or matching parts. *Home Activity:* Ask your child to find a picture in a magazine or newspaper that shows two matching parts.

Make the shapes show symmetry.

Draw to show the matching part.

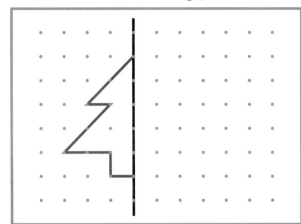

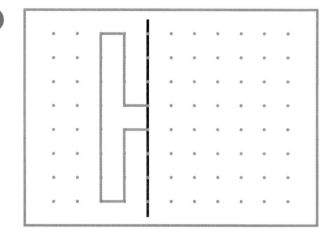

**Mixed Practice** Trace each shape.

Flip the pattern block. Trace again.

Draw one line of symmetry for the new shape.

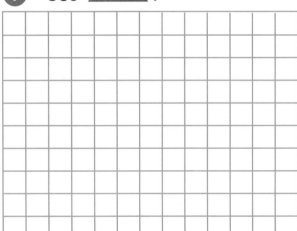

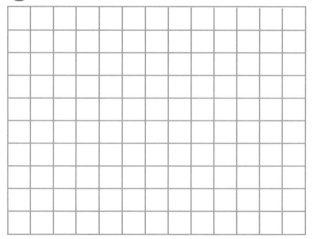

## Problem Solving  Visual Thinking

Draw as many lines of symmetry as you can.

**Notes for Home:** Your child completed shapes to show symmetry. *Home Activity:* Ask your child to draw a picture of a sandwich to show matching parts.

Name _____

## Use Logical Reasoning

Read the riddle. Then draw the shape it describes.

I read the whole
riddle first
before I started
to draw.

**①** I have 3 corners
and 3 sides. I am
green on the inside
with blue dots.

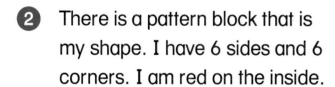

**②** There is a pattern block that is
my shape. I have 6 sides and 6
corners. I am red on the inside.

**③** My shape shows symmetry.
I have no corners. I have
black and yellow stripes.

**Talk About It** How does it help to read the whole
riddle first before you begin to draw the shape?

**Notes for Home:** Your child drew shapes to fit a description. *Home Activity:* Describe an object
in your home and have your child identify it.

Read the riddle. Then draw the shape it describes.

**4** If you traced around the face of a cube, you would draw my shape. I have a line of symmetry drawn through my middle. I am gray.

**5** There is a pattern block that is my shape. You can make me by putting 2 triangles together. I am brown all over.

**6** I have 5 sides and 5 corners. You can make me by putting a square and a triangle together. I am black.

**7** I am not a square, but I have 4 sides and 4 corners. Part of me is yellow, and part is purple.

**Journal**

**8** Draw your own shape. Tell a friend how to draw it. Don't let your friend see your drawing!

**Notes for Home:** Your child drew shapes to fit a description. *Home Activity:* Ask your child to draw a shape that has 3 sides and is two colors.

Name _____

# Problem Solving: Use Logical Reasoning

**Learn** • • • • • • • • • • • •

Which cracker am I?

I am yellow.

I have less than 4 corners.

*I cross out the crackers that don't match the clues.*

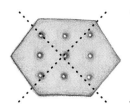  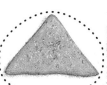  

**Check** • • • • • • • • • • • • • • • • • • • • • • •

Solve the riddles. Cross out pictures that don't match the clues. Circle the answers.

**1** Which cracker am I?
I have more than 3 sides.
I am not yellow.
I have more than 4 corners.

**2** Which cracker am I?
My shape shows symmetry.
I have more than 3 corners.

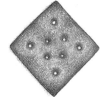 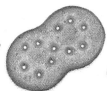  

**3** Which cracker am I?
I have corners. I am not
congruent to another cracker.

**Talk About It** How does crossing out pictures help you to solve the riddles?

**Notes for Home:** Your child used logical reasoning to solve riddles. *Home Activity:* Ask your child to solve this riddle: I have no corners. Am I a circle, square, or triangle? (circle)

PROBLEM SOLVING

Solve the riddles. Cross out pictures that don't
match the clues. Circle the answers.

**4** Which cracker am I?
I have more than 3 corners.
I do not have holes.

  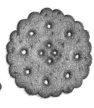 

**5** Which cracker am I?
I have no corners.
I have no stripes.

   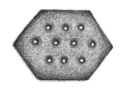

**6** Which cracker am I?
I am not a rectangle.
I am brown.
I have 3 sides.

## Write About it

**7** Write a riddle about
4 different shapes.

Draw your shapes.

_____

_____

_____

_____

**Notes for Home:** Your child practiced using logical reasoning to solve riddles.
*Home Activity:* Use different objects and ask your child to tell you a riddle about them.

# Mixed Practice
### Lessons 1–7

Write how many faces, corners, and edges for this solid.

**1** _____ faces          **2** _____ corners          **3** _____ edges

**4** Draw a shape that is congruent.

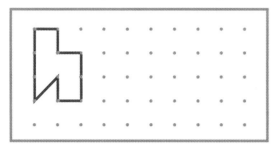

**5** Write **slide, flip,** or **turn.**

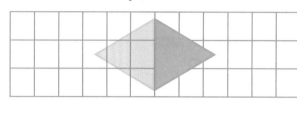

_____

Make the shapes show symmetry. Draw matching parts.

**6**

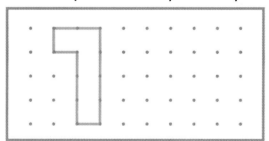

**7**

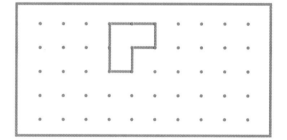

## Problem Solving

Solve the riddle. Cross out the pictures that don't
match the clues. Circle the answer.

**8** I have more than 1 side.
I have 4 corners.
I have only 1 line of symmetry.
I have holes.

## Journal

**9** Draw a triangle. Then draw what happens
when you flip, slide, and turn the triangle.

 **Notes for Home:** Your child practiced identifying and drawing shapes. *Home Activity:* Ask your child
to draw a building that includes a square, a rectangle, a triangle, and a circle.

MIXED PRACTICE

Name _____

# Cumulative Review
### Chapters 1–12

## Concepts and Skills

Write the number.

**1** thirty-nine _____

**2** seventy-two _____

**3** sixty _____

---

Find the nearest ten.
Estimate the sum.

**4**
```
   48
 + 13
```
Think: ☐
☐
+ ☐

48 + 13 is about _____.

**5**
```
   52
 + 39
```
Think: ☐
☐
+ ☐

52 + 39 is about _____.

---

## Problem Solving

Solve.

**6** Cheese costs 38¢. Crackers cost 29¢. How much would both cheese and crackers cost?

_____ ¢

**7** You need 18 banana slices and 27 apple slices for a fruit salad. How many slices do you need?

_____ slices

---

**Notes for Home:** Your child reviewed reading and writing words, estimating sums, solving problems, and estimating lengths. *Home Activity:* Ask your child to use a ruler to measure the length of a fork and a spoon.

Name _____

**Learn**

I made 4 equal parts. Everyone will get a piece that is the same size.

Oops! I made 4 parts, but they are not the same size.

**Check**

Write the number of parts. Then circle **equal** or **not equal**.

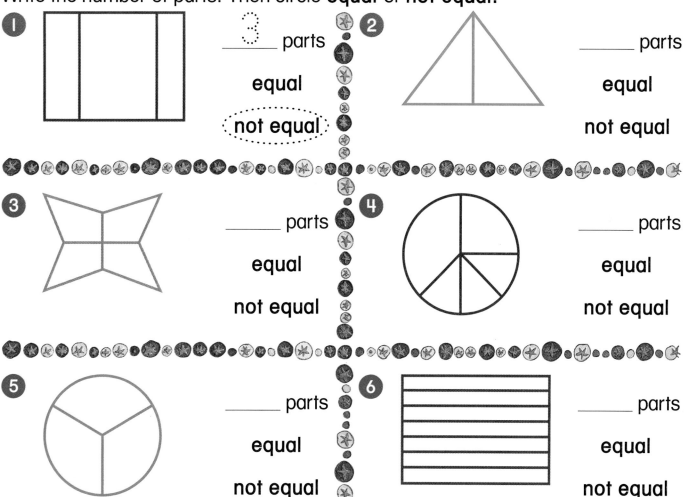

**1** _3_ parts

equal

(not equal)

**2** _____ parts

equal

not equal

**3** _____ parts

equal

not equal

**4** _____ parts

equal

not equal

**5** _____ parts

equal

not equal

**6** _____ parts

equal

not equal

**Talk About It** What are 3 ways you could divide a square into 4 equal parts?

**Notes for Home:** Your child identified the number of parts in a shape and decided if the parts are equal or not equal. *Home Activity:* Ask your child to draw a circle divided into 4 equal parts and another circle divided into 4 parts that are not equal.

**Practice** • • • • • • • • • • • • • • • • • •

Write the number of equal parts and
the new shapes that are made.

 **7**

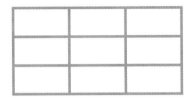 

_9_ equal parts  _____ equal parts  _____ equal parts

 rectangles

_____  _____

---

Draw equal parts. Color each part a different color.

 **8**

3 equal parts  2 equal parts  4 equal parts

---

 **9**

    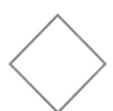

8 equal parts  6 equal parts  2 equal parts

---

## Problem Solving Visual Thinking

**10** Draw 4 equal parts to make the new shapes.

Make squares.  Make rectangles that  Make triangles.
are not squares.

 **Notes for Home:** Your child divided shapes into a number of equal parts. *Home Activity:* Ask your child
to draw rectangles divided into 2, 3, 4, and 6 equal parts.

**464** four hundred sixty-four

# Unit Fractions

**Learn**  • • • • • • • • • • • • • • • • • • • • • • • • • • • • • • • • • •

The parts are equal. You can write a fraction.

<table>
<tr><td style="text-align:center">halves</td><td style="text-align:center">thirds</td></tr>
</table>

 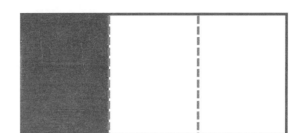

I of 2 equal parts is blue.

One half is blue. $\frac{1}{2}$ is blue.

I of 3 equal parts is red.

One third is red. $\frac{1}{3}$ is red.

**Check**  • • • • • • • • • • • • • • • • • • • • • • • • • • • • • • •

Fold paper to show equal parts. Shade one part.

| | How many equal parts? | Draw to show how you folded and shaded. | Write the fraction for the shaded part. |
|---|---|---|---|
| **1** | 4 | | $\frac{1}{4}$ of ____ equal parts is shaded. _One_ fourth is shaded. |
| **2** | 6 | | ☐ of ____ ☐ equal parts is shaded. _____ sixth is shaded. |

**Talk About It** What does the fraction $\frac{1}{10}$ mean?

 **Notes for Home:** Your child learned about fractions as parts of a whole. *Home Activity:* Ask your child to draw pictures of sandwiches cut into halves and fourths. Ask your child to name the fraction for each part.

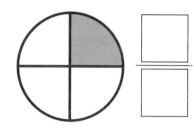

Write the fraction that tells how much is shaded.

**3**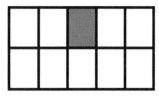

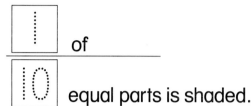

$\dfrac{1}{10}$ of _____ equal parts is shaded.

**4**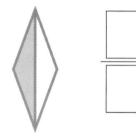

**5**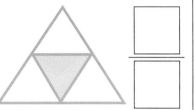

**6**

**7**

**8**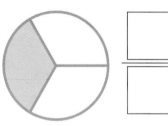

**9**

**10**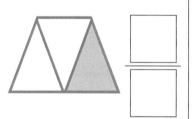

**11**

**12**

**13**

## Problem Solving Critical Thinking

**14** Each cracker has 4 equal parts.

How are the parts of the two crackers alike?

How are they different?

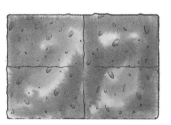

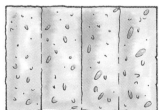

Name _____

# Fractions

**Learn** • • • • • • • • • • • • • • • • • • • • • • • • • • • • • •

*I spread jelly on 2 of the 4 equal parts.*

2 of
4 equal parts have jelly.

_two_ fourths of the cracker has jelly.

**Check** • • • • • • • • • • • • • • • • • • • • • • • • • • • • • •

Write the fraction that tells how much is shaded.

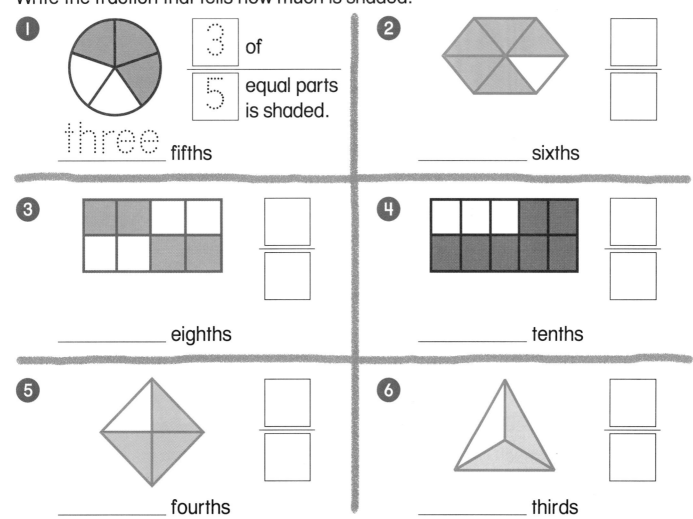

**1** 3 of
5 equal parts is shaded.

_three_ fifths

**2** _____ sixths

**3** _____ eighths

**4** _____ tenths

**5** _____ fourths

**6** _____ thirds

**Talk About It** What are 3 ways you could show $\frac{3}{8}$ of this shape?

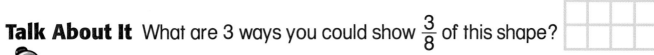

**Notes for Home:** Your child wrote fractions to describe how much of a shape was shaded.
*Home Activity:* Ask your child to tell you what $\frac{5}{6}$ means. (5 out of 6 equal parts)

## Practice

Write the fraction that tells how much you shaded.

**7** Shade 3 parts.

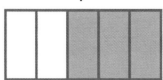 

**8** Shade 2 parts.

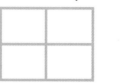 

**9** Shade 6 parts.

 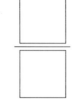

**10** Shade 9 parts.

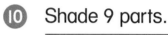 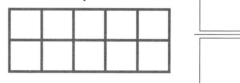

**11** Shade 1 part.

 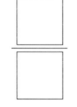

**12** Shade 2 parts.

 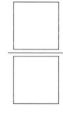

**13** Shade 3 parts.

 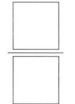

**14** Shade 1 part.

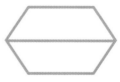 

## Problem Solving

**15** Solve.

You have $\frac{1}{3}$ of a granola bar left. How much did you already eat?

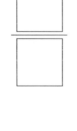

**Write your own** problem about a fraction of a pizza. Have a friend solve it.

_____

_____

_____

**Notes for Home:** Your child practiced writing fractions. *Home Activity:* Ask your child to fold a paper into 4 equal parts, shade some parts, and name the fraction that describes how much of the paper was shaded.

**468** four hundred sixty-eight

**For additional practice, see Skills Practice Bank, page 538, Set 2.**

Name _____

Practice Game

# Fraction Concentration

**Players** 2

**What You Need**

Gameboard

Crayon ▌▌purple▌▌

Cards labeled with one
fraction on each card

$\frac{1}{2}$  $\frac{1}{3}$  $\frac{2}{3}$  $\frac{1}{4}$  $\frac{2}{4}$  $\frac{1}{8}$  $\frac{2}{8}$  $\frac{3}{8}$  $\frac{4}{8}$  $\frac{5}{8}$  $\frac{6}{8}$  $\frac{3}{4}$

I can't color in $\frac{1}{3}$ now,
so I'll skip my turn.

## How to Play

① Lay out cards facedown.

② Players take turns.
Each player turns one card
over and colors that fraction
on his or her gameboard.
Then the player puts the
card back facedown.

③ The player who colors
in three rows first wins.

| one |
|---|

 **Notes for Home:** Your child played a game to practice naming fractions. *Home Activity:* Ask your child to draw pictures to show the fractions $\frac{2}{3}$ and $\frac{3}{4}$.

PRACTICE

Name _____

Write the number of parts.
Then circle **equal** or **not equal.**

**1**  _____ parts

equal

not equal

**2** 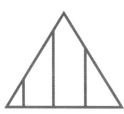 _____ parts

equal

not equal

Draw equal parts. Color each part a different color.

**3**

6 equal parts      4 equal parts      2 equal parts

Write the fraction for the parts that are shaded.

**4**

_____ thirds

**5**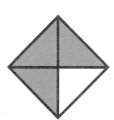

_____ fourths

Shade some of the equal parts.
Write the fraction for the shaded parts.

**6** Shade 1 part.

**7** Shade 5 parts.

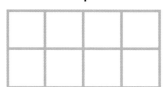

 **Notes for Home:** Your child practiced writing fractions. *Home Activity:* Ask your child to fold a paper into 8 equal parts, color some parts, and name the fraction.

PRACTICE

Name _____

**Learn** • • • • • • • • • • • • • • • • • • • • • • • • • •

About how much of the tostada is left?

I think about the whole tostada to help me estimate.

about $\frac{1}{4}$

about $\frac{1}{2}$

about $\frac{9}{10}$

The part that is left is about the same size as the part that is missing.

**Check** • • • • • • • • • • • • • • • • • • • • • • • • • •

How much is left? Circle the best estimate.

**1**

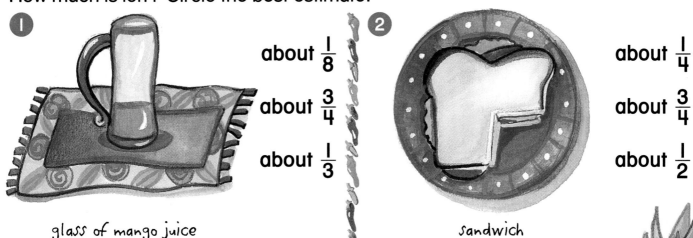

about $\frac{1}{8}$

about $\frac{3}{4}$

about $\frac{1}{3}$

glass of mango juice

**2**

about $\frac{1}{4}$

about $\frac{3}{4}$

about $\frac{1}{2}$

sandwich

**Talk About It** About how much of the pineapple slice is left? About how much was eaten? Explain how you know.

**Notes for Home:** Your child learned to estimate fractions. *Home Activity:* Ask your child to use a fraction to tell you what part of a food item is left.

How much is **left**? Circle the best estimate.

**3**

about $\frac{1}{4}$

about $\frac{2}{3}$

about $\frac{1}{6}$

pitcher of water

**4**

about $\frac{1}{2}$

about $\frac{1}{4}$

about $\frac{3}{4}$

tamale pie

How much **was eaten**? Circle the best estimate.

**5**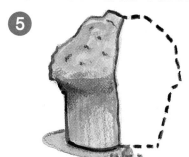

about $\frac{3}{4}$

about $\frac{7}{8}$

about $\frac{1}{2}$

cornbread muffin

**6**

about $\frac{1}{3}$

about $\frac{1}{2}$

about $\frac{2}{3}$

burrito

## Problem Solving Visual Thinking

**7** Lena and Jesse had sandwiches that were the same size.

Lena ate 2 parts of her sandwich. Jesse ate 1 part of his. Did Lena eat more than Jesse? Explain.

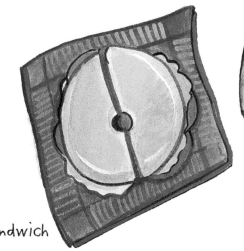

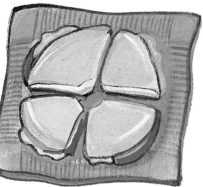

Lena's Sandwich

Jesse's Sandwich

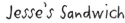

**Notes for Home:** Your child estimated what fraction of a food item remains. Ask your child to tell you what part of a slice of bread remains after half of the slice has been eaten.

Name _____

# Explore a Fraction of a Set

**Explore** • • • • • • • • • • • • • • • • • • • • • • • • • • •

How much of the set of counters is red? How much is yellow?

| 4 of | 2 of |
|---|---|
| 6 counters are red. | 6 counters are yellow. |

Four sixths are red.    Two sixths are yellow.

Take some counters.   Sort them by color.   Write the fractions.

| Draw the counters. | Write the fractions. | |
|---|---|---|
| **1** | ☐ of ☐ counters are red. | ☐ of ☐ counters are yellow. |
| **2** | ☐ of ☐ counters are red. | ☐ of ☐ counters are yellow. |
| **3** | ☐ of ☐ counters are red. | ☐ of ☐ counters are yellow. |

**EXPLORE**

**Share** • • • • • • • • • • • • • • • • • • • • • • • • • • •

How are fractions of a set like fractions of a whole?

How are they different?

 **Notes for Home:** Your child explored finding the fractions of red and yellow counters in a group of counters. *Home Activity:* Ask your child to draw a group of squares in two different colors, and then tell the fraction of the group for each color.

**Chapter 12 Lesson 12**                     four hundred seventy-three **473**

**Connect** • • • • • • • • • • • • • • • • • • • • •

There are 3 green peppers.
There are 4 peppers in all.

> I can write fractions that tell about the group of peppers!

$\frac{3}{4}$ of the peppers are green, and $\frac{1}{4}$ is yellow.

Write the fractions that tell about each group.

**4**

$\frac{2}{3}$ of cabbages are green.

☐ of ☐ cabbages is purple.

**5**

☐ of ☐ apples are yellow.

☐ of ☐ apples are green.

**6**

☐ of ☐ bananas are yellow.

☐ of ☐ bananas are green.

**7**

☐ of ☐ pears is green.

☐ of ☐ pears is yellow.

## Problem Solving

**8** Draw 6 grapes.
Color some purple.
Color the rest green.
What fraction is green?

☐ of ☐ grapes are green.

**Notes for Home:** Your child wrote fractions to describe how much of a group of objects is one color. *Home Activity:* Ask your child to draw a group of circles in two different colors and write a fraction to tell how much of the group is one color.

Name _____

# Fraction of a Set

**Learn** • • • • • • • • • • • • • • • • • • • • • • • • • • • •

There are 3 glasses of purple juice.

There are 2 glasses of orange juice.

There are five glasses in all.

$\frac{3}{5}$ are purple.    $\frac{2}{5}$ are orange.

**Check** • • • • • • • • • • • • • • • • • • • • • • • • • • • • • •

Color each group to show the fractions.

**1**

$\frac{3}{4}$ orange  $\frac{1}{4}$ yellow

**2**

$\frac{2}{6}$ brown  $\frac{4}{6}$ red

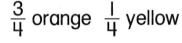

**3**

$\frac{4}{8}$ green  $\frac{4}{8}$ purple

**4**

$\frac{1}{3}$ blue  $\frac{2}{3}$ green

**5**

$\frac{1}{5}$ yellow  $\frac{4}{5}$ red

**6**

$\frac{1}{2}$ purple  $\frac{1}{2}$ yellow

**Talk About It** $\frac{5}{6}$ of the apples in a bowl are yellow. How many apples

are there in all? Explain how you know.

**Notes for Home:** Your child colored objects to show a fraction. *Home Activity:* Ask your child to draw 5 circles and color $\frac{2}{5}$ red and $\frac{3}{5}$ blue.

**Chapter 12 Lesson 13**

four hundred seventy-five  **475**

First find the
number in all!

**7** Draw a group of apples.
Color $\frac{5}{6}$ yellow. Color $\frac{1}{6}$ red.

**8** Draw a group of muffins.
Color $\frac{1}{4}$ orange. Color $\frac{3}{4}$ brown.

**9** Draw a group of crackers.
Color $\frac{1}{3}$ yellow. Color $\frac{2}{3}$ orange.

## Mental Math

Solve.

**10** I have 5 eggs. 3 are white and the rest are brown. How many eggs are brown?

_____ eggs

What fraction of my eggs are brown?

☐/☐ are brown.

**Notes for Home:** Your child drew groups of objects and colored them to show a fraction.
*Home Activity:* Ask your child to draw a group of his or her favorite food item, draw some of them one color, and tell the fraction shown by his or her picture.

# Explore Probability

**Explore** • • • • • • • • • • • • • • • • • • • • • • • • • • • •

Which color are you more likely to pick?

Don't peek!

Put red cubes and yellow cubes in a bag.
Reach in and pick one cube. Color the graph to
show what you picked. Put the cube back in
the bag. Pick 10 times in all. Write your results.

Put 20 red cubes and 10 yellow cubes in a bag.

**1**

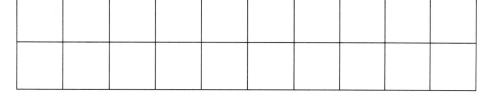

_____ red

_____ yellow

**2** Put 20 red cubes and 2 yellow cubes in a bag.

_____ red

_____ yellow

**3** Put 10 red cubes and 10 yellow cubes in a bag.

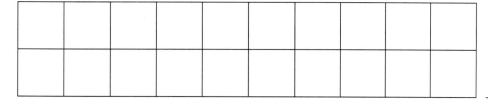

_____ red

_____ yellow

**Share** • • • • • • • • • • • • • • • • • • • • • • • • • • •

Compare your results with your classmates.
How are they alike? How are they different?

**Notes for Home:** Your child explored probability by picking cubes from a bag. *Home Activity:* Ask your
child to put 15 of one item and 5 of a second item in a bag. Pick an item and return it to the bag.
Repeat 10 times. Ask your child to describe the results.

EXPLORE

There are fewer yellow cubes in this bag. It's least likely you'll pick yellow!

**EXPLORE**

**4** Put red, blue, and yellow cubes in a bag. Make the blue cubes least likely to be picked. Use 20 cubes in all.

Pick 1 cube. Record your results. Put the cube back. Pick 20 times in all.

| Number of cubes in my bag | My results |
|---|---|
| R _____ | R _____ |
| B _____ | B _____ |
| Y _____ | Y _____ |

**5** Put red, blue, and yellow cubes in a bag. Make the blue cubes most likely to be picked. Use 20 cubes in all.

Pick 1 cube. Record your results. Put the cube back. Pick 20 times in all.

| Number of cubes in my bag | My results |
|---|---|
| R _____ | R _____ |
| B _____ | B _____ |
| Y _____ | Y _____ |

**Journal**

**6** Suppose you put 10 red cubes, 10 yellow cubes, and 10 blue cubes in a bag. You pick a cube 12 times. Which color do you think you would pick the most? Explain.

 **Notes for Home:** Your child put red, blue, and yellow cubes in a bag and predicted which color was most likely or least likely to be picked. *Home Activity:* Ask your child to put 3 red crayons and 1 blue crayon in a bag. Have your child predict which color is more likely to be picked.

Name _____

# Problem Solving: Make a Prediction

**Learn** • • • •

How can you predict
what is more likely
to happen?

*The spinner has more
green than yellow, so
it's more likely to land
on green.*

**Check** • • • • •

Red     Blue

1. Look at the red and blue spinner.
   Predict. If you were to spin once,
   would this spinner be more likely to
   land on red or blue?     _____

2. What makes you think so?

   _____

   _____

3. Predict. If you were to spin 12 times,
   how many times would the spinner land on red?_____     On blue? _____

4. Spin 12 times. Color a square for each spin. Write the results.

   | | | | | | |
   |---|---|---|---|---|---|
   | | | | | | |

   _____ red

   _____ blue

**Talk About It** How did you predict the number of times
the spinner would land on red?

**Notes for Home:** Your child predicted which colors a spinner would land on, and then tested that
prediction. *Home Activity:* Ask your child to draw two spinners using the colors red and yellow. Ask
them to make the first spinner more likely to spin red and the second spinner more likely to spin yellow.

PROBLEM SOLVING

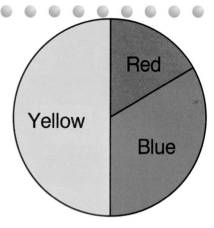

**5** Predict. If you were to spin once, would this spinner be most likely to land on red, blue, or yellow?

_____

**6** What makes you think so?

_____

_____

**7** Predict. If you were to spin
12 times, how many times
would the spinner land on red?_____ on blue? _____ on yellow? _____

**8** Spin 12 times. Color a square for each spin.
Write the results.

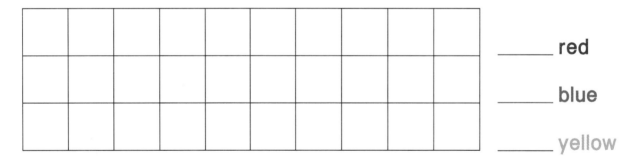

_____ red

_____ blue

_____ yellow

## Write About It

**9** Name something that is certain
to happen in the next 5 minutes. _____

**10** Name something that cannot
happen in the next 5 minutes. _____

**11** Name something that is likely
to happen in the next 5 minutes. _____

**Notes for Home:** Your child practiced making predictions. *Home Activity:* Ask your child to predict which is more likely to happen within the next day: your child will eat a meal or your child will travel to another country.

**For additional practice, see Skills Practice Bank, page 538, Set 3.**

PROBLEM SOLVING

Name _____

# Mixed Practice
## Lessons 8-15

How many equal parts in each shape?

**1**

_____ equal parts        _____ equal parts        _____ equal parts

---

Write the fraction that tells how much is shaded.

**2** 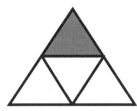    **3**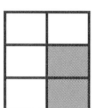

---

How much is left?

Circle the best estimate.

**4**    about $\frac{1}{2}$

about $\frac{1}{4}$

Draw a group of grapes.

Color $\frac{4}{6}$ purple. Color $\frac{2}{6}$ green.

**5**

---

## Problem Solving

**6** Predict. If you were to spin this spinner 20 times, would it be most likely to land on blue, yellow, or red more times? _____

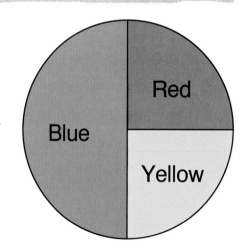

## Journal

**7** You and a friend cut a cookie in half.

Could your friend get a bigger part? Explain.

**Notes for Home:** Your child practiced finding the number of equal parts, identifying fractions, and making a prediction. *Home Activity:* Ask your child to draw 5 shirts so that $\frac{3}{5}$ of the shirts are blue.

MIXED PRACTICE

Name _____

# Cumulative Review
### Chapters 1–12

## Concepts and Skills

Add or subtract.

**1**
$$75 + 9$$ $$23 + 18$$ $$78 - 56$$ $$40 + 30$$ $$60 - 9$$ $$54 - 48$$

**2**
$$37 + 28$$ $$45 - 20$$ $$54 + 32$$ $$50 + 18$$ $$66 - 37$$ $$59 - 29$$

## Problem Solving

**3** Ramona brought fruit for the class. She brought 24 oranges and 12 bananas. How many pieces of fruit did she bring in all?

_____ pieces of fruit

**4** Ralph helped his grandma make green beans. He started with 67 beans. He cut 38 of them. How many more beans did Ralph need to cut?

_____ beans

---

### Test Prep

Fill in the ○ for the correct answer.

**5** Choose the correct symbol to compare the numbers.

26 ○ 54

○          ○          ○
<          =          >

**6** Which numbers are in order from greatest to least?

○ 17, 109, 38, 342

○ 6, 17, 38, 109, 342

○ 342, 109, 38, 17, 6

---

CUMULATIVE REVIEW

# Chapter 12 Review

## Vocabulary

**1** Circle the shape you would make if you traced one face of the cube.

 |

**2** Divide the circle into fourths.

Shade $\frac{3}{4}$.

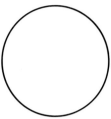

## Concepts and Skills

**3** Draw a shape that is congruent to this shape. Draw a line of symmetry on your shape.

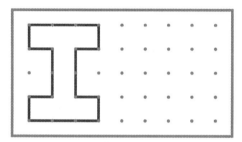

**4** How was the shape moved? Write **slide**, **flip**, or **turn**.

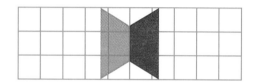

_____

Write the fraction that tells how much is shaded.

**5**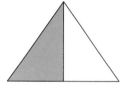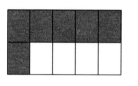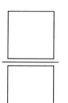

## Problem Solving

**6**  Color $\frac{8}{9}$ of the tiles red. Color the rest blue. Are you **more likely** to pick a red tile or a blue tile out of the bag? _____

**7** Solve the riddle. Circle the answer.
I have more than 3 sides.
I am not yellow. I have more than one line of symmetry.

 **Notes for Home:** Your child reviewed vocabulary, concepts, skills, and problem solving from Chapter 12. *Home Activity:* Ask your child to draw a rectangle, divide it into a number of equal parts, and then describe one or more parts using fractions.

**CHAPTER REVIEW**

Name _____

# Chapter 12 Test

Circle the shape you would make if you traced one face of the objects.

**1**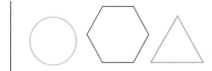

**2**

**3** Draw a shape that is congruent to this shape. Draw a line of symmetry on your shape.

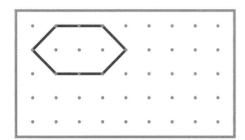

**4** How was the shape moved? Write **slide**, **flip**, or **turn**.

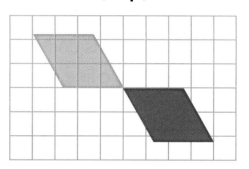

_____

**5** Write the fraction that tells how much is shaded.

 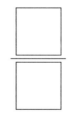 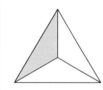 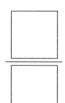 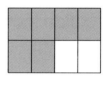 

**6**  Color $\frac{4}{6}$ of the tiles yellow.

Color the rest green. Are you

**more likely** to pick a green tile

or a yellow tile out of the bag? _____

Solve the riddle. Circle the answer.

**7** I have fewer than 6 corners.
I have more than 3 sides.
I am not a square.

 **Notes for Home:** Your child was tested on Chapter 12 skills, concepts, and problem solving. *Home Activity:* Ask your child to draw two shapes, tell you if the shapes have matching parts, and draw a line to show the matching parts if they do.

Name _____

# Performance Assessment
## Chapter 12

Find an object in your classroom that is a
rectangular prism. Tell about your object.

**1** My object is a _____ .

**2** It has _____ faces.

**3** It has _____ edges.

**4** It has _____ corners.

**5** Use another piece of paper.
Trace a face of your object.

**6** Draw 2 lines of symmetry
so that your shape has 4 parts
that are equal in size.

**7** Color 3 of the parts red.

**8** Color one part yellow.

**9** Write a fraction
that tells how much
is red.
[ ]
[ ]

**10** Write a fraction
that tells how much
is yellow.
[ ]
[ ]

## Problem Solving Critical Thinking

**11** Color the tiles so that $\frac{10}{12}$ of the
group is green and the rest is blue.
[ ]
[ ]

**12** What fraction of the tiles is blue?

**13** Would you be more likely to pick a
green tile or a blue tile? Explain.

_____

_____

**Notes for Home:** Your child did an activity that tested Chapter 12 skills, concepts, and problem solving.
*Home Activity:* Ask your child to describe an object in your home that is the shape of a cube.

PERFORMANCE ASSESSMENT

Name _____

Explore with a
COMPUTER

# Picture This!

## Computer Skills You Will Need

**Use a mouse.**

**Draw.**

**Select and move objects.**

**Change the size.**

Use your drawing program.

1. Draw a picture using shapes. You can move shapes so that they are inside other shapes. You can *drag* shapes to make them larger or smaller.

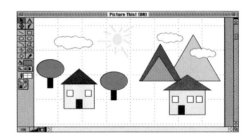

2. Ask a friend to use your picture to complete this chart.

*My picture has:*

| | Circles | Triangles | Squares | Other Rectangles |
|---|---|---|---|---|
| | | | | |

3. Make a pattern using shapes. Ask a friend to tell what comes next.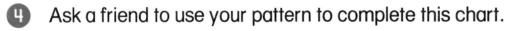

4. Ask a friend to use your pattern to complete this chart.

*My pattern has:*

| | Circles | Triangles | Squares | Other Rectangles |
|---|---|---|---|---|
| | | | | |

**Tech Talk** How would you draw this design?
Do you think there is more than one way? Explain.

**Visit our Web site.  www.parent.mathsurf.com**

# Sym-mat-ry!

You can use symmetry to make interesting place mats.

## What You Need

colored paper   scissors

## What You Do

1. Take a piece of colored paper. Fold it in half.

2. Draw a shape along the edges of one side.

3. Cut along your line. Unfold the paper.

4. Describe what happened. Find a line of symmetry.

Fold down

# MathSoup

Scott Foresman - Addison Wesley    My Math Magazine    No. 12

## Take a Bite!

Look at the pictures of these "buildings." Tell how many cubes are in each building.

**1**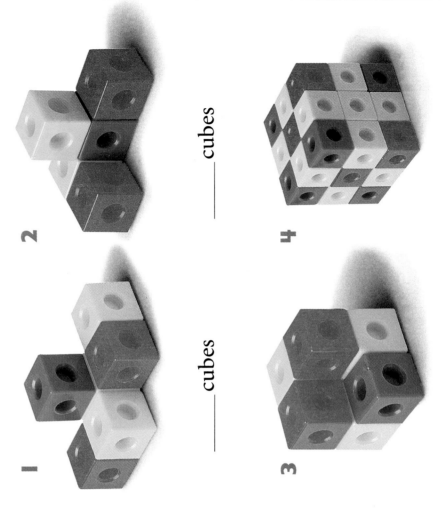

\_\_\_\_ cubes

**2**

\_\_\_\_ cubes

**3**

\_\_\_\_ cubes

**4**

\_\_\_\_ cubes

**5** Make your own model building with cubes. Ask another person to count the cubes.

**Notes for Home:** Your child counted the number of cubes used to form solid figures. *Home Activity:* Ask your child to compare the number of cubes used in Exercises 1 and 4. (Exercise 4 has 21 more cubes.)

# Putting It All Together

Tangrams are a kind of puzzle from China. A large square is cut into different shapes. The shapes can be arranged to form different pictures.

Cut out the tangram below, then cut along the lines to make pieces. See if you can arrange the pieces to make the pictures shown.

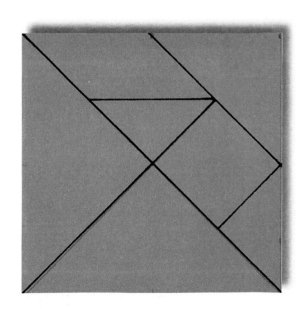

**Notes for Home:** Your child made pictures using different shapes. *Home Activity:* Ask your child to identify some of the shapes used in the tangram, such as the square and triangles.

# Cube Count

Many buildings look like rods and cubes that are put together.

This building in Montreal, Canada, looks like many cubes.

The Sears Tower in Chicago looks like rods that are attached.

1 a fish

2 a cat

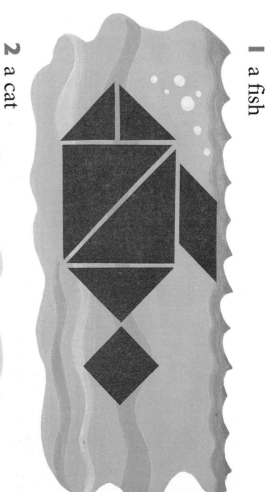

3 Make up your own picture! Show it to a friend or family member. Have them guess what the picture is.

3

# Super Sandwich

What is your favorite sandwich? peanut butter and jelly? How about ham and cheese?

Did you know there is a special day for sandwiches? National Sandwich Day is every year on November 3.

Write the fraction for one part of each sandwich.

**1** _____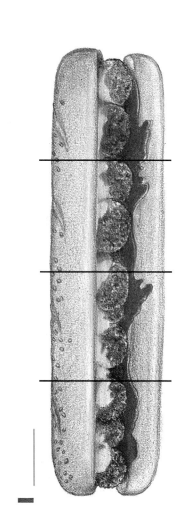

**2** _____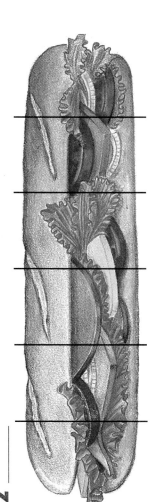

Draw lines to divide each sandwich into the given fraction.

**3** halves

**4** thirds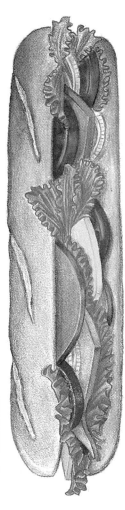

**5** Someone ate part of this sandwich. $\frac{1}{3}$ is left. How much was eaten?

_____

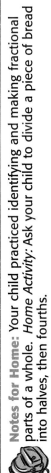

**Notes for Home:** Your child practiced identifying and making fractional parts of a whole. *Home Activity:* Ask your child to divide a piece of bread into halves, then fourths.

**CHAPTER**

**13**

# Multiplication and Division Concepts

Summer Fun

## Math at Home

Dear Family,
Our class is starting Chapter 13. We will be multiplying and dividing. Here are some activities we can do together.

2 eyes, socks
3 _____
4 _____
5 fingers
6 _____
7 days in a week

### Hunting for Groups
Help your child look around your home and make a list of things that come in groups. Keep the list handy so that your child can continue to add to it.

### Snack Time
At snack time, have your child show how to make equal groups. For example, ask your child how to divide 8 crackers equally between 2 people.

**Community Connection**
When you are outside with your child, look for examples of equal groups. Ask your child to tell how many in all. For example, 5 cars with 4 wheels each is 20 wheels in all.

💻💻 **Visit our Web site. www.parent.mathsurf.com**

© Scott Foresman Addison Wesley

Name _____

# Explore Joining Equal Groups

**Explore** ● ● ● ● ● ● ● ● ● ● ● ● ● ● ● ● ● ● ● ● ● ● ● ● ●

Use pattern blocks to make a design.
Draw it here.

How many pattern blocks did you use? _____

Make the same design more times.

|   | Make this many. | How many pattern blocks in all? |
|---|---|---|
| **1** | 2 | |
| **2** | 3 | |
| **3** | 4 | |
| **4** | 5 | |

**Share** ● ● ● ● ● ● ● ● ● ● ● ● ● ● ● ● ● ● ● ● ● ● ● ● ●

How did you find the total number of pattern

blocks when you made your design 5 times?

**Notes for Home:** Your child used pattern blocks to explore putting together equal groups.
*Home Activity:* Ask your child to use objects such as buttons to make 2 groups of 3 and then
tell how many in all.

**E X P L O R E**

**Chapter 13 Lesson 1**

four hundred ninety-three

**493**

You can add to find how many sails in all.

$3 + 3 + 3 + 3 = 12$

Each of these sailboats has 3 sails. The groups of sails are equal.

**EXPLORE**

Use pattern blocks to make the sails.

Find how many sails in all.

| | | Draw the sails. | How many sails in all? |
|---|---|---|---|
| **5** | 1 boat | | 3 |
| **6** | 2 boats | | $3 + 3 =$ _____ |
| **7** | 3 boats | | $3 + 3 + 3 =$ _____ |
| **8** | 4 boats | | $3 + 3 + 3 + 3 =$ _____ |

**Talk About It** What patterns do you see in your answers?

**Notes for Home:** Your child made equal groups and added to find how many in all. *Home Activity:* Ask your child to use objects to make 3 groups of 4 objects each. Ask your child to add to find how many objects in all. (12)

Name _____

# Addition and Multiplication

**Learn** • • • • • • • • • • • • • • • • • • • • • • • • • • • • • •

When groups are equal, you can
add or multiply to find how many in all.

6 is the product.

How many wheels?

2 + 2 + 2 = 6 wheels        3 × 2 = 6 wheels
3 groups of 2 is 6.          3 times 2 is 6.

**Check** • • • • • • • • • • • • • • • • • • • • • • • • • • • • • •

Use Snap Cubes. Find how many in all.
Draw to show your work.

**1** 4 water balloons
in each pail

_4_ + _4_ + _4_ = _12_ balloons

3 groups of 4 is 12.    _3_ × _4_ = _12_ balloons

**2** 3 tennis balls in each can

____ + ____ + ____ + ____ + ____ = ____ balls

5 groups of 3 is 15.    ____ × ____ = ____ balls

**Talk About It** Could you write a multiplication
sentence for 2 + 2 + 2 + 4? Explain.

 **Notes for Home:** Your child used addition and multiplication to find how many in several groups.
*Home Activity:* Ask your child to find the total numbers of flowers if there are 3 flowers in each of 3 pots.

**Chapter 13 Lesson 2**                    four hundred ninety-five **495**

Find how many in all. You can use Snap Cubes.

**3** How many legs?
4 groups of 2

____ + ____ + ____ + ____ = ____

____ × ____ = ____ legs

**4** How many children?
2 groups of 3

____ + ____ = ____

____ × ____ = ____ children

**5** How many kites?
4 groups of 3

____ + ____ + ____ + ____ = ____

____ × ____ = ____ kites

**6** How many balloons?
3 groups of 5

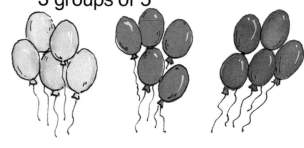

____ + ____ + ____ = ____

____ × ____ = ____ balloons

## Problem Solving Visual Thinking

Can you multiply to find how many in all? Tell why or why not.

**7**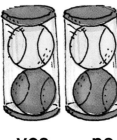

**yes    no**

**8**

**yes    no**

**9**

**yes    no**

 **Notes for Home:** Your child added and multiplied to find the total number in several groups.
*Home Activity:* Ask your child to write a multiplication sentence to find the total number of crackers for 2 packs of crackers with 4 crackers in each pack.

Name _____

# Explore Building Arrays

**Explore** • • • • • • • • • • • • • • • • • • • • •

Use Snap Cubes. Make equal rows.

Color to show your rows.

Write how many.

Remember, rows go across.

 ❶

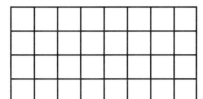

_____ equal rows      _____ in each row

_____ in all

❷

_____ equal rows      _____ in each row

_____ in all

 ❸

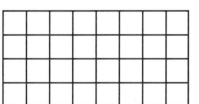

_____ equal rows      _____ in each row

_____ in all

❹

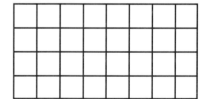

_____ equal rows      _____ in each row

_____ in all

**Share** • • • • • • • • • • • • • • • • • • • • •

How are these alike?

How are they different?

 **Notes for Home:** Your child colored equal rows on a grid and found how many squares in all. *Home Activity:* Have your child use objects to show you 2 rows of 6 and then find how many objects in all.

**Chapter 13 Lesson 3**                                              four hundred ninety-seven   **497**

2 rows of 5 chairs

$2 \times 5 = 10$

There are

10 chairs in all.

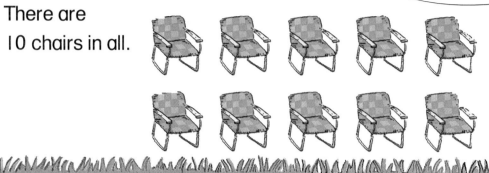

These rows are equal. You can multiply to find how many in all.

Color equal rows. Write how many. Find the product.

5 Show 3 rows of 4

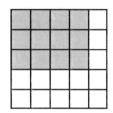

_3_ rows

_4_ in each row

$3 \times 4 = \underline{12}$

6 Show 4 rows of 2

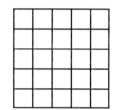

_____ rows

_____ in each row

$4 \times 2 = \underline{\quad}$

7 Show 5 rows of 5

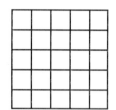

_____ rows

_____ in each row

$5 \times 5 = \underline{\quad}$

## Problem Solving

8 Draw groups to show $3 \times 5$.

How many in all? _____

9 Draw groups to show $5 \times 7$.

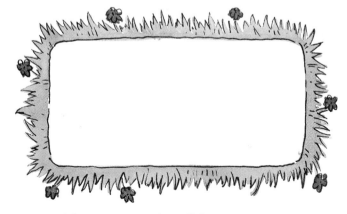

How many in all? _____

**Notes for Home:** Your child colored equal rows on a grid and completed a multiplication number sentence. *Home Activity:* Ask your child to draw a picture which shows 6 groups of 4.

© Scott Foresman Addison Wesley

Name _____

**Learn** ● ● ● ● ● ● ● ● ● ● ● ● ● ● ● ● ● ● ● ● ● ● ● ● ●

You can multiply the numbers in any order and get the same product.

Both rides hold 6 people!

$3 \times 2 = \underline{6}$ $2 \times 3 = \underline{6}$

**Check** ● ● ● ● ● ● ● ● ● ● ● ● ● ● ● ● ● ● ● ● ● ● ● ● ●

You can use Snap Cubes. Make equal rows.
Color each row. Find the product.

**1** 3 rows of 5          5 rows of 3          **2** 2 rows of 4          4 rows of 2

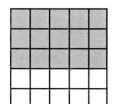

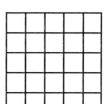

$3 \times 5 = \underline{\hphantom{00}}$ $5 \times 3 = \underline{\hphantom{00}}$ $2 \times 4 = \underline{\hphantom{00}}$ $4 \times 2 = \underline{\hphantom{00}}$

**3** 3 rows of 4          4 rows of 3          **4** 1 row of 5          5 rows of 1

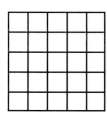

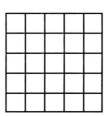

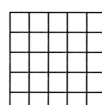

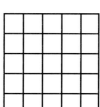

$3 \times 4 = \underline{\hphantom{00}}$ $4 \times 3 = \underline{\hphantom{00}}$ $1 \times 5 = \underline{\hphantom{00}}$ $5 \times 1 = \underline{\hphantom{00}}$

**Talk About It** Does 4 rows of 3 Snap Cubes have
more Snap Cubes than 3 rows of 4 Snap Cubes? Explain.

**Notes for Home:** Your child colored rows to show multiplication facts, and completed number
sentences. *Home Activity:* Ask your child to arrange small objects such as buttons or beans to show
$2 \times 6$ and $6 \times 2$.

Find the product. You can use Snap Cubes.

**5**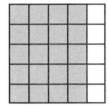

$5 \times 4 =$ _____    $4 \times 5 =$ _____

**6**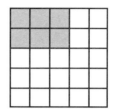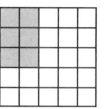

$2 \times 3 =$ _____    $3 \times 2 =$ _____

 **Write your own.** Use the same numbers.

Color different rows. Write different multiplication sentences.

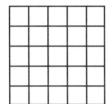          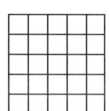

_____ $\times$ _____ = _____          _____ $\times$ _____ = _____

**7** $5 \times 4 =$ _____        **8** $4 \times 6 =$ _____        **9** $3 \times 8 =$ _____

$4 \times 5 =$ _____           $6 \times 4 =$ _____           $8 \times 3 =$ _____

## Problem Solving Patterns

**10** Find the products. What patterns do you see?

$1 \times 3 =$ _____        $2 \times 3 =$ _____        $3 \times 3 =$ _____        $4 \times 3 =$ _____

 **Notes for Home:** Your child found answers to related multiplication facts. *Home Activity:* Ask your child to use objects to show you 4 groups of 3 and 3 groups of 4.

Name _____

**Buckets of Beans**

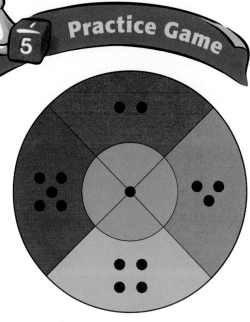

5    2
4    3

Number of Buckets

Number of Beans in each Bucket

**Players** 2 or 3

## What You Need

beans or counters

pencil

paper clip ⬭

## How to Play

1. Spin each spinner.

2. Multiply to find how many beans in all. Write a number sentence.

3. If your product is correct, take that many beans or counters.

4. After each turn, add to find your total number of beans.

5. The first player to get a total of 50 or more wins!

| Number Sentence | Total |
|---|---|
| ____ × ____ = ____ | |
| ____ × ____ = ____ | |
| ____ × ____ = ____ | |
| ____ × ____ = ____ | |
| ____ × ____ = ____ | |
| ____ × ____ = ____ | |
| ____ × ____ = ____ | |
| ____ × ____ = ____ | |

**PRACTICE**

**Notes for Home:** Your child played a game to practice multiplication facts. *Home Activity:* Ask your child to tell you how he or she found the numbers in the column labeled **Total**.

Name _____

Find how many in all. You can use Snap Cubes.

**1** How many beach balls?
2 groups of 6

 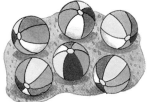

____ + ____ = ____

____ × ____ = ____

**2** How many arms?
3 groups of 5

____ + ____ + ____ = ____

____ × ____ = ____

Find the product. You can use Snap Cubes.

**3**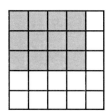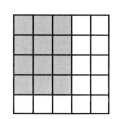

$3 \times 4 =$ ____    $4 \times 3 =$ ____

**4**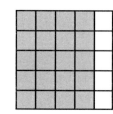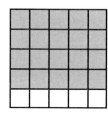

$5 \times 4 =$ ____    $4 \times 5 =$ ____

**5** $2 \times 5 =$ ____

$5 \times 2 =$ ____

**6** $4 \times 2 =$ ____

$2 \times 4 =$ ____

**7** $5 \times 3 =$ ____

$3 \times 5 =$ ____

## Number Sense

**8** Ellen and her friends are jumping rope. How many feet are jumping rope?

____ feet

**Notes for Home:** Your child practiced using multiplication. *Home Activity:* Ask your child to write and solve a pair of multiplication facts that use the same numbers.

PRACTICE

# Multiplication in Vertical Form

**Learn**

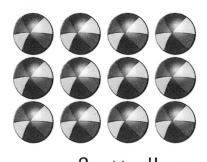

When you multiply, you can write the facts in two ways.

3 × 4 = _12_
rows · balls in each row · balls in all

4  balls in each row
× 3  rows
12  balls in all

**Check**

Find the products.

**1** 2 rows of 8

2 × 8 = ____

8
× 2 rows

**2** 4 groups of 2

4 × 2 = ____

2
× 4 groups

**3** 5 groups of 3

5 × 3 = ____

3
× 5 groups

**4** 3 rows of 6

3 × 6 = ____

6
× 3 rows

## Talk About It

Describe a picture that shows this multiplication fact.  7 × 3 = 21

**Notes for Home:** Your child found the answer to multiplication facts written two different ways.

*Home Activity:* Ask your child to show you two ways to write 6 times 2. (6 × 2; × 6 with 2 on top)

Write the number sentence.

**5** 2 rows of 7

$\underline{2} \times \underline{7} = \underline{14}$

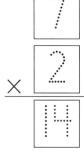

$$\begin{array}{r} 7 \\ \times\ 2 \\ \hline 14 \end{array}$$

**6** 4 groups of 5

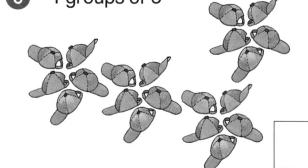

____ × ____ = ____

**PRACTICE**

**7** 4 rows of 4

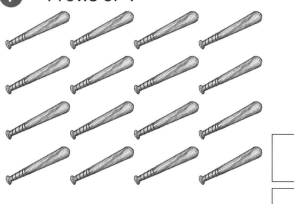

____ × ____ = ____

$\times$

**8** 5 rows of 2

____ × ____ = ____

$\times$

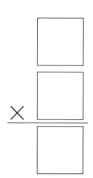

## Problem Solving Patterns

**9** Draw the next larger square. Write the number sentence.

$2 \times 2 = 4$    $3 \times 3 = 9$    $4 \times 4 = 16$    ____ × ____ = ____

**Notes for Home:** Your child wrote multiplication facts in two ways. *Home Activity:* Ask your child to draw 3 groups of 5 and then write the multiplication fact for the picture two ways. ($3 \times 5$; $\begin{array}{r} 5 \\ \times 3 \end{array}$)

**For additional practice, see Skills Practice Bank, page 539, Set**

Name _____

**Learn**  • • • • • • • • • • • • • • • • • •

**PROBLEM SOLVING GUIDE**
Understand • Plan • Solve • Look Back

Lesley has 4 bean plants,
4 carrot plants, and 4 pepper plants.
How many plants does she have in all?

There's more than one way to solve this problem!

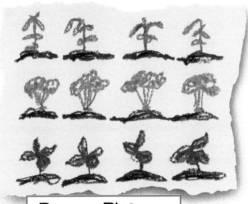

Draw a Picture.

$3 \times 4 = 12$ plants
Write a Number Sentence.

Use Objects.

**Check**  • • • • • • • • • • • • • • • • • • • • • • • • • •

Choose a way to solve each problem. Show what you did.

**1** Nolan's garden has 4 rows
of corn. Each row has 5 plants.
How many corn plants does
he have?

**2** Sandra planted 3 seeds in
each flower pot. She had 6 pots.
How many seeds did she plant?

**Talk About It** What other ways could you solve these problems?

**Notes for Home:** Your child chose strategies to solve word problems involving multiplication.
*Home Activity:* Ask your child to choose a way to find how many toys in all if there are 4 boxes
with 3 toys in each. (12)

PROBLEM SOLVING

Choose a way to solve each problem.
Show what you did.

**3** 5 children pick 2 pumpkins each. How many pumpkins do they pick in all?

**4** Tamara plants 3 sunflowers in each of 7 pots. How many sunflowers does she plant in all?

**5** Leah picks 5 bowls of strawberries. Eric picks 5 bowls of blueberries. Malik picks 5 bowls of blackberries. How many bowls of berries do they pick in all?

## Estimation

**6** About how many flowers are in the garden?

Circle the best estimate.

about 15        about 50        about 90

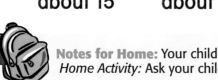

**Notes for Home:** Your child chose strategies to solve problems involving multiplication.
*Home Activity:* Ask your child to explain how he or she chose the answer for Exercise 6.

© Scott Foresman Addison Wesley

# Mixed Practice

**Lessons 1–6**

## Concepts and Skills

Find how many in all. You can use Snap Cubes.

**1** How many shells?

4 groups of 3

_____ + _____ + _____ + _____ = _____

_____ × _____ = _____

---

Color equal rows. Find the product.

**2** 4 rows of 5          5 rows of 4

$4 \times 5 =$ _____          $5 \times 4 =$ _____

**3** 3 rows of 2          2 rows of 3

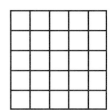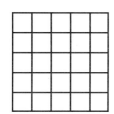

$3 \times 2 =$ _____          $2 \times 3 =$ _____

## Problem Solving

Draw a picture to solve the problem.

**4** There are 6 buckets on a beach blanket.
Each bucket has 3 shovels in it.
How many shovels are there in all?

_____ × _____ = _____

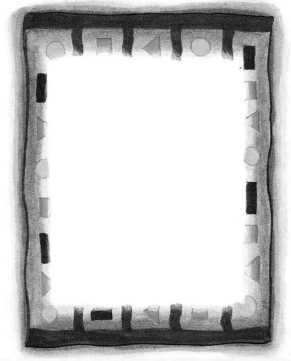

**Journal**

**5** Write a story to tell about $3 \times 4 = 12$.

**Notes for Home:** Your child practiced using pictures and drawing pictures to solve multiplication problems. *Home Activity:* Ask your child how the pictures in Exercise 2 would be different if they showed $4 \times 3$ and $3 \times 4$.

MIXED PRACTICE

Name _____

# Cumulative Review
## Chapters 1–13

## Concepts and Skills

Write the fraction that tells how much you shaded.

**1** Shade 6 parts.

 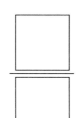

**2** Shade 2 parts.

 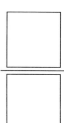

## Getting Ready for Next Year

Copy each problem on a separate piece of paper. Add or subtract.

**3**

| 420 | 653 | 592 | 314 | 817 | 617 |
|---|---|---|---|---|---|
| + 119 | − 428 | − 161 | + 227 | − 252 | + 212 |

**4**

| 584 | 216 | 987 | 375 | 714 | 504 |
|---|---|---|---|---|---|
| + 53 | + 429 | − 654 | + 264 | + 82 | + 162 |

---

### Test Prep

Fill in the ○ for the correct answer.

Which shape would you make if you traced a face of each object?

**5**
- ○ △
- ○ □
- ○ (trapezoid)
- ○ ○

**6**
- ○ △
- ○ □
- ○ (trapezoid)
- ○ ○

**7**
- ○ (rectangle)
- ○ △
- ○ ○
- ○ (trapezoid)

 **Notes or Home:** Your child reviewed fractions, solids, and addition and subtraction. *Home Activity:* Ask your child to share a piece of fruit or other food item so that he or she has $\frac{2}{3}$ and you have $\frac{1}{3}$.

508    five hundred eight

Name _____

# Explore Making Equal Groups

Use 12 counters. How many ways
can you make equal groups?
Draw one of your ways.

**Share**

Tell about the other ways you found to make equal groups.

**Notes for Home:** Your child used counters to make equal groups. *Home Activities:* Ask your child
to use 8 objects to make equal groups.

On their hike, 3 children picked 18 berries. They shared them equally. How many berries did each child get?

Start by giving one to each child. Keep sharing until they are gone.

Each child gets __6__ berries.

Use counters to make equal groups. Draw a picture to show your work.

**1** 12 people share 3 picnic blankets. How many people on each blanket?

__4__ people

**2** 8 children share 2 picnic tables. How many children at each table?

____ children

**3** 4 children share 16 water balloons. How many balloons for each child?

____ balloons

**4** 5 children share 10 hot dogs. How many hot dogs for each child?

____ hot dogs

**Talk About It** Could 4 children share 17 crackers equally? How do you know?

**Notes for Home:** Your child drew pictures to share amounts equally. *Home Activity:* Ask your child to use 6 objects and show how to share them equally among 6 people.

**EXPLORE**

**510** five hundred ten

## Share and Divide

**Learn** • • • • • • • • • • • • • • • • • • • • • • • • •

5 children share 15 hoops equally.
How many hoola hoops will each child get?

When you share equally, you *divide*.

15 divided by 5 equals __3__

15 ÷ 5 = __3__ hoops.

**Check** • • • • • • • • • • • • • • • • • • • • • • • • • •

Use counters to make equal groups. Draw to show your work.
Write the number sentence.

**1** 12 bean bags in 4 buckets

12 ÷ 4 = 3 bean bags

**2** 16 beads on 2 necklaces

____ ÷ ____ = ____ beads

**3** 10 balloons shared by 2 children

____ ÷ ____ = ____ balloons

**4** 9 yo-yos in 3 boxes

____ ÷ ____ = ____ yo-yos

**Talk About It** How did you find how many yo-yos went in each box?

**Notes for Home:** Your child drew pictures to share groups equally and completed division sentences.
*Home Activity:* Ask your child to draw a picture and write a division sentence to show 9 balls shared equally by 3 children.

## Practice

You can use counters. Draw a picture to show equal groups.
Write the number sentence.

**5** 20 pieces of chalk in 4 boxes

$\underline{20} \div \underline{4} = \underline{5}$ pieces

**6** 12 birds on 2 branches.

____ ÷ ____ = ____ birds

**7** 25 marbles in 5 bags

____ ÷ ____ = ____ marbles

**8** 15 toy cars in 3 cases

____ ÷ ____ = ____ toy cars

**9** 12 children on 3 swing sets

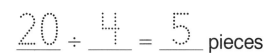

____ ÷ ____ = ____ children

**10** 8 kites shared by 2 children

____ ÷ ____ = ____ kites

## Problem Solving

Solve. You can use counters.

**11** Tanesha has 18 water balloons to give
away. If she gives 2 to each friend,
how many friends will get water balloons?

____ friends

**Notes for Home:** Your child drew pictures and completed number sentences to divide.
*Home Activity:* Ask your child to write a division sentence using the numbers 18, 3, and 6.

**For additional practice, see Skills Practice Bank, page 539, Set 2.**

Name ______________________________

Reading for Math

## Compare and Contrast

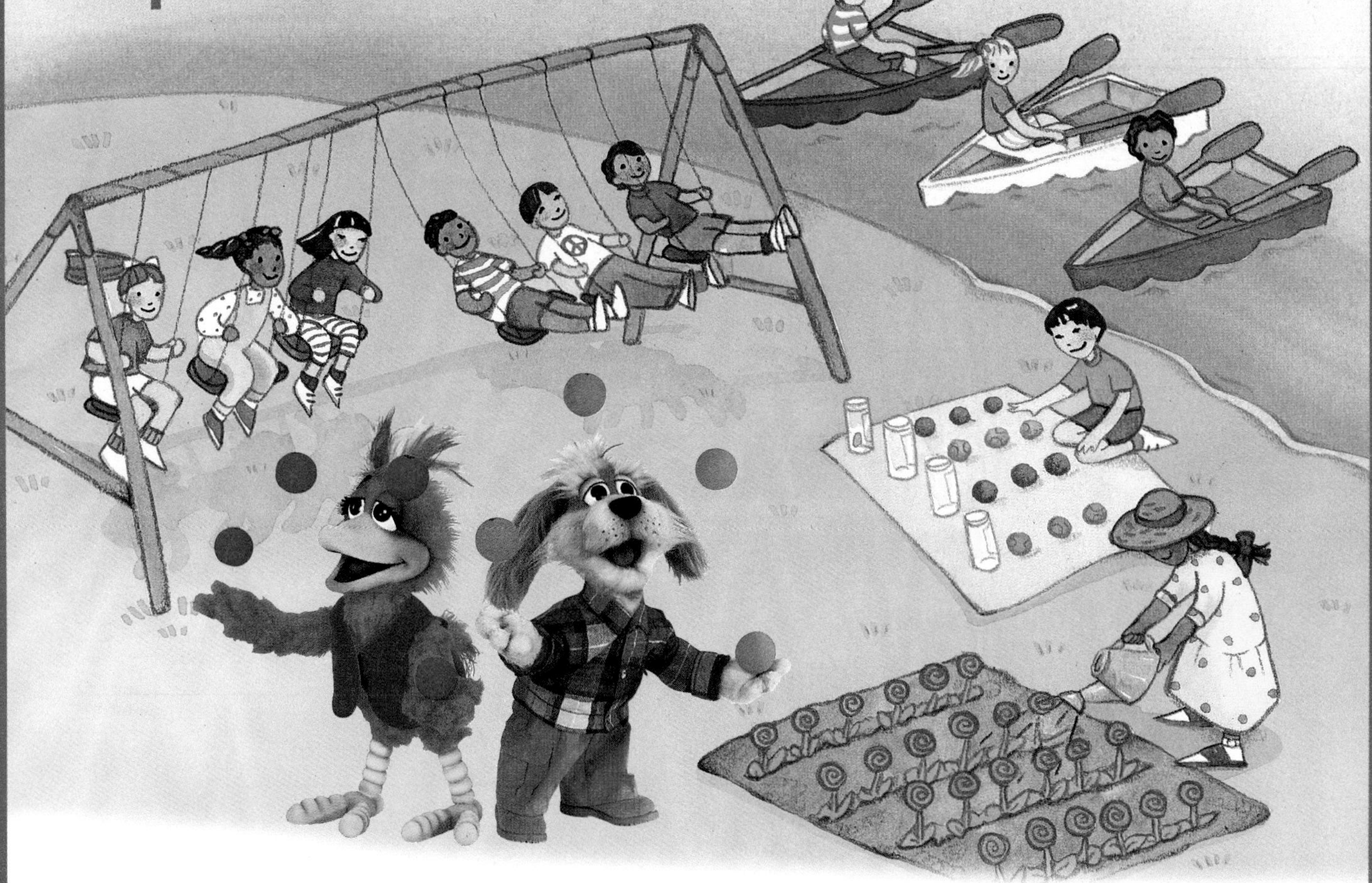

Use the picture. Tell multiplication stories. Tell division stories.

1. How are multiplication and division stories alike?

______________________________

______________________________

______________________________

2. How are multiplication and division stories different?

______________________________

______________________________

______________________________

**Notes for Home:** Your child compared multiplication and division stories. *Home Activity:* Show your child 2 equal groups such as 2 groups of 3 spoons each. Ask your child to make up a multiplication story and a division story using the items.

Use the picture.

**3** Tell a multiplication story.
How do you know it is a multiplication story?

_____

_____

_____

**4** Tell a division story.
How do you know it is a division story?

_____

_____

_____

**Journal**

**5** Write a story that shows multiplication. Write a story that shows division. Compare your stories with a friend.

**Notes for Home:** Your child compared multiplication and division. *Home Activity:* Ask your child to draw a simple picture with equal groups in it and tell multiplication and division stories about it.

Name _____

# Problem Solving: Choose an Operation

**Learn** • • • • • • • • • • • • •

**PROBLEM SOLVING GUIDE**
Understand • Plan • Solve • Look Back

There are 6 tents.
Each tent has 3 children inside.
How many children are there?

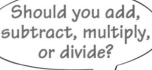
Should you add, subtract, multiply, or divide?

6 ÷ 3 = 2          6 × 3 = 18          6 − 3 = 3

**Check** • • • • • • • • • • • • • • • • • • • • • • • • • • • • •

Circle the number sentence that solves the problem.

**1** 2 children are hiking.
3 more children join them.
How many children are hiking?

2 × 3 = 6          3 − 2 = 1          2 + 3 = 5

**2** On a camping trip, 5 people
shared 10 boxes of raisins equally.
How many boxes did each
person get?

10 + 5 = 15          10 ÷ 5 = 2          2 × 5 = 10

**Talk About It** In the problem about tents, how
would you use addition to find the answer? Explain.

 **Notes for Home:** Your child circled the number sentence that solves a word problem.
*Home Activity:* Ask your child to write a word problem that could be solved by dividing.

**Chapter 13 Lesson 9**                    five hundred fifteen   **515**

Circle the number sentence that helps you solve the problem.

**3** 5 children are fishing.
Each child catches 3 fish.
How many fish do the
children catch in all?

$5 \times 3 = 15$          $5 - 3 = 2$          $15 \div 3 = 5$

**4** There are 8 children around
a campfire. 2 children go
into their tents. How many
children are still around
the campfire?

$8 + 2 = 10$          $8 \div 2 = 4$          $8 - 2 = 6$

**5** 10 people want to share
2 canoes equally.
How many people will
go in each canoe?

$10 + 2 = 12$          $10 \div 2 = 5$          $10 - 2 = 8$

## Tell a Math Story

Tell a story for each number sentence.

**6** $4 \times 2 = 8$          **7** $12 \div 2 = 6$          **8** $17 - 9 = 8$

**Notes for Home:** Your child identified a number sentence that could be used to solve a word problem.
*Home Activity:* Ask your child to write a word problem that could be solved by multiplying.

# Mixed Practice
### Lessons 7–9

## Concepts and Skills

You can use counters to make equal groups.
Draw to show your work. Write the number sentence.

**1** 8 people share 2 beach towels.
How many people on each towel?

_____ ÷ _____ = _____ people

**2** 12 shells go in 3 buckets.
How many shells in each bucket?

_____ ÷ _____ = _____ shells

## Problem Solving

Circle the number sentence that solves the problem.

**3** There are 6 children.
Each child has 3 balloons.
How many balloons are there?

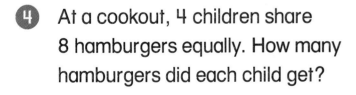

$6 - 3 = 3$       $18 ÷ 3 = 6$       $6 × 3 = 18$

**4** At a cookout, 4 children share
8 hamburgers equally. How many
hamburgers did each child get?

$4 × 2 = 8$       $8 ÷ 4 = 2$       $8 + 4 = 12$

## Journal

**5** Write a story for this number sentence.    $6 ÷ 2 = 3$

**Notes for Home:** Your child practiced multiplying and dividing. *Home Activity:* Ask your child to draw a picture for $12 ÷ 3 = 4$.

Name _____

# Cumulative Review
## Chapter 1–13

## Concepts and Skills

Draw a shape that is congruent to each shape.

**1**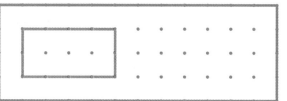

**2**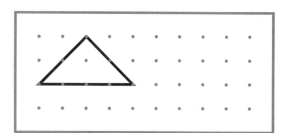

## Problem Solving

**3** Dan brought 16 oranges and 20 bananas to the picnic. How many pieces of fruit did he bring?

_____ pieces of fruit

**4** At summer camp, 53 children went canoeing. 27 children went hiking. How many more children went canoeing?

_____ children

## Getting Ready for Next Year

Copy each problem on a separate piece of paper.
Add.

**5**

| 21 | 15 | 23 | 64 | 18 | 19 |
|----|----|----|----|----|----|
| 32 | 12 | 17 | 29 | 48 | 31 |
| + 14 | + 45 | + 52 | + 6 | + 10 | + 49 |

---

### Test Prep

Fill in the ○ for the correct answer.

Add or subtract.

**6**
$$415 + 326$$
○ 701
○ 731
○ 741
○ 811

**7**
$$526 - 352$$
○ 174
○ 234
○ 274
○ 284

**8**
$$982 - 657$$
○ 335
○ 225
○ 425
○ 325

 **Notes for Home:** Your child reviewed congruence, addition, subtraction, and word problems.
*Home Activity:* Ask your child to draw two shapes that have the same size and shape, or that are congruent.

# Chapter 13 Review

## Vocabulary

**1** Find the product.
Write the number sentence.

There are 4 trees with 3 children in each tree. How many children are in the trees?

____ × ____ = ____ children

**2** Divide.
Write the number sentence.

12 people share 4 row boats equally. How many people are in each boat?

____ ÷ ____ = ____ people

## Concepts and Skills

**3** Color equal rows. Find the product.
4 rows of 3

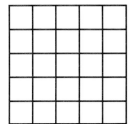

4 × 3 = ____

**4** Find the product.
3 groups of 6

3 × 6 = ____

6
× 3
___

## Problem Solving

**5** Choose a way to solve the problem. Show what you did.

At the beach, 2 children collect 5 seashells each. How many seashells do they have?

**6** Circle the number sentence that solves the problem.

2 friends share 4 boxes of raisins equally. How many boxes of raisins for each friend?

4 + 2 = 6         4 ÷ 2 = 2         4 × 2 = 8

**Notes for Home:** Your child reviewed vocabulary, concepts, skills, and problem solving from Chapter 13. *Home Activity:* Ask your child to write a multiplication story and a division story using the numbers 10, 5, and 2.

**CHAPTER REVIEW**

Name _____

# Chapter 13 Test

Find how many in all. Write the number sentence.

**1** How many clams?

2 groups of 5

____ + ____ = ____

____ × ____ = ____

**2** Color equal rows. Find the product.

3 rows of 5

____ × ____ = ____

**3** Find the product.

4 groups of 3

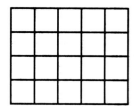

4 × 3 = ____          $\begin{array}{r} 3 \\ \times\, 4 \\ \hline \end{array}$

**4** Draw to show equal groups. Write the number sentence.

10 children on 2 blankets

____ ÷ ____ = ____ children

**5** Choose a way to solve the problem. Show what you did.

Calvin plants 3 rows of flowers with 6 flowers in each row. How many flowers does he plant in all?

**6** Circle the number sentence that solves the problem.

4 children share 16 balloons equally.
How many balloons does each child get?

4 × 4 = 16          16 + 4 = 20          16 ÷ 4 = 4

**Notes for Home:** Your child was tested on Chapter 13 skills, concepts, and problem solving.
*Home Activity:* Ask your child to tell a word problem using the numbers 12, 6, and 2.

CHAPTER TEST

520   five hundred twenty

Name _____

# Performance Assessment
## Chapter 13

Show What You Know

Take number cards.

Write a story.

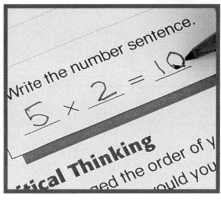
Write the number sentence.

| Activity 1 | Activity 2 |
|---|---|
| Take two number cards from Bag 1. | Start with the number 12. Pick one number card from Bag 2. |
| ① Write a multiplication story that uses your numbers. | ③ Write a division story that uses your numbers. |
| _____<br>_____<br>_____<br>_____ | _____<br>_____<br>_____<br>_____ |
| ② Write the number sentence.<br><br>_____ × _____ = _____ | ④ Write the number sentence.<br><br>_____ ÷ _____ = _____ |

## Critical Thinking

If you changed the order of your numbers
in Activity 1, how would your story change?

**Notes for Home:** Your child did an activity that tested Chapter 13 skills, concepts, and problem solving.
*Home Activity:* Ask your child to write a multiplication story about objects in your home.

**Explore with a CALCULATOR**

# Your Town Counts!

**Keys You Will Use**  ON/C  ×  +  =

About how many people do you think are in your city or town? You can use your calculator to help you estimate.

**1** Each person in your room stands for a family. Find how many people the students in your class represent. Add to find the total number.

**2** Estimate how many people the students in your school represent. Multiply the total number of people your class represents by the number of classes in your school.

| Name | Total in Family |
|------|------|
| Louisa | 3 |
| Eric | 2 |
| Jesse | 4 |
| Bree | 5 |
| John | 3 |
| Total in Class | |

_____ × _____ = _____

actual people     actual        estimated
your class        number        number
represents        of classes    of people

**3** Estimate how many people are in your town. Find out how many schools there are in your city or town. Multiply your estimate of the total number of people your school represents by the number of schools in your city or town.

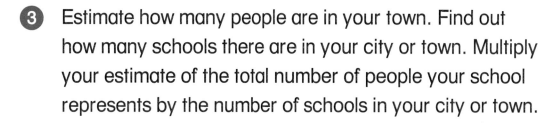

_____ × _____ = _____

estimated        actual        estimated
number           number        number of people
of people        of schools    in my town

**4** Find out the actual number of people in your city or town. Compare your estimate to the actual number. Was your estimate higher or lower than the actual number?

**Tech Talk** How could you solve the above problem without the  × key?

⌨ **Visit our Web site.** www.parent.mathsurf.com

# What a Square!

If you can arrange dots to form an array in the shape of a square, you have formed a square number.

Here are the first four square numbers. Use multiplication to tell about the number of dots.

**1**

$1 \times 1 =$ ____

**2**

____ $\times$ ____ $=$ ____

**3**

____ $\times$ ____ $=$ ____

**4**

What do you think the next two square numbers are? Draw an array, then use multiplication to tell about the number of dots.

Fold down

Hot Shot!

Math Surf

Scott Foresman - Addison Wesley

My Math Magazine    No. 13

Justin began playing in tournaments when he was six years old. He almost always finishes in first, second, or third place! Many hours of practice help Justin enjoy many hours of summer fun!

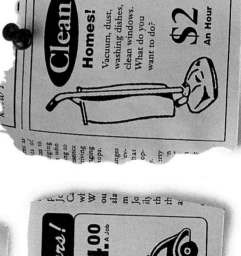

# Pay Your Way

It's summer! What do you want to do? Go out to eat? To pay for your summer fun, sometimes you have to do summer work.

The advertisements show different jobs you can do to earn money.

LAWN MOWERS

**Yard Work!**

Rake and bag grass trimmings.

**$6** A Job

**Water Plants**

**$2** A Day

Earn extra money this summer. Water plants for out-of-town folks!

**Clean Homes!**

Vacuum, dust, washing dishes, clean windows. What do you want to do?

**$2** An Hour

**Wash Cars!**

Hey Kids! Wash and shine cars in your spare time.

**$4.00** A Job

**Notes for Home:** Your child practiced multiplying and dividing. *Home Activity:* Ask your child to multiply 3 × 4, then divide the product by 2. (6)

**2**

# Just Fore Fun!

Have you ever played miniature golf? Justin Carter's favorite game is golf—not miniature golf, but full-sized golf on real golf courses.

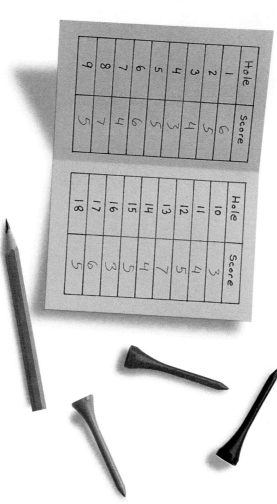

| Hole | Score |
|------|-------|
| 1 | 6 |
| 2 | 5 |
| 3 | 4 |
| 4 | 3 |
| 5 | 5 |
| 6 | 6 |
| 7 | 4 |
| 8 | 7 |
| 9 | 5 |

| Hole | Score |
|------|-------|
| 10 | 3 |
| 11 | 4 |
| 12 | 5 |
| 13 | 7 |
| 14 | 4 |
| 15 | 5 |
| 16 | 3 |
| 17 | 6 |
| 18 | 5 |

Suppose Justin got these scores in one round of golf.

1 On how many holes did Justin score 3?
Multiply to find his total score for these holes.

2 Multiply to find Justin's total score for the holes where he scored 4, 5, 6, and 7.

3 Add your answers to find Justin's score for the entire round.

Use the advertisements to answer these questions.

1 Your neighbors go on vacation. You water their plants for 5 days. How much do you earn?

_____

2 You and a friend do 1 job of yard work. When you are finished, you divide the money equally. How much do you each earn?

_____

3 You and a friend clean your home for 2 hours. Then you wash 2 cars. How much do both of you earn in all?

_____

Divide the money you earned equally. How much do you each earn?

_____

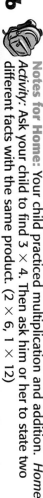

**Notes for Home:** Your child practiced multiplication and addition. *Home Activity:* Ask your child to find 3 × 4. Then ask him or her to state two different facts with the same product. (2 × 6, 1 × 12)

6

# It's in the Bank!

Do you like basketball? How about miniature golf? Here's a game that combines them. It's called Bankshot.

In Bankshot, you must bank, or bounce, the basketball off different backboards.

Each basket, or station, has three circles by it. You shoot twice from each circle and earn different points for each shot.

## Shots Made

| | Farthest Circle (3 points a shot) | Middle Circle (2 points a shot) | Nearest Circle (1 point a shot) |
|---|---|---|---|
| Station 1 | 2 | 1 | 2 |
| Station 2 | 1 | 2 | 2 |
| Station 3 | 1 | 2 | 2 |
| Point Totals | —— points | —— points | —— points |

1  Suppose you are playing Bankshot. The table shows the number of shots you made at the first three stations. Find your total points for each circle.

2  Add your point totals to find your total score.

—— points

**Notes for Home:** Your child practiced multiplying and adding to find totals.
*Home Activity:* Ask your child to add the products for $3 \times 3$ and $4 \times 2$. (17)

# Skills Practice Bank
### Chapter 1

**Set 1** Use after page 8.

Count by 2s, 5s, or 10s.

Write the numbers.

**1** 2, 4, _____, _____, _____

**2** 12, 14, _____, _____, _____

**3** 10, 20, _____, _____, _____

**4** 15, 20, _____, _____, _____

**Set 2** Use after page 12.

Continue the pattern. Color the numbers.

**1**

| 1 | 2 | 3 | 4 | 5 | 6 | 7 | 8 | 9 | 10 |
|---|---|---|---|---|---|---|---|---|----|
| 11 | 12 | 13 | 14 | 15 | 16 | 17 | 18 | 19 | 20 |
| 21 | 22 | 23 | 24 | 25 | 26 | 27 | 28 | 29 | 30 |
| 31 | 32 | 33 | 34 | 35 | 36 | 37 | 38 | 39 | 40 |
| 41 | 42 | 43 | 44 | 45 | 46 | 47 | 48 | 49 | 50 |

**Set 3** Use after page 22.

**1** Use the tally chart to make a bar graph.

| Favorite Game | |
|---|---|
| Jump Rope | IIII |
| Tag | III |
| Hide-and-Seek | HHT I |

| Favorite Game | | | | | | |
|---|---|---|---|---|---|---|
| Jump Rope | | | | | | |
| Tag | | | | | | |
| Hide-and-Seek | | | | | | |

1 2 3 4 5 6

**2** How many more children chose
**Hide-and-Seek** than **Jump Rope?** _____ more

# Skills Practice Bank
## Chapter 2

**Set 1** Use after page 44.

Add.

**1**
| 4 | 7 | 8 | 9 | 5 | 8 | 9 |
|---|---|---|---|---|---|---|
| + 1 | + 2 | + 0 | + 2 | + 3 | + 3 | + 1 |

**2**
| 3 | 5 | 3 | 2 | 3 | 4 | 1 |
|---|---|---|---|---|---|---|
| + 9 | + 2 | + 6 | + 9 | + 5 | + 3 | + 7 |

---

**Set 2** Use after page 58.

Subtract.

**1**
| 6 | 9 | 7 | 8 | 11 | 12 | 10 |
|---|---|---|---|----|----|----|
| − 1 | − 2 | − 0 | − 2 | − 1 | − 0 | − 2 |

**2**
| 5 | 12 | 8 | 7 | 10 | 9 | 6 |
|---|----|---|---|----|---|---|
| − 2 | − 1 | − 0 | − 2 | − 1 | − 2 | − 1 |

---

**Set 3** Use after page 68.

Circle **add** or **subtract.**

Write the number sentence. Solve.

**1** 10 children jumped rope.
2 children went home.
How many children were left?

**add**    **subtract**

_____ children

**2** 8 children played hide-and-seek.
3 more children joined them.
How many children are there?

**add**    **subtract**

_____ children

**528**    five hundred twenty-eight

Name _____

# Skills Practice Bank
**Chapter 3**

**Set 1** Use after page 92.

Add. Write the addition sentence.

 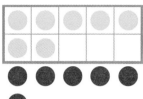

_____ + _____ = _____

_____ + _____ = _____

---

**Set 2** Use after page 94.

❶ Malik is cleaning his room.
Find all the ways he can
put 7 toys in two boxes.
Each box can hold up to 6 toys.
Write your numbers in the list.
You can use 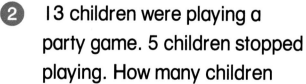 to help.

| Box 1 | Box 2 |
|-------|-------|
|       |       |
|       |       |
|       |       |
|       |       |
|       |       |
|       |       |

---

**Set 3** Use after page 102.

Write a number sentence. Solve.

❶ 8 children were playing a
party game. 5 more children
joined them. How many
children were playing then?

_____

❷ 13 children were playing a
party game. 5 children stopped
playing. How many children
were playing then?

_____

# Skills Practice Bank
### Chapter 4

**Set 1** Use after page 122.

Complete each fact family. Add or subtract.

**1** $9 + 5 =$ ___    **2** $7 + 6 =$ ___    **3** $9 + 8 =$ ___

$5 + 9 =$ ___    $6 + 7 =$ ___    $8 + 9 =$ ___

$14 - 5 =$ ___    $13 - 6 =$ ___    $17 - 8 =$ ___

$14 - 9 =$ ___    $13 - 7 =$ ___    $17 - 9 =$ ___

**Set 2** Use after page 136.

Add.

**1** $5 + 5 + 4 =$ ___    **2** $6 + 3 + 2 =$ ___

$4 + 3 + 4 =$ ___    $8 + 0 + 2 =$ ___

**Set 3** Use after page 144.

Write each number sentence. Solve.

**1** There are 14 prizes on the shelf.
People win 6 prizes.
How many prizes are left?

_____ prizes

4 more prizes are put on the shelf.
How many prizes are there now?

_____ prizes

**2** Joe brings 4 sandwiches
to the picnic. Bonnie brings
8 more. How many sandwiches
are at the picnic?

_____ sandwiches

6 of the sandwiches are eaten.
How many sandwiches are left?

_____ sandwiches

# Skills Practice Bank
## Chapter 5

**Set 1** Use after page 162.

Write the number.

**1** eight _____   **2** seventeen _____   **3** forty-five _____

Write the word.

**4** 7 _____   **5** 14 _____   **6** 23 _____

---

**Set 2** Use after page 166.

Use the graph to answer the questions.

**1** How many leaves did Bridget collect?

_____ leaves

**2** How many more leaves did Clara collect than Lamar?

_____ more

| Leaf Collections | |
|---|---|
| Clara | 🍁 🍁 🍁 🍁 🍁 |
| Lamar | 🍁 🍁 🍁 |
| Bridget | 🍁 🍁 🍁 🍁 🍁 🍁 |

Each 🍁 means 10 leaves.

---

**Set 3** Use after page 176.

Write the numbers in order from least to greatest.

**1** 53   38   47        _____   _____   _____

**2** 41   70   28        _____   _____   _____

**3** 86   90   82        _____   _____   _____

**4** 79   59   97        _____   _____   _____

Name _____

# Skills Practice Bank
**Chapter 6**

**Set 1** Use after page 206.

Count the money. Write how much in all.

 **1**

_____ ¢

**2**

_____ ¢

**Set 2** Use after page 208.

**1** Chris needs 25¢ to buy milk for lunch.
Complete the list to find all the ways
to make 25¢.

| | | |
|---|---|---|
| | | |
| | | |
| | | |
| | | |

**Set 3** Use after page 214.

**1** Use quarters and dimes to show $1.00.
Draw the coins. Write how many.

<br><br><br><br><br>

There are _____ quarters and _____ dimes in $1.00.

**SKILLS PRACTICE BANK**

Name

# Skills Practice Bank
## Chapter 7

**Set 1** Use after page 240.

Draw the clock hands.

Write the ending time.

**1** Start 5:00

2 hours later

Stop ____:____

**Set 2** Use after page 244.

Use the table. Solve the problems.

Write each answer.

| Computer Club Schedule | | |
|---|---|---|
| Day | Starts | Ends |
| Monday | 3:00 | 4:00 |
| Tuesday | 3:00 | 4:00 |
| Wednesday | 3:00 | 5:00 |
| Thursday | 3:00 | 4:00 |
| Friday | 3:00 | 6:00 |

**1** On how many days does the Computer Club meet for only one hour?

______ days

**2** For how many hours does the Computer Club meet on Friday?

______ hours

**Set 3** Use after page 248.

Write the time for each clock.

**1** 

____:____

**2** 

____:____

**3** 

____:____

**4** 

____:____

# Skills Practice Bank
## Chapter 8

**Set 1** Use after page 286.

Add. Then circle the sum if you regrouped.

|  | tens | ones |
|---|---|---|
| **1** | ☐ | |
| | 2 | 3 |
| + | | 8 |

|  | tens | ones |
|---|---|---|
| **2** | ☐ | |
| | 5 | 4 |
| + | | 5 |

|  | tens | ones |
|---|---|---|
| **3** | ☐ | |
| | 7 | 7 |
| + | | 7 |

|  | tens | ones |
|---|---|---|
| **4** | ☐ | |
| | 8 | 3 |
| + | | 6 |

**Set 2** Use after page 298.

Add.

**1**

| 15 | 53 | 40 | 14 | 62 | 20 |
|---|---|---|---|---|---|
| 22 | 8 | 12 | 18 | 10 | 9 |
| + 41 | + 31 | + 38 | + 21 | + 17 | + 47 |

**Set 3** Use after page 300.

55¢   30¢   40¢   35¢   39¢

Solve. Show each guess. Then check each guess.

**1** Brett has 67¢.

He wants to buy 2 toys.

What can he buy?

Brett can buy the _____ and the _____ .

Name _____

# Skills Practice Bank
**Chapter 9**

**Set 1** Use after page 324.

Subtract. Circle the difference if you regrouped.

| tens | ones | | tens | ones | | tens | ones | | tens | ones |
|------|------|--|------|------|--|------|------|--|------|------|
| ☐ | ☐ | | ☐ | ☐ | | ☐ | ☐ | | ☐ | ☐ |
| 2 | 4 | | 4 | 2 | | 7 | 5 | | 6 | 4 |
| − | 8 | | − 1 | 7 | | − 3 | 9 | | − 5 | 2 |

| tens | ones | | tens | ones | | tens | ones | | tens | ones |
|------|------|--|------|------|--|------|------|--|------|------|
| ☐ | ☐ | | ☐ | ☐ | | ☐ | ☐ | | ☐ | ☐ |
| 8 | 7 | | 9 | 3 | | 7 | 2 | | 4 | 9 |
| − 3 | 6 | | − 3 | 9 | | − 5 | 5 | | − 3 | 8 |

**Set 2** Use after page 336.

Subtract. Regroup if you need to.

|   | 26 | 50 | 62 | 70 | 84 | 96 |
|---|----|----|----|----|----|----|
|   | − 19 | − 23 | − 41 | − 28 | − 18 | − 62 |

**Set 3** Use after page 344.

Solve. Cross out the information you do not need.

① A dolphin can swim about 37 miles per hour.
A trout can swim about 15 miles per hour.
People can swim about 5 miles per hour.
How much faster can a dolphin swim than a trout?

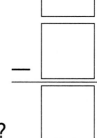

☐ miles per hour

SKILLS PRACTICE BANK

# Skills Practice Bank
## Chapter 10

**Set 1** Use after page 366.

Compare the numbers. Write >, <, or =.

❶ 132 ◯ 231     418 ◯ 481     642 ◯ 624

❷ 770 ◯ 770     301 ◯ 279     883 ◯ 880

---

**Set 2** Use after page 384.

Subtract. Regroup if you need to.

❶
$$\begin{array}{r} 418 \\ -\ 327 \end{array} \qquad \begin{array}{r} 742 \\ -\ 127 \end{array} \qquad \begin{array}{r} 415 \\ -\ 210 \end{array} \qquad \begin{array}{r} 618 \\ -\ 453 \end{array} \qquad \begin{array}{r} 886 \\ -\ \ \ 94 \end{array}$$

---

**Set 3** Use after page 388.

Use the picture to answer the questions.

❶ Reggie needs 250 beads for an art project. Which bags could he choose? Circle them in red.

❷ Stephanie needs 175 beads to make a craft. Which bags could she choose? Circle them in blue.

SKILLS PRACTICE BANK

# Skills Practice Bank
## Chapter 11

**Set 1** Use after page 412.

**1** Mark an **X** on the shape that you estimate
has the greatest perimeter. Measure the lengths
of the sides. Add to find the perimeter.
Circle the shape with the greatest perimeter.

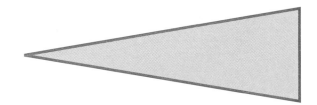

_____ inches around

_____ inches around

---

**Set 2** Use after page 416.

**1** Use 12 🪙.
Make a shape that is a rectangle
and has a perimeter of 14 units.
Draw to show what you did.

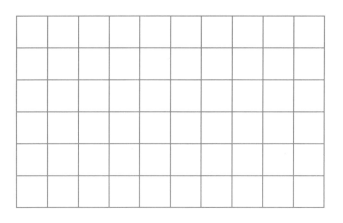

---

**Set 3** Use after page 424.
Solve.

**1** Dalia needs 2 quarts of milk
for a recipe. Color the number
of cups she could fill.

**2** Bernard has 6 pints of juice.
Color the number of quarts
that hold the same amount.

# Skills Practice Bank
**Chapter 12**

**Set 1** Use after page 452.

Draw a shape that is congruent to each shape.

 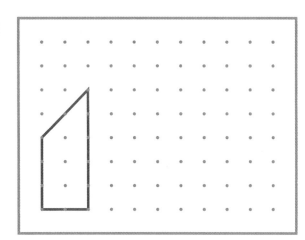

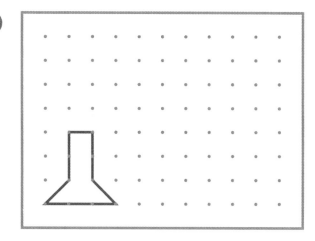

**Set 2** Use after page 468.

❶ Write the fraction that tells how much is shaded.

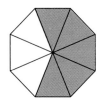 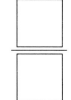

❷ Write the fraction that tells how much you shaded. Shade 4 parts.

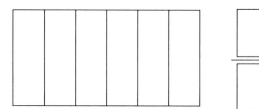

**Set 3** Use after page 480.

❶ Predict. If you were to spin 12 times, how many times would the spinner land

on orange? _____    on red? _____

on purple? _____

❷ Spin 12 times. Write the results.

_____ orange    _____ red

_____ purple

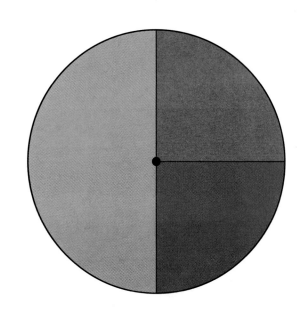

SKILLS PRACTICE BANK

Name _____

# Skills Practice Bank
## Chapter 13

**Set 1** Use after page 504.

Write the number sentence.

**1** 6 groups of 2 balls

____ × ____ = ____    × ☐/☐/☐

**2** 3 rows of 5 Snap Cubes

____ × ____ = ____    × ☐/☐/☐

**Set 2** Use after page 512.

You can use counters.

Draw a picture to show equal groups.

Write the number sentence.

**1** 12 children in 3 wagons

____ ÷ ____ = ____ children

**2** 16 children in 4 rowboats

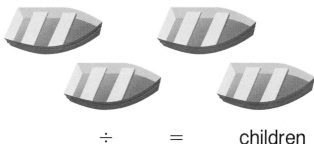

____ ÷ ____ = ____ children

**Set 3** Use after page 516.

Circle the number sentence that solves the problem.

**1** 15 children were making crafts.
5 children left to go on a hike.
How many children were still
making crafts?

$15 + 5 = 20$

$15 ÷ 5 = 3$

$15 - 5 = 10$

Name _____

# Basic Facts Review

**Set 1** Use after page 53.

Add.

**1**
$$
\begin{array}{r} 2 \\ +7 \end{array}
\qquad
\begin{array}{r} 6 \\ +3 \end{array}
\qquad
\begin{array}{r} 9 \\ +3 \end{array}
\qquad
\begin{array}{r} 8 \\ +1 \end{array}
\qquad
\begin{array}{r} 3 \\ +7 \end{array}
\qquad
\begin{array}{r} 2 \\ +9 \end{array}
\qquad
\begin{array}{r} 5 \\ +2 \end{array}
$$

**2**
$$
\begin{array}{r} 10 \\ +0 \end{array}
\qquad
\begin{array}{r} 5 \\ +4 \end{array}
\qquad
\begin{array}{r} 11 \\ +1 \end{array}
\qquad
\begin{array}{r} 2 \\ +6 \end{array}
\qquad
\begin{array}{r} 7 \\ +1 \end{array}
\qquad
\begin{array}{r} 12 \\ +0 \end{array}
\qquad
\begin{array}{r} 9 \\ +1 \end{array}
$$

**3** $4 + 6 = $ _____   $3 + 5 = $ _____   $7 + 3 = $ _____

**4** $2 + 8 = $ _____   $1 + 8 = $ _____   $5 + 6 = $ _____

**Set 2** Use after page 69.

Subtract.

**1**
$$
\begin{array}{r} 7 \\ -2 \end{array}
\qquad
\begin{array}{r} 8 \\ -0 \end{array}
\qquad
\begin{array}{r} 9 \\ -2 \end{array}
\qquad
\begin{array}{r} 11 \\ -2 \end{array}
\qquad
\begin{array}{r} 10 \\ -0 \end{array}
\qquad
\begin{array}{r} 9 \\ -1 \end{array}
\qquad
\begin{array}{r} 10 \\ -2 \end{array}
$$

**2**
$$
\begin{array}{r} 12 \\ -6 \end{array}
\qquad
\begin{array}{r} 11 \\ -5 \end{array}
\qquad
\begin{array}{r} 10 \\ -7 \end{array}
\qquad
\begin{array}{r} 9 \\ -0 \end{array}
\qquad
\begin{array}{r} 12 \\ -3 \end{array}
\qquad
\begin{array}{r} 11 \\ -4 \end{array}
\qquad
\begin{array}{r} 9 \\ -6 \end{array}
$$

**3** $8 - 0 = $ _____   $12 - 5 = $ _____   $10 - 3 = $ _____

**4** $11 - 6 = $ _____   $8 - 4 = $ _____   $11 - 1 = $ _____

**BASIC FACTS REVIEW**

Name _____

**Set 3** Use after page 95.

Add.

**1**

| 6 | 9 | 7 | 8 | 9 | 3 | 9 |
|---|---|---|---|---|---|---|
| + 6 | + 4 | + 5 | + 8 | + 3 | + 7 | + 1 |

**2**

| 9 | 8 | 7 | 4 | 6 | 1 | 4 |
|---|---|---|---|---|---|---|
| + 6 | + 5 | + 7 | + 8 | + 7 | +10 | + 7 |

**3**

| 4 | 9 | 8 | 7 | 3 | 5 | 8 |
|---|---|---|---|---|---|---|
| + 4 | + 2 | + 2 | + 9 | + 5 | + 5 | + 9 |

**4**

| 6 | 2 | 7 | 9 | 8 | 6 | 4 |
|---|---|---|---|---|---|---|
| + 8 | +10 | + 5 | + 9 | + 4 | + 5 | + 7 |

**5** 10 + 0 = _____ 5 + 6 = _____ 8 + 8 = _____

**6** 2 + 9 = _____ 4 + 4 = _____ 5 + 7 = _____

**7** 6 + 3 = _____ 9 + 4 = _____ 8 + 9 = _____

**8** 9 + 9 = _____ 5 + 8 = _____ 11 + 1 = _____

**9** 6 + 6 = _____ 2 + 7 = _____ 4 + 8 = _____

**10** 5 + 9 = _____ 4 + 6 = _____ 5 + 5 = _____

Name _____

**Set 4** Use after page 107.
Add or subtract.

**1**   7    14      **2**   9    15      **3**   9    14
   +7   &minus;7        +6   &minus;6        +5   &minus;5

**4**   9    18      **5**   6    14      **6**   8    16
   +9   &minus;9        +8   &minus;8        +8   &minus;8

**7**  12   10    9    8    9   10    8
  &minus;5   &minus;3   +4   +6   +5  &minus;0   +7

**8**   9    7   15   13    6   11   10
   +8   +7  &minus;9   &minus;7   +6   &minus;1   &minus;7

**9**  10 + 0 = ____    12 &minus; 4 = ____    8 + 4 = ____

**10**  9 + 8 = ____    17 &minus; 8 = ____    6 + 7 = ____

**11**  2 + 9 = ____    8 + 8 = ____    15 &minus; 9 = ____

**12**  12 + 0 = ____    9 &minus; 5 = ____    7 + 8 = ____

**13**  11 &minus; 3 = ____    4 + 8 = ____    4 + 9 = ____

BASIC FACTS REVIEW

Name _____

**Set 5** Use after page 129.

Complete each fact family.

① $6 + 7 =$ ___

$7 + 6 =$ ___

$13 - 7 =$ ___

$13 - 6 =$ ___

② $4 + 8 =$ ___

$8 + 4 =$ ___

$12 - 4 =$ ___

$12 - 8 =$ ___

③ $8 + 7 =$ ___

$7 + 8 =$ ___

$15 - 7 =$ ___

$15 - 8 =$ ___

④  $\begin{array}{r} 9 \\ + 9 \\ \hline \end{array}$  $\begin{array}{r} 18 \\ - 9 \\ \hline \end{array}$

⑤  $\begin{array}{r} 7 \\ + 7 \\ \hline \end{array}$  $\begin{array}{r} 14 \\ - 7 \\ \hline \end{array}$

⑥  $\begin{array}{r} 6 \\ + 6 \\ \hline \end{array}$  $\begin{array}{r} 12 \\ - 6 \\ \hline \end{array}$

**Set 6** Use after page 145.

Add. Circle the numbers you would add first.

①  $\begin{array}{r} 4 \\ 7 \\ + 4 \\ \hline \end{array}$  $\begin{array}{r} 2 \\ 8 \\ + 6 \\ \hline \end{array}$  $\begin{array}{r} 3 \\ 4 \\ + 5 \\ \hline \end{array}$  $\begin{array}{r} 7 \\ 3 \\ + 3 \\ \hline \end{array}$  $\begin{array}{r} 9 \\ 6 \\ + 1 \\ \hline \end{array}$  $\begin{array}{r} 3 \\ 5 \\ + 5 \\ \hline \end{array}$  $\begin{array}{r} 5 \\ 8 \\ + 4 \\ \hline \end{array}$

Find the missing numbers in each fact family.

② ___ $+ 9 = 17$

$17 - 9 =$ ___

$9 +$ ___ $= 17$

$17 -$ ___ $= 9$

③ ___ $+ 6 = 13$

$13 - 6 =$ ___

$6 +$ ___ $= 13$

$13 -$ ___ $= 6$

④ ___ $+ 5 = 14$

$14 - 5 =$ ___

$5 +$ ___ $= 14$

$14 -$ ___ $= 5$

five hundred forty-three **543**

# Picture Glossary

**after**

1, 2, 3, 4, 5

4 comes **after** 3.

**area**

The number of square units
in a shape

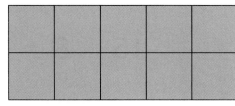

10 square units

**bar graph**

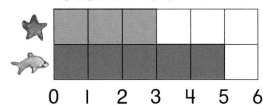

**Sea Animals We Like**

0  1  2  3  4  5  6

**before**

1, 2, 3, 4, 5

2 comes **before** 3.

**between**

1, 2, 3, 4, 5

3 comes **between** 2 and 4.

**cent (¢)**

A penny is 1 cent.

**centimeter**

I'm about
1 centimeter long.

0   1   2   3   4   5   6   7

**cone**

**count back**

3, **2**

3 − 1 = 2

**count on**

3, **4**

3 + 1 = 4

**cube**

**cup**

**cylinder**

**difference**

$$7 - 1 = 6$$

$$\begin{array}{r} 7 \\ -\ 1 \\ \hline 6 \end{array}$$

└── **difference** ──┘

**dime**   10¢

**divide**

$12 \div 3 = 4$

**dollar**  $1.00

↑ decimal point

**doubles**
$4 + 4 = 8$
$8 - 4 = 4$

**doubles plus one**
$7 + 7 = 14$, so $7 + 8 = 15$.

**equal sign** =
$2 + 3 = 5$

**estimate**
$42 + 21$ is about 60.

**even**
2, 4, 6, 8, and 10 are **even** numbers.

**fact family**
$2 + 4 = 6$        $6 - 4 = 2$
$4 + 2 = 6$        $6 - 2 = 4$

**foot**
A **foot** is 12 inches.

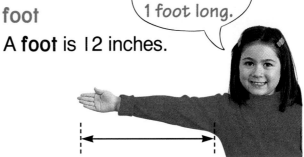

My arm is more than 1 foot long.

**fraction**

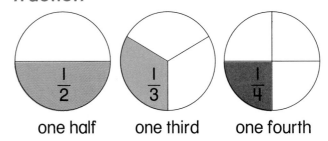

$\frac{1}{2}$        $\frac{1}{3}$        $\frac{1}{4}$

one half        one third        one fourth

**greater than** >
$99 > 32$

**greatest**
47        36        **51**
51 is the **greatest** number.

**half dollar**

50¢

**half hour**

PICTURE GLOSSARY

**hour**

**hundreds**

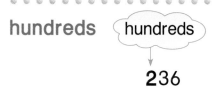

**2**36

**inch**

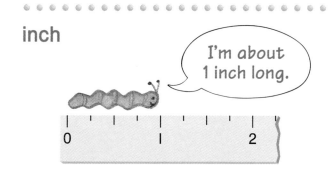

I'm about 1 inch long.

**kilogram**

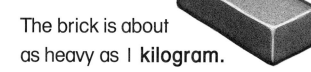

The brick is about as heavy as 1 **kilogram.**

**least**

22     **12**     19

12 is the **least** number.

**less than <**

23 < 56

**line of symmetry**

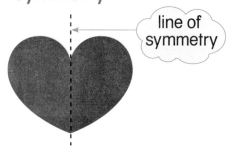

line of symmetry

**liter**

**meter**

A golf club is about 1 meter long.

A **meter** is 100 cm.

**minute**

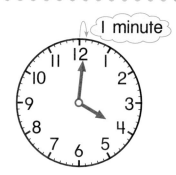

1 minute

**multiply**

$3 \times 4 = 12$

**nickel**

  5¢

**odd**

1, 3, 5, 7, and 9 are **odd** numbers.

## pattern

## penny

 1¢

## perimeter

The distance around is the **perimeter.**

## pictograph

**Our Boats**

Tim

Maria

Each 🛥 means 1 boat.

## pint

One pint is 2 cups.

## pound

The bread weighs about 1 **pound.**

## product

$3 \times 4 = 12$ ⟵ **product**

## pyramid

## quart

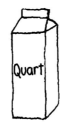 

One quart is 4 cups.

## quarter

25¢

## rectangular prism

## sphere

## sum

$$2 + 3 = 5 \longleftarrow \textbf{sum} \longrightarrow \begin{array}{r} 2 \\ + 3 \\ \hline 5 \end{array}$$

## tally marks

卌 ||

## turnaround facts

$3 + 4 = 7$        $4 + 3 = 7$

## yard

A **yard** is 3 feet.

A baseball bat is about 1 **yard** long.

# Credits

## Illustration

**Allen, Elizabeth** 51, 52, 67, 68

**Becker, Pamela** 199, 202, 208, 210

**Belcher, Cynthia** 40, 273, 311, 317, 333, 344, 373

**Berrett, Lisa** 40, 41, 42, 51, 54, 56, 60, 62, 63, 64, 67, 69, 70, 103, 104, 105, 165, 166, 167, 182, 189, 190, 271, 285, 286, 303, 304, 313, 317, 318, 340, 346, 402, 433, 435, 436

**Bettoli, Delana** 474, 475, 476, 481

**Bolton, Jennifer** 126, 127, 128, 131, 135, 137

**Broda, Ron** 231

**Brooks, Nan** 79, 99, 100

**Cable, Annette** 119, 120, 121, 122, 124, 141, 142, 143, 148, 459, 460, 461, 462, 483, 484, 491, 493, 494, 495, 509

**Carter, Abby** 211, 212, 221

**Dieterichs Morrison, Shelley** 37, 47, 431, 432, 433, 436

**Dinges, Michael** 273, 274, 277, 278, 288

**Dugan, Karen** 117, 233, 234, 235, 238, 239, 243, 244, 247, 248, 249, 385, 386, 387, 388, 389

**Egan, Tim** 172, 178, 294

**Freeman, Nancy** 155

**Galkin, Simon** 455, 456, 463, 464, 467, 468, 501, 502, 503, 504, 505, 506, 507

**Harris, Diane Teske** 363, 371, 373, 378

**Hirashima, Jean** 321, 322

**Jeanotilla, Carol** 37

**Karas, Brian** 103, 104, 105

**Kotik, Kenneth** 1

**Laden, Nina** 155, 170, 183, 184, 365, 366, 367, 368, 369, 370, 379, 382

**Lash-Ruff, Michelle** 192, 204, 226

**Levine, Melinda** 267

**Mauterer, Erin** 445, 446, 447, 448, 451, 452, 453, 454, 465, 466

**Melmon, Deborah Haley** 79, 84, 95, 96, 101, 102, 219, 220, 231, 471, 472, 481

**Moffatt, Judy** 267, 311

**Oversat, Laura** 79, 90, 92, 108

**Parnell, Miles** 79, 87, 88, 110

**Polfus, Roberta** 401, 402, 408, 410

**Raymond, Victoria** 443

**Rockwell, Barry** 315, 316, 328, 335, 343

**Romero, Javier** 32

**Roth, Roger** 200, 201, 205, 206, 213, 214

**Schneider, Jennifer** 7, 8, 510, 511, 512, 513, 514, 515, 516, 517, 519, 520

**Sheperd, Roni** 14, 15, 16, 24, 25

**Snider, Jackie** 79, 107, 109

**Steiger, Terry** 155, 171, 399, 407, 419, 421, 422, 426, 496, 497, 498, 499

**Sullivan, Don** 79, 89, 91, 93, 94, 320, 323, 324, 331, 332, 337, 338

**Swan, Susan** 79, 98

**Thompson, Emily** 180, 181, 184, 187, 299, 300, 301, 406, 417, 420, 421

**Verzaal, Dale C.** 17, 18, 27, 29, 30

**Weissman, Bari** 89

**Williams, Toby** 117

**Wolf, Elizabeth** 39, 40, 42, 47, 48, 56, 59, 60, 62, 64, 65, 66, 156, 161, 162, 166, 167, 179, 186, 189, 190, 197, 269, 270, 279, 280, 284, 287, 292, 293, 298, 355, 399, 401, 403, 404, 409, 411, 415, 419, 423, 424, 425, 427, 428, 429, 430, 437, 540, 541, 542

## Math Soup Illustration

**Chapter 1**
**Steve Mach** 2, 3, 6, 7
**Troy Thomas** 4, 5
**Nadine Bernard Westcott** 1

**Chapter 2**
**Geri Bourget** 4, 5
**Jennifer Hewitson** 1, 2, 3
**Laura Oversat** 7

**Chapter 3**
**Dusan Petricic** 8
**Jean and Mou-sien Tseng** 4, 5
**Nadine Bernard Westcott** 6

**Chapter 4**
**Lonni Sue Johnson** 8
**Steve Mach** 6, 7
**Dorthy Stott** 5

**Chapter 5**
**Geri Bourget** 3, 5

**Chapter 6**
**Steve Mach** 8
**Stanley Martucci** 1, 6

**Chapter 7**
**Lonni Sue Johnson** 6

**Chapter 9**
**Barry Rockwell** 3, 4, 6, 7, 8

**Chapter 10**
**Kate Evans** 8

**Chapter 11**
**Mary Lynn Blasuta** 2
**Jennifer Bolten** 1
**Abby Carter** 8
**Ruta Dangavietis** 6
**Georgia Shola** 4

**Chapter 12**
**Stanley Martucci** 4
**Barry Rockwell** 3

**Chapter 13**
**Terri Starrett** 2

## Photography

Unless otherwise acknowledged, all photos are the property of Scott Foresman - Addison Wesley. Math Soup photography created expressly for Scott Foresman - Addison Wesley by Fritz Geiger and Michael Walker.

**Cover** Gail Shumway/FPG

Myrleen Ferguson/PhotoEdit 1(Row 2, l)
John Eastcott/YVA Momatiuk/The Image Works, 1(Row 2, c)
David Young-Wolff/PhotoEdit 1(Row 3, cl)
Comstock 1(Row 3, cr)

Roy Morsch/Stock Market 1(Row 3, r)
Paul Conklin/PhotoEdit 1(Row 4, l)
Jim Cummins/FPG 1(Row 4, cl)
Bryan F. Peterson/Stock Market 1(Row 4, r)
Tom Prettyman/PhotoEdit 48(t)
Elena Rooraid/PhotoEdit 48(b)
David Wells/The Image Works 84
Bill Aron/PhotoEdit 106
D. Greco/The Image Works 143
Bob Daemmrich 199(t)
Bob Daemmrich/Stock Boston 202(b)
David Young-Wolff/PhotoEdit 206(l)
Michael Newman/PhotoEdit 206(r)
Richard Pasley/Stock Boston 208(t)
Lawrence Migdale/Stock Boston 212
Comstock 240
Superstock 314, 318, 320, 321, 328(r) 329, 334, 336, 340, 342(l)
Mickey Gibson/ANIMALS ANIMALS 317
Fritz Prenzel/ANIMALS ANIMALS 327(t)
ANIMALS ANIMALS 328(l)
Ken Cole/ANIMALS ANIMALS 342(r)

## Math Soup Photography

**Chapter 2**
HMS Images/Image Bank 4

**Chapter 3**
Richard T. Nowitz 1, 3

**Chapter 4**
Randall Hyman 2

**Chapter 5**
Les Morsillo 4–5
Michael Okoniewski 7(tr)
Michael Gullett 7(bl)

**Chapter 6**
Paul F. Gero 1, 4–5

**Chapter 7**
Keith Ayres 2

**Chapter 8**
National Geographic Society/
    Photo: Franklin J. Viola 3
All car photos by Jeffrey Dworin 4–5
I. N. Phelps Stokes Collection/New York Public
    Library, Astor, Lenox and Tilden Foundations 6(t)
From the Collections of the Henry Ford Museum and
    Greenfield Village 6(b)
Library of Congress 7(t)
UPI/Corbis-Bettmann 7(b)

**Chapter 9**
Tim Davis/Tony Stone Images 1
Ted Benson/Modesto Bee 2

**Chapter 10**
Lawrence Migdale 1, 2, 3
Bob Smith 6, 7

**Chapter 12**
Jim Cummins/Tony Stone Images 1
Christopher Morrow/Stock Boston 6(t)
Cameramann International 6(b)

**Chapter 13**
Courtesy of Bankshot 4
K. D. Lawson 7